Fabric-by-Fabric
One-Yard
Wonders

Cottons, Knits, Voiles, Corduroy, Fleece, Flannel, Home Dec, Oilcloth, Wool, and Beyond

Rebecca Yaker and Patricia Hoskins

Photography by Tara Donne

Photo styling by Raina Kattelson

Storey Publishing

*The mission of Storey Publishing is to serve our customers by
publishing practical information that encourages
personal independence in harmony with the environment.*

Edited by Deborah Balmuth and Nancy D. Wood
Art direction and book design by Jessica Armstrong

Cover and interior photography by © Tara Donne, except for authors' photograph by Gene
    Pittman; pages 131, 220, and 348 by Mars Vilaubi; and fabric borders throughout by Greg
    Nesbit Photography, except for those on pages 240, 242, 254, and 256 by Mars Vilaubi
Photo styling by Raina Kattelson
Illustrations by Missy Shepler

Indexed by Nancy D. Wood

Storey Publishing
210 MASS MoCA Way
North Adams, MA 01247
www.storey.com

Printed in China by R.R. Donnelley
10 9 8 7 6 5 4 3 2

Library of Congress Cataloging-in-Publication Data

Yaker, Rebecca.
  Fabric-by-fabric one-yard wonders / by Rebecca Yaker and Patricia Hoskins.
    p. cm.
  Includes index.
  ISBN 978-1-60342-586-5 (hardback)
  1. Machine sewing. 2. Textile fabrics. I. Hoskins, Patricia. II. Title.
TT713.Y34 2011
646.2'044—dc23
                                             2011024750

CONTENTS

CHAPTER 1

Fabric Fundamentals

Like you, we are so excited to see the different types of fabrics being created by our favorite contemporary print designers. When you want a perfect-for-fall corduroy skirt, summery sheer top, cozy fleece mitts, or an easy springy knit, you're no longer confined to dull solids or gaudy colorways. You can now find lively printed corduroys, velveteens, voiles, and coated cottons from some of your most loved fabric designers!

The Wild World of Fabrics

As exciting as these new fabrics are, they often have complex sewing and care rules. This easy-to-follow manual will introduce you to the wild world of wonderful fabrics, some of which you might not even be familiar with, and teach you all you need to know for the best sewing success. For instance, just how do you press corduroy without crushing the pile? How can you cut knits without having the fabric stretch and curl out of shape as you go? And what kinds of things can you make with oilcloth other than tablecloths?

Well, read on for the answers to these and many more questions. In this book we have tips and tricks for working with so many different kinds of fabrics, including: lightweight fabrics such as voiles; quilting cottons; heavyweight home decorating fabrics; flannels; pile fabrics such as corduroy and velveteen; coated fabrics such as oilcloth; fleece; knits; and woolens.

Of course there are far more fabric types than we are able to cover in this book, so simply use the information provided as the foundation in your quest to work with assorted fabrics. A mind-boggling array of silks, wools, knits, leathers, and man-made fabrics awaits you!

Making Your Sewing Machine Work for You

Your sewing machine was designed and built for precision; it's up to you to ensure that it delivers. Whether your machine is new or old, mechanical, electronic or computerized, it's important to familiarize yourself with its basic functions. The key functions you need to know are how to thread your machine, how to wind and insert bobbins, and how to change the needle. The rest will come with time, patience, and practice.

If you have your manual, read it, keep it within arm's reach, and refer to it regularly. We can't stress enough just how important the manual is, because it explains the nuances and special functions of your specific machine. Even though you most likely know how to use your sewing machine, you might be tickled to find additional tips and tricks in your manual that you just didn't know about. Above all else, remember that your sewing machine is your friend and partner in creativity, and you must communicate and work together.

Stay sharp! Always make sure that you choose the appropriate needle for the project at hand. Generally speaking, you need a needle that is fine enough to enter the fabric without leaving a puncture hole and strong enough to go through the fabric without bending. The wrong size or a damaged needle might break, mar, or tear the fabric, and will almost certainly result in skipped stitches, poor stitch quality, or even no stitches at all. In addition to the size of the needle, pay attention to the type. For the most part, you'll use a universal needle for most sewing projects and a ballpoint for sewing on knitted or stretch fabrics. The best practice is to start each project with a new needle, as needles tend to wear down and dull with use. You'll thank yourself later.

ballpoint   universal

Stitch Smarts

Stitch length is another matter of importance. Adjust the length of the stitch depending on the type of fabric, as well as the type of sewing you are doing. As a general rule, the heavier the fabric, the longer the stitch length. Regarding the fabrics discussed in this book, voile fabrics require the shortest stitch length, while heavyweight home decor and corduroy fabrics require the longest.

That said, even when sewing only one fabric, it may be necessary to use different stitch lengths within the same project to achieve different results. For example, it's a good idea to use a shorter stitch length along curved edges to ensure a smoother curve. Topstitching typically requires a longer stitch length than seams. Basting requires yet a longer stitch length, as the stitches are temporary and you will most likely want to remove them later. Gathering fabric requires the longest stitch length of all. Refer to the Fabric Type Cheat Sheet on page 13 to fully understand seam stitch length as it pertains to fabric you are working with.

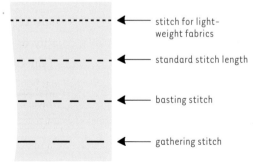

stitch for light-weight fabrics

standard stitch length

basting stitch

gathering stitch

Type A or Type B? Also of importance is stitch type. The bulk of your sewing will be done with a straight stitch, but you may want to venture beyond. When working with knits, for example, set your machine for

TIME FOR A TUNE-UP

Please don't neglect basic do-it-yourself sewing machine maintenance. It's a good idea to free your machine of lint, especially in the bobbin area, as this will fix (and prevent) many a sewing headache. One way to cut down on lint buildup is to cover your machine when it's not in use. Most machines also come with a lint brush, so you can brush the lint out of the machine. Don't blow on the lint because that can force the lint deeper into the machine. Also, don't forget about sewing machine oil and keeping your machine lubricated. Check your manual for the right way to keep your machine lubed and to see if your particular machine even requires oiling (many newer machines don't). And if you can't oil it yourself, take your machine to a professional. It's a good idea to have your machine serviced professionally about once a year.

a stretch stitch or small zigzag stitch when sewing seams. This will prevent your seams from breaking. Depending on your sewing machine, you may have several additional decorative stitches. Experiment and have fun!

Don't be so tense! Sewing machine tension can also be a tricky detail that is best not overlooked. It's crucial to pay attention to, and familiarize yourself with, both the top needle (upper) tension, as well as the bobbin (lower) tension. Perfect tension is when both the upper and lower threads are perfectly balanced, and are drawn into the fabric the same amount (the bobbin thread does not float on the bottom of the fabric and the upper thread does not float on top of the fabric).

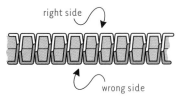

BALANCED TENSION

right side

wrong side

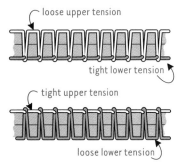

loose upper tension

tight lower tension

tight upper tension

loose lower tension

Once again, your sewing machine manual will come in handy. Most manuals have a chart detailing the appropriate tension adjustments for working with specific fabrics. Take care that your tension is not too loose, because the threads can pull out completely, or too tight, resulting in puckered seams. Always test the tension on a scrap of the same fabric you are using in your project, using the same thread and needle.

Best Foot Forward

Your sewing machine probably came with the standard (a.k.a. zigzag) presser foot, as well as a few additional feet. If not, it's a good idea to invest in some specialty presser feet that were designed for working with different fabric types. A Teflon foot, which looks just like your standard foot, is useful when working with

hard-to-handle, stickier fabrics, such as oilcloth and other coated fabrics. Additionally, there is a wide range of foot options out there for specific tasks and applications such as cording, making buttonholes, darning, gathering, and inserting invisible zippers, just to name a few. Probably, there's a foot for every task!

Take the driver's seat. Speaking of feet, take your time and don't be a lead foot! As with your automobile, the speed at which your sewing machine stitches is variable. Let up on the speed (unless you are under a serious time crunch); it's best to sew at a steady, controlled rate. This way, you can stop any mistakes before they get too out of hand. When you don't stitch at an even pace, the result is likely to be uneven and less than ideal. We can't stress enough that your sewing machine is your friend and partner in creativity. Enjoy your ride together!

A satin stitch foot is slightly longer than the standard presser foot with a larger opening that allows dense stitching through medium to heavyweight fabrics.

A walking foot helps feed heavier fabrics and fabrics that tend to shift through your machine, because it feeds the fabric layers evenly.

A roller foot has actual rollers to provide better friction when feeding some fabrics, like leather and vinyl, through your machine.

Making & Using the Sewing Patterns

For each project in this book, the sewing pattern will appear in one of two ways:

* You'll be told to look for a full-size pattern in the pattern envelope. When you find the pattern pieces, pay close attention to the markings. Some pieces have an edge labeled with asterisk symbols and the note: "Mirror along this line." These pieces represent half of the entire piece. To make the entire piece, you will need to trace one side, then flip the piece over on the mirror line to trace the other side. You'll also notice some pattern pieces are nested within other pattern pieces. You will find it easiest to redraft these nested pieces onto sew-in interfacing, pattern-making paper, or tissue paper instead of cutting them out.

* You'll be given instructions for drafting your own pattern from a set of measurements. You may do this directly on your fabric or play it safe and draft it first on sew-in interfacing, pattern-making paper, or tissue paper. If it's a project you love, and you think you'll be making it again and again, draft it on paper. When drafting your pattern pieces, use a ruler for straight edges and a curved ruler for curved and rounded edges. In general, take care that your lines are neat and tidy and that your measurements are precise.

Please note that some projects in this book require the use of both pattern piece types; you might need to find a pattern piece in the envelope and also draft a piece based on the dimensions provided.

Pattern notations. Take note of all marks on the paper pattern pieces. Specifically, watch for asterisks, notches, dots, darts, tucks, pleats, and other notations. Transfer all marks to the wrong side of your cut fabric pieces before removing the paper pattern piece.

Notches and dots will help you put the project together smoothly and help eliminate any confusion. Before marking, refer to the Fabric Type Cheat Sheet (*see page* 13) for the appropriate marking tools for your fabric. Test the suggested marking tool on a fabric scrap or in a corner of the fabric to make sure the marks don't bleed through to the right side.

To mark fabrics cut right side up in a single layer, simply place a piece of tracing paper, right side up, under the paper pattern piece and fabric. For fabrics cut in a double layer with right sides together, use two pieces of tracing paper, placing one right side up under the fabric and the other right side down between the paper pattern and top layer of fabric. Some heavy fabrics may require you to mark one layer at a time. In all cases, gently use your tracing wheel to transfer markings.

TRICK

We've got a sneaky trick to help you mark dots. Use a paper punch to punch out holes in your paper pattern pieces where the marked dots appear. You can then easily mark the fabric at the center of the punched-out circle while the pattern template is still pinned on your fabric. For notches, you can cut around the notches or make a small clip into the seam allowances.

Best Sewing Practices

There are many details that should not be overlooked when sewing. Although this may be overwhelming at first, you will find that the below practices quickly become second nature. You will not even think twice when it comes to pinning your projects, clipping curves, or pressing as you sew. You'll be thrilled with the finished results.

Thread. Pay close attention to the thread you select for your sewing project. Threads vary by weight, luster, and fiber content. These factors affect the look of the stitches and, potentially, the tension of your sewing machine (*see page* 8). The tried-and-true thread choices that work with nearly every fabric are cotton-wrapped polyester or 100 percent polyester thread. The polyester core ensures strong, durable seams while the cotton wrap provides smoothness and luster, making this an ideal choice for an all-purpose thread. You may also use 100 percent cotton threads, which are lustrous, smooth, and have little or no stretch, for machine- or hand-sewing natural woven fabrics.

You will also find an assortment of special-purpose threads for specific applications such as sewing with denim, silk, nylon, metallic, elastic, and more. Experiment to determine what thread works best for your project. It's always a good idea to do a little test sewing on a swatch of the actual project fabric to determine the correct thread tension (*see page* 8). Getting these details right ahead of time will ensure the best possible results!

Pins. Always pin or otherwise clip your pieces together before and while you sew. We know, it seems tedious and cuts into the fun sewing time, but you will be absolutely amazed by the professional results you'll achieve when you take the time to pin your projects before you sew them. You will find it most convenient to put the pins perpendicular to the edge of your fabric. This makes them easy to remove while sewing, and less damaging to your machine if you accidently sew over them. That said, the best practice is to remove the pins before you sew over them. If you don't, you might break your needle on a pin, and that's a drag, to say the least. Keep in mind that for some fabric types (*see page* 13), pinning isn't recommended, but you can always use clips (hem clips, binder clips, paper clips, you name it) as alternatives.

Feed dogs. Don't pull your fabric while sewing. Your sewing machine has been designed to move your fabric along as you stitch. The feed dogs (located in your sewing machine's throat plate) and the presser foot work together to make this happen. Pulling your fabric as you stitch will result in uneven stitches, screwy tension, and an unhappy sewing machine.

If the fabric does not feed through easily, it may be time for a service call. There will be instances where you are working with multiple layers of heavy fabrics, such as home dec, denim, or corduroy, when the fabric seems stuck and your feed dogs aren't doing their job. In these instances, there are special tools you can use, such as a roller or walking foot, or a Jean-a-ma-jig (a product designed to help your machine handle heavyweight fabrics, kind of like a shim) for sewing over bulky seams. They are addressed in the appropriate fabric chapter.

Backstitching. Backstitching is crucial! A backstitch is required of most fabrics at the beginning and end of every seam to lock the stitches. Usually ⅛" to ¼" of backstitching should be enough to do the trick. However, when working with lightweight or easily perforated fabrics, you might find it better to leave a long tail at the beginning and end of each seam and tie the threads into a knot by hand. This will eliminate bulk and unnecessary stress on fragile fabrics. On coated fabrics, this technique will minimize perforation of the material at the seams.

Turning corners. When stitching around corners (such as collar points or bag corners), slow down as you approach the corner. Stop with your needle in the down position once the needle is a seam allowance width away from the raw edge of the fabric. Lift the presser foot and pivot the fabric on the needle. Lower the presser foot and resume stitching. This will guarantee neat corners, and save both time and thread while stitching. On heavier weight materials (home decor, heavy woolens, vinyl), *rounding* the corner stitches instead of pivoting will make the corners appear sharper once the project is turned right side out.

Trimming, clipping, and notching. Notch and clip the seam allowance around curves and trim corners to ease fullness. Clipping (*see the glossary*) is done to reduce tension on concave seams (inward curves), while notching (*see the glossary*) is used to make convex seams (outward curves) lie flat. You will also find it necessary to trim corner seam allowances at a 45-degree angle close to the intersection of the two stitching lines. One quick tip is to use pinking shears to remove some of that excess fabric within curved seam allowances. But whatever you do, don't clip through your stitching line!

Pressing. Embrace the iron as the silent partner in your sewing projects. You need this partner to achieve great-looking results. It's as simple as this: press as you stitch – the success of your project depends on it. Skipping the pressing step will make your projects look "homemade" as opposed to "handcrafted." You might hate ironing, but please know that pressing is something different entirely. Ironing is done on a finished garment, while pressing is done as you create it, to mold and shape your work in progress. When the instructions direct you to press a seam allowance open, or in a certain direction, pay attention. These steps are crucial to your finished project. Keeping all your seams neat and even as you work will definitely pay off. Invest in an iron with a nice steam button to make pressing so much easier; you won't be sorry.

Your Sewing Pantry

Here's a list of the 48 essentials we think you'll want to have on hand, not just to complete your projects, but to ensure a frustration-free sewing experience every time! Just as you wouldn't attempt to cook a fabulous recipe without your essential cooking utensils, and just as you keep your kitchen stocked with a smattering of basic ingredients, so must you keep your sewing pantry stocked with some fundamental sewing necessities. Of course, you don't have to run out and buy everything for your first project, but build up your sewing pantry as you master the various projects and techniques that go into making them.

31 Equipment Must-Haves

1. Sewing machine and assorted feet: zigzag, zipper, and walking feet are definitely at the top of the list. A magnetic seam guide and other machine accessories are handy, too — especially long tweezers, a small screwdriver, a brush, and oil.

2. Sewing machine needles for various fabric weights

3. Seam ripper

4. 60" tape measure

5. Point turner (knitting needle or chopstick can be used in a pinch)

6. Fabric shears (7" to 9" blade)

7. Pinking shears

8. Trimming scissors (4" blade)

9. Rotary cutter (go wild and get a pinking blade!)

10. Cutting mat

11. Clear quilter's ruler (3"×18" is great, or 5"×24")

12. Hand-sewing needles (assorted, including embroidery needles)

13. Tailor's chalk, fabric marker, and/or soap slivers

14. Carbon paper and tracing wheel

15. Tissue, tracing paper, sew-in interfacing, or other pattern-making paper

16. Paper scissors

17. Transparent tape

18. Drafting tape

19. Straight pins (dressmaker's, quilter's, or similar)

20. Clips (such as binder clips or paper clips)

21. Pattern weights

22. Safety pins

23. Iron and ironing board

24. Pressing cloth

25. Curved ruler (French curve)

26. Bodkin (used to feed elastic and ribbon through casings — you can also use a large safety pin)

27. Lighter (used to prevent fraying on polyester webbing, Cordura, and other man-made materials)

28. Pincushion (wrist-strap and magnetic versions make cleaning up spilled pins a cinch)

29. Thimble (metal, leather, plastic — experiment to find the most comfortable option for you)

30. Bobbins (always have a few prewound in your most used thread colors)

31. Hammer or clapper for flattening bulky seams

17 Necessary Notions

1. Spools of thread in assorted colors

2. Elastic in various widths: ¼", ½", ¾", 1"

3. Zippers in assorted lengths: metal, polyester, invisible

4. Interfacing: sew-in and fusible, including double-sided fusible

5. Various closures, such as buttons, hooks and eyes, snaps, buckles, D-rings

6. Velcro

7. Twill tape

8. Rickrack

9. Bias tape (homemade or store-bought): single-fold and double-fold

10. Bias tape maker (available in 5 sizes: ¼", ½", ¾", 1", 2")

11. Ribbons and trims in assorted widths

12. Embroidery floss

13. Decorative buttons

14. Fabric scraps

15. Webbing

16. Liquid fabric sealant (such as Fray Check)

17. Fabric glue (such as Fabri-Tac)

Fabric Type Cheat Sheet

Fabric	Needle size/type	Seam stitch length	Stitch tips	Sewing machine	Marking	Pressing	Laundering	Special equipment
Light-weight Cotton	universal 60/8–70/10	1.25–2mm	no backstitch; knot threads	roller foot, straight stitch foot, or offset needle (move to left or right of center)	no wax, all other marking types ok	cooler than cotton	preshrink	tissue stitching if puckered seams are a problem
Quilting-weight Cotton	universal 70/10–80/12	2–2.5mm	—	standard foot	no wax, all other marking types ok	cotton	preshrink	—
Home Dec	universal 90/14–110/18	3mm	round corners; hammer seams flat	walking foot, roller foot	no wax, all other marking types ok	cotton, linen	preshrink	Jean-a-ma-jig for getting over bulky seams
Flannel	universal 80/12	2–2.5mm	—	standard foot	no wax, all other marking types ok	cotton	preshrink	—
Woven Pile	universal 70/10–80/12	2.5–3mm	may need to push fabric toward presser foot	standard foot, walking foot, roller foot	no wax, all other marking types ok	towel as pressing cloth	preshrink cottons	pattern weights
Coated	universal sharp 70/10–140/16; leather needle for vinyl	3–3.5mm	—	Teflon foot, roller foot	chalk, drafting tape	finger-press, low heat, pressing cloth	no	pattern weights, temp adhesive, clips
Fleece	universal sharp or ballpoint 70/10–90/14	2.5–3mm	—	walking foot, satin stitch foot	drafting tape, fabric marker	finger-press	low/no heat	mark right/wrong side
Knits	ballpoint 70/10–80/12	stretch stitch or small zigzag	jersey: no backstitch; knot threads	walking foot, serger	scissor snip on fabric edge, soap, chalk	press and lift, setting for fabric composition	in some cases, preshrink 2x	clips to keep seams from curling
Wool	universal 80/12–90/14	2–3mm	—	standard foot, walking foot	drafting tape	pressing cloth(s), wool setting with steam	hand wash or dry clean	mark right/wrong side; soap seams and creases

CHAPTER 2

LIGHTWEIGHT COTTONS

Lightweight cotton fabrics often feel luxurious and light on the skin, perfect for summer apparel! Voile and lawn are two lightweight plain-weave fabrics that fabric manufacturers have recently started to produce in popular contemporary prints. Voile is soft and fairly sheer. Lawn is finely woven, with a high thread count, and often with a slight sheen.

Fabric Facts

Most of the projects in this chapter were made with voile, lawn, or gauze, but you can use several lightweight fabrics with specially woven and/or embroidered textures that offer a nice change of pace. Among them are dotted Swiss, dobby, and eyelet, all of which have great surface interest. Double gauze is another great lightweight woven fabric, available primarily from Japanese fabric manufacturers. Gauze has a loose, open weave (fewer threads per inch) and its individual warp threads are twisted. Two layers of gauze are tacked together at regular intervals to create double gauze, so it isn't as sheer. Here are some things to know about lightweight cotton fabrics.

Attributes

Lightweight cottons are somewhat fragile and can be easily damaged by dull or large sewing machine needles, feed dogs, and/or presser feet. Seams have a tendency to pucker, but a tension adjustment often corrects the problem. Seam slippage, where the fabric pulls away or separates at the seam, can also be a problem, particularly on close-fitting garments (*see* Stitch Types, Tips, and Machine Settings *for some quick fixes*). Since these fabrics are often sheer or semi-sheer, your seam allowances will show through on the right side of the finished project, so keep them neat!

Needle Type(s)

Use a 60/8, 65/9, or 70/10 universal needle. Always use a new needle when starting a new project.

Sewing Machine Accessories

To avoid pulling the fabric into the throat plate, try using a roller foot or straight stitch foot. Alternatively, use a standard presser foot but adjust the needle position to the left or right of center, if your machine has that option for straight stitching.

Stitch Types, Tips, and Machine Settings

Use 1.25mm–2mm stitch length for most seaming. Avoid backstitching whenever possible to minimize the threat of puckering and damage to your fabric. Instead, leave thread tails long at the beginning and end of your seams and knot the thread tails before trimming them. Knots, instead of backstitching, minimize bulk at the seams and the fewer holes in the fabric can help prevent seam slippage. If you are having a problem with puckered seams and seam slippage, and can't seem to correct it with tension settings or a new needle, try tissue-stitching your seams. Tissue-stitching simply involves adding a layer of tissue paper to the seam. After the seam is stitched, carefully remove the tissue, but avoid pulling at the stitches and distorting them or the fabric. Staystitch along curved seams to help pattern pieces retain their shape.

Marking

Like most cotton fabrics, wax-based marking methods are not suitable for lightweight woven fabrics; all other marking types are fine.

Cutting

Make sure all of the fabric is on your work surface while pinning the patterns and cutting them out. If the fabric hangs off the table, it can stretch and distort. If the fabric has sheen, treat it as a napped fabric. If your fabric is particularly slippery, try placing a piece of flannel (or a flannel-backed tablecloth or similar material) on your work surface, underneath your working fabric to help hold it in place and keep it from sliding around. Of course, take care not to cut through the flannel work surface!

Interfacing

When projects call for the use of lightweight woven fabrics, they typically want to highlight the sheerness, lightness, and drape of the fabric; therefore, interfacing is rarely used.

Special Equipment

Use well-sharpened shears, and very fine or new pins on light and delicate fabrics.

Seams

Self-finished seams, such as French seams and flat-felled seams, are best. Trim seams whenever possible to ¼" or less.

Pressing and Ironing

Although made of cotton fibers, which can withstand high heat, press lightweight cotton fabrics at a slightly cooler setting than the cotton setting. Lightweight fabrics always want a cooler iron than heavier fabrics of the same composition (fiber type); otherwise, you run the risk of scorching or burning the fabric. Press a fabric scrap first to test the iron settings and your pressing style.

Fabric Care

Preshrink all cottons before cutting and sewing, especially if you are making an item you intend to launder! Otherwise, consult the care instructions as recommended by the manufacturer.

HALTER WRAP

Designed by Don Morin

*This versatile halter is the perfect lightweight top for summer beach parties.
Or dress it up with some jewels and wear it to your much-anticipated holiday
party. The perfect pairing with pants, skirts, or shorts, this forgiving wrap
style has a flattering shape and a fit that looks great on all body types.*

MATERIALS

* Locate the pattern in the envelope (sheet #1)
* 1 yard of 54/60" voile, double gauze, or other lightweight fabric
* 1 spool of coordinating thread

Sizes – XS, S, M, L, XL

Seam allowance – ½" unless otherwise specified

FABRIC NOTES: *double-faced fabric is ideal for this wrap halter because both sides of the fabric will be visible when wrapped. Not suitable for obvious one-way patterns and diagonal stripes.*

① Determine Your Size

Sizing is determined according to your bust measurement.

	X-Small	Small	Medium	Large	X-Large
Bust size	32"	34"	36"	38"	40"

② Measure, Mark, and Cut

Lay out your fabric in a single layer with the right side facing up. Position the pattern pieces according to the layout and cut them out. Transfer markings from the pattern pieces to the wrong side of the fabric.

* **Front** (cut 2, one reversed)
* **Back** (cut 1)
* **Neck band** (cut 1)
* **Front facing** (doubles as a casing for the neck band) (cut 2)
* **Back facing** (cut 1)

NOTE: *Position the grainline arrow on the pattern pieces along the straight grain of the fabric.*

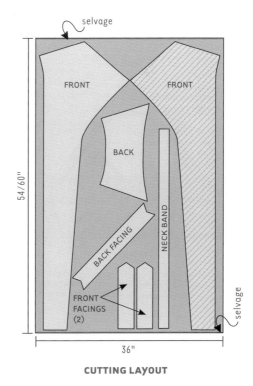

CUTTING LAYOUT

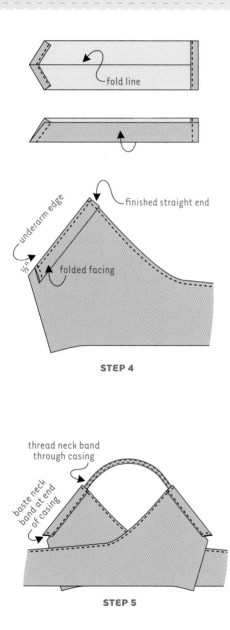

STEP 4

STEP 5

❸ Make the Neck Band

Fold the neck band in half lengthwise with right sides together and stitch along the long edge. Turn the neck band right side out, and press. Edgestitch along both long edges. Set the neck band aside.

❹ Stitch the Front Pieces

* Stitch a narrow double-fold ¼" hem along the long curved edge of both front pieces. Set the front pieces aside.
* Turn both short ends of each front facing ½" to the wrong side and stitch the folded edges in place. Fold and press the front facing strips in half lengthwise with the wrong sides together.
* Aligning the raw edges, position a facing piece on the right side of a front piece along the underarm edge, with the straight finished end of the facing at the point on the front piece (the pointed end of facing will be ½" away from the side seam edge). Stitch the pieces together. Repeat for the remaining front piece and front facing.
* For each front piece, press the facing/casing and seam allowance up (away from the front piece) and edgestitch the facing, catching the seam allowance in the stitching.

❺ Attach the Neck Band

Thread each end of the neck band through the casings created with the front facings. Baste the neck band in place at the end of both casings with a ¼" seam.

⑥ Attach the Back Facing

* Staystitch along both short ends of the back facing with a ½" seam allowance. Clip the center points on both short ends to, but not through, the staystitch line.

* Turn under both short ends of the back facing ½" to the wrong side and stitch the folded edge in place.

* Fold the back facing piece in half lengthwise with the wrong sides together. Aligning the raw edges, position the back facing piece on the right side of the back piece along the upper edge ½" from each side edge of the back piece. Stitch the pieces together.

* Press the facing and seam allowance up, away from the back piece and edgestitch the facing, catching the seam allowance in the stitching.

½"   ½"

back

STEP 6

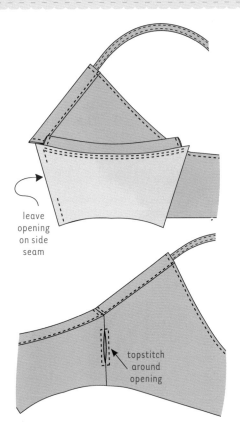

leave opening on side seam

topstitch around opening

STEP 7

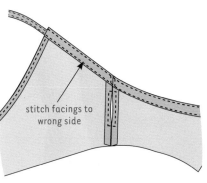

stitch facings to wrong side

STEP 8

⑦ Stitch the Side Seams

* With the right sides together, align the side seam raw edges of the front and back pieces, taking care to carefully match up the facings. Stitch the right side seam below the facing pieces, leaving a 5"-6" opening as shown. Do not stitch the front and back facing pieces together.

* Stitch the left side seam from top to bottom, below the facing pieces, without leaving an opening. Again, do not stitch the front and back facing pieces together.

* Press the seam allowances open. Edgestitch around the opening in the right side seam.

* Fold the raw edges of all the side seam allowances to the wrong side and edgestitch for clean finished seams.

⑧ Finish the Facings

Press the front and back facings to the wrong side of the halter. Stitch the entire facings in place, close to the folded edge, taking care not to catch the neck band in the stitching. Note that the facings are not stitched together at the side seams (this will not be possible, as there is not extra fabric to overlap).

⑨ Hem the Edges

Stitch a narrow ¼" double-fold hem along the short straight edges of the front pieces, and along the bottom edge of the halter.

THE "O" TUNIC

Designed by Tanja and Suada Ivacic

This beautiful tunic is the perfect top for summer evenings. The style is simple, yet with a touch of French flair. What's not to love with the subtle gathering details, the bell sleeves, and the delightful front neck shaping. Your little girlie is going to be "O" so thrilled with this feminine and stylish tunic.

MATERIALS

* Locate the pattern in the envelope (sheet #2)
* 1 yard of 54/60" voile, double gauze, or other lightweight fabric
* 1 spool of coordinating thread
* 1 button, ¾" in diameter

Sizes – 2T, 3T, 4T, 5T

Seam allowance – ½" unless otherwise specified

1 Determine Your Child's Size

Measure your child's chest to find the right size.

	2T	3T	4T	5T
Chest size	18"-20"	21"-22"	22"-23"	23"-24"

2 Measure, Mark, and Cut

Fold your fabric in half lengthwise with the right sides together, aligning the selvages. Position the pattern pieces and mark the additional front facing listed below, following the layout. Transfer the markings from the pattern pieces to the wrong side of the fabric.

* **Front yoke** (cut 4)
* **Back yoke** (cut 2)
* **Sleeve** (cut 2)
* **Lower front** (cut 1 on fold)
* **Lower back** (cut 1 on fold)

Measure and mark the following directly onto the fabric:

* **Front facing** 4¼" × 2¼" (cut 1)

NOTE: *Position the grainline arrow on the pattern pieces along the straight grain of the fabric.*

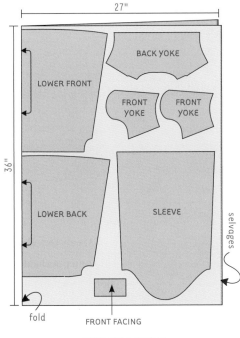

CUTTING LAYOUT

❸ Make the Front Slit

* To finish the center front slit opening, center and pin the front facing on the center of the front piece, with the right sides together, aligning the top raw edges. Stitch the two pieces together along the marked lines as indicated on the front pattern piece. Using sharp scissors, cut a slash through both layers, in between the stitching lines to the bottom point. Be very careful to clip to, but not through, the stitching.

* Turn the front facing through this opening, to the wrong side of the front piece and press. Edgestitch along the finished edges of the front slit.

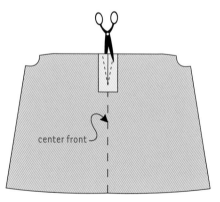

center front

STEP 3

❹ Stitch the Darts

Fold and pin the darts on the back yoke along the center of each dart with the right sides together. Stitch on the marked lines. Press each dart toward the center back. Repeat on the remaining back yoke piece.

❺ Attach the Yokes

* Use a basting stitch to gather the top raw edge of the lower back piece between the two stars as indicated on the pattern. Adjust the gathers so that the top of the lower back piece is the same size as the bottom edge of the back yoke piece. Pin the top edge of the lower back and bottom edge of one back yoke with the right sides together and distribute the gathers evenly. Stitch the pieces together and press the seam allowances up, toward the back yoke.

* Repeat this step to gather and stitch the top raw edges of the lower front piece, on both sides of the slit, to the bottom edges of two front yoke pieces. Align the finished edges of the slit opening with the line indicated on the pattern. Press the seam allowances up toward the yoke.

STEP 5

6 Stitch the Shoulder Seams

Pin and stitch the shoulder seams of the front and back yoke pieces with the right sides together. Press the seam allowance open. Repeat with the second set of front and back yoke pieces to create the yoke facing.

7 Attach the Facing

* Fold and press the bottom raw edges of the yoke facings ½" to the wrong side. With the right sides together, pin the front and back neck edges of the yoke and yoke facings. Stitch the pieces together along the neck edge and around the front curves.
* Notch the curved seam allowances. Turn the facing to the inside of the tunic, and press. Baste the yokes together around armhole edges with a ¼" seam allowance.
* Pin the bottom edge of front and back yoke facings to cover the seam allowances. Edgestitch around all finished edges of the yoke, catching the bottom edges of the yoke facing in the stitching.

STEP 7

8 Attach the Sleeves

Use a basting stitch to gather the top raw edge of the sleeve cap between the two stars as indicated on the pattern. Adjust the gathers so they are evenly distributed. With the right sides together, pin the raw edge of the sleeve cap to the armhole opening of the tunic, matching the center mark on the sleeve with the shoulder seam on the tunic. Stitch the pieces together and press the seam allowance toward the sleeve. Repeat with the second sleeve.

9 Stitch the Side Seams

With the right sides together, stitch the front to the back along the side and underarm seams. Press the seams toward the back of the tunic.

10 Hem the Edges

* Make a narrow ¼" double-fold hem along both of the sleeve edges.
* Also make a double-fold hem on the bottom edge of the tunic, pressing under ¼", then another ¾". Stitch close to the folded edge.

11 Add the Button and Buttonhole

Make a horizontal buttonhole in the right front yoke referring to the placement line on the pattern piece. Position and stitch the button on the left yoke, as it corresponds to the buttonhole placement.

Gazillions of Gathers Pillow

Designed by Caroline Sanchez

This pillow is a perfect shortcut way to create a pillow with an incredible amount of gathers, without having to do any of the actual gathering yourself! By using an elastic thread in your bobbin, you can create a timeless shirred fabric with gathers that are guaranteed to be perfectly even. Once you get the hang of it, you'll be adding shirring to many of your projects, just you wait!

MATERIALS

* 1 yard of 44/45" voile, double gauze, or other lightweight fabric
* 1 spool of coordinating thread
* 1 spool of elastic thread
* 16" square pillow form

Finished dimensions – 16" square
Seam allowance – ½" unless otherwise specified

① Measure, Mark, and Cut

Lay out your fabric in a single layer with the wrong side facing up. Using a ruler and washable fabric pen or tailor's chalk, measure and mark the following pieces directly on the fabric, with straight edges along the grainline:

* **Front** 18" × 30" (cut 1)
* **Front facing** 17" × 17" (cut 1)
* **Back** 17" × 12" (cut 2)

② Prepare the Bobbin

Load your bobbin with elastic thread. To do this, manually wind the elastic thread onto your bobbin by hand, giving it a very slight stretch as you wind. Throughout the course of stitching the pillow, you will need to wind more than one bobbin of elastic thread to get you through the project.

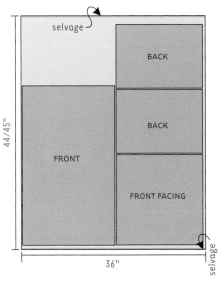

CUTTING LAYOUT

③ Mark and Stitch the Shirring Lines

✳ Lay the front piece right side up on a flat surface. Use a disappearing fabric pen to mark horizontal lines 1" apart across the width of the front piece.

✳ Set your machine to a long stitch length (something close to a basting stitch). Your elastic thread should be loaded in the bobbin and a basic coordinating thread to match your fabric loaded in the top of the machine. Begin sewing along the marked lines, backstitching at the beginning and end of each stitch line. When you finish stitching (and backstitching) one line of shirring, lift your presser foot and turn the fabric around to begin sewing in the opposite direction on the next marked line. This minimizes waste of the elastic thread, and also results in fewer threads to clip until you are completely done with the shirring. Be sure to stretch your fabric flat in front of the needle as you sew. Continue in this fashion until all the lines are stitched.

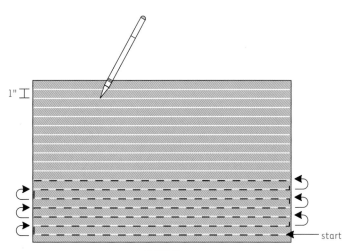

STEP 3

④ Shrink up the Gathered Front

Spritz the disappearing ink stitching lines with water and be sure they are completely gone before pressing, as heat can cause the lines to become permanent. Using steam, press the fabric on the right side while it's wet to shrink up your elastic a little more and create even more texture. (Applying heat directly on the elastic will damage it, so always press on the right side.) Pin the front piece to your ironing board, stretching it as flat as possible ahead of your iron. Continue pressing until you've steamed all the water out of your fabric.

⑤ Stabilize the Shirred Pillow Front

The front facing will help stabilize the stretchy pillow front. Stitch the pieces together as follows:

✳ With the wrong sides facing, position the shirred front and the front facing pieces together with the shirred front on top. Pin the side raw edges together. In one direction your shirred fabric may be scrunched up smaller than the 17" square – if this is the case, simply stretch it to make it fit.

✳ Once all edges are aligned, baste a ¼" seam around the perimeter. You may find it easier to stitch if the facing side is on top. This way you can guarantee a finished 17" square. If extra fabric from the front piece extends beyond the front facing, simply trim it away after you have stitched the two pieces together.

⑥ Create the Pillow Envelope Back

✻ Press under one long edge of a back piece ¼" to the wrong side, then press under another ¾" (creating a double-fold hem). Stitch close to the folded edge. Repeat along one long edge of the second back piece.

✻ With the right sides facing up, layer the two hemmed back pieces on top of each other, overlapping the hemmed edges by 5", to create a 17" square. Stitch a scant ¼" seam across the top and bottom overlaps to hold the pieces together.

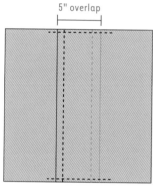

STEP 6

⑦ Assemble the Pillow

With the right sides together, pin the envelope back to the pillow front and stitch around all four sides. Clip the corners, trim the seam allowance to ¼", and zigzag the raw edges. Turn the pillow cover right side out and stuff your pillow form inside. Now you have a stunning pillow with a texture you won't be able to resist running your hands over!

cap sleeve bolero

Designed by Rebecca Yaker

Reminiscent of your favorite knitted shrug, this cap sleeve bolero is a more tailored version. Wear it with jeans, skirts, and slacks. It's a great way to infuse a little patterning into any outfit. It won't necessarily add warmth, but it will add pizzazz!

MATERIALS

* Locate the pattern in the envelope (sheet #1)
* 1 yard of 54/60" voile, double gauze, or other lightweight fabric
* 1 spool of coordinating thread
* 3 buttons, ¾" in diameter

Sizes – XS, S, M, L

Seam allowance – ½" unless otherwise specified

❶ Determine Your Size

Sizing is determined according to the bust measurement.

	XS	S	M	L
Bust Size	32"	34"	36"	38"

❷ Measure, Mark, and Cut

Fold your fabric in half lengthwise with the right sides together, aligning the selvages. Using the paper pattern pieces provided, and measuring/marking the additional bias strip listed below, follow the layout and place the pieces accordingly. Cut out the pieces. Transfer the markings from the pattern pieces to the wrong side of the fabric before removing the paper pattern pieces.

* **Front** (cut 2)
* **Back** (cut 1 on fold)
* **Sleeve** (cut 2)
* **Collar** (cut 2)
* **Front facing** (cut 2)
* **Back facing** (cut 1 on fold)

Also measure and mark the following directly onto the fabric:

* **Bias strip** 15" × ¾"
  (cut 2 on bias)

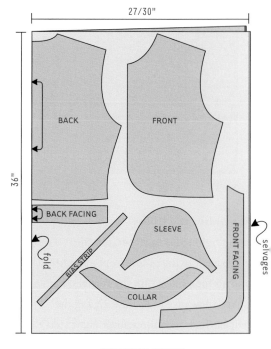

CUTTING LAYOUT

NOTE: *Position the grainline arrow on the pattern pieces along the straight grain of the fabric.*

③ Make the Pleats

On the front pieces, fold the fabric with the right sides together, aligning and pinning the pleat lines. Stitch the pleats from top to bottom along the 1½" pleat lines (two pleats per front piece). Press the finished pleats toward the side seams. Repeat with the four pleats on the back piece. Press the back pleats toward the center back.

④ Stitch the Shoulder and Side Seams

With the right sides together, stitch the bolero fronts to the back along the shoulder and side seams. Press the seam allowances open.

⑤ Make and Attach the Sleeves

* Use a basting stitch to gather the top raw edge of the sleeve cap between the two dots indicated on the pattern piece. Pull the gathering thread so the gathered distance between the two dots is 2" and the gathers are evenly distributed. Stitch the gathers in place with a regular stitch length and a ¼" seam allowance. Remove the basting stitches.
* With right sides together, align the raw edge of the sleeve cap with the armhole opening of the bolero, matching the front and back edges of the sleeve with the front and back of the bolero. Also, match the center mark on the sleeve with the shoulder seam. Note that the front and back edges of the sleeve do not extend all the way to the side seam. Instead, the sleeve should stop approximately 1" before the side seam on both the front and back of the bolero.
* Stitch the sleeve in place with a ½" seam allowance. Stitch again, this time using a slightly narrower seam allowance to reinforce this seam. Trim the seam allowance close to the second stitching line and press the seam allowance toward the sleeve. Repeat with the second sleeve.

⑥ Finish the Sleeve Edges

Fold and press one long edge and both short edges of one of the bias strips ¼" to the wrong side. With the right sides together, pin the long, unfolded edge of the bias strip around the sleeve opening. Stitch the two pieces together with a ¼" seam allowance. Press the bias strip to the inside of the sleeve, so the wrong sides are together. From the right side of the sleeve, topstitch the bias strip in place with a scant ¼" seam allowance. Repeat with the other bias strip and sleeve opening.

⑦ Make and Attach the Facings

* With the right sides together, pin and stitch the front and back facings together at the side seams, and press the seam allowances open.
* Staystitch around the inner curved edge of the facing pieces with a ¼" seam allowance. Turn and press the inner edge of the front and back facings to the wrong side along the staystitching.
* With the right sides together, pin the facing to the bolero, aligning the raw edges. Stitch the pieces together with a ½" seam allowance. Also, stitch the pieces together along the neck edge, from the outside edge to the center front (marked) line; clip the seam allowances vertically at the center front.

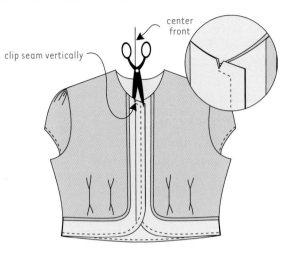

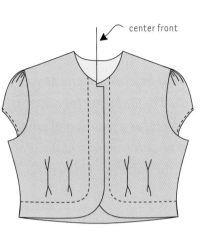

STEP 7

* Clip the corners and notch along the curved edges within the seam allowance. Press the facing to the wrong side of the bolero. From the right side, stitch the facing in place with a 1¼" seam allowance, or if that is difficult for you to do neatly, turn the bolero to the wrong side and stitch the facing in place close to the folded edge.

⑧ Make and Attach the Collar

* On one of the collar pieces, press the bottom edge ½" to the wrong side. This piece is now the collar facing.
* Pin the collar and collar facing pieces with the right sides together and stitch along the top and curved side edges, leaving the bottom edge unstitched. Notch along the curved edge, turn the collar right side out, and press.

* With the right sides together, align the bottom raw edge of the collar along the neck edge of the bolero, matching the center backs. The front edges of the collar should extend to the center front line on the front pieces of the bolero. Stitch the collar and neck edge together, taking care not to catch the collar facing in the stitching.
* Press the seam allowances up toward the collar, so the folded edge of the collar facing covers them. Pin the folded edge of the collar facing in place and, from the right side of the bolero, edgestitch along the bottom edge of the collar, catching the folded edge of the collar facing in the stitching. Neatly edgestitch along the finished top edge of the collar.

⑨ Make Buttonholes and Attach Buttons

Make three vertical buttonholes in the right front according to the placement lines as indicated on the pattern piece. Position and stitch the buttons on the left front, as they correspond to the buttonhole placement.

FLIRTY SKIRTY

Designed by Tina Michalik

You've likely seen this skirt everywhere! Maybe you also noticed the large price tag often attached to it at your favorite little boutique. Well lucky for you, you can now make it for a fraction of what that price tag reads, and it won't take more than an afternoon to make. Pair it with your favorite boots in the fall, or sandals in the summer. This versatile style transcends seasons!

MATERIALS

* 1 yard of 44/45" voile, double gauze, or other lightweight fabric (not suitable for one-way designs)
* 1 spool of coordinating thread
* 3"-wide elastic band, long enough to comfortably fit around your waist
* 2⅛ yards of ⅝"-wide ribbon (optional)
* 2⅛ yards of 1¼"-wide lace (optional)

Sizes – custom fit, according to your hip and waist measurements. Finished length is approximately 24", including the waistband height.

Seam allowance – ½" unless otherwise specified

① Measure, Mark, and Cut

Fold your fabric in half lengthwise, with the right sides together, aligning the selvages. Using a ruler and washable fabric pen or tailor's chalk, measure and mark the following pieces directly onto the wrong side of the fabric, with straight edges along the grainline. Cut them out:

* **Skirt front/back** 21" × 35" rectangles (cut 2)

② Stitch the Sides

With the right sides together, stitch the skirt front to the skirt back along both side seams (the 21" edges). Press the seams open.

③ Make the Elastic Waistband

To determine how much elastic you need for the waistband, stretch it gently around your waist at the location you intend to wear your skirt. You want the elastic to be stretched enough so that it sits on your waist snugly, yet comfortably. Position the raw ends of the elastic with the right sides together and stitch them with a zigzag stitch. Turn the elastic band right side out.

④ Gather the Top Edge of the Skirt

Use two rows of basting stitches to gather the top raw edge of the skirt. Pull the basting threads until the top edge of the skirt measures 1" larger than your hip measurement and adjust the gathers until they are evenly distributed. Stitch along the top edge of the skirt with regular stitch length to secure the gathers. Remove the basting stitches.

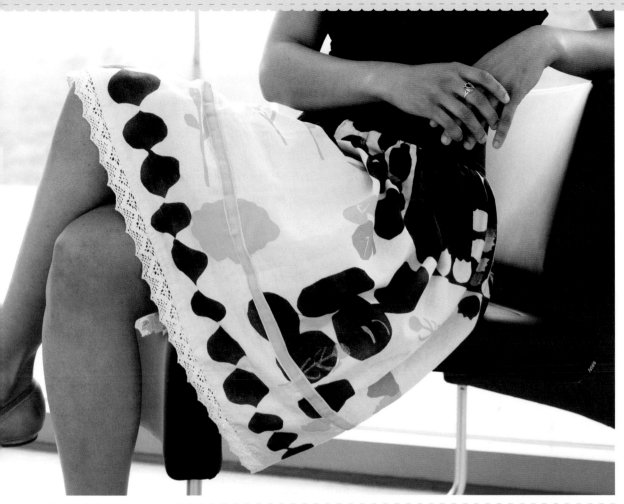

⑤ **Attach the Waistband to the Skirt**

With the right sides facing up, position the elastic waistband on the top gathered edge of the skirt, overlapping the elastic over the skirt by ½". Pin the waistband to the skirt in four places: center front, center back, and both side seams. Using a large zigzag stitch, with the elastic facing up, stitch the elastic to the skirt from one pin to the next, stretching the elastic as you sew so that the skirt is eased onto the elastic. Stitch all the way around the top edge of the skirt (bottom edge of the elastic) so that the elastic band is completely attached to the skirt.

⑥ **Hem the Skirt and Embellish**

Hem the skirt with a narrow ¼" double-fold hem. Depending on the style you like, you may choose to add decorative trim. We pinned and stitched yellow ribbon 5" up from the hem all the way around, then stitched a strip of lace to the wrong side of the hem.

SCRUFFLE SCARF

Designed by Pamela McFerrin

Every girl needs some ruffles in her life. Whether paired with a pink polka dot dress or a black leather motorcycle jacket, ruffles seem to top off any outfit. This pretty, raw-cut scarf is so easy, you can sew by day and be stylin' by night.

MATERIALS

* 1 yard 44/45" voile, double gauze, or other lightweight minimal-fray fabric
* 1 spool of coordinating thread
* 1 spool of contrasting thread (optional)

Finished dimensions – approximately 64" long × 5½" wide

Seam allowance – ½" unless otherwise specified

1 Measure, Mark, and Cut

With the right sides together, fold your fabric in half lengthwise, aligning the selvages. Measure and mark the following pieces directly on the wrong side of the fabric, with straight edges along the grainline. Cut them out.

* **Scarf base** 6" × 32½" (cut 2 on fold)
* **Ruffle strip** 2" × 44" (cut 10 on fold)

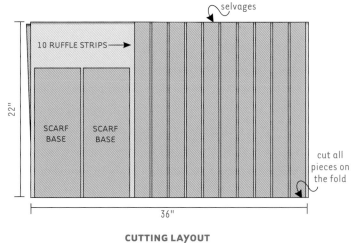

CUTTING LAYOUT

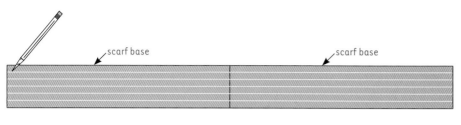

scarf base   scarf base

STEP 3

② Make the Ruffles

* With a 36" length of thread knotted at one end, hand-sew a long basting stitch down the center of one ruffle strip with coordinating thread. Knot the opposite end so that thread and strip measure 32½". Arrange the gathers evenly along the length. Repeat for the remaining ruffle strips.

* Pin two ruffle strips with the right sides together along the narrow ends and stitch to make one long ruffle strip. Repeat to create five pairs of joined ruffle strips.

③ Create the Scarf Base

Stack the scarf base pieces with the right sides together, and stitch along one short end to make one long piece. Mark horizontal placement lines every 1" along the length of the scarf base as shown.

④ Complete the Scarf

* On the right side of the scarf base, pin the center seam of one ruffle strip along the first placement mark, aligning the short ends. Using contrasting thread if desired, stitch the ruffle to the base, following the basting stitch as a guide.

* Stitch the remaining ruffle strips to the remaining placement marks in similar fashion, taking care not to catch the edges of adjoining ruffle strips in your stitching.

smocked sundress

Designed by Lorraine Teigland

Gingham-style checkered fabric is timeless, and perfect for this simple sundress as it showcases smocking beautifully. Don't have any experience smocking? No problem! Learn a few basic stitches with this project. Using a fabric with regularly spaced checks will help simplify the smocking process.

MATERIALS

* Locate the pattern in the envelope (sheet #1)
* 1 yard of 54/60" lightweight fabric (*see* Fabric Notes)
* 1 spool of coordinating thread
* Perle cotton embroidery thread in 3 shades (light, medium, and dark)
* 1 yard of rickrack

Sizes – 2/3, 4/5, 6/7
Seam allowance – ½" unless otherwise specified

FABRIC NOTES: *A regimented check fabric with ¼" to ½" squares, such as a gingham-style check, works best in the smocking process*

① Determine Your Child's Size

Measure your child's chest to find the right size.

	2/3	4/5	6/7
Chest size	21"–22"	23"–24"	25"–26"

② Measure, Mark, and Cut

Lay out your fabric in a single layer with the wrong side facing up. Set aside the dress front pattern piece for now. Lay out the remaining paper pattern pieces and measure/mark two additional pieces as listed below, following the cutting diagram. Transfer the markings from the pattern pieces to the wrong side of the fabric before removing the paper pattern pieces.

* **Dress back** (cut 1)
* **Back yoke** (cut 1)
* **Front yoke** (cut 1)

* **Pockets** (cut 2)
* **Pocket binding** (cut 2)

Also measure and mark the following:

* **Front** 26" × 25" (cut 1)
* **Bias strips (for shoulder ties)** 2" × 30" (cut 2, pieced)

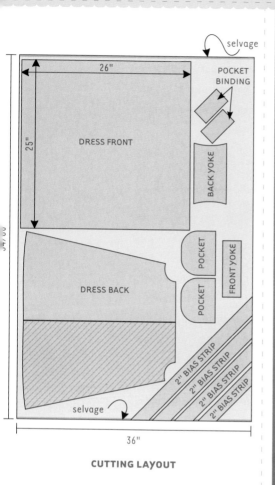

CUTTING LAYOUT

NOTES: *Mirror the Dress Back along the line indicated on the pattern. Cut the bias strips from the remaining section of fabric. You will need to piece the strips together to achieve the necessary finished length. Position the grainline arrow on the pattern pieces along the straight grain of the fabric.*

BASIC SMOCKING TUTORIAL

Cable stitch. This is a tight embroidery stitch worked in double rows that joins alternating columns of gathers, creating single pleats. It is a great foundation stitch to hold individual pleats in place.

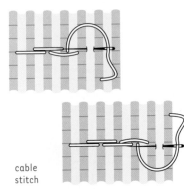

cable
stitch

Honeycomb stitch. This is a very elastic stitch and creates a pattern of triangles. You will notice a diagonal stitch concealed on the wrong side of the fabric.

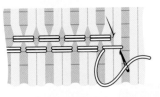

honeycomb stitch

Diamond stitch. This stitch pattern alternately employs tight horizontal stitches and loose diagonal stitches. It holds sections of pleats together.

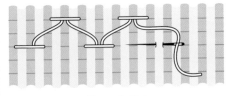

diamond stitch

French knot. This fundamental embroidery stitch is used to create polka dots, flower centers, and more. Bring the needle through to the front of the fabric, but before pulling it out all the way, wrap the needle three or four times with the embroidery thread. Pull the needle through the thread wraps, and a French knot is formed.

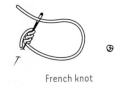

French knot

Lazy daisy stitch. This is actually a detached chain stitch, often used in multiples to create flower shapes, such as the daisy.

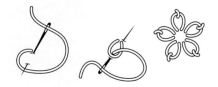

lazy daisy

⑤ Smock the Front Piece

* Position the dress front pattern piece as far to the left as possible on the right side of the front piece cut in the previous step. Using a washable fabric pen, mark the outline of the left side of the dress front; then remove the paper pattern.

* Using the checkered pattern of the fabric as smocking placement lines, begin smocking about ½" from the top edge and about ½" from the armhole edge. You may find it easiest to use the line between the rows of checks and work your smocking on that line.

* Using the pearl cotton, begin smocking on the left side of the dress front, working the stitches left to right. Follow the schematic for the order and combination of stitches used on this dress, beginning with two rows of the cable stitch (*see* Basic Smocking Tutorial *on page* 38).

Row	Stitch	Thread Color
1	Cable	light color embroidery thread
2	Cable	light color embroidery thread
3	Diamond	dark color embroidery thread
4	Diamond	medium color embroidery thread
5	Diamond	medium color embroidery thread
6	Diamond	dark color embroidery thread
7	Honeycomb	light color embroidery thread
8	Honeycomb	light color embroidery thread
9	Honeycomb	light color embroidery thread
10	Honeycomb	light color embroidery thread

NOTE: *In between rows 4 and 5, add the lazy daisy and French knots as indicated in the schematic, using the light color embroidery thread.*

* Continue each row of smocking across the front piece until the width of the smocking stitches is the same as the width of the front yoke piece minus 1". (This 1" difference is to accommodate the armhole binding, which will be added in a later step.) When you have completed the smocking pattern, baste ½" from the top across the top edge of the smocking; this helps hold the pleats in place when adding binding in a later step.

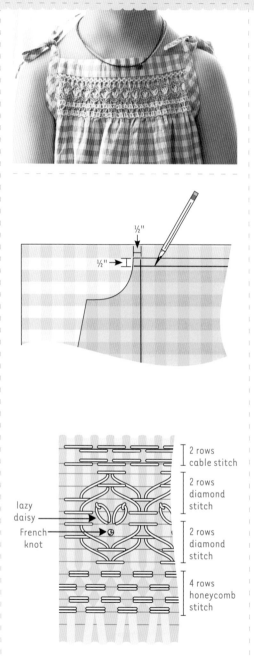

½"

½"

lazy daisy

French knot

2 rows cable stitch

2 rows diamond stitch

2 rows diamond stitch

4 rows honeycomb stitch

STEP 3

④ Cut Out the Dress Front

Position the front pattern piece on the smocked fabric, aligning the left edge of the pattern piece with the left edge marked in the previous step. Cut out the dress front.

⑤ Smock the Pockets

* Use the smocking techniques detailed in the smocking tutorial to work four smocking rows per the diagram, starting ½" down from the top edge of the pocket and 1½" from the left edge. Smock the first row using a cable stitch. End the smocking 1½" before the right edge of the pocket. The finished width across the top of the pocket, after smocking, should be 4¾".
* At the completion of the four rows of smocking, baste ¼" from the bottom edge of the pocket to hold the pleats in place. Repeat with the second pocket.

Row	Stitch	Thread Color
1	Cable	light color embroidery thread
2	Cable	light color embroidery thread
3	Diamond	dark color embroidery thread
4	Cable	dark color embroidery thread

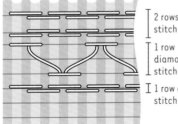

2 rows cable stitch

1 row diamond stitch

1 row cable stitch

STEP 6

⑥ Bind and Attach the Pockets

* Press one long edge of the pocket binding piece ½" to the wrong side.
* With the right sides together, align the top edge of the pocket with the unturned edge of the pocket binding piece and stitch them together. Press the binding up, away from the pocket, and over to the wrong side of the pocket along the fold line, so that the binding covers the seam allowance. From the right side of the pocket, edgestitch the pocket binding in place.
* Press the side and bottom raw edges of the pocket ½" to the wrong side. Position the pocket on the dress front, according to placement marks on the paper pattern piece. Edgestitch the pocket in place.
* Repeat with the second pocket.

⑦ Attach the Front Yoke

* Press one long edge of the front yoke ½" to the wrong side.
* With right sides together, align the top edge of the dress front with the unturned edge of the front yoke and stitch them together. Press the yoke up, away from the dress, and over to the wrong side of the dress along the fold line, so that the yoke covers the seam allowance. From the right side of the dress, edgestitch the front yoke in place along both long edges.

❽ Attach the Back Yoke

* Use a basting stitch to gather the top raw edge of the dress back. The finished gathered width should be equal to the width of the back yoke piece. Adjust the gathers so they are evenly distributed.
* Press one long edge of the back yoke ½" to the wrong side.
* With the right sides together, align the top gathered edge of the dress back with the unturned edge of the back yoke and stitch them together. Press the yoke up, away from the dress, and over to the wrong side of the dress along the fold line, so that the yoke covers the seam allowance. From the right side of the dress, edgestitch the back yoke in place along the top and bottom long edges.

❾ Stitch the Side Seams

With the right sides together, stitch the dress front to the dress back along both side seams. Press the seams open.

❿ Bind the Dress

* Press the short ends of both bias strips ½" to the wrong side. Fold the bias strips in half lengthwise with the wrong sides together and press. Open the binding pieces with the wrong sides facing up and press each long edge to the center crease. Fold the binding in half lengthwise again, along the original fold line.

* Mark the halfway point on each of the bias strip pieces. Pin the halfway point of one bias strip to the armhole at the side seam. Continue pinning the binding in place along the armhole, fully encasing the raw edges between the folds of the bias strips. The ends will extend off the dress in both the front and back. Edgestitch all of the edges along the entire piece of the binding to finish the armhole edge and create shoulder ties. Repeat this step with the remaining bias strip and the other armhole.
* Try on the dress and tie the binding in bows over each shoulder.

⓫ Hem the Dress

* Make a double-fold hem by pressing the bottom edge of the dress ¼", then under an additional ¾".
* On the right side of the dress, pin rickrack trim along the bottom edge, ⅝" from the folded edge. Stitch the rickrack in place, catching the folded hem in your stitching line.

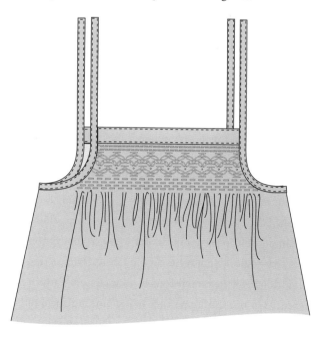

STEP 10

PARTY LAMP SHADE

Designed by Rebecca Yaker

It can be very difficult to find an attractive lamp shade in a color or pattern that suits your personal decor. Well, who knew making one could be so easy? Simply use a white lamp shade that you already own, or pick one up from the store and get to work! Although not recommended, your new, improved lamp shade will also double as a smashing party hat!

MATERIALS

* 1 yard of 44/45" voile, double gauze, or other lightweight fabric (not suitable for a one-way design)
* White conical or drum-style lamp shade
* Permanent clear fabric glue in a squeeze bottle
* All-purpose spray adhesive
* Paper for making patterns
* Pinking shears
* ⅜"-wide decorative ribbon, enough to go around the lamp shade twice, plus 1" (optional)

Finished dimensions – custom fit

Seam allowance – ½" unless otherwise specified

① Make the Lamp shade Pattern Piece

Lay your lamp shade on its side on a large piece of pattern-making paper. Starting at the seam, where the existing shade is glued together, place a mark on the paper at the top and bottom of the lamp shade. Slowly roll the shade along the paper, tracing a line along the top and bottom edge of the shade until you have traced the entire top and bottom edge of the shade, and reached the seam again. Add ½" seam allowance along all the edges of the newly created shade pattern piece.

② Measure, Mark, and Cut

Lay out your fabric in a single layer with the right side facing up. Position the paper pattern from step 1 on your fabric. Note that grain-line is unimportant in this project. Simply place your pattern piece at the necessary angle so that it fits on the fabric. (The cutting layout is representational, as the dimensions of your custom pattern piece will be different.) Cut out the lamp shade using pinking shears. Using a fabric pen, mark the ½" seam allowance on the wrong side of the lamp shade fabric piece.

* **Lamp shade** (cut 1)

selvage

44/45"

LAMP SHADE

selvage

36"

CUTTING LAYOUT

❸ Adhere the Fabric to the Lamp Shade

* Fold and press one short end of the lamp shade fabric ½" to the wrong side. Apply a small amount of fabric glue underneath this folded edge to hold it in place.
* Working in a well-ventilated area, place the lamp shade fabric on a flat surface with the wrong side facing up. Starting at one end, and working in small sections, apply a light coating of spray adhesive to the fabric.
* Place the lamp shade on top of the fabric, within the marked seam allowances and so the short, unfolded end of the fabric aligns with the seam of the lamp shade. Adhere the fabric to the lamp shade by rolling the shade along the fabric, pressing the fabric in place firmly as you roll. Take care to ensure that the fabric is smooth as you position it on the lamp shade. Also note that the lamp shade must stay within the marked ½" seam allowances. If the fabric shifts or wrinkles, simply lift it off the lamp shade and reposition it.

* The folded short end of the shade will cover the initial raw edge. If necessary, apply a small amount of fabric glue to the wrong side of the folded edge to hold it firmly in place.

❹ Finish the Top and Bottom Edges

Run a small bead of fabric glue along the inside bottom lip edge of the lamp shade. Carefully fold the ½" seam allowance along the bottom edge to the inside of the shade, sticking it in place. (Note that the use of pinking shears in step 2 will give the edge a nice finished look and prevent fraying.) Repeat with the seam allowance along the top edge of the shade.

❺ Add Decorative Trim

You may decide that your fantastic, new lamp shade could also use some decorative trim. Simply decide on the desired location, and adhere the trim with fabric glue. For this project, the trim was placed around the circumference of the shade ¾" from the top and bottom edges.

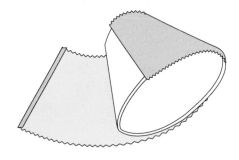

Hi-Fi Habitat

Designed by Gene Pittman

Okay, so you have an MP3 player and some speaker pods, but you're not quite sure where to place them. Look no further, as this project provides the perfect solution. Your mini stereo system is about to be wall mountable and very aesthetically pleasing when you use your favorite yard of fabric. Don't have an MP3 system? Skip the speaker covers and make multiples of the cube covers to display your favorite knickknacks!

MATERIALS

* 1 yard of 44/45" voile, double gauze, or other lightweight fabric
* 3 wall-mountable shadow box cubes
* Permanent clear fabric glue in a squeeze bottle
* Staple gun with ¼" staples

Finished dimensions – custom fit for your MP3 player and speaker pods

Seam allowance – ½" unless otherwise specified

❶ Select the Wall Cubes

Select three wall-mountable shadow box cubes. One must be large enough to accommodate your MP3 player and dock (if you use one), while the remaining two cubes must be able to accommodate your speakers. (Note that the intended speakers for this project are the palm-size pod variety.) If you are, or know, a crafty woodworker, you could always have the cubes custom built.

❷ Determine the Pattern Piece Sizes

* For the speaker covers (two identical sizes): wrap the measuring tape around a cube from the inside lip on one side to the inside lip on the opposite side. Since the cubes are square, this will be the length and width of each speaker cover piece.
* For the MP3 cube exterior: Measure in the same way as the speaker covers. In our example, this cube is larger than the speaker cubes.
* For the MP3 cube interior: Find the length by measuring the inside on all sides, and add 1"; the width will be the height of the cube plus 1".

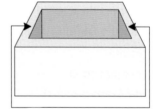

measure the exterior

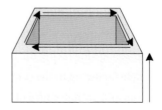

measure the interior + height

STEP 2

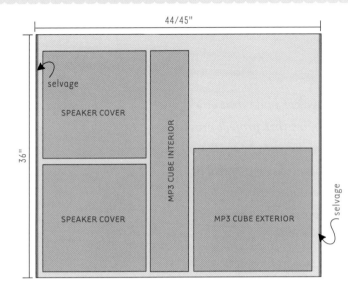

CUTTING LAYOUT

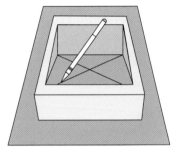

STEP 5

3 Measure, Mark, and Cut

Lay out your fabric in a single layer with the wrong side facing up. Using a ruler and disappearing ink fabric marking pen or tailor's chalk, measure and mark the pattern pieces directly onto the fabric, then cut them out. (The pieces shown on the layout are representational, as the dimensions of your custom pattern pieces will be different.)

* **Speaker cover** (cut 2)
* **MP3 Cube exterior** (cut 1)
* **MP3 Cube interior** (cut 1)

4 Cover the Speaker Cube

* Lay out one of the speaker cover fabric pieces on a flat surface with the wrong side facing up. Position the speaker cube with wrong side facing up in the center of the fabric.
* On the top and bottom edges of the cube, pull the fabric up and over to the back of the cube. Staple the fabric in place at 2" intervals, making sure that the fabric remains taut.

* On the sides of the cube, pull the fabric up and over to the back of the cube, neatly folding the excess fabric in the corners as if wrapping a package. Work on one side at a time to ensure that you are satisfied with the way the fabric lies in the corners. Staple the fabric in place on the back of the cube in 2" intervals. Again, make sure the fabric remains taut. Repeat with the second speaker cube.

5 Cover the Exterior of the MP3 Cube

* Lay out the cube exterior fabric piece on a flat surface with the wrong side facing up. Position the MP3 cube with wrong side facing up in the center of the fabric. Using a fabric pen, draw diagonal lines from corner to corner on the inside of the cube.
* Attach the fabric to the cube in the same manner as the speaker covers.

✳ Using sharp scissors, neatly cut along the diagonal lines in the center of the cube. Apply fabric glue to the wrong side of each of the cut fabric triangles and press them in place on the inside edges of the cube. Trim away any excess fabric that extends beyond the back of the cube.

⑥ Cover the Interior of the MP3 Cube

✳ Fold and press all the raw edges of the MP3 cube interior fabric piece ½" to the wrong side. Apply a small amount of fabric glue underneath all four folded edges to hold them in place. This piece will perfectly fit inside the cube to cover and finish the inside edges.

✳ Abut one short edge of the interior piece with a corner inside the cube. Apply fabric glue to the wrong side of the interior piece and glue it in place. Continue applying glue to the wrong side of the interior piece, pressing it in place along all the inside edges of the cube. Both folded short ends will meet at the same corner.

✪ Mount Your Stereo Display Units

Using the mounting hardware provided with the wall cubes, mount the three units on your wall in a danceable location. Place your speakers behind the speaker cubes and your MP3 player in the MP3 cube. Your speakers are now concealed and some of your favorite fabric is on display. Rock on!

CHAPTER 3

QUILTING-WEIGHT COTTONS

Quilting cottons are 100% cotton, light to medium-weight, plain-weave fabrics. They are often called sheeting by the trade, though technically sheeting can be a light, medium, or heavyweight fabric. Quilting-weight cottons are by far the most common and readily available fabrics for home sewers. Why do we love them so much? Because they are the loveliest prints!

Fabric Facts

There is an endless assortment of whimsical prints in amazing hues, and we just can't stop ourselves from buying more, which is why quilting-weight cottons probably represent the largest part of our personal fabric stashes!

Attributes

Quilting weights and other plain-weave cotton fabrics are not very elastic, though they have great natural stretch on the bias (and some give on the crossgrain). They are fairly durable and very easy to sew. On the downside, quilting cottons wrinkle easily, don't have great drape, and are prone to shrinkage, which is why preshrinking is so important! Like any cotton fabric, quilting-weight cottons can rot over time, but this is something you probably don't need to worry about in your lifetime. Quilting cottons can also soil easily, but on a positive note, they are easily laundered. Fraying and seam slippage can also be problematic, particularly with lower-quality goods. That said, it is best to avoid lower-quality fabrics as they are frequently off-grain (meaning the warp and weft threads are not perfectly perpendicular), which means they hang funny and prints can be trickier to match.

Needle Type(s)

Use a 70/10 or 80/12 universal needle.

Sewing Machine Accessories

Standard presser foot is fine; other feet may be called for in project construction instructions.

Stitch Types, Tips, and Machine Settings

2-2.5mm stitch length for seams, longer for topstitching.

Marking

Like most cotton fabrics, wax-based marking methods are not suitable for quilting-weight fabrics; all other marking types are fine.

Cutting

No special equipment or techniques required. For fabrics cut in a double layer, fold the yardage with the right sides together. Scissors or rotary cutter work well.

Interfacing

No particular interfacing requirements; fusible or sew-in are fine.

Seams

You do want to finish your hem and seam allowances to prevent fraying. Options include pinked edges, zigzag stitching, serged edges, or turned and stitched edges. For hems, single-fold or double-fold the hem allowances. Pinking shears do a great job at seam finishing.

Pressing and Ironing

Cotton (hot) setting, with steam; you'll need steam to remove stubborn wrinkles.

Fabric Care

Preshrink all cottons before cutting and sewing, especially if you are making an item you intend to launder! Otherwise, consult the care instructions recommended by the manufacturer.

RETRO BAG

Designed by Sue Kim

A pleated number with a vintage touch, this fun, feminine bag features an extra-long strap that can be worn diagonally across the torso. Pleating appears on just the front of the bag, for easier and quicker construction. The strap is designed to allow you to add a pretty decorative ring or buckle to jazz it up.

MATERIALS

* Locate the pattern in the envelope (sheets #1 and 2)
* 1 yard of 44/45" quilting-weight cotton fabric (not suitable for one-way designs)
* 1 spool of coordinating thread
* 1 yard of 22" medium-weight fusible interfacing
* One 3"-wide decorative ring
* 1 magnetic snap, ½" or ¾" in diameter

Finished dimensions — 11½" tall × 13½" wide
Seam allowance — ½" unless otherwise specified

1 Measure, Mark, and Cut

Lay out your fabric in a single layer with the right side facing up. Position the pattern pieces, and measure and mark the additional pieces as shown. Cut out the pieces, and transfer the markings from the pattern pieces to the wrong side of the fabric.

* **Exterior top front** (cut 1)
* **Exterior bottom front** (cut 1)
* **Lining/exterior back** (cut 3)

Measure and mark the following directly onto the fabric:

* **Strap** 5" × 44" (cut 1)
* **Holder** 7" × 5" (cut 1)
* **Pocket** 5" × 6" (cut 2)

Cut from Interfacing:

* **Lining/exterior back** (cut 2)

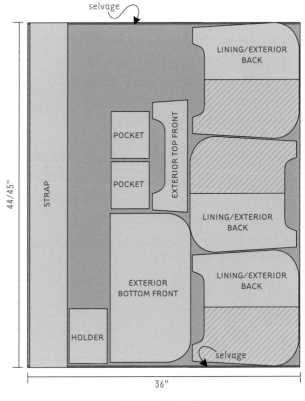

CUTTING LAYOUT

NOTE: *Position the grainline arrow on the pattern pieces along the straight grain of your fabric. Mirror the lining back pieces along the line indicated on the pattern.*

② Apply the Interfacing

Fuse the interfacing to the wrong side of two lining/exterior back pieces following the manufacturer's instructions. These will become the bag lining.

③ Make the Front Pleats

Working from the right side of the exterior bottom front, fold and pin each pleat on the indicated fold line over to the matching placement line. When you look at the pleats from the front, they should all be folded toward the center. Baste the pleats in place close to the raw edges.

④ Stitch the Front Pieces Together

Pin the exterior top front to the exterior bottom front with the right sides together, aligning the sides and straight raw edges. Stitch and press the seam allowances toward the top, pressing on both the wrong and the right sides of the piece. Topstitch on the top panel ⅛" away from the seam.

⑤ Stitch the Front and Back Exteriors

Pin the pleated front to the remaining lining/exterior back piece (without interfacing), with the right sides together and the raw edges aligned. Stitch along the sides and bottom, leaving the top open. Press the seam allowance open. Turn the bag right side out and press again.

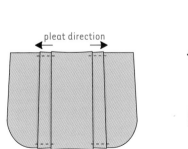

pleat direction

STEP 3

topstitch

STEP 4

⑥ Make the Holder

* Press both long raw edges of the holder ½" to the wrong side, then fold the holder in half lengthwise with the wrong sides together. Press and edge-stitch along both long edges.

* Thread one end of the holder through the ring and fold it in half widthwise, aligning the raw edges. Smooth the bag exterior flat at the side seams and pin the ends of the holder to the right side of the bag at the strap location. Baste the holder in place with an edgestitch.

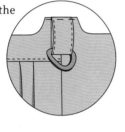

⑦ Stitch the Strap

* Press one short edge and both long edges of the strap ½" to the wrong side. Fold the strap in half lengthwise with the wrong sides together. Press, and edge-stitch along the three finished edges.

* Pin the unfinished edge of the strap to the bag exterior at the remaining strap location. Baste it in place with an edgestitch. Set the bag exterior aside.

⑧ Make the Pocket

* Pin the pocket pieces with the right sides together, and stitch along the side and bottom edges. Clip the corners and turn the pocket right side out. Push out the corners with a turning tool.

* Fold the top raw edges ½" to the wrong side and press. Edgestitch the top closed.

* Center the pocket on the right side of one lining piece, 4" down from the top edge, with the topstitched edge of the pocket at the top. Edgestitch along the sides and bottom, leaving the top edge open.

⑨ Construct the Lining

* Center each half of the magnetic snap on the right side of the lining pieces, 2" from the top edge. Attach them, following the manufacturer's instructions.

* Pin the two lining pieces with the right sides together, aligning all the raw edges. Stitch the sides and bottom. Press the seam allowances open.

⑩ Assemble the Bag

* Insert the exterior bag into the lining with the right sides together, aligning the side seams and top raw edges. Make sure the strap and holder are sandwiched between the layers. Stitch around the top opening of the bag, leaving a 5" opening on one side for turning.

* Notch the curves and turn the bag right side out. Tuck the lining into the bag exterior. Press the raw edges of the opening ½" to the wrong side, and continue pressing all around the top edge. Edgestitch around the top edge, closing the opening in the stitching.

⑪ Finish the Strap

Insert the loose end of the strap into the ring from the outside to the inside. Try on the bag and adjust the strap length as desired. Topstitch the end of the strap to secure it at the desired location, or hand-sew it with a slipstitch if you don't want the stitching to show on the outside of the strap.

HOT PaD APRON

Designed by Destri Bufmack

Can't find your hot pads when you need them? This apron has hot pads built right in for perfect protection. The pleats keep the fabric positioned for easy access to your hot pads and make the apron wide enough to be fully utilitarian.

MATERIALS

* 1 yard of 44/45" quilting or home dec weight fabric
* ½ yard of insulated batting
* 1 spool of coordinating thread

Finished dimensions – 19" long × 44" wide at bottom edge, with 87" ties

Seam allowance – ¼" unless otherwise specified

❶ Measure, Mark, and Cut

Fold your fabric in half with the right sides together, aligning the selvages. Measure and mark the following pieces directly on the wrong side of your fabric, as shown.

* **Apron** 20" × 44" (cut 1 on fold)
* **Hot pad** 9" square (cut 4)
* **Waistband/ties** 3½" × 44" (cut 2 on fold)

Cut from insulated batting:

* **Hot pad lining** 9" square (cut 4)

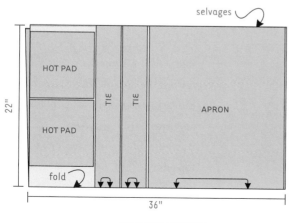

CUTTING LAYOUT

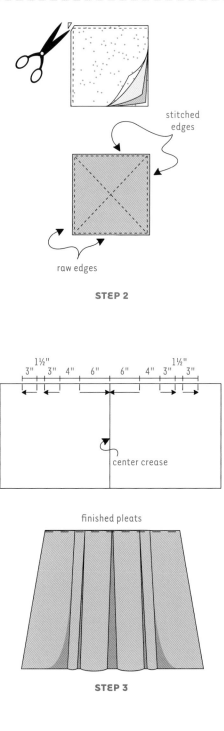

STEP 2

STEP 3

② **Make the Hot Pads**

Pin two hot pad squares with the right sides together. Pin two lining squares to the fabric squares so there are four layers. Stitch the layers together on two adjoining sides, leaving the other two sides unstitched (they will be finished later). Clip the corner where the seams meet, turn the hot pad right side out, and press. Edgestitch around all the sides, including the two sides with the raw edges. Topstitch an X through the center (from each corner to its opposite corner). Repeat for the remaining hot pad and liners.

③ **Make the Pleats**

* Fold the apron in half widthwise, aligning the 20" edges, and mark a center crease. Open the apron and smooth it flat. Make pleat placement marks as shown in the diagram.

* For the center pleat, fold the fabric on each side of the crease so that the 6" marks meet at the center. Pin the folds in place and press.

* For the remaining four pleats, fold the fabric at the 3" marks so the pleats fold toward the outside edges, away from the center. Press. Pin the folds in place and press.

* Baste the pleats in place, close to the top edge.

④ Attach the Hot Pads to the Apron

* Fold and press the side and bottom raw edges of the apron ¼" to wrong side, then fold and press another ½" to the wrong side.

* Tuck the exposed raw edges of each hot pad into the folds at each bottom corner of the apron. Stitch along the sides and bottom of the apron to hem, being sure to catch the hot pads in the stitching.

* Tack each hot pad to the apron with small zigzag or hand stitch at the center of the topstitched X. This stitch will show through on the right side of the apron, so use a coordinating thread color. The stitch prevents the hot pads from flopping out at the bottom of the apron, and allows you to "wear" the hot pads more like mitts when you use them.

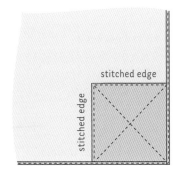

STEP 4

⑤ Make and Attach the Waistband/Ties

* Pin the waistband pieces with the right sides together along one short edge. Stitch to make one long waistband, and press the seam open. Fold and press all the raw edges ¼" to the wrong side.

* Unfold one long pressed edge and pin it to the apron with the right sides together and the waistband seam aligned with the apron center crease marking.

* Stitch the waistband to the apron. Press the seam allowance toward the waistband; at the same time re-press the entire bottom edge ¼" to the wrong side. Edgestitch around the entire waistband/tie ends.

* To shape the tie ends, make a diagonal fold 2" from the bottom of each tie end, so the wrong sides are together. Edgestitch the loose edges together.

ORGANIZER WALLET

Designed by Elizabeth Dronen

Can your wallet hold change, cards, and a checkbook? This one sure can! Create your own fabulous, functional wallet, complete with a space to hold your creative project ideas. This cute and useful accessory makes a great gift for yourself and your best friend, since you can make two with just one yard of fabric.

MATERIALS

* 1 yard of 44/45" quilting-weight cotton fabric
* 1 spool of coordinating thread
* Scrap of lightweight fusible interfacing
* ⅛ yard of medium-weight fusible interfacing
* ¼ yard of heavyweight double-sided fusible web
* Magnetic snap (and tool)
* 7" zipper

Finished dimensions – 4" high × 7½" wide (when closed)

Seam allowance – ⅜" unless otherwise specified

① Measure, Mark, and Cut

Lay out your fabric in a single layer with the wrong side facing. Measure and mark the following pieces directly on the wrong side of your fabric as shown in the cutting layout diagram. (If you are making a second identical wallet for a friend, fold the fabric in half and cut an extra set of pieces.) Refer to the labeled drawing of the wallet as reference for the location of each piece.

* **Wallet interior/exterior**
  9" × 8½" (cut 2)
* **Zipper pocket**
  4½" × 8½" (cut 4)
* **Card pocket 1**
  4½" × 8½" (cut 2)
* **Card pocket 2**
  4" × 8½" (cut 1)
* **Card pocket 3**
  3½" × 8½" (cut 1)
* **Card pocket 4**
  3" × 8½" (cut 1)
* **Snap tabs**
  5" × 2½" (cut 2)

Cut from lightweight fusible interfacing:
* **Zipper reinforcement**
  1" × 7½" (cut 2)

Cut from medium-weight fusible interfacing:
* **Pocket interfacing**
  4 ½" × 8½" (cut 2)

Cut from heavyweight double-sided fusible web:
* **Snap tab interfacing**
  4" × 2" (cut 1)
* **Wallet interfacing**
  8" × 7½" (cut 1)

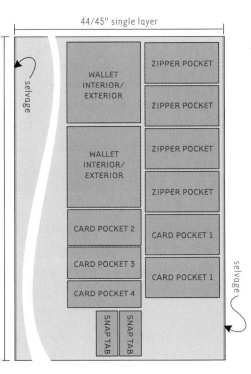

44/45" single layer

selvage

ZIPPER POCKET

WALLET INTERIOR/ EXTERIOR

ZIPPER POCKET

ZIPPER POCKET

WALLET INTERIOR/ EXTERIOR

ZIPPER POCKET

CARD POCKET 2

CARD POCKET 1

CARD POCKET 3

CARD POCKET 1

CARD POCKET 4

SNAP TAB

SNAP TAB

selvage

CUTTING LAYOUT

NOTE: *The wavy line in the layout indicates extra fabric that is not shown.*

A Card Pocket 1
B Zipper Pocket
C Snap Tab
D Card Pocket 3
E Card Pocket 4
F Card Pocket 2

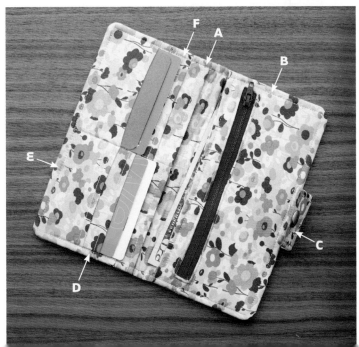

STEP 2

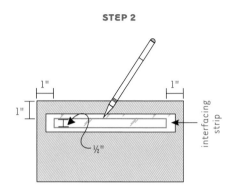

drawing zipper placement lines

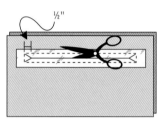

cutting the zipper opening

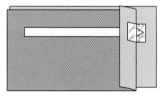

tacking side triangles to inside fabric layer

② Make the Zipper Slot

* On the wrong side of two zipper pocket pieces, center a zipper reinforcement strip of interfacing ¾" down from the top raw edge. Fuse following the manufacturer's instructions.
* On the wrong side of one of the interfaced pieces, draw a ½"-wide rectangle as shown, 1" from the top and 1" from each side edge. This piece will become the zipper pocket lining.
* Pin the second interfaced piece (which will become the zipper pocket exterior) to the zipper pocket lining with the right sides together and the drawn rectangle facing up.
* Pin and stitch along the marked lines, using a short stitch length and following the edges of the rectangle exactly.
* Cut a line through all the layers in the center of the rectangle, stopping ½" from each end. Make angular cuts as shown toward each of the four corners. Be very careful to clip right up to, but not through, the stitching lines.
* Pull one fabric layer through the opening so that both pieces are right side out. Press all around the cut-out rectangle. Tack the side triangles to the inside fabric layer.

DESIGNER TIP: *Before putting in the zipper, you can reduce the bulk in your new wallet by stitching a bar tack across the zipper teeth just above the bottom metal stop. Then cut off the stop. This will also make the zipper easier to sew.*

③ Stitch the Zipper

Pin the zipper behind the zipper pocket with the right side of the zipper facing out through the opening. Make sure the bar tacking (*see* Designer Tip) is not visible in the opening. Edgestitch around the opening to stitch the zipper in place; catch the zipper tape in the stitching.

4 Finish the Zipper Pocket

* Interface one of the remaining zipper pockets with a pocket interfacing and pin it to the zipper pocket exterior with the right sides together. Pin the last zipper pocket piece on top with the right side up, so that the top two layers have the wrong sides together.
* Stitch along the top edge.
* Flip the layers so that the zipper exterior is once again on top and the last two zipper pieces are behind the zipper, and press. Edgestitch along the top edge and baste the remaining three sides together with an edgestitch.

5 Make the Credit Card Pockets

* Interface a card pocket 1 with the remaining pocket interfacing. Pin both card pocket 1 pieces with the right sides together, aligning the raw edges. Stitch the top edge. Flip the pocket right side out and press. Edgestitch along the top edge.
* Stitch a narrow ¼" double-fold hem on the top of card pockets 2, 3, and 4.
* Pin credit card pockets 1 and 2 with their right sides facing up, aligning the bottom and side edges, while making sure the top edges are parallel.

* Mark a line across pocket 2 that is 2½" down from the topmost edge. Stitch along the line to form the bottom edge of pocket 2.
* Add credit card pocket 3 to the top in similar fashion, this time marking and stitching a line 3" down from the topmost edge.
* Add the last credit card pocket and baste the unfinished edges (sides and bottom) together, close to the raw edges.
* Mark or press a vertical line down the center of the pockets and topstitch along the marked line to divide the pockets.

2½"

setting up credit card pockets

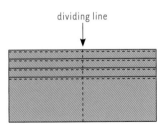

dividing line

stitching credit card pockets

STEP 5

6 Assemble the Inside Pieces

Lay a wallet interior right side up on your work surface. Place the credit card pocket assembly on one half, with the right side facing up and the raw edges aligned. Place the zippered pocket on the other half with the right side facing up and the raw edges aligned. Baste the layers together on all four sides, close to the raw edges. Refer to the photograph for pocket placement.

7 Make the Snap Tab

* Interface one snap tab with the heavyweight interfacing following manufacturer's instructions, centering it ¼" from each raw edge.
* Pin the snap tabs with the right sides together, and stitch three sides with a scant ¼" seam allowance just outside of the interfacing. Leave one end open for turning.
* Clip the corners and trim the seam allowances. Turn the snap tab right side out and press all around to fuse the reverse side of the interfacing to the second fabric layer. Edgestitch along the three finished sides.
* Mark the snap placement ¾" from the finished short end of the tab, and install the female half of the snap according to the manufacturer's instructions.

8 Complete the Wallet

* Interface the remaining wallet exterior with heavyweight interfacing, centering it ½" from each raw edge.
* Mark the snap placement on the right side of the interfaced exterior 1½" from the top 8½" edge, centered from each side. Install the male half of the snap according to the manufacturer's instructions.
* Pin the interior and exterior with the right sides together, making sure the snap edge of the exterior lines up with the card pockets on the interior.
* Stitch around all the edges with a ½" seam allowance, leaving an opening at the center of the zippered pocket edge for turning and for the snap tab. Use a short stitch length for strength and backstitch at each corner.
* Clip the corners and trim the seam allowances except at the opening.
* Turn the wallet right side out. Insert the snap tab in the opening and pin it in place, testing that the wallet closes and snaps properly. Press all around to fuse the reverse side of the interfacing to the second fabric layer.
* Topstitch all the way around, closing the opening as you stitch. Use an 18/110 or denim machine needle if necessary to sew through all the layers.

camp shirt

Designed by Nina Martine Robinson

Update this classic shirt style for your little person with whimsical prints and patterns. This easy-to-wear style is loose fitting with a one-piece collar. It's a great style for both girls and boys. It's also the perfect way to incorporate some fun prints into your little one's wardrobe!

MATERIALS

* Locate the pattern in the envelope (sheet #2)
* 1 yard of 44/45" quilting-weight cotton fabric
* 1 spool of coordinating thread
* 4 buttons, ½" in diameter, or 4 snaps (size 16)

Sizes – 3T, 4T, 5T

Seam allowance – ½" unless otherwise specified

1 Determine Your Child's Size

Measure the chest to find the right size.

	3T	4T	5T
Chest size	22"	23"	24"

2 Measure, Mark, and Cut

Fold your fabric in half lengthwise with the right sides together, aligning the selvages. Position the pattern pieces according to the layout and cut them out. Transfer markings from the pattern to the wrong side of the fabric before removing the pattern.

* **Front** (cut 2)
* **Back** (cut 1 on fold)
* **Sleeve** (cut 2)
* **Collar** (cut 2 on fold)
* **Back facing** (cut 1 on fold)

NOTE: *Position the grainline arrow on the pattern pieces along the lengthwise grain of the fabric.*

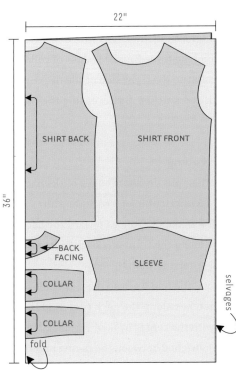

CUTTING LAYOUT

❸ Stitch the Shoulder Seams

With the right sides together, pin and stitch the front to the back along the shoulder seams. Trim the seam allowances to ¼" and press both toward the back of the shirt.

❹ Attach the Sleeves

With the right sides together, pin the curved edge of the sleeve to the armhole opening on the shirt, matching the notches and the center of the sleeve cap to the shoulder seam. Stitch and press the seam allowances toward the sleeve.

❺ Make and Attach the Collar

* Pin the collar pieces with the right sides together and stitch along three edges, leaving the notched edge unstitched. Clip the corners and notch along the curved edge. Turn the collar right side out and press. Baste across the raw edges with a ¼" seam allowance. Edgestitch along the three finished edges of collar.
* Pin the raw edge of the collar to the right side of the neckline, matching the center back and notches. Baste, easing the collar to fit the neck edge.

❻ Make and Attach the Facing

* With the right sides together, pin the short edges of the back facing piece to the front facings (cut in one with the shirt front). Stitch and press the seam allowances toward the back facing. Turn the raw edge along the front and back facings ¼" to the wrong side and stitch to finish the edge.
* Fold the front facings along the fold lines so the right sides are together, matching the notches along the neck edge, and the center back of the shirt with the center back of the back facing. The collar will be sandwiched between the facing and the shirt. Stitch along the neck edge through all the layers. Clip the corners and notch the curved edge. Leave the facings with the wrong side out until after the shirt is hemmed.

❼ Stitch the Side Seams

With the right sides together, stitch the front to the back along the side and underarm seams. Press the seams toward the back of the shirt.

❽ Hem the Shirt

Turn the bottom edge of the shirt (including the front facing) ¼" to the wrong side and press. With the right sides of the shirt and facings still together, stitch the bottom edge of the front facing and shirt together with a ¾" seam allowance. Clip the corners. Turn and press the facings to the inside of the shirt so that wrong sides are together. Turn and press the remaining bottom edge of the shirt ¾" to the wrong side. Topstitch on the right side of the shirt ⅝" from the bottom edge.

❾ Hem the Sleeves

Turn and press the sleeve edges ¼" to the wrong side, then turn an additional ¾" and stitch close to the folded edge.

❿ Add the Buttons or Snaps

If using buttons, make horizontal buttonholes on the left front according to the placement marks on the pattern piece. Position the buttons on the right front, ½" in from the finished edge, as they correspond to the buttonholes. If using snaps, position them the same way, with the female snaps on the left front and male snaps on the right front.

convertible Diaper clutch

Designed by Jolene Lightfoot

Do those bulky diaper bags get you down? While sometimes necessary, avoid them when you can with this light, compact clutch. The unfolded clutch is the changing pad, with a pocket built right in for diapers, wipes, and balm. Easy to move from bag to bag, or carry on its own, and such a space saver!

MATERIALS

* 1 yard of 44/45" quilting-weight cotton fabric
* 1 spool of coordinating thread
* ⅓ yard of fusible fleece
* ½ yard of fusible interfacing
* One 1" swivel clasp
* One 1" D-ring
* Zipper foot (optional)
* Walking foot (optional)
* 1 snap
* Cereal bowl, glass, or other template for rounding corners

Finished dimensions – 24" long × 12" wide
Seam allowance – ¼" unless otherwise specified

① Measure, Mark, and Cut

Fold your fabric in half lengthwise with the right sides together, aligning the selvages. Measure and mark the following pattern pieces directly on the wrong side of your fabric, as shown in the cutting layout. Then cut them out.

* **Body** 24" × 12" (cut 2)
* **Pocket** 7" × 12" (cut 2)
* **Binding** 2¼" × 44" (cut 2 on fold)

Open the fabric to form a single layer, and measure and mark the following pattern pieces directly on the wrong side of the remaining fabric.

* **Wristlet strap** 13" × 4" (cut 1)
* **D-ring tab** 4" × 3" (cut 1)

From fusible interfacing, cut:
* **Pocket** 7" × 12" (cut 2)
* **Wristlet strap** 11" × 4" (cut 1)
* **D-ring tab** 4" × 3" (cut 1)

From fusible fleece, cut:
* **Body** 24" × 12" (cut 1)

CUTTING LAYOUT

STEP 3

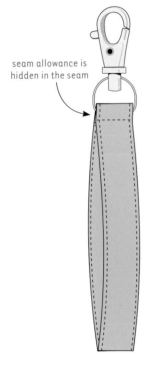

seam allowance is
hidden in the seam

STEP 4

② Interface the Pieces

* Fuse the fleece to the wrong side of a body fabric piece following the manufacturer's instructions.
* Match up the interfacing pieces with the corresponding fabric pieces and fuse each interfacing piece to the wrong side of the fabric.

③ Make the D-Ring Tab

* Fold the D-ring tab in half lengthwise with the wrong sides together and press. Open and press each long side to meet at the center crease. Refold the tab in half lengthwise, and press. Edgestitch both long edges.
* Slide the D-ring on the tab and fold the tab in half widthwise, aligning the short raw edges. Stitch across the width just below the D-ring; use a zipper foot if desired. Set the tab aside.

④ Make the Wristlet Strap

* Fold, press, and stitch the wristlet strap piece the same way as the D-ring tab to produce a double-fold strap. Slide the swivel clasp on the strap, fold the strap in half, aligning the short raw edges, and stitch along the raw edge to form a loop.
* Press the seam allowances open and flip the loop so the raw edges are inside the loop.
* Slide the clasp so it is directly over the seam. Stitch across the loop just below the clasp, catching the seam allowances in the seam. Set the strap aside.

⑤ Make the Pocket

* Pin the two pocket pieces with the right sides together, aligning all raw edges. Stitch across one long edge. Press the seam allowances open. Turn the pocket right side out and press the seam once more, then edgestitch along the finished edge. This will be the top of the pocket.

* Round the opposite corners (along the raw edges) by placing a bowl or other circle template in each corner and tracing it with a pencil. Cut along the lines.

6 Quilt the Clutch Body

* Using the same circle template or the rounded pocket corners as a guide, round all four corners of both body pieces.
* Use tailor's chalk or a fabric marker to draw quilt lines as desired on the right side of one body piece. (The project shown features crossing diagonal lines about 2" apart.)
* Center the male snap 5¾" from a short edge of one body piece and attach according to the manufacturer's instructions. This will be the bottom of the clutch.
* Pin the body pieces with the wrong sides together, aligning rounded corners and raw edges. Stitch along marked quilting lines.

7 Assemble the Clutch

* Lay the quilted body on a work surface with the snap side facing down. Pin the pocket on top of the body on the same end as the snap, aligning the raw edges. Baste the pocket in place close to all three raw edges of the pocket.

* Along one long side, measure 14¼" up from the bottom (snap) edge and mark the D-ring tab placement. Pin the tab at this mark on the snap side of body, with the raw edges aligned. Baste the tab in place with an edgestitch.

8 Make and Attach the Binding

* Pin the two binding strips with the right sides together and stitch along one short edge. Press the seam allowances open. Fold one short end of the binding ¼" toward the wrong side and press. Fold the strip in half lengthwise, with the right sides together, and press.
* To attach, pin the folded end of the binding to the snap side of the body with the right sides together and the raw edges aligned. Stitch all the way around the outer edge, catching the D-ring tab in the stitching. When you reach the start of the stitching, overlap the ends ½" and trim the excess binding.
* Turn the binding to the pocket side of the body and press. Hand-sew the binding in place with a slipstitch.

9 Complete the Clutch

Fold the body in thirds with the pocket on the inside. Mark the point where the top of the clutch meets the male snap. Install the female snap at the mark following the manufacturer's instructions. Fill the clutch with wipes and diapers.

TUXEDO DRESS

Designed by Alexis Meschi

Do you have a T-shirt you love so much, you wish it were a dress? Why not marry it with some fabric for a superadorable look. This dress features a unique, hidden drawstring, which eliminates the need for a zipper and allows the dress to be fitted. Pair it with your favorite boots and hit the town!

MATERIALS

* 1 yard of 44/45" quilting-weight cotton fabric
* A great-fitting T-shirt
* ⅛ yard of coordinating fabric (for inner ruffle)
* 1 spool of coordinating thread
* Scrap of lightweight fusible interfacing, 6" × 10"
* 2 or 3 buttons, ⅜" in diameter
* 1 yard of cording for drawstring

Sizes — custom fit to your size

Seam allowance — ½" unless otherwise specified

① Cut Your T-Shirt

Try on your T-shirt and determine the natural waistline. Measure and mark from the bottom, a line 1½" below the natural waistline all around the T-shirt. Cut the bottom portion of the T-shirt off at the marking. Save the bottom portion of the T-shirt to use for the ruffles.

② Measure, Mark, and Cut

Fold your fabric in half lengthwise with the right sides together, aligning the selvages. Measure and mark the following pattern pieces directly onto your fabric and cut them out.

* **Skirt front/back** 25" × 42" (cut 1 on fold)
* **Outer ruffle** 3" × 32" (cut 1 on fold)

NOTE: *The 25" cutting dimension is the length of the finished skirt. You may cut your skirt longer than 25"; there is enough fabric to cut it up to 33" long.*

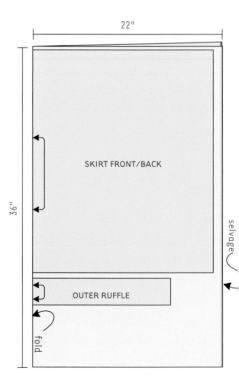

CUTTING LAYOUT

Cut the following from the remaining T-shirt fabric:

* **Middle ruffle** 1½" × 27" (cut 1; you may need to piece the fabric to achieve this length)
* **Faux placket** 3¼" × 8" (cut 1)

Cut the following from the coordinating fabric:

* **Inner ruffle** 3" × 25" (cut 1)

Cut the following from fusible interfacing:

* **Interfacing** 5½" × 9½"

③ **Attach the Interfacing**

Following the manufacturer's instructions, fuse the interfacing to the center of the wrong side of the T-shirt front, just below the neck edge. This will help stabilize the ruffled bib.

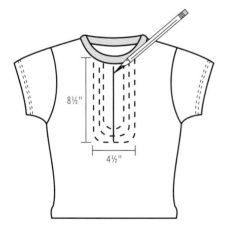

STEP 3

④ **Make and Attach the Ruffled Bib**

Mark the following stitching lines with a disappearing ink fabric marker or tailor's chalk. On the right side of the T-shirt front, draw placement lines in a U-shape that are 2¼" on each side of center and 8½" down from the neck edge. This will be the stitching line for the outer ruffle. Draw a second stitching line ¾" inside of the first stitching line for the middle ruffle. Draw a third stitching line ½" inside the second stitching line for the inner ruffle. Then make the ruffles as follows.

TIP: *It might help to mark a straight line down the center of the T-shirt before marking the stitching lines.*

* **Outer ruffle** Fold the outer ruffle in half lengthwise with the right sides together. Stitch across both short ends, leaving the long edge open. Clip the corners, turn the ruffle right side out, and press. Use a basting stitch to gather the long raw edges of the ruffle. Position the raw edges of the ruffle along the marked placement line and adjust the gathers so they are evenly distributed along the line. Stitch the ruffle in place close to the raw edges.

* **Middle ruffle** Use a basting stitch to gather one long side of the middle ruffle (all edges of this ruffle will be left unfinished). Position the ruffle along the middle marked line, and adjust the gathers so they are evenly distributed. Stitch the middle ruffle in place.

* **Inner ruffle** Prepare this ruffle the same way as the outer ruffle. Position the raw edge of the ruffle along the inner marked line and adjust the gathers so they are evenly distributed along the line. Stitch the inner ruffle in place.

⑤ **Add the Faux Placket**

Press all four edges of the faux placket ½" to the wrong side. Pin the placket in the center of the ruffles, covering the seam allowance of the inner ruffle. Edgestitch the placket in place along all four sides. Hand-sew evenly spaced buttons down the center of the faux placket piece to complete the look.

Alternatively, you may also recycle an existing button placket from another shirt in your wardrobe (as was done for the sample pictured for this project). Simply cut a 3¼" × 8" section of placket off your existing top, which should include ½" on all sides for turning under. Prepare and stitch as described above.

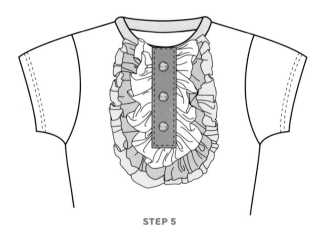

STEP 5

⑥ **Make the Skirt**

With the right sides together, stitch the side seam of the skirt. Press the seam allowances open. Use a basting stitch to gather the top raw edge of the skirt. The finished gathered top edge of the skirt must be at least 2" larger than your hip measurement. Adjust the gathers so they are evenly distributed.

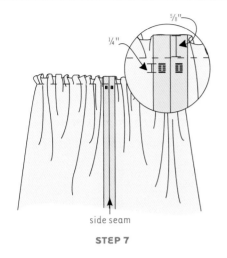

STEP 7

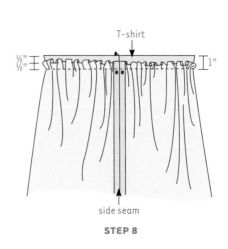

STEP 8

❼ Make the Casing Opening

Make one ¼"-long buttonhole on each side of the side seam, ⅝" down from the top edge of the skirt. These buttonholes will accommodate the drawstring added in step 10.

❽ Attach the Skirt

Pin the T-shirt and skirt with the right sides together and the skirt on top of the T-shirt, matching the skirt seam to one of the T-shirt side seams. The raw edge of the T-shirt should extend ½" above the top raw edge of the skirt. Stretch the T-shirt slightly to fit the gathered edge of the skirt. Stitch, with a 1" seam allowance, using the edge of the T-shirt as a guide.

❾ Stitch the Casing

Press both seam allowances down, toward the skirt. Pin the seam allowances in place, and stitch ¾" below the waistline seam to form the casing.

❿ Insert the Drawstring

Using a safety pin, thread the drawstring through the casing opening. Knot the ends of the drawstring to prevent it from slipping back inside the casing. Turn the dress right side out. Cinch the drawstring to your desired size when wearing the dress.

⓫ Hem the Dress

Make a double-fold hem by pressing under the bottom edge of the skirt ¼", then another 2". Stitch the hem in place, close to the folded edge. As an optional step, add a bit of contrasting trim to the bottom edge of the skirt, to tie in the color of the T-shirt.

PRETTY PINAFORE

Designed by Caroline Critchfield

What a darling concept! This little gem of a dress is perfect for spring and is cut from just one pattern piece. The pinafore itself is very comfortable and allows perfect freedom of movement for a little girl under age two. It's quite versatile and can be worn alone or over a top and leggings.

MATERIALS

* Locate the pattern in the envelope (sheet #2)
* 1 yard of 44/45" quilting-weight cotton fabric
* 1 spool of coordinating thread
* 1 package of ¼"-wide double-fold bias tape
* Scrap of complementary fabric and a button for the flower (optional)

Sizes – 12, 18, and 24 months
Seam allowance – ½" unless otherwise specified

❶ Determine Your Child's Size

Measure the waist and chest to find the right size.

	12 months	18 months	24 months
Chest size	18"	19"	20"
Waist size	20"	20½"	21"

❷ Measure, Mark, and Cut

Fold your fabric in half lengthwise with the right sides together, aligning the selvages. Using the pattern provided, follow the layout, and place the piece accordingly. Cut out the pinafore.

* **Pinafore** (cut 1 on fold)

NOTE: *Position the grainline arrow on the pattern piece along the straight grain of the fabric.*

❸ Sew the Shoulder Seams

Fold the pinafore with the right sides together, aligning the shoulder seams. Take care that the back of the pinafore is crisscrossed and overlaps. Stitch the shoulder seams together and press the seams open.

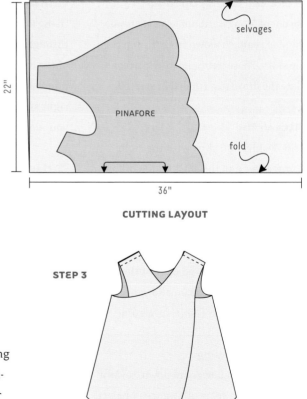

CUTTING LAYOUT

STEP 3

④ Apply the Bias Tape

Attach bias tape to all the raw edges of the pinafore, which you can do with one long strip from start to finish. Here are some pointers:

* Choose a spot on the back of the pinafore concealed by the overlap to begin attaching the bias tape. Unfold the double-fold bias tape and fold over the short end at the beginning of the tape to the wrong side and pin a few inches of the tape to the fabric, aligning raw edges, with the right sides together.

* Stitch in the crease of the bias tape, easing it into place following the raw edge of the pinafore. As you approach the inside corner of a scallop along the bottom edge of the pinafore, stop with your needle down in the fabric at the pivot point. Lift the presser foot and pivot the fabric to continue the line.

* Once you've completed the entire perimeter, overlap the end of the tape at the beginning point and cut the tape.

* Press the bias tape away from the pinafore, and to the wrong side of the garment, pinning where necessary to hold it in place. From the right side of the pinafore, stitch close to the inside folded edge of the bias tape. Take care around the scalloped edges to ensure that the bias tape fully encases the raw edges.

* Apply heat and steam from an iron to smooth out all the edges and curves.

⑤ Embellish with a Flower

* To make a flower embellishment, cut the contrasting fabric scrap into a 3" × 21" strip. Fold the fabric strip in half lengthwise with the wrong sides together.

* Use a needle and thread to make a running stitch through both layers along one short end of the fabric strip. Gather the thread tightly, and continue the running stitch for approximately 3" along the long raw edge of the folded fabric strip. Gather the thread tightly and tie a knot to secure the first petal of the flower.

* Continue working in 3" increments the entire length of the fabric strip, knotting the thread after each 3" segment to create the individual petals. The final petal should include the opposite short end of the folded fabric strip.

* Form a ring with the seven petals and stitch the short ends together on the back of the flower.

* Hand-sew a decorative button to the center front of the flower and glue a small circle of felt to the back of the flower to conceal your stitches. This brooch may be sewn to the dress, or pinned on so that it can be easily removed for laundering.

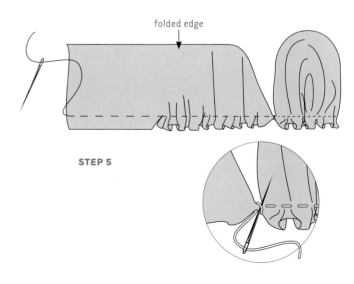

folded edge

STEP 5

DRAWSTRING TIDY CADDY

Designed by Paula Ozier

The padding in this caddy allows it stand up on its own, making it perfect for toys, craft projects, and almost anything! Once it's full, cinch it closed and take it on the go. When empty, collapse it and hang it from a hook or stand it on a shelf. Make this project with a nondirectional fabric or a border print, since the pieces are cut sideways on the fabric.

MATERIALS

* Locate the pattern in the envelope (sheet #2)
* 1 yard of 44/45" quilting-weight cotton fabric
* 1 spool of coordinating thread
* ½ yard of cotton batting or felt padding
* 30" of ribbon, ¼" or ⅜" wide

* 1 cord stop
* One ½"-diameter jingle bell or bead (optional)
* Walking foot (optional)

Finished dimensions – 11½" high × 7" wide × 7" deep
Seam allowance – ½" unless otherwise specified

❶ Measure, Mark, and Cut

Fold your fabric in half lengthwise with the right sides together, aligning the selvages. Position the pattern piece according to the layout, and measure and mark the straps. Cut out the pieces.

* **Side** (cut 8)
* **Straps** 1½" × 10" (cut 4)

NOTE: *Position the grainline arrow on the pattern piece along the crossgrain of the fabric.*

Cut from batting or felt:
* **Side padding** (cut 4)
* **Strap padding** 1" × 11" (cut 2)

❷ Make the Straps

* Pin two strap pieces with the right sides together. Stitch both long edges with a ¼" seam allowance. Turn the tube right side out and press.
* Thread one strap padding piece through the tube with a safety pin, so that both ends of the padding overhang the strap by ½". Take care not to twist the padding. Press the padded tube flat.
* Topstitch parallel lines the length of the strap every ¼".
* Repeat with the remaining strap and padding pieces. Set the straps aside.

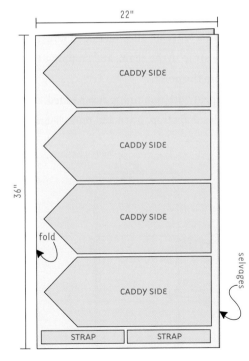

CUTTING LAYOUT

❸ Attach the Padding

Pin a side padding piece to the wrong side of a fabric side piece, aligning the points and side raw edges. The fabric will extend beyond the padding by 6". Baste the pieces together along the sides and point with a ¼" seam allowance. Repeat this process with three more fabric side and padding pieces. These become the caddy exterior.

❹ Make the Caddy Exterior

* Pin two padded sides, with the right sides together, along one side to the tip of the point. Sandwich one unfinished strap end between them, 1" below the top edge of the padding, and pin. Stitch with a ½" seam allowance, catching the strap in the seam, and stopping ½" from the point.
* Repeat with remaining two padded sides and strap. Open and press seams.

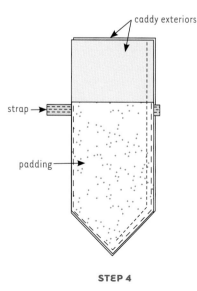

STEP 4

* Pin the two stitched pieces with the right sides together, aligning the seams, points, and raw edges. Make sure the free end of each strap is pinned to an opposite raw edge.
* Stitch one side with ½" seam allowance, catching the free end of the strap in the seam and stopping ½" from point. The end of the seam should meet the previously stitched seam, since both seams stopped ½" from the point. Stitch the remaining seam the same way.
* Press the seams and clip the seam allowance at the corners. You have now created an open-top box that can stand on its own; keep it inside out (padding on the outside, handles on the inside) for now.

❺ Make the Lining

Pin two unpadded fabric sides with the right sides together. Stitch one long side down to the point with ½" seam allowance, stopping ½" from point, the same as for the exterior but without the straps. Repeat with the remaining unpadded sides, then stitch the two halves of the lining together in the same manner. Press the seams and clip the seam allowance at the corners. Turn the lining right side out.

❻ Attach the Lining to the Exterior

* Insert the lining inside the exterior so the right sides are together, aligning the seams and corners. Square off the corners by pushing the lining into each bottom corner with your finger.
* Mark a stitching line 3" from the top raw edges of the exterior and lining pieces and stitch along it, leaving a 3" opening for turning. Don't trim the seam allowance; it adds body to the top of the caddy.
* Turn the caddy right side out through the opening. Push the lining into the exterior and square off the corners again. Press all around, including the top seam, making sure the 3" seam allowance lies flat in between the layers.

⑦ Create the Drawstring Casing

Edgestitch the top edge, starting at one end of the 3" opening. Stitch all around, closing most of the opening, but leave a ½" gap; backstitch on both sides of the gap. Repeat this stitching, including the ½" gap, 1½" below the first stitching line. Stitch one more line ½" below the second stitching line, this time leaving no gap.

⑧ Add the Drawstring

Attach a safety pin to one end of the ribbon, and thread it through the gaps in the first two lines of stitching, then through the casing around the caddy, and back out through the first gap. Thread the cord stop and bead several inches down one end of the ribbon. Thread this same end of the ribbon back through the cord stop. Knot the ends of the ribbon together securely; then manipulate the ribbon so the knot is hidden in the drawstring casing. Stitch the gap at the top edge of the bag closed.

PERSONALIZED GARMENT BAG

Designed by Lisa Cox

With just one yard of fabric, you can make a garment bag that fits a jacket or a child's dress! What a great way to keep dust off and store out-of-season or seldom-worn clothing. The single initial appliqué adds an extra-special personal touch. In addition to quilting-weight cotton, you can use home decor weight fabric, or even coated cotton for when you are traveling or want extra protection.

MATERIALS

* 1 yard of 44/45" quilting-weight fabric
* 5" square scrap of contrasting fabric for alphabet letter
* 1 spool of coordinating thread
* ¼ yard paper-backed fusible web
* 6" square of white or light colored cotton fabric
* ⅔ yard ½"-wide or jumbo rickrack or ribbon
* 32" zipper
* 5" narrow ribbon
* Dinner plate, approximately 9" diameter, or similar circle template for rounding corners
* Garment hanger

Finished dimensions – 35" long × 21" wide

Seam allowance – ½" unless otherwise specified

① Measure, Mark, and Cut

Fold your fabric in half with the right sides together, aligning the selvages. Cut the pieces listed below, which will use all of the fabric.

* **Garment bag** 36" × 22" (cut 2)

Cut from white (light) fabric:

* **Letter backing** 6" diameter circle (cut 1)

Cut from fusible web:

* **Letter** 5" square
* **Letter backing** 6" diameter circle (cut 1)

❷ Create the Appliqué

* Apply the 5" square of fusible web to the wrong side of the 5" square of contrasting fabric following the manufacturer's instructions.
* Using your favorite computer font, print a letter that is approximately 4" at its largest dimension, and cut it out to use as a paper pattern. You can also draw a letter freehand, if you prefer.
* Trace the letter, reversed, on the paper side of the fusible web attached to the contrasting fabric. Cut out the letter shape from the contrasting fabric and peel off the paper backing.
* Center the letter on the right side of the backing circle and press to fuse. Satin stitch around the edges of the letter.

❸ Appliqué the Letter to the Garment Bag

* Apply the 6" circle of fusible web to the wrong side of the white or light colored backing fabric. Peel off the paper backing. Center the backing on the right side of one garment bag piece, 5" down from the top edge. Press to adhere.
* Pin rickrack around the circumference of the circle, covering the raw edge of the fabric and overlapping the rickrack ends. Topstitch the rickrack in place. Alternatively, you can satin stitch the letter backing to the garment bag.

❹ Make the Garment Bag

* Round both corners of one of the short ends of both garment bag pieces with a circle template. These short ends now become the top of the garment bag. (Make sure you round the corners closest to the appliqué.)
* Press the raw edge on the right side of the garment bag front ¼" to wrong side.
* Press the raw edge on the left side of the garment bag back ¼" to wrong side.
* Starting ¾" from the bottom raw edge, pin the folded edges of the garment bag front and back to each side of the zipper tape. Edgestitch the folded edges to the zipper tape with a zipper foot. (The zipper stop should be at the bottom of the garment bag and the top of the zipper should reach to a few inches from the top of the bag.)
* Pin the front and back pieces with the right sides together, aligning all the raw edges. Stitch from the top of the zipper all the way around to the bottom of the zipper, leaving a 2" gap at the center of the top edge for a coat hanger hook to pass through. Clip the curves and press the seam allowances open, including the seam allowances at the top gap. Turn the garment bag right side out and press. Edge finish the seam allowances with a serger or with pinking shears. Hand-tack the seam allowances down at the top gap to secure them.
* Fold the narrow ribbon in half, thread it through the zipper tab, and knot it close to the zipper tab to form a decorative zipper pull.
* Slip the garment bag over your favorite blouse (already on a clothes hanger, of course) and hang!

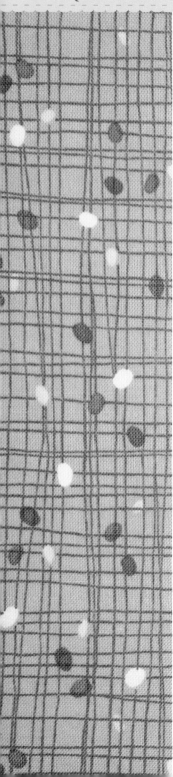

kanzashi CLOCK

Designed by Katherine Donaldson

Kanzashi is a time-honored Japanese craft in which fabric is folded into flower petals. While traditionally used to make hair ornaments, for this project the fabric flower petals are large enough to frame a clock kit, creating a wall clock that is more art than timekeeper.

MATERIALS

* Locate the pattern in the envelope (sheet #1)
* 1 yard of 44/45" quilting-weight fabric
* 1 spool of coordinating thread
* Two 6" squares of ⅛"-thick cardboard
* Glue gun
* Utility knife

* Quartz clock kit, with approximately a 2¼" square "movement" (the box encasing the motor)
* Felt, fabric scraps, ribbon, beads, or other embellishment if desired (optional)

Finished dimensions – 13" across

Seam allowance – ½" unless otherwise specified

❶ Measure, Mark, and Cut

Lay out your fabric in a single layer with the wrong side facing up. Pin the clock face pattern piece close to the selvage and cut it out. Transfer the markings to the wrong side of the fabric. Next to the clock face, cut a circle with a 1½" diameter for the movement lining. Measure and mark the petal pieces with the straight edges along the straight and crossgrain lines. Cut out the pieces.

* **Clock face** (cut 1)
* **Petals** 10" square (cut 12)
* **Movement lining** 1½" diameter circle (cut 1)

Cut from cardboard using utility knife:

* **Clock face support** (cut 1)
* **Star template** (cut 1, leaving the clock movement cutout uncut for now)

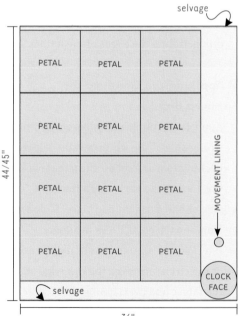

selvage

PETAL | PETAL | PETAL
PETAL | PETAL | PETAL
PETAL | PETAL | PETAL
PETAL | PETAL | PETAL

44/45"

MOVEMENT LINING

CLOCK FACE

selvage

36"

CUTTING LAYOUT

DESIGNER NOTES

You can fussy cut (*see the glossary*) the center and "petals" to make some interesting looks and highlight the fabric print. Quilting-weight cottons work great, but silks, brocades, and other fancy fabrics make a great base too. Feeling particularly creative? Try a lovely decorative paper for the clock face, or embroider, paint, or bead number markers onto each of the petals. This is not your average everyday straitlaced office clock!

STEP 2

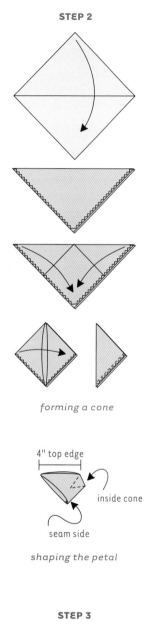

forming a cone

4" top edge

inside cone

seam side

shaping the petal

STEP 3

② Make Petals

As you fold the petals, don't press the folds; you want to create a soft and loose looking organic petal. To make each petal, do the following:

* Fold one petal in half diagonally with the wrong sides together, and zigzag stitch along the cut edges to prevent fraying.
* Fold the side points to the bottom point. Then fold the fabric in half again, one side corner to the other. Straight stitch ⅜" from the zigzag stitched edges to form a cone.
* Turn the wide, open end of the cone right side out, leaving about 2" of the tip of the cone unturned inside.
* Holding the seam side of the cone at the bottom, lightly flatten the cone into a truncated triangle and measure along the top edge. Push in or pull out the tip of the cone until the top edge of the petal is about 4" long.

③ Assemble Petal Ring

* Place the star template on a work surface with the cutout placement marking facing up. With the front of a petal facing you, push the inner unturned cone section of the petal all the way onto one of the points of the star template. This will flatten and unfold the top edge of the petal.
* Check to make sure the top of the petal is centered on the arm, the folds are neat, and the petal is still 4" long when the tip is pulled to a point.
* Repeat with the remaining petals.
* With the glue gun, gently squeeze hot glue between the top of the cardboard and the flower petal, pushing the petal down gently until the glue holds. Take care to wipe off excess glue and don't burn yourself!
* Hand-tack the petals to each other 3" up from the bottom glued edge and ¾" back from the front folded edge with a small stitch through the adjoining outer layers of each petal. Be sure not to catch the front layer of fabric in your stitch. Knot the ends of the thread together and clip them so they don't show from the front.

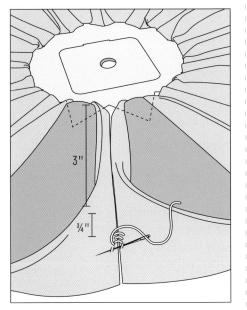

STEP 3

④ Make Clock Face

* Cut away the clock movement cutout at the placement mark, adjusting the size as necessary for your movement. Take care not to bend the cardboard as you cut.

* Center the movement lining circle on the fabric clock face with the right sides together. Machine- or hand-stitch the two pieces together along the ⅜" stem hole circle marked on the clock face.

* With sharp scissors, poke a small hole in the center of the ⅜" circle and clip as close to the stitching as possible, all around the circle.

* Push the lining through the hole so that the fabrics are wrong sides together and the opening has a finished fabric edge. Press the opening flat.

* Hand-sew a running stitch along the marked gathering line on the wrong side of the fabric clock face, leaving the thread tails long.

* Place the fabric clock face on top of the cardboard clock face with the right side facing up. Pull the raw edges of the movement lining scrap through the hole in the cardboard clock face.

* Smooth the fabric on the front of the clock face and pull the gathering thread tight to wrap the outer edge of the fabric around the edge of the cardboard face. The lining on the back of the cardboard will not lie flat, and that's okay. It's there to line the hole and keep the center of your clock face from fraying. Knot the gathering thread tightly and trim the thread ends.

⑤ Complete the Clock

* Mount the clock movement to the completed clock face following the manufacturer's instructions, leaving the hands off for now.

* Place the clock face assembly on the petal ring, checking to make sure they fit together and that the petals line up the way you like.

* Lift the clock face and put a generous dab of glue at the base of each of the flower petals on the petal ring.

* Slide the clock face back on the petal ring, fitting the movement through the hole in the petal ring. Press the two pieces of cardboard together firmly until the glue sets.

* Tug the folds straight at the base of each flower petal and shape the ends.

* Put the hands on your clock, and give yourself a round of applause!

Logan's Guitar

Designed by Jess Durrant

A rockin' gift for the budding musician! This stuffed toy guitar replicates a Fender Jaguar, with a classic electric guitar shape. But watch out, the other kids may demand an entire band's worth of instruments when you're done!

MATERIALS

* Locate the pattern in the envelopes (sheets #1 and 2)
* 1 yard of 44/45" quilting-weight cotton fabric
* 1 spool of coordinating thread
* One 12" × 9" light colored felt scrap
* Small felt scrap in contrasting color
* Two 12-ounce bags of fiberfill
* Embroidery floss
* Yardstick or dowel, cut to approximately 20" length (optional)
* 3 buttons, ½" diameter (optional)

Finished dimensions – 22" tall (including neck) × 9½" wide × 2" thick

Seam allowance – ¼" unless otherwise specified

❶ Measure, Mark, and Cut

Fold your fabric in half lengthwise with the right sides together, aligning the selvages. Position the body, gusset, and neck pattern pieces to the fabric as shown and cut them out. Transfer the markings from the pattern pieces to the wrong side of fabric. For variety, the gusset can be cut from a different fabric, as in the sample.

* **Body** (cut 2)
* **Neck** (cut 2)
* **Gusset** (cut 1 on fold)

Cut from 12" × 9" felt:
* **Pickguard** (cut 1)
* **Bridge** (cut 1)
* **Neck** (cut 1)

Cut from contrasting felt:
* **Pickup** (cut 2)

NOTE: *Position the grainline arrows on the pattern pieces along the lengthwise grain of the fabric. The Neck and Pickguard are on sheet #1; the Body, Gusset, Bridge, and Pickup are on sheet #2.*

❷ Appliqué the Guitar Face

Appliqué the two pickup pieces onto the pickguard as shown in the project, using an edgestitch. Appliqué the pickguard and bridge onto the right side of one guitar body with an edgestitch. This piece becomes the guitar front.

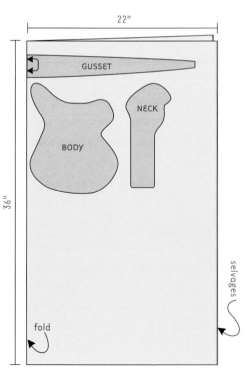

CUTTING LAYOUT

③ Assemble the Guitar Body

✳ With the right sides together, pin and stitch the gusset to the front body, starting at one neck opening placement dot at the top and ending at the other placement dot.

✳ Stitch the other long edge of the gusset to the remaining body in the same fashion, this time leaving an opening at the bottom, as marked on the pattern, for turning and stuffing.

✳ Notch all the curves and turn the guitar body right side out.

④ Assemble the Neck

✳ Layer the fabric neck pieces with the right sides together, and the felt neck piece sandwiched between them, aligning all the raw edges. Pin, then stitch them together from one placement dot to the other, leaving the short end open for turning and stuffing.

✳ Turn the neck right side out and press. Press the raw edges of the opening ¼" to the wrong side.

✳ If you want to use a dowel or yardstick for a stiffer neck, insert it now into the neck and stuff firmly all around it, keeping the dowel centered. (The dowel will extend several inches out of the neck opening.)

⑤ Complete the Guitar

✳ Insert the exposed end of the dowel into the neck opening of the body, until the folded edges of the neck cover the opening and overlap the guitar front and back.

✳ Hand-sew the neck to the body with a slipstitch or blanket stitch. This may prove easier if the body is at least partially stuffed.

✳ Stuff the body through the opening in the bottom, keeping the dowel centered.

✳ Hand-sew the opening closed with a slipstitch or whipstitch.

✳ Hand-sew three buttons at the top of the neck.

IF YOU LIKE: *Select some embroidery thread in different colors and embroider frets and strings onto the neck.*

PLAYDAY FROCK

Designed by Rachel Knoblich

Here's a fun design for a sweet and simple little girl's summer dress — feminine, yet not overly frilly. The pullover style has no buttons, zippers, or ties, making it perfect for every day. During the cooler months, it also works well layered over another top and leggings.

MATERIALS

* Locate the pattern in the envelope (sheet #3)
* 1 yard of 44/45" quilting-weight cotton fabric
* 1 spool of coordinating thread
* ⅔ yard of ¼"-wide elastic
* ½ yard of ½"-wide single-fold bias tape

Sizes – 1-2, 3-4, 5-6
Seam allowance – ½" unless otherwise specified

① Determine Your Child's Size

Measure the chest to find the right size.

	1-2	3-4	5-6
Chest size	21"	23"	25"
Finished length	20"	22"	24"

② Measure, Mark, and Cut

Lay out your fabric in a single layer with the right side facing up. Position the pattern pieces according to the layout and cut them out. Transfer the markings from the pattern to the wrong side of the fabric.

* **Dress front** (cut 1)
* **Dress back** (cut 1)
* **Sleeve** (cut 2)
* **Pocket** (cut 2)

Cut the elastic as follows:

* **For size 1-2:** 19"
* **For size 3-4:** 20"
* **For size 5-6:** 21"

NOTE: *Position the grainline arrow on the pattern pieces along the lengthwise grain of the fabric.*

selvage

44/45"

SLEEVE

DRESS BACK

SLEEVE

POCKET

DRESS FRONT

POCKET

selvage

36"

CUTTING LAYOUT

NOTE: *Mirror the Dress Back and Front along the line indicated on the pattern.*

❸ Make and Attach the Pockets

* Stitch a narrow ¼" double-fold hem along the top straight edge of each pocket.
* Staystitch ¼" from the curved edge of each pocket. Clip the seam allowance to, but not through, the stitching. Turn and press the seam allowance to the wrong side of the pocket. The staystitching will help form a smoother edge when pressing around the curve.
* Pin both pockets on the front according to the placement marks on the pattern. Edgestitch the pockets in place along the side and bottom edges.

❹ Stitch the Sides

With the right sides together, pin the front to the back along both side seams. Stitch, then press the seams open.

❺ Make and Attach the Sleeves

Finish the lower, curved edge of each sleeve with a narrow ¼" double-fold hem. With the right sides together, pin the sleeve side seams to the armhole openings of the dress, aligning the notches. Stitch the seams and turn the dress right side out.

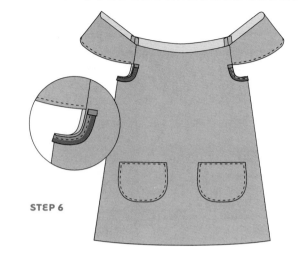

STEP 6

❻ Bind the Armhole

* Cut two pieces of single-fold bias tape, each 1" longer than the raw edge of the armhole opening. Turn and press both short ends of the bias tape ½" to the wrong side. Open one long folded edge of the bias tape. On the right side of the dress, align the raw edge of the bias tape with the raw edge of the armhole opening, pinning it from the front sleeve edge to the back sleeve edge. Stitch along the pressed crease of the bias tape.
* Turn and press the bias tape to the inside of the armhole. Stitch the bias tape in place from the right side of the dress with a ⅜" seam allowance.

❼ Create the Neckline Casing

Press under the top edge of the dress (front, back, and top edges of sleeves) ¼", then press under another ½". Stitch close to the folded edge of the casing; leave a 1" opening along the back to insert the elastic through. Thread the elastic through the casing, overlap the ends of the elastic ½", and stitch the ends together securely. Stitch the casing opening closed.

❽ Hem the Frock

Stitch a ½" double-fold hem on the bottom edge of the dress.

MANDARIN DRESS

Designed by Daljeet Kaur

This unlined, half-wrap dress for girls is Chinese inspired and features pretty buttons instead of traditional frog closures. The wrap styling is perfect for the immodest sitting posture of a two-year-old, as it allows for plenty of movement. The bias binding around the collar, front opening, and armholes provides the perfect touch of contrast.

MATERIALS

* Locate the pattern in the envelope (sheet #3)
* 1 yard of 44/45" quilting-weight cotton fabric (not suitable for one-way patterns)
* 1 spool of coordinating thread
* Small piece of lightweight woven, fusible interfacing (for the collar)
* 2 yards of ¼"-wide double-fold bias tape
* 14" length of elastic cording
* 4 buttons, ½" in diameter

① Determine Your Child's Size

Measure the chest to find the right size.

	2	3	4
Waist size	21"	22"	23"
Finished length	18"	19¾"	21¾"

② Measure, Mark, and Cut

Lay out your fabric in a single layer with the right side facing up. Position the pattern pieces according to the layout and cut them out. Transfer the markings from the pattern, including the button loop placement, to the wrong side of fabric.

* **Right front** (cut 1)
* **Left front** (cut 1)
* **Back** (cut 1)

* **Collar** (cut 2)

Cut from interfacing:

* **Collar** (cut 1)

Sizes – 2, 3, 4
Seam allowance – ¼" unless otherwise specified

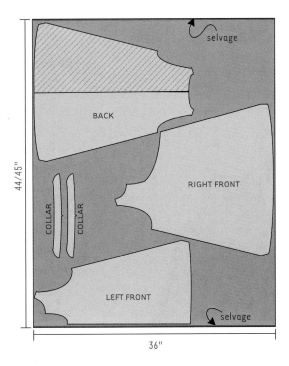

CUTTING LAYOUT

NOTE: *Position the grainline arrow on the pattern pieces along the lengthwise grain of the fabric. Mirror the Dress Back along the line indicated on the pattern.*

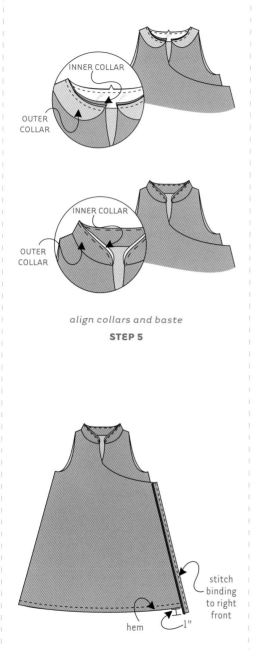

align collars and baste
STEP 5

stitch
binding
to right
front

hem 1"

STEP 6
stitch binding to right front

③ Attach the Fronts and Back

* With the right sides together, pin the left front and right front to the back piece at the shoulders and stitch. Press the shoulder seams toward the back of the dress.

* With the right sides together, pin the front pieces to the back piece at the side seams and stitch. Press the side seams toward the back of the dress.

④ Hem Two Edges

* At the inside straight edge of the left front, stitch a ¼" double-fold hem.

* Stitch a ½" double-fold hem along the bottom edge of the entire dress.

⑤ Attach the Collar

* Fuse the interfacing onto the wrong side of one collar piece following the manufacturer's instructions. The interfaced collar becomes the inner collar piece.

* Pin the inner and outer collar pieces with the right sides together and the dress neckline sandwiched between the two collars, aligning all the neck edges. Take care to match the notch at the center of the collar with the center back of the dress. Stitch through all three layers with a ¼" seam allowance.

* Turn and press the collar pieces up, away from the dress. The collar pieces will now be wrong sides together. Baste the top raw edges of the collar together with a ⅛" seam allowance.

⑥ Bind the Right Front Edge

* Unfold the double-fold bias tape and pin it along the raw edge starting at the top straight edge of the right front with right sides together. Pin the entire length of the right front piece, leaving a 1" tail of bias tape extending beyond the bottom edge. Stitch the bias tape in the crease closest to the raw edge.

* Press the bias tape away from the right front and press the 1" tail at the bottom edge up. Fold the bias tape to the wrong side of the right front and pin. For very precise and neat stitches, stitch close to the inside folded edge of the trim from the right side of the front. If you are unable to catch the bias tape when you stitch from the right side, stitch with the wrong side up, along the edge of the bias tape.

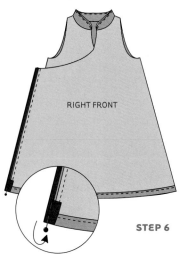

RIGHT FRONT

STEP 6

⑦ Bind the Neck Opening and Collar

* Starting from the bottom edge of the keyhole opening on the left front piece, unfold the bias tape and pin it along the raw edge with the right sides together. Leave a ½" tail of bias tape extending beyond the edge of the left front. Continue pinning the bias tape in place around the top edge of the

collar, and then along the keyhole neckline of the right front. Trim the bias tape, leaving a ½" tail extending beyond the edge of the right front.

* Turn the dress over so the wrong side is facing up. Fold the ½" tails of bias tape to the wrong side and pin them in place. Press the bias tape away from the garment, fold it over to encase the raw edges of the left and right fronts and collar, and stitch in place, as in step 6.

⑧ Bind the Armholes

* Pin the bias tape along the armhole edges, encasing all the fabric raw edges the same as for the side front, keyhole edges and neck opening. Overlap the bias tape slightly where the ends meet, taking care to turn and press the short raw edge to the wrong side. Stitch the bias tape in place, making sure to catch the back of the bias tape in the stitching.

⑨ Attach the Button Loops and Buttons

* Cut the elastic cording into four 3½" lengths. Fold each elastic piece in half and knot the two ends together. Note that you must have about ½" of the looped cord to work with. Make sure the knot is very secure.

* Using needle and thread, secure the elastic loops onto the wrong side of the right front at the placement marks. Make two running stitches over the cord at the bottom of the loop, just above the knot. Trim the "legs" of the cord to about ⅛".

* Determine the button placement by closing the front of the dress and marking button position on the left front. Securely sew on the buttons.

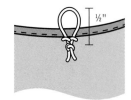

STEP 9

CRAYON AMMO BELT & BAG

Designed by Tracey Citron

*A "his and hers" set for artistic siblings, perhaps?
Your little one will love the ammo-style crayon belt,
while the crayon tote works for girls or boys who
want extra crayon storage and a special bag to stash
their coloring books, paper, and other treasures.*

MATERIALS

* 1 yard of 44/45" quilting-weight cotton fabric
* 1 spool of coordinating thread

Finished dimensions – Bag is 9½" square; Ammo Belt is 6½" × 20½"
Seam allowance – ¼" unless otherwise specified

➊ Measure, Mark, and Cut

Fold your fabric in half lengthwise with the right sides together,
aligning the selvages. Measure and mark the following pattern
pieces directly on the wrong side of your fabric, with the straight
edges positioned along the grainline.

* **Bag**: 10" square (cut 4)
* **Strap/tie** 2" × 21" (cut 4)
* **Ammo belt** 6" × 21" (cut 2)
* **Bag crayon pocket**
  7" × 10" (cut 2)
* **Ammo belt crayon pocket**
  7" × 21" (cut 1 on fold)

The Bag

➊ Make the Crayon Pockets

* Fold each bag crayon pocket in half with the wrong sides
  together, forming two pieces that are 3½" × 10". The folded
  edges will become the top of each crayon pocket.
* Pin each folded pocket onto the right side of a bag square,
  aligning the side and bottom raw edges.
* With a fabric marker or chalk, and starting 1" from one side
  edge, measure and mark vertical crayon pocket stitch lines ¾"
  apart across the entire width of each pocket. Stitch along each
  marked line, being sure to backstitch at the top of the pocket
  each time for reinforcement.

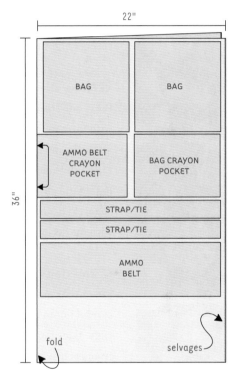

CUTTING LAYOUT

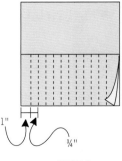

STEP 1

② Stitch the Exterior

Pin the two bag pieces with the attached crayon pockets with the right sides together, aligning all the raw edges. Stitch along the side and bottom edges, being sure to catch the pocket raw edges in the seam. Leave the top edge open. Clip the corners and turn the bag right side out.

③ Make the Straps

Press one strap/tie piece in half lengthwise with the wrong sides together. Open up the strap/tie and press both long raw edges to the wrong side so they meet at the crease. Refold the strap in half lengthwise and edgestitch along both long edges. Repeat with the second strap.

④ Position the Straps

Pin one strap on each side of the bag, being careful not to twist the handles. With the right sides together, pin the strap ends 2" from each side seam and ½" beyond the top, raw edge of the bag.

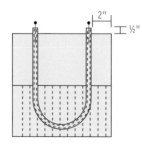

STEP 4

⑤ Assemble the Bag and Lining

* Pin the remaining bag pieces (the lining) with the right sides together, aligning all the raw edges. Stitch along the side and bottom edges. Clip the corners.

* Insert the exterior into the lining with the right sides together, aligning the side seams. The straps should lie between the fabric layers. Stitch around the top edge, leaving a 3" opening for turning on one side.

* Turn the bag right side out, push the lining into the exterior, and extend the straps. Press.

* Edgestitch around the top edge, closing the opening as you stitch. Fill the pockets with crayons and the bag with coloring books, scrap paper, and whatever other treasures your little one desires!

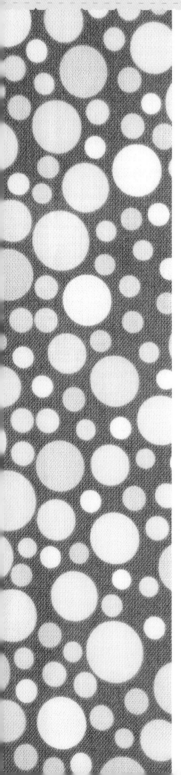

The Ammo Belt

❶ Make the Crayon Pocket

* Fold the ammo belt crayon pocket in half with the wrong sides together, forming a 3½" × 21" piece. The folded edge will become the top edge of the pocket.
* Pin the folded pocket onto the right side of one ammo belt piece, aligning the side and bottom raw edges.
* With a fabric marker or chalk, and starting 1" from one side edge, measure and mark vertical crayon pocket stitch lines ¾" apart across the entire width of the pocket.
* Stitch along each marked line, being sure to backstitch at the top of the pocket each time for reinforcement.

❷ Make the Belt Ties

Press one strap/tie piece in half lengthwise with the wrong sides together. Open up the tie and press both long raw edges to the wrong side to meet at the crease. Refold the tie in half lengthwise and edgestitch along both long edges. Tie a knot close to one finished short edge. Repeat with the second tie.

❸ Position the Ties

Place one tie on the right side of pocketed ammo belt piece. The raw edge should align with the top of the crayon pockets on one short side of the belt, and extend beyond the belt raw edge by ½". Baste it in place. Attach the remaining tie to the opposite side in similar fashion.

❹ Assemble the Belt

* Pin the ammo belt pieces with the right sides together, aligning all the raw edges and tucking the ties between the two pieces. Stitch all around, leaving a 4" opening along the top edge for turning. Be sure not to catch the free ends of the ties in the stitching.
* Clip the corners and turn the ammo belt right side out. Push out the corners with a turning tool.
* Fold the raw edges of the opening ¼" to the wrong side and press all around. Edgestitch along the top edge, closing the opening as you stitch. Add crayons as ammo and tie it on!

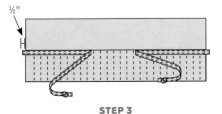

STEP 3

CHILD'S CHEF HAT & APRON

Designed by Cindy Hopper

You can never have too many fun, handmade gift ideas for children. This chef hat and apron is the perfect gift for a little up-and-coming chef. You might consider packaging the set with cookie decorating supplies for the aspiring young baker in your life!

MATERIALS

* Locate the pattern in the envelope (sheet #1)
* 1 yard of 44/45" quilting-weight cotton fabric
* 1 spool of coordinating thread
* ¼ yard of ½"-wide Velcro
* ¼ yard of light- or medium-weight fusible interfacing
* 3" piece of ½"-wide double-fold bias tape

Finished dimensions – Chef's Hat fits up to a 22" head size; Apron is 13" × 11" not including waistband

Seam allowance – ½" unless otherwise specified

① Measure, Mark, and Cut

Lay out your fabric in a single layer with the right side facing up. Position the apron pattern according to the layout, and measure and mark the additional straight pieces with straight edges along the grainline of the fabric. Draw an 18" diameter circle as indicated. Cut out the pieces. Transfer the markings from the pattern to the wrong side of fabric.

* **Apron (cut 2)**
* **Ruffle** 4" × 43" (cut 1)
* **Waistband** 5" × 25" (*see* Exceptions, then cut 1)
* **Hat crown** 18"-diameter circle (cut 1)
* **Hat band** 8" × 24" (cut 1)

Also cut from interfacing:

* **Hat band** 8" × 24" (cut 1)

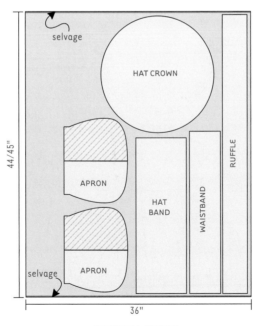

CUTTING LAYOUT

NOTE: *Position the grainline arrow on the pattern piece along the lengthwise grain of the fabric. Mirror the Apron along the line indicated on the pattern.*

EXCEPTIONS

The waistband is designed to fit a 20"–23" waist. If your child's waist is larger, add 5" to his/her actual waist measurement and cut the waistband to that length.

Chef's Hat

❶ Prepare the Hat Band

Fuse interfacing to the wrong side of the hat band, following the manufacturer's instructions. Fold and press each long edge of the band ½" to the wrong side. Fold the band in half lengthwise so the right sides are together. Stitch across each short end, starting at the folded edge and stopping ½" from the pressed edges. Clip the corners, turn the band right side out, and press. Set the band aside.

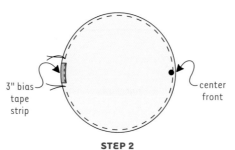

3" bias tape strip

center front

STEP 2

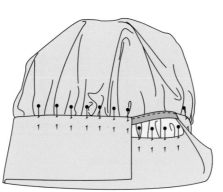

STEP 3

❷ Prepare the Hat Crown

* Stitch the 3" piece of bias tape anywhere along the edge of the hat crown, fully encasing a 3" portion of the raw edge. Mark the point opposite the center of the bias tape as the center front. Use a basting stitch to gather the edge of the hat crown, starting and stopping on either side of the bias tape.

* Pull the basting thread to gather the hat crown edge to 22", not including the 3" section encased with bias tape. Adjust the gathers so they are evenly distributed. Stitch around the circumference of the hat crown with a regular stitch length to secure the gathers. Remove the basting thread.

❸ Attach the Crown and Band

* Align the center of the hat band with the center front mark on the hat crown. Slip the raw edge of the crown in between the open folded edges of the hat band and pin.

* Continue pinning the hat band and crown together, sandwiching the raw edge of the crown in between the folded edges. Approximately ½" of both ends of the bias tape will also be sandwiched between the hat band folds. Pin the layers together securely.

* Edgestitch around all four sides of the hat band, through all the layers, securing the hat crown to the hat band.

④ Finish the Chef Hat

Stitch two 2" pieces of loop Velcro to the left underside of the hat band, parallel to the bottom and top edges. Fold the left side of the band over as far as the bias tape opening will allow, overlapping the right side to determine hook Velcro placement. Stitch the corresponding hook Velcro to the top side on the right end of the hat band. This makes the hat adjustable.

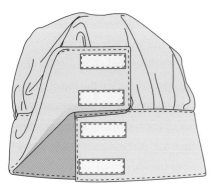

STEP 4

Apron

① Make and Attach the Ruffle

* Fold the ruffle in half lengthwise with the right sides together. Stitch across both short ends. Clip the corners, turn the ruffle right side out, and press. Find and mark the center of the ruffle.

* Use a basting stitch to gather the raw edge of the ruffle.

* Pin the ruffle to the right side of one apron piece, along the curved edge, matching the center marks. To make the ruffle ends taper, angle the ends of the ruffle off the edge of the apron at the marks indicated on the pattern. Adjust the gathers so they are evenly distributed between the marked points.
* Baste the apron and ruffle together with a ¼" seam allowance.
* Pin the apron pieces with the right sides together, sandwiching the ruffle between the two layers. Stitch around the outside curved edge of the apron, leaving the top edge unstitched. Notch the curved seam allowance, turn the apron right side out, and press.
* Edgestitch close to the seam, along the finished edge of the apron.

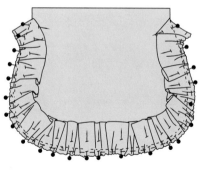

STEP 1

2 Make the Waistband

Fold each long edge ½" to the wrong side. Fold the waistband in half lengthwise with the right sides together and stitch across both short ends. Clip the corners, turn the waistband right side out, and press.

3 Attach the Waistband

* With both right sides facing up, position the apron along the left edge of the waistband. Place the top raw edge of the apron between the layers of the waistband and pin.
* Edgestitch around all four sides of the waistband to secure the top of the apron in the waistband. Be sure to catch the back of the waistband in the stitching.
* Stitch a 2" piece of loop Velcro to the left end of the waistband on the wrong side. Stitch a 3" piece of hook Velcro to the right end of the waistband on the right side. This makes the waist adjustable.

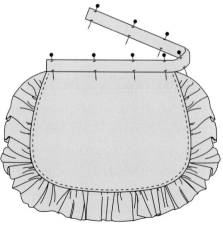

STEP 3

CupCake Apron

Designed by Sharon Madsen

You probably have a favorite apron that you like to wear in the kitchen. How about wearing an apron specific to the food you are preparing? This will certainly be your apron of choice when you're whipping up everyone's favorite cupcakes! It's feminine and flirty, with a touch of whimsy, à la the cupcake pocket on the front of the apron. Too cute!

MATERIALS

* Locate the pattern in the envelope (sheet #2)
* 1 yard of 44/45" quilting-weight cotton fabric
* 1 spool of coordinating thread
* 3 yards of rickrack

* 12" × 12" scrap fabric for cupcake pocket
* 4" × 9" scrap fabric for frosting
* 9" × 7" scrap for front panel facing

Finished dimensions – 28" wide × 17" long, not including ties
Seam allowance – ½" unless otherwise specified

① **Measure, Mark, and Cut**

Lay out your fabric in a single layer with the right side facing up. Measure and mark the following pattern pieces directly on the wrong side of the fabric, then cut them out. Pattern pieces are provided for the front panel and the cupcake pocket facing and frosting.

* **Front panel** (cut 1)
* **Apron center** 11" × 21" (cut 1)
* **Apron side** 11" × 34" (cut 2)
* **Waistband** 4" × 12" (cut 1)
* **Ties** 34" × 4" (cut 2)

Cut the following from scrap fabric:

* **Front panel facing** 9" top length × 6" bottom length × 7" height (cut 1 trapezoid shape)
* **Cupcake pocket** 6" × 12" (this piece will be pintucked and shaped)
* **Cupcake pocket facing** (cut 1)
* **Cupcake frosting** (cut 2)

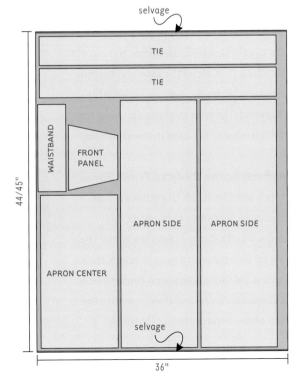

CUTTING LAYOUT

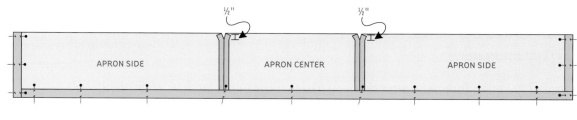

STEP 2

❷ Assemble the Apron Body

* With the right sides together, stitch the apron side panels to each side of the center panel. Start each seam ½" down from the top edge. Press the seam allowances open.
* Turn and press the side and bottom edges ¼" to the wrong side and then an additional ¾" and pin in place.
* On the right side of the apron, pin rickrack trim along the side and bottom edges, ⅝" from the bottom folded edge. Topstitch the trim in place, catching the folded edge of the hem in the stitching.

❹ Attach Apron Body to Front Panel

* Use a basting stitch to gather each of the three sections of the apron body individually. Baste across the top of the apron side piece, cut your threads, then across the top of the apron center piece, cut your threads, and finally, across the top of the second apron side piece.

* Pull the threads to gather the apron side pieces to 6½" and the apron center to 5".
* With the right sides together, pin the apron center section to the 6" side of the front panel, and the apron sides to the side angled edges of the front panel. Adjust the gathers to fit evenly. Stitch along the bottom and side edges of the front panel in one continuous seam, pivoting at the corners. Press the seam allowances toward the front panel.
* Fold and press the bottom and side edges of the front panel facing piece ½" to the wrong side. On the wrong side of the apron, pin the front panel facing over the front panel with the wrong sides together, covering the seam allowances. Invisibly hand-sew the facing in place.

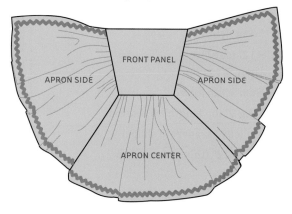

STEP 4

5 Make the Waistband and Ties

* Fold the tie pieces in half lengthwise with the right sides together. Stitch along one short edge and the long edge of each tie piece, leaving one short edge open. Clip the corners, turn the ties right side out, and press.
* Baste the ties onto the waistband with the right sides together, raw edges aligned, ½" up from the bottom edge.
* Press the top and side (including ties) edges of the waistband ½" to the wrong side.

STEP 5

6 Attach the Waistband to the Apron

* With the right sides together, pin the waistband to the top edge of the apron front panel, matching center fronts. The waistband will extend along both sides of the hemmed edge of the apron for about 1½" to 2". Stitch the pieces together.
* Press the waistband up, away from the apron. Fold waistband in half with the wrong sides together so the pressed edge covers the seam allowance. Edgestitch around all four sides of the waistband.

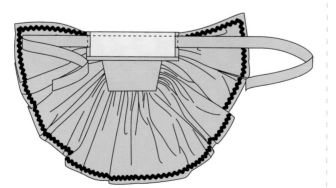

STEP 6

7 Make the Cupcake Pocket

* Beginning 2" from the right side, stitch vertical pintucks every 1" on the 6" × 12" piece of fabric. Press the pintucks to one side. Use the cupcake pocket pattern piece to cut a pocket from the pintucked fabric.
* With the right sides together, stitch the cupcake pocket and the cupcake facing pieces together around all four sides, leaving a 2" opening along the bottom edge for turning. Clip the corners, turn the pocket right side out, and press.
* With the right sides together, stitch the frosting pieces along the top curved edge, leaving the scalloped edge unsewn. Clip the curves, turn the frosting right side out, and press.
* With the right sides facing up, pin the frosting on the cupcake pocket along the placement line. Using a narrow, tight zigzag stitch (or satin stitch), stitch the frosting to the pocket along scalloped bottom edge of the frosting piece.
* Center and pin the cupcake pocket on top of the front panel and edgestitch it in place along the side and bottom edges.

bees Knees POCKeT BaG

Designed by Candace Davis

Here's a simple purse that's cute enough to take everywhere, and with enough streamlined pockets for everything you need!

MATERIALS

* Locate the pattern in the envelope (sheet #4)
* 1 yard of 44/45" quilting-weight cotton fabric
* 1 spool of coordinating thread
* Small scrap of fusible interfacing for snaps
* 1 magnetic snap

Finished dimensions – 10" high × 12" wide
Seam allowance – ½" unless otherwise
    specified

❶ Measure, Mark, and Cut

Lay out your fabric in a single layer with the wrong side facing up. For the best use of the fabric, measure and mark two straps and two inside pockets along one cut edge as shown in the layout. Then, position and trace around the outside pocket pattern piece, flip it over and trace the mirror image. Measure and mark the exterior and lining pieces, as shown in the layout. Cut out the pieces.

* **Outside pocket** (cut 2, one reversed)
* **Exterior/lining** 11" × 13" (cut 4)
* **Inside pocket** 5" × 8" (cut 2)
* **Strap** 5" × 30" (cut 2)

NOTE: *Position the grainline arrow on the pattern piece along the straight grain of the fabric.*

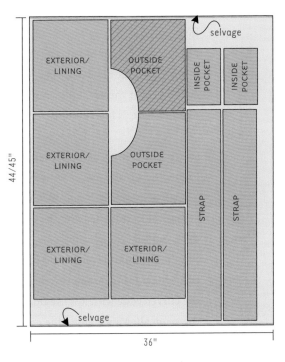

CUTTING LAYOUT

❷ Make the Inside Pockets

* Fold all the raw edges of each inside pocket ½" to the wrong side and press. Topstitch around all the edges to hem the pockets.
* Center one inside pocket on a lining piece 4" from the top edge. Edgestitch it in place on both sides and across the bottom, leaving the top edge open.
* Repeat with remaining inside pocket and lining.

❸ Add Magnetic Snaps

* Mark a dot on the right and wrong side of each lining piece, centered from side to side and 1½" from the top edge. Fuse a scrap of interfacing to the wrong side of each lining piece, centered over the dot, following the manufacturer's instructions.
* Attach each half of the magnetic snap to the right side of each lining piece, centered over the dot, following the manufacturer's instructions.

❹ Make the Lining and Exterior

* Pin the two lining pieces with the right sides together. Stitch the sides and across the bottom, leaving the top edge open. Set the lining aside.
* Pin the two outside pocket pieces with the right sides together. Stitch along the curved edge with a ¼" seam. Clip the seam allowance along the curve. Turn the pocket right side out and press. Topstitch around the curve.
* Pin the completed outer pocket to one exterior piece and baste the layers together with an edgestitch along the sides.
* Pin the exterior pieces with the right sides together (and the outside pocket sandwiched between them), and stitch along the sides and across the bottom, leaving the top open. Catch the edges of the outside pocket in the stitching. Turn the exterior right side out.

❺ Make the Straps

Press each strap piece in half lengthwise with the wrong sides together. Open the strap and press each long raw edge in to meet in the center. Refold the strap in half lengthwise and press. Topstitch around the edges of each strap.

❻ Attach the Straps

Pin both ends of one strap to the right side of an exterior piece 2" in from each side with the raw edges aligned, making sure the strap is not twisted. Stitch the strap ends in place ⅛" from the top edge. Repeat on the remaining exterior with the second strap.

❼ Assemble the Bag

* Slide the exterior bag inside the lining so the right sides are together (straps sandwiched between the layers). Stitch around the top edge, leaving a 4" opening for turning.
* Turn the bag right side out through the opening, and push the lining into the exterior. Press and topstitch around the top edge of the bag, closing the opening as you go.

CHAPTER 4

Home Dec Fabrics

Heavyweight woven fabrics, often called home decor or upholstery-weight fabrics, are the perfect choice for lifestyle projects such as home decor items, apparel, and accessories to name a few. They are manufactured in many variations, from plain weave to twill weave, and even some satin weave versions, and all of them are available in glorious prints and rich solids!

Fabric Facts

Probably the most familiar heavyweight woven fabric is denim, which is a twill weave, characterized by its white warp threads and blue fill threads. In addition to denim and related twills, another popular decorator-weight fabric is canvas, most commonly a strong, closely woven, plain-weave fabric used for durability. Heavyweight oxford cloth is also readily available in fabulous prints, and is quite similar to canvas in look, although lighter in weight. Midweight and heavyweight cotton sateen has a satin weave and resembles satin in construction, but is stronger and more durable due to its fiber content and yarn size. Cotton sateen is somewhat lustrous and has more drape than other home dec fabrics.

Barkcloth is a classic, retro heavyweight fabric with a nubby texture, slightly resembling tree bark. Tropical, floral, and geometric barkcloth designs circa 1930–1960 have been making a resurgence, and many are available as reprints. You can also find heavier linen and linen-cotton blends with great prints on the market today, particularly from Japanese manufacturers. There are many other home decor weight fabric options worth exploring, nearly all of which adhere to the following guidelines.

Attributes

Grainline is very important, especially with denims and heavier weight fabrics. Cutting off-grain can result in the fabric feeding unevenly through the sewing machine. Most heavyweight woven fabrics are not very elastic (but do stretch on the bias), and are quite durable. They typically don't drape well (the heavier the fabric, the less drape it will have), and can rot over time. Fraying edges can also be troublesome, with twill weave fabrics more prone to fraying than plain-weave variations. Linen and linen blend home decor weight fabrics are lovely, but are even more prone to wrinkling than cotton and have a higher shrinkage rate. Like cotton, linen is also prone to fraying.

Needle Type(s)

Use a 100/16 or 110/18 universal needle; 90/14 is acceptable for lighter home decor fabrics such as sateen or lighter weight twills.

Sewing Machine Accessories

A walking foot or roller foot should be used to help feed multiple fabric layers through the machine evenly.

Stitch Types, Tips, and Machine Settings

Use a stitch length of 3mm for seams, and longer for topstitching. Hammer the seams of heavyweight denims and other heavyweight fabrics flat before topstitching to minimize skipped stitches. Slightly round the corners of square projects, so when they are turned right side out, the corners will be smoother.

Marking

Like most cotton fabrics, wax-based marking methods are not suitable for heavyweight fabrics; all other marking types are fine.

Cutting

Pattern weights can be helpful on heavier fabrics, since pins can be hard to manipulate or may bend and/or distort the fabric. Standard scissors or rotary cutters all work fine. Some pronounced twill weaves should be treated as a napped fabric.

Interfacing

There are no particular interfacing requirements; fusible or sew-in are both suitable, depending on your preference or the project instructions. On the other hand, heavy-weight fabrics have so much body on their own, interfacing is often not necessary, unless the project is meant to be overly structured.

Special Equipment

A Jean-a-ma-jig or similar shim can be used to help the presser foot move smoothly and the machine stitch consistently at the intersection of multiple layers, particularly at the beginning of a seam or at a corner.

Seams

Finish seam allowances with a serger, zigzag stitch, or bind the seam edges to prevent fraying. Press the seams open to reduce bulk. Hammer or pound the seams flat to soften the fibers, making it easier to sew through multiple layers.

Pressing and Ironing

Set your iron to a high heat, cotton setting (or linen for linen-blends). Use a pressing cloth with linens and press on the wrong side of the fabric to prevent shine.

Fabric Care

Preshrink all cottons, and most other fabrics, before cutting and sewing, especially if you are making an item you intend to launder! Otherwise, consult the care instructions as recommended by the manufacturer.

THE DAY OUT BAG

Designed by Sue Kim

Perfect for a girls' day out, this zippered bag is just the right size to carry the day's necessities. A loop on the outside can be used to clip keys, a cell phone case, or anything else you might want to keep handy.

MATERIALS

* Locate the pattern in the envelope (sheet #2)
* 1 yard of 44/45" nondirectional heavyweight home decor fabric
* 1 spool of coordinating thread
* 2½ yards of 22"-wide medium-weight fusible interfacing
* One 22" all-purpose zipper
* Zipper foot

1 Measure, Mark, and Cut

Lay out your fabric in a single layer with the wrong side facing up. Position the pattern piece according to the layout, and measure and mark the additional pieces as listed. Cut out the pieces and transfer the markings from the pattern to the wrong side of fabric.

* **Exterior/lining (cut 2)**

Additional pieces:

* **Side panel** 3½" × 4" (cut 4)
* **Zipper panel** 23" × 2" (cut 4)
* **Pocket** 4½" × 6" (cut 2)
* **Loop** 4" × 3" (cut 1)
* **Strap** 17½" × 4½" (cut 2)

Cut from fusible interfacing:

* **Exterior/lining** (cut 1)
* **Side panel** 3½" × 4" (cut 2)
* **Zipper panel** 23" × 2" (cut 2)

Finished dimensions – 8" tall × 19" wide × 3" deep
Seam allowance – ½" unless otherwise specified

NOTE: *Mirror the Exterior/Lining pieces along the line indicated on the pattern.*

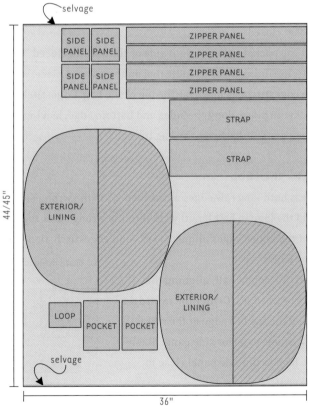

CUTTING LAYOUT

❷ Interface the Fabric

* Fuse interfacing to the wrong side of one exterior/lining. This interfaced piece becomes the exterior.
* Fuse interfacing to the wrong side of two side panels. These become the exterior side panels.
* Fuse interfacing to the wrong side of two zipper panels. These become the exterior zipper panels.

❸ Make the Pocket and Lining

* Pin the pocket pieces with the right sides together, and stitch on three sides, leaving one long (top) edge open. Clip the corners and turn the pocket right side out. Use a chopstick or similar tool to push out the corners.
* Press the top raw edges ½" to the wrong side. Edgestitch the pocket closed.
* Pin the pocket onto the right side of the noninterfaced exterior/lining piece as indicated on the pattern piece, with the edgestitched edge near the top of the bag. Edgestitch the pocket in place along the sides and bottom edge, leaving the top open. This becomes the bag lining.

❹ Make the Loop

* Press both long raw edges of the loop ½" to the wrong side. Fold the loop in half lengthwise with the wrong sides together and the folded edges aligned. Press and edgestitch along both long edges.
* Fold the loop in half, aligning the short raw edges. Center the raw edges along the top (4") edge of the right side of one exterior side panel. Baste the loop to the side panel close to the edge.

baste the loop

STEP 4

❺ Make and Attach the Straps

* To make each strap, press both long raw edges ½" to the wrong side and press. Fold the straps in half lengthwise with the wrong sides together and the folded edges aligned. Press and edgestitch the long edges together.
* Pin the straps on opposite sides of the exterior as indicated on the pattern, with the raw edges aligned. Make sure the straps are not twisted. Baste the straps in place close to the raw edge.

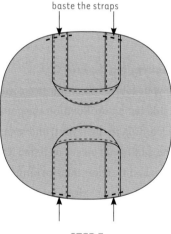

baste the straps

STEP 5

Install the Zipper

* Close the zipper and pin it on the interfaced zipper panel with the right sides together, aligning one zipper tape edge with one panel raw edge. If the length of the zipper tape overhangs the panel by more than ½", trim the zipper to fit.

* Stitch the zipper and zipper panel together, with the zipper foot close to the zipper coil. Open the zipper and press the seam allowance toward the panel. Edgestitch along the zipper panel seam.

* Repeat to attach the remaining exterior zipper panel to the opposite side of the zipper tape.

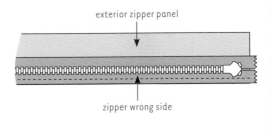

exterior zipper panel

zipper wrong side

STEP 6

⑦ Attach the Side Panels

* With the right sides together, pin one short end of the zipper panel to the edge of the exterior side panel with the loop, aligning the raw edges. Stitch and press the seam allowances toward the side panel.

* Repeat with the second side panel (no loop).

* Topstitch the side panels ¼" from the seam.

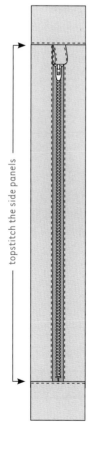

topstitch the side panels

STEP 7

⑧ Construct the Exterior

* Fold the assembled zipper/side panel in half widthwise and press it gently to mark the center with a crease. Unfold. Do the same with the bag exterior to mark the center of each curved edge with the handles. Pin the center of each short raw edge of the assembled zipper/side panel to the bag exterior, right sides together, at each side panel marking. Stitch, starting and stopping ½" from each corner. Clip the bag exterior seam allowance.

* Pin one long edge of the assembled zipper/side panel to one curved edge of the bag exterior with the handles, aligning the raw edges and matching the center crease marks.

* Notch the zipper panel seam allowances to ease the curves. Stitch, starting and stopping ½" from each side panel marking, and backstitch over the straps.

* Open the zipper a few inches and attach the other side of the zipper panel to the other side of the bag exterior in the same way.

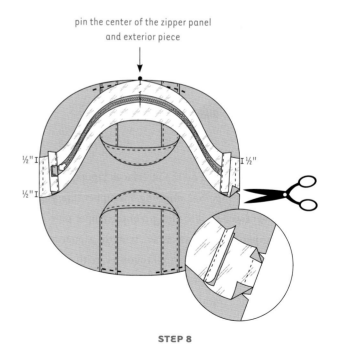

pin the center of the zipper panel and exterior piece

½" I

½" I

I ½"

STEP 8

9 Stitch the Zipper Panel Lining

* Press one long edge of each remaining zipper panel ½" to the wrong side.

* Lay out the panels side by side, with the folded edges to the inside, about ½" apart.

* Pin one remaining side panel to the zipper panels, with the right sides together, aligning the top raw edge of the side panel with the short raw edges of both zipper panels. The side raw edges of the side panel should align with the outside raw edges of the zipper panels.

* Stitch the panels together and press the seam allowances toward the side panel.

* Attach the remaining side panel to the opposite end of zipper panels in similar fashion.

* Topstitch the side panels ¼" from the seam.

10 Assemble the Lining

Attach the zipper panel lining to the bag lining piece in the same manner as the exterior of the bag, in step 8. Disregard the reference to the straps and loop.

11 Complete the Bag

* Turn the bag exterior right side out through the zipper opening. Insert the lining, still wrong side out, into the exterior with wrong sides together, aligning all the seams and corners.

* Hand-tack the lining to the exterior at each of the corners, so the lining lies smooth inside the bag.

* Turn the top of the bag inside out slightly, so you can see the folded edge of one zipper panel lining and the wrong side of the zipper tape.

* Hand-sew each zipper panel lining to the wrong side of zipper tape with a slipstitch or whipstitch, taking care that your stitches don't come through to the bag exterior.

stitch the front and back panels

STEP 8

½" fold

STEP 9

CHARMING BAG

Designed by Sue Kim

A delightful bag with a button detail, perfect for showing off two big, bold, meant-to-be-noticed buttons! You may just channel Audrey Hepburn à la Breakfast at Tiffany's with this charming number.

MATERIALS

* Locate the pattern in the envelope (sheet #3)
* 1 yard of 44/45" home decor fabric
* 1 spool of coordinating thread
* 1 yard of 22"-wide medium-weight fusible interfacing
* 1 magnetic snap, ½" or ¾" in diameter
* 2 large decorative buttons, 2" in diameter

Finished dimensions – 16" wide × 12" tall (handle included)

Seam allowance – ½" unless otherwise specified

① Measure, Mark, and Cut

Fold your fabric in half lengthwise with the right sides together, aligning the selvages. Position the pattern pieces, and measure and mark the additional pocket piece as shown. Cut out the pieces, and transfer the markings from the pattern pieces to the wrong side of the fabric.

* <u>Exterior center panel</u> (cut 2)
* <u>Exterior side panel</u> (cut 4)
* <u>Handle</u> (cut 2)
* <u>Lining</u> (cut 2)
* <u>Pocket</u> 6" × 5" rectangle (cut 2)

Cut from interfacing:

* <u>Lining</u> (cut 2)

NOTE: *Position the grainline arrow on the pattern pieces along the straight grain of the fabric.*

② Interface the Lining

Fuse the interfacing to the lining pieces, following the manufacturer's instructions.

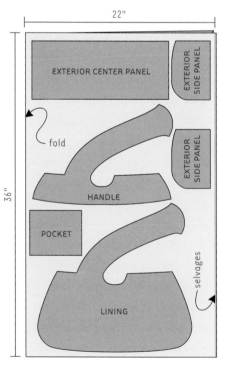

CUTTING LAYOUT

3 Pleat the Exterior Center Panel

* Working with one center panel at a time, fold and pin the top pleats on the pleat lines, as indicated by the arrows. When you look at the pleats from the front, they should all be folded toward the center. Baste them in place close to the top raw edge. Repeat with the remaining center panel.

* Fold and baste the bottom pleats following the same process.

4 Stitch the Side Panels to the Exterior Center Panel

* Pin a side panel to one short end of the center panel with the right sides together, aligning the straight side raw edges. Stitch, and press the seam allowances toward the side panel.

* On the right side, topstitch the side panel ⅛" from the seam.

* Attach another side panel to the opposite end of this center panel in the same fashion.

* Repeat for remaining center and side panels.

attaching the side panel

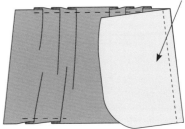

⑤ Attach the Handle

* Mark the center of the handle along the bottom edge and the center of the exterior pieces. Pin one assembled exterior and one handle with the right sides together, aligning the bottom raw edge of the handle with the top raw edge of the exterior and matching the center marks.
* Stitch the seam and clip the seam allowances along the entire curve. Press the seam allowances toward the handle. Topstitch along the handle ⅛" above the seam.
* Repeat for the remaining exterior and handle.

⑥ Assemble the Exterior

Pin the two exteriors, including the handles, with the right sides together, aligning all the raw edges. Stitch the side and bottom edges, leaving the top and handle open.

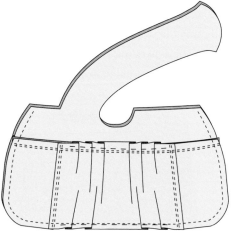

STEP 6

⑦ Make the Pocket

* Pin the two pocket pieces with the right sides together, aligning the raw edges. Stitch the sides and bottom, leaving the top edge open. Clip the corners and turn the pocket right side out, pushing out the corners. Fold the top raw edges ½" to the wrong side. Edgestitch along the top edge to close the pocket.
* Pin the pocket onto the right side of one lining piece at the placement marks. Edgestitch along the side and bottom edges to attach the pocket to the lining.

⑧ Make the Lining

* Pin the lining pieces with the right sides together, aligning the raw edges. Stitch the side and bottom edges, leaving a 5" opening at the center bottom raw edge for turning. Leave the top and handle open and unstitched. Press the seams open and turn the lining right side out.
* Attach the corresponding pieces of the magnetic snap to the right side of the lining pieces at the placement marks, following the manufacturer's instructions. Make sure they align before attaching.

⑨ Finish the Bag

* Insert the lining into the exterior so the right sides are together, aligning the top and handle raw edges. Pin the pieces together. Stitch around the top and handles, and clip the corners and curves.
* Turn the bag right side out through the opening in the lining. Push out the corners and curves in the handle and press.
* Hand-sew the opening in the lining closed with a slipstitch.
* Tuck the lining into the exterior and press once more. Edgestitch all around the top edge and handles.
* Stitch the handle ends to their respective sides of the bag with a box stitch, as shown in the photograph. Then, hand-sew the buttons over the box stitching for embellishment.

smart Girl's set

Designed by Lauren Kurtz and Madeline Warr

The on-the-go girl will love carrying her essentials in one handy wristlet with an easy open zipper strap. The phone case doubles as a wallet; it has a padded pocket for her phone and two for her credit cards, business cards, and cash. The sunglasses case protects her shades, and the lip gloss case keeps her makeup at the ready.

MATERIALS

* Locate the pattern in the envelope (sheet #3)
* 1 yard of 44/45" home decor fabric
* 1 spool of coordinating thread
* ½ yard of lightweight fusible interfacing
* Scraps of cotton batting

For the Wristlet:
* 1 spring hook
* 1 large jump ring
* 9" zipper

For the Phone Case:
* 1 button, 1⅛" in diameter
* 1" square of Velcro

For the Sunglasses Case:
* 1 button, ¾" in diameter
* 1" square of Velcro

For the Lip Gloss Case:
* 1 button, ¾" in diameter
* 1" square of Velcro

Finished dimensions – see instructions for each project

Seam allowance – ¼" unless otherwise specified

① Measure, Mark, and Cut

Lay out your fabric in a single layer with the wrong side facing up. Fold over the top edge 18", leaving 8" of a single layer of fabric at the bottom. Position the pattern pieces, and measure and mark the additional pieces as shown on page 120. Cut out the pieces, and transfer the markings from the pattern pieces to the wrong side of fabric. Separate the pieces by project.

For the Wristlet:
* <u>**Wristlet lining**</u> (cut 2)
* <u>**Wristlet body**</u> (cut 2)
* <u>**Wristlet upper band**</u> 5" × 12½" (cut 2)
* <u>**Wristlet strap**</u> 14" × 2½" (cut 1)

For the Phone Case:
* <u>**Phone Case flap**</u> (cut 2)
* <u>**Phone Case front**</u> 11" × 4½" (cut 1)
* <u>**Phone Case back**</u> 5½" × 4½" (cut 2)
* <u>**Phone Case medium pocket**</u> 9" × 4½" (cut 1)
* <u>**Phone Case small pocket**</u> 7" × 4½" (cut 1)
* <u>**Phone Case strap**</u> 1½" × 4½" (cut 1)

For the Sunglasses Case:
* <u>**Sunglasses Case flap**</u> (cut 2)
* <u>**Sunglasses Case**</u> 6½" × 9" (cut 2)

For the Lip Gloss Case:
* <u>**Lip Gloss Case back/flap**</u> (cut 2)
* <u>**Lip Gloss Case front**</u> 6" × 6½" (cut 1)

NOTE: *Position the grainline arrow on the pattern pieces along the straight grain of the fabric and make sure the straight edges of the measured and marked pieces are on the straight fabric grain.*

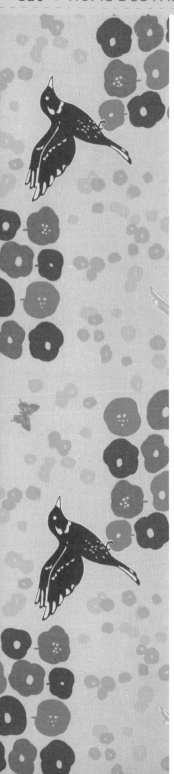

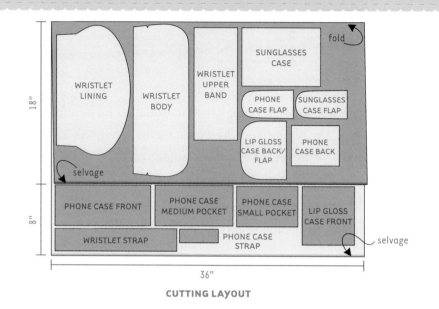

CUTTING LAYOUT

Wristlet

Finished dimensions – 8" tall × 14" wide

❶ Cut the Interfacing

Use the pattern or the cut fabric as a guide for cutting the following pieces from interfacing. Fuse all of the interfacing to their corresponding fabric pieces following the manufacturer's instructions.

* **Wristlet body** (cut 2)
* **Wristlet upper band** 5" × 12½" (cut 2)
* **Wristlet strap** 14" × 2½" (cut 1)

❷ Make the Pleats

On each wristlet body, fold and press the pleats in the direction indicated on the pattern. Machine-baste along the upper edge to secure the pleats. The pleats should fold away from the center front.

pleats fold away from the center

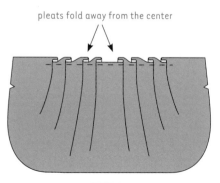

STEP 2

❸ Attach the Upper Bands

Fold and press each upper band in half lengthwise with the wrong sides together. Pin a folded band on top of a wristlet body with the right sides facing up and the folded edge of the band overlapping the pleated raw edge slightly. Edgestitch the band to the body close to folded edge of the band. Repeat with the remaining band and body pieces.

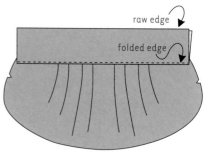

STEP 3

❹ Make the Strap

Fold the wristlet strap in half lengthwise with the wrong sides together, and press. Open and press the long raw edges to the wrong side to meet at the crease. Fold the strap in half again lengthwise and edgestitch along both long edges. Set the strap aside.

❺ Attach the Zipper

* Pin the wrong side of the zipper to the right side of one lining piece, so the edges of both are aligned. Baste the zipper in place.
* Pin one of the wristlet bodies to the zipper/lining piece with the right sides together and the top raw edges aligned, sandwiching the zipper between the two layers. Stitch along the top edge, catching the zipper tape in the stitching.
* Fold and press the wristlet body back so the wrong sides of the lining and wristlet body are together, exposing the other side of the zipper. Repeat the two previous steps to attach the remaining lining and wristlet body pieces to the opposite side of the zipper.

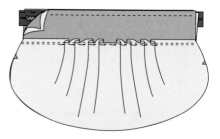

STEP 5

❻ Stitch the Wristlet and Lining

* Fold the wristlet body pieces so the right sides are together, aligning the raw edges. Take care to move the lining pieces out of the way.
* Insert one end of the strap between the top band layers near the zipper, aligning raw edges and centering the strap along the short edge of the band. Pin it in place so the strap is sandwiched between layers and hidden from view.

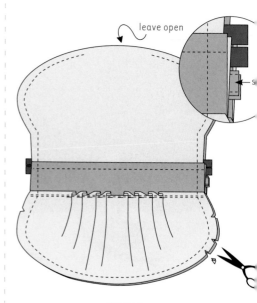

STEP 6

* Pin the lining pieces with the right sides together, pushing the metal ends of the zipper toward the lining side.

* Pin around the entire perimeter (lining and wristlet), leaving a 4" opening for turning at the bottom of the lining.

* Starting at one end of lining opening, stitch the entire perimeter of lining and wristlet body, being sure only to catch one end of the strap in the stitching, and stopping at the opposite end of the 4" opening.

NOTE: *When stitching near the zipper, stitch only over the zipper tape; do not stitch over any metal parts.*

* Trim any excess bulk from the zipper and notch the curves.

⑦ Finish the Wristlet

* Turn the wristlet right side out through the opening and press all around. Press the raw edges at the opening ½" to the inside. Edgestitch the opening closed by machine, or slipstitch it by hand.

* Fold the free end of the strap ½" to one side, then fold it again another 1". Press. Slide the spring hook into the second fold and edgestitch the layers to secure the spring hook.

* Attach the jump ring to the zipper pull, and then attach the spring hook to the jump ring.

Phone Case

Finished dimensions — 5" tall × 3¾" wide

① Cut the Interfacing and Batting

Use the pattern or the cut fabric as a guide for cutting the following pieces:

From interfacing:

* **Phone Case flap** (cut 1)

From batting:

* **Phone Case back** 5½" × 4½" (cut 2)

② Make the Flap

* Interface one flap following the manufacturer's instructions.

* Stitch the hook side of the Velcro square to the right side of this flap at the placement mark.

* Pin the flaps with the right sides together, and stitch around, leaving the straight edge open. Notch the curved seam allowances and turn the flap right side out. Press. Edgestitch around the finished edges.

③ Make the Back Panel

Pin the back pieces with the right sides together. Insert the flap between the layers, aligning the top edges and centering the flap. Pin the back and flap layers to one of the batting pieces, aligning all the edges, and stitch along the top edge. Turn the back right side out.

④ Make the Front Panel

Fold the front in half widthwise with the wrong sides together, forming a piece that is 5½" × 4½". Insert the remaining batting piece between the layers, and edgestitch along the top folded edge, being sure to catch the batting in the stitching.

⑤ Make the Pockets

* Fold the medium pocket in half widthwise with the wrong sides together, forming a piece 4½" square. Edgestitch along the top folded edge.
* Fold the small pocket in half widthwise with the wrong sides together, forming a piece 3½" × 4½". Edgestitch along the top folded edge.
* Stitch the loop side of the Velcro square to the small pocket 1" down from the top folded edge and centered from each side.

⑥ Make the Strap

Fold the strap in half lengthwise with the wrong sides together, and press. Open and fold the long raw edges to the wrong side to meet at the crease. Refold the strap lengthwise and edgestitch along both long edges. Set the strap aside.

⑦ Layer the Pockets

Position the medium pocket on the front, aligning the side and bottom raw edges. Position the small pocket on top of the medium pocket, aligning the side and bottom raw edges. Baste the layers together along the side and bottom edges.

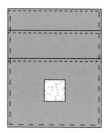

STEP 7

⑧ Finish the Phone Case

* Pin the front and back with the right sides together, so that the pockets and Velcro square face the back.
* Fold the strap in half and insert it between the front and back ½" from the top, aligning the raw edges.
* Stitch through all the layers along the side and bottom edges, leaving the top open. Turn the phone case right side out and press.
* Hand-sew a decorative button to the outside of the flap, matching the Velcro placement. Or, you can use a fabric scrap and make a fabric-covered button.

insert strap

STEP 8

Sunglasses Case

Finished dimensions – 6" high × 4" wide

❶ Cut the Interfacing and Batting

Use the pattern or the cut fabric as a guide for cutting the following pieces:

From interfacing:

* **Sunglasses Case flap** (cut 1)

From batting:

* **Sunglasses Case**
  6½" × 9" (cut 1)

❷ Make the Flap

* Interface one flap following the manufacturer's instructions.
* Stitch the hook side of the Velcro to the right side of this flap at the placement mark.
* Pin the flaps with the right sides together, and stitch around, leaving the straight edge open. Notch the curved seam allowances and turn the flap right side out. Press. Edgestitch around the sewn edges.

❸ Attach the Flap to Sunglasses Case

* Pin cotton batting to the wrong side of one sunglasses case piece. Baste around all four sides, close to the raw edges.
* Fold the batted piece in half to form a 4½" × 6½" rectangle, and press to mark the center line. Open up the piece.
* Make a placement mark 2" to the right of the center crease along the top 9" edge. Center the flap on this new placement mark with the top raw edges aligned. Baste the flap in place.

❹ Create the Sunglasses Case

* Pin the sunglasses case pieces with the right sides together and the flap sandwiched between them. Stitch the top edge. Turn the case right side out and edgestitch along the top edge. Baste all the layers together close to the remaining three raw edges.
* Attach the loop side of the Velcro to the outside of the sunglasses case, on the other side of the center crease, 3½" from the top edge and 2" from the side, as shown.

❺ Stitch the Side

Fold the sunglasses case in half along the center crease with the right sides (exteriors) together. Stitch along the sides and bottom, leaving the top edge open. Turn the sunglasses case right side out and press. Hand-sew a decorative or fabric-covered button to outside of the flap, matching the Velcro placement.

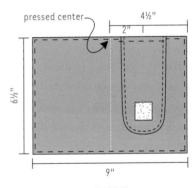

STEP 3

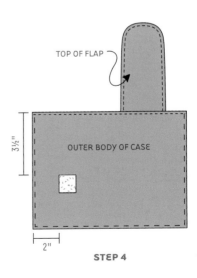

STEP 4

Lip Gloss Case

Finished dimensions – 3" high × 6¼" wide

❶ Attach the Velcro Hook Side

Stitch the hook side of the Velcro to the right side of one back/flap at the placement mark. Press the bottom straight edge ¼" to the wrong side. Set the piece aside.

❷ Stitch the Back to the Front

* Pin the 6½" straight edge of the other back/flap (without Velcro) to a same-size end of the front with the right sides together. Stitch the seam and press the seam allowances toward the flap.
* Lay the stitched piece on a flat surface with the right side up. Fold the bottom edge of the front piece ¼" to the wrong side. Then align the folded edge with the seam and pin it in place.
* Pin the back/flap pieces with the right sides together, aligning raw edges.
* Stitch the outer raw edges around the entire piece. Trim the bottom corners and notch the curves.

❸ Finish the Case

* Turn the case right side out through the opening and push out all the corners. Hand-sew the opening closed; this doesn't need to be neat because it will be inside the case and won't show.
* Test-fold the case, turning the front up to the start of the curved flap, and then fold the flap over the front. Once you are pleased with the proportion, mark where the loop half of the Velcro needs to go to align with the hook half. Unfold the case and stitch the Velcro in place.
* Refold the front of the case to the start of the curved flap and pin. Edgestitch around the entire perimeter of the case.
* Hand-sew a decorative button to the outside of the flap, matching the Velcro placement.

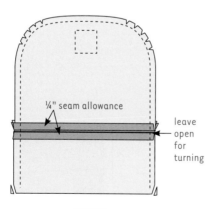

¼" seam allowance

leave open for turning

STEP 2

Jet Set

iPod/MP3 Cozy designed by Megan Risley

Ticket Portfolio designed by Sally Mortensen

Bright Bag Tag, Cheery Passport Cover, and Travel Tissue Pack designed by Nicole Kaplan

Vacation Valet Travel Tray designed by Sally Mortensen and Nicole Kaplan

Perk up your travel time with six coordinated items that will make your life easier. Choose fabric that is colorful, durable, and a little bit retro; perfect for jet-setting! All of these items can be made from just one yard of 44/45" medium or heavyweight home decorating fabric and a smattering of notions!

MATERIALS

* Locate the pattern in the envelope (sheet #1)
* 1 yard of 44/45" home decor cotton fabric
* 1 spool of coordinating thread
* ½ yard of lightweight batting
* ½ yard of 20/22"-wide medium-weight fusible interfacing
* 1 yard of 22"-wide heavyweight fusible interfacing

For the iPod/MP3 Cozy:

* 1" of ½"-wide coordinating grosgrain ribbon (optional)
* 1" lobster clip (optional)
* 1" of ¾"-wide Velcro

For the Ticket Portfolio:

* 1" of ¾"-wide Velcro
* ¾"- or 1"-diameter fabric-covered button

For the Bright Bag Tag:

* 12"–15" of ½"-wide sturdy ribbon or bias tape
* Cardstock, trimmed to 2½" tall × 4" wide or business card for name and address

For the Cheery Passport Cover:

* 32" of ½"-wide double-fold bias tape
* Pinking shears (optional)
* One passport (you may have to adjust the measurements to fit a non-US passport)

For the Travel Tissue Pack:

* ¾ yard of ½"-wide double-fold bias tape
* 1 package of travel-size tissues

For the Vacation Valet Travel Tray:

* 1½ yards of ½"-wide double-fold bias tape
* One 6¾" square of stiff plastic or stiff interfacing such as Peltex or Timtex
* 4 pairs of gripper snaps and attachment tool

Finished dimensions – see instructions for each project

Seam allowance – ¼" unless otherwise specified

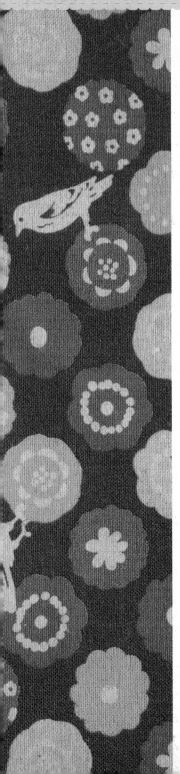

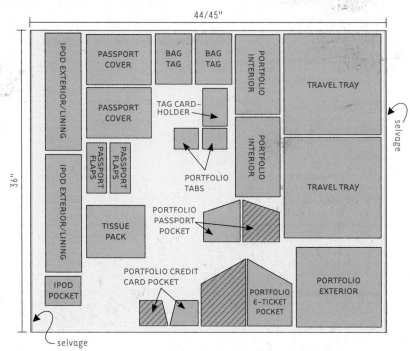

CUTTING LAYOUT

NOTE: *When cutting 2 of each portfolio pocket, cut 1 reversed as shown.*

- - -

❶ Measure, Mark, and Cut

Lay out your fabric in a single layer with the wrong side facing up. Position the pattern pieces, and measure and mark the additional pieces as shown. Mark the straight lines of the pattern pieces parallel to the straight grain of the fabric. Cut out the pieces and separate them by project.

For the iPod/MP3 Cozy:
- **iPod exterior/lining** 14" × 4½" (cut 2)
- **iPod pocket** 3½" × 4½" (cut 1)

For the Ticket Portfolio:
- **Portfolio e-ticket pocket** (cut 2)
- **Portfolio passport pocket** (cut 2)
- **Portfolio credit card pocket** (cut 2)
- **Portfolio exterior** 9½" × 10½" (cut 1)
- **Portfolio interior** 9½" × 5½" (cut 2)
- **Portfolio tab** 2½" × 3" (cut 2)

For the Bright Bag Tag:
- **Bag tag** 6" × 4½" (cut 2)
- **Tag cardholder** 4½" × 3" (cut 1)

For the Cheery Passport Cover:
- **Passport cover** 6" × 8" (cut 2)
- **Passport flaps** 6" × 2½" (cut 2)

For the Travel Tissue Pack:
- **Tissue pack** 6¼" × 7¼" (cut 1)

For the Vacation Valet Travel Tray:
- **Travel tray** 12" square (cut 2)

iPod/MP3 Cozy

Finished dimensions – 5½" tall × 4" wide

① Cut the Interfacing and Batting

Use the cut fabric as a guide for cutting the following pieces:

From medium-weight fusible interfacing:

* **Exterior/lining** 14" × 4½" (cut 1)
* **Pocket** 3½" × 4½" (cut 1)

From batting:

* **Exterior/lining** 14" × 4½" (cut 1)

② Make the Exterior

* Fuse interfacing to the wrong side of one exterior/lining following the manufacturer's instructions. This piece becomes the exterior.
* Stitch one Velcro half to the right side of the exterior, ¾" down from the top raw edge and centered from side to side.
* With fabric marker or chalk, mark a pocket placement line on the right side of the exterior, 5¾" down from the top raw edge and running across the width of the piece.
* If you wish to add the clip, also mark the ribbon/clip placement on the right side 3¼" from the bottom raw edge and centered from side to side.

③ Attach the Clip (Optional)

Skip this step if you do not want a clip on your cozy:

* Fold each short end of the ribbon ¼" to the wrong side and press. Thread the ribbon though the lobster clip and fold it in half.
* Stitch the pressed ribbon ends to the exterior at the marked spot, with the clip facing the bottom raw edge.

④ Make the Pocket

* Fuse interfacing to the wrong side of the pocket. Fold the top raw edge ½" to the wrong side and press; edgestitch it in place. Fold the bottom raw edge ½" to the wrong side and press.

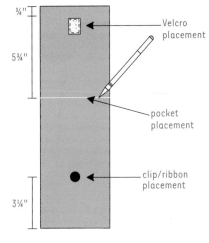

¾"

5¾"

3¼"

Velcro placement

pocket placement

clip/ribbon placement

STEP 2

* Place the pocket, right side up, on the right side of the exterior, aligning the pocket's bottom folded edge with the placement line. Stitch along the bottom edge with an edgestitch to secure. Leave the sides unstitched.

⑤ Attach the Velcro to the Lining

Stitch the remaining Velcro half to the remaining, noninterfaced lining piece, 1" down from the top raw edge of the right side of the fabric and centered side to side.

⑥ Complete the Cozy

* Pin the exterior and lining pieces with the right sides together, raw edges aligned and the exterior on top. Make sure the Velcro side (top edge) of the lining is pinned to the ribbon side (bottom edge) of the exterior.
* Pin the batting on top of both fabric layers, again aligning the raw edges.

* Stitch around all the sides with ¼" seam allowance, leaving a 2"
  opening on one long side for turning. Clip the corners, turn the
  cozy right side out, and press.
* Place the cozy on a work surface with the lining facing up and
  the Velcro at the top. Fold the bottom of the cozy up at the bottom
  edge of the pocket to form the body of cozy. Edgestitch all around
  to form the body and close the opening.
* Fold the top edge down to form a flap, aligning the Velcro halves.

Ticket Portfolio

Finished dimensions — 9" tall × 4¼" wide

❶ Cut and Apply Interfacing

Use the cut fabric pieces as a guide for cutting one piece of heavyweight fusible interfacing for every cut fabric piece, except the tab.
Fuse the interfacing to the wrong side of the corresponding fabric
piece following the manufacturer's instructions.

❷ Make the Pockets

* Pin the two e-ticket pocket pieces with the right sides together,
  aligning the raw edges. Stitch along the angled edge. Turn the
  pocket right side out and press. Edgestitch along the angled
  side. Do the same with the two passport pocket pieces.
* Pin the credit card pocket pieces with the right sides together,
  aligning the raw edges. Stitch along the top, angled side, and
  bottom, leaving the straight side open for turning. Clip the
  corners and turn the pocket right side out. Turn the raw edges
  of the opening ¼" to the wrong side and press. Edgestitch
  along the angled side.
* With both right sides facing up, pin the e-ticket pocket to one
  interior piece, matching the side and bottom edges. Baste it in
  place along the sides and bottom, close to the raw edges, leaving the top angled edge open.
* With both right sides facing up, pin the passport pocket to the
  remaining interior, aligning the bottom raw edges and centering

it from side to side. Edgestitch along both
sides to attach. Pin the credit card pocket
above the passport pocket, 1" from the top
raw edge and centered from side to side.
Edgestitch along the top, straight side, and
bottom to attach, leaving the angled side open.

❸ Finish the Interior

Pin the interior pieces with the right sides
together, along one long edge for the center
seam. Stitch, and press the seam open.

❹ Make the Tab Closure

* Center and stitch one Velcro half to the right
  side of one tab piece, ½" from one short edge.
* Pin the two tab pieces with the right sides
  together, aligning the raw edges. Stitch along
  both long edges and the short edge with the
  Velcro square, leaving the other short edge
  open for turning. Clip the corners and turn
  the tab right side out. Push the corners out to
  square the piece. Edgestitch along all three
  finished sides, leaving the raw edge open.

⑤ Make the Exterior

* Place the exterior on a work surface with the right side facing up. The longer 10½" edges are the top and bottom edges; the shorter 9½" edges are the sides.
* Center and pin the tab on the left side of the rectangle with the Velcro facing up and the raw edges aligned. Baste the tab in place close to the raw edge.
* Stitch the remaining Velcro half to the right side of the opposite side of the exterior, ¾" in from the right raw edge and centered from top to bottom.

⑥ Finish the Portfolio

* Pin the exterior and interior with the right sides together, aligning the raw edges. Stitch around all of the sides, leaving a 3" opening along the top edge for turning. Clip the corners and turn the portfolio right side out. Push the corners out to square the piece.
* Turn the raw edges of the opening ¼" to the wrong side and press. Edgestitch around all the edges, closing the opening with the stitching. Topstitch down the center of the portfolio.
* If you want a button embellishment, cover a button from a cover-your-own-button kit with a scrap of fabric, following the manufacturer's instructions. Hand-sew the button to the outside of the tab closure.

Bright Bag Tag
Finished dimensions – 5½" tall × 4" wide

① Cut and Apply the Interfacing

Use the cut fabric pieces as a guide for cutting medium-weight fusible interfacing for all three pieces. Fuse the interfacing to the wrong side of each piece, following the manufacturer's instructions.

② Assemble the Cardholder

* Fold one short end of the cardholder ¼" to the wrong side. Press and hem with an edgestitch.
* Center and pin the cardholder, right side up, on the right side of one tag piece. Stitch around the three raw edges of the cardholder using a satin or zigzag stitch. Leave the hemmed edge unstitched.

③ Assemble the Tag

* Pin the tag pieces with the right sides together, aligning all the raw edges. Stitch around three sides with a scant ¼" seam allowance, leaving the short side corresponding to the open edge of the cardholder unstitched for turning. Clip the corners and turn the tag right side out. Fold the raw edges of the opening ¼" to the wrong side and press.
* Fold the 12"-15" piece of ribbon in half widthwise and insert the ends at least 1" into the tag opening. Edgestitch around the tag, closing the opening and catching the ribbon in the stitching.

✱ Finishing Touches

Write your contact information on the cardstock and insert it into the cardholder. Fasten the tag to your luggage by looping the ribbon around the luggage handle and tucking the tag through the ribbon.

Cheery Passport Cover
Finished dimensions — 6" tall × 4" wide

❶ Cut and Apply the Interfacing

Use the cut fabric pieces as a guide for cutting medium-weight fusible interfacing for all four pieces. Fuse the interfacing to the wrong side of each fabric piece, following the manufacturer's instructions.

❷ Pink the Edges

Use pinking shears to trim one long side of each flap, creating a decorative edge (optional). As an alternative, you could also make a ¼" single-fold hem.

❸ Attach the Flaps

Pin both flaps, right side up, on opposite ends of the right side of one cover piece, aligning the raw edges. The pinked or finished edge of each flap should face inward. Baste in place around all four sides of the cover piece, close to the raw edges.

❹ Assemble the Passport Cover

Pin the cover pieces with the wrong sides together, aligning all the raw edges. Encase all the raw edges with the bias tape and edgestitch, making sure to catch the back of the bias tape in the stitching. Miter or fold the bias tape at each corner and overlap the end of the bias tape over the beginning. Insert the first and last pages of a passport between the flaps.

Travel Tissue Pack
Finished dimensions — 4" tall × 6½" wide

❶ Cut and Apply the Interfacing

Use the cut fabric piece as a guide for cutting one piece of medium-weight fusible interfacing. Fuse the interfacing to the wrong side of the fabric piece.

❷ Assemble the Pack

* Encase the two short raw edges of the cover with bias tape and edgestitch, being sure to catch the back of the bias tape in the stitching.
* Fold the cover in half with the wrong sides together, aligning the short bound raw edges. Press to mark the center. Open the cover and fold the short bound raw edges to the wrong side to meet at the center crease. Press.
* Cut two pieces of bias tape long enough to finish the raw edges plus ½", and fold the narrow ends of the bias tape ¼" to the wrong side. Encase the remaining, double layer of raw edges on both ends with bias tape and edgestitch, being sure to catch the back of the bias tape in stitching.
* Insert tissues into the finished pack.

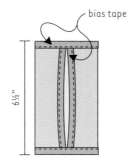

bias tape

6½"

STEP 2

Vacation Valet Travel Tray
Finished dimensions — 12" square

① Cut and Apply the Interfacing

Use the cut fabric pieces as a guide for cutting medium-weight fusible interfacing for both pieces. Fuse the interfacing to the wrong side of each piece following the manufacturer's instructions.

② Create the Base

* Pin the base pieces with the wrong sides together, aligning all the raw edges. With a washable fabric marker or chalk, mark four stitching lines, each 2½" from the outside edges. The lines will create a 7" square in the center of the base.
* Stitch three of the four stitching lines. Slip the plastic between the fabric layers into the stitched square. Stitch the fourth side, enclosing the plastic between the layers.

③ Add the Snaps

Using a snap fastener kit, attach a pair of snaps in each corner, 1" from each outside edge and ½" away from the stitching lines. All of the snap fastenings should face upward.

④ Finish the Tray

* Fold the short raw ends of the bias tape to the wrong side for a clean finish. Encase the raw edges of the fabric with bias tape, folding or mitering the corners, and stitch, being sure to catch the back of the bias tape in the stitching.
* Fasten the snaps to create a tray (the stitching lines will act as fold lines for the base of the tray). Unsnap and lay flat for easy packing!

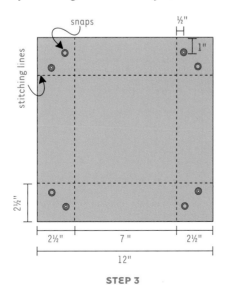

STEP 3

HANGING BOOK DISPLAY

Designed by Katherine Donaldson

This project provides a great way to show off both your favorite fabric and your favorite children's picture books. Hang it on the wall for everyone to see. The pockets cover only the bottom of the book covers, with a floating dowel higher up to keep them from toppling forward, so most of the book covers are visible. Use it as a special place to keep track of library books, or as a rotating display of your personal library to tempt young readers.

MATERIALS

* 1 yard of 44/45" home decor weight fabric in a sideways or nondirectional print
* 1 spool of coordinating thread
* 3⅓ yards of 1½"-wide cotton webbing, in coordinating color
* 4 large grommets or eyelets, at least ¼" in diameter
* 3 dowels, ¼" in diameter, each cut to 32" long
* 3 dowels, ⅜" in diameter, each cut to 31½" long
* Sandpaper, if needed, to smooth dowel ends
* Wood stain or craft paint and paintbrush for painting dowels (optional)
* Craft glue (optional)

Finished dimensions – 25" tall × 34" wide
Seam allowance – ½" unless otherwise specified

❶ Measure, Mark, and Cut

Lay out your fabric in a single layer with the wrong side facing up. Cut and square off your fabric as neatly and evenly as possible to make one piece that is 36" × 44/45". The fabric selvages become the book display's top and bottom edges; so don't trim them off. Also cut the following from webbing:

* **Four** 25½" lengths for reinforcement straps
* **Six** 2" lengths for dowel loops

❷ Prepare the Dowels

* Make sure the cut ends of the 32"-long dowels are sanded smooth. Stain or paint them in a coordinating color if desired.
* Because the 31½"-long dowels will be completely encased in the fabric, they do not need to be sanded or painted.

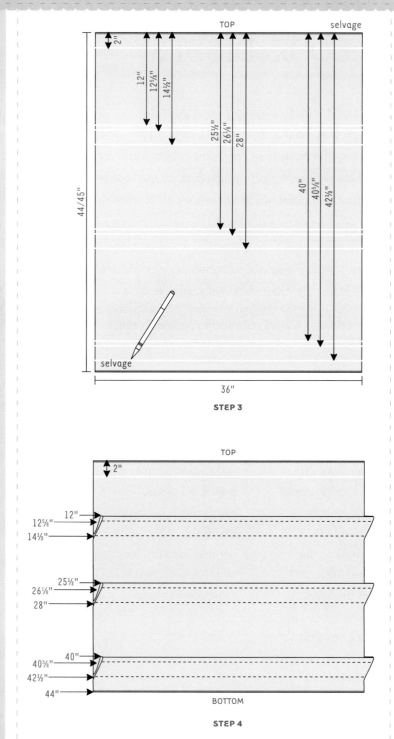

STEP 3

STEP 4

❸ Mark the Pocket Lines

Orient the fabric so that the selvages are at the top and bottom and the right side of the fabric is faceup. Since the construction lines are marked on the right side of the fabric, be sure to use a removable or disappearing fabric marking method. Measuring down from the top selvage edge, mark the following lines across the entire width of the fabric:

* **Top fold** 2"
* **First pocket** 12", 12⅝", and 14½"
* **Second pocket** 25½", 26⅛", and 28"
* **Third pocket** 40", 40⅝", and 42½"

❹ Stitch the Pocket Flaps

* Fold the fabric with the wrong sides together at the 12" mark. Stitch along the 12⅝" and 14½" lines. This forms the first pocket and dowel channel. Be sure to stitch at least ⅝" from the fold to allow enough room for the thicker ⅜" dowel (test the fit to be sure, particularly if using thicker fabric). Unfold the fabric at the seam and press the flap up, toward the top edge.
* Make the second and third pockets in similar fashion, folding at the first line in the grouping and stitching at the second and third lines. You should now have three sewn flaps with ⅝" dowel channels at the top of each.

⑤ Attach the Reinforcement Straps

* Place the display wrong side up, with the pocket flaps facing toward the top of the fabric. On the wrong side of the fabric, mark the strap placement on the 2" line across the top, as shown in the illustration. Measure the first four points from the left side, and the remainder from the right side.

* Starting 2" from the top, place the short end of each 25" length of webbing along the marked line between the placement marks. Pin the webbing straight down, equidistant from the cut edge, taking care not to pin down the pocket flaps.

* Fold each pocket (on the right side) out of the way and edgestitch the webbing in place within each section between the pocket flaps. After stitching each section, make sure you haven't caught any of the pockets in your stitching; they should be free to flap up and down.

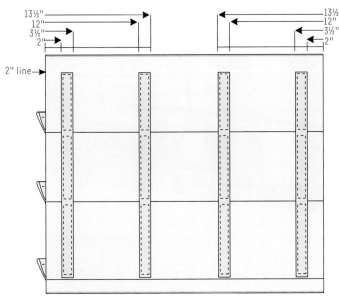

STEP 5

⑥ Hem the Top and Bottom Edges

* Fold the bottom pocket down, and the bottom edge to the wrong side along the stitching line, so that the selvage is now against the back of the book display. Stitch to secure ½" from the selvage edge through both layers to hem the bottom edge, keeping the pocket free of all stitching. (No need for a double-fold hem, as the selvage won't unravel.)

* Fold the top edge 2" to the wrong side, covering the tops of the webbing strips. Stitch to secure ½" from the selvage edge.

⑦ Attach the Grommets

Mark grommet placement ¾" down from the top hemmed edge and centered over each webbing strip. Apply four grommets at these marks, following the manufacturer's instructions.

⑧ Finish the Pockets

* On the right side of the display, fold the pocket flaps up toward the top edge and pin them in place. On the top pocket, stitch directly over the dowel seam, starting from the raw edge and stopping once you've crossed the first piece of webbing. Backstitch. Do the same on the opposite side of the top pocket.

* Repeat for both sides of the second and third pockets.

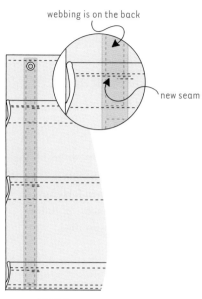

webbing is on the back

new seam

STEP 8

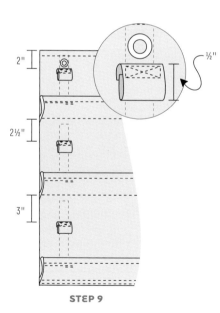

2"

2½"

3"

½"

STEP 9

⑨ Attach the Dowel Loops

* Fold the bottom raw edge of each 2" length of webbing up so that it lies ⅜" below the top raw edge. Fold the top raw edge down over the bottom raw edge and baste the edges in place.
* Place one folded dowel loop on the right side of the display, 2" below the top edge of the fabric and in line with the webbing reinforcement stitching done in step 5. The loop should face down. Stitch the loop in place with a box stitch; the stitching should be ½" above the bottom of the loop to ensure room for the dowel.
* Place a second folded dowel loop 2½" below the bottom of the first pocket and stitch in a similar fashion.
* Place a third folded dowel loop 3" below the bottom of the second pocket and stitch in a similar fashion.
* Repeat this process along the opposite side of the book display.

⑩ Insert and Secure the Pocket Dowels

* Hem the left raw edge by pressing ½" to the wrong side and then another 1" so that the folded edge of the hem meets the edge of the outer reinforcement strap. Edgestitch the hem in place, closing off the dowel channels on the left side.
* Insert the three ⅜" dowels into the fabric channels at the top edge of the three pockets and push them as far as you can toward the left seam. Hem the right raw edge with a double-fold hem as you did the left edge, edgestitching to close off the dowel channels on the right side. A zipper foot will make stitching easier.
* Adjust the pocket dowels so they are centered between the left and right hems.

⑪ Insert the Loop Dowels

Insert the three ¼" dowels into the webbing dowel loops. While the dowels should stay in place, you might want to tack them in place with a bit of craft glue. Hang your book display, fill it with books, and admire your little library!

FOLD OVER BaG

Designed by Anna Graham

This casual and fun, perfectly sized bag cleverly holds everything inside without need of a closure. Simply fold over the top to keep everything secure and unfold to open!

MATERIALS

* 1 yard of 44/45" home decor cotton fabric in a nondirectional print
* 1 scrap of cotton for pocket (optional; can use main fabric)
* 1 spool of coordinating thread
* 1 package of double-fold bias tape (or make your own)
* ½ yard of medium-weight fusible interfacing
* 48" length of 1½"-wide webbing
* Five grommets, ⅜" inside diameter

Finished dimensions – 14 ½" tall × 13" wide when folded over

Seam allowance – ½" unless otherwise specified

① Measure, Mark, and Cut

Fold your fabric in half lengthwise with the right sides together, aligning the selvages. Measure and mark the following pattern pieces directly on the wrong side of your fabric, so the straight edges line up with the grainline.

* **Bag exterior** 14" × 22" (cut 2)
* **Bag lining** 14" × 22" (cut 2)

Cut from scrap cotton:

* **Pocket** 11" × 8½" (cut 1)
* **Pull tab** 6" × 2½" (cut 1) (optional)

Cut from interfacing:

* **Pocket interfacing** 11" × 8½" (cut 1)
* **Reinforcement interfacing** 6" × 8" (cut 1)

Cut from bias tape:

* **Pocket binding** 9" strip
* **Bag binding** 32" strip

② Make the Inside Pocket

* Fuse the pocket interfacing to the wrong side of the pocket following the manufacturer's instructions.
* Fold each long side of the pocket ½" to wrong side and press. Fold the pocket in half with wrong sides facing, matching the short raw edges, and press.

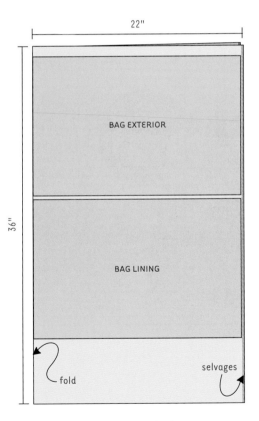

CUTTING LAYOUT

* Encase the raw edges together in bias tape, leaving ¼" of bias tape extending past each side. Fold the raw edges of the bias tape to the wrong side of the pocket and stitch the binding in place, making sure to catch the back of the tape in the stitching.

* Center and pin the bound top pocket edge 13" from the top edge of one lining piece. Edgestitch the pocket in place along the side and bottom edges. If you want a divided pocket, add another line of stitching down the center of the pocket.

* Apply reinforcement interfacing to the wrong side of the lining where the pocket is attached, being sure to cover the stitching lines. This helps secure the pocket to the lining.

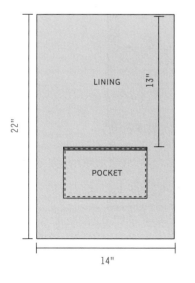

STEP 2

❸ Stitch the Sides

Pin the exterior pieces with the right sides together. Stitch the long sides and bottom of the bag, leaving the top edge open. Repeat with the lining pieces.

❹ Make the Gussets

* Leave the exterior bag wrong side out. Measure and mark a 1½" square in each bottom corner of the exterior piece. Cut out the squares and press the side seams and bottom seams open.

* Pull the bag sides apart at each cutout and pinch the side and bottom seams together, lining up the seams and raw edges. Stitch across each corner of the bag to create gussets, and zigzag stitch within the seam allowances to reinforce the gussets. (*See page* 238 *for another example of sewing a gusset.*)

* Repeat the process to make gussets in the lining.

⑤ **Assemble the Bag**

* Turn the exterior bag right side out. Place the lining into the exterior so the wrong sides are together, aligning the side seams.
* Open the bias tape and press one short end ½" to the wrong side. Refold the bias tape.
* Starting with the unfolded raw end of bias tape, encase the top raw edge of the bag in the bias tape. The bias will wrap around the top of the bag so that the folded and pressed end will cover the beginning of the binding. Stitch the bias tape in place, making sure to catch the back of the tape in the stitching.
* Fold the top 6½" of the bag over to one side and press.

⑥ **Make the Pull Tab (Optional)**

* Fold all the sides of the pull tab ½" to the wrong side and press. Then fold it in half widthwise with the wrong sides together to form a 1½" × 2½" rectangle. Press.
* Center the tab on the right side of one side of the bag flap exterior, positioning it so that half of the tab extends past the bound edge. Edgestitch all around the tab, stitching the tab shut and attaching it to the bag at the same time.
* Attach one grommet to the extending end of the tab following the manufacturer's instructions.

⑦ **Attach the Strap**

* Cut the webbing to any desired length. (The shown sample, with a 48" length of webbing, allows the bag to be worn in a cross-body style.)
* Bind the short ends of the webbing with the remaining bias tape, or even different color bias tape. Alternately, you may choose to fold over the raw edges and zigzag stitch.
* Pin the webbing in place, centering it on the side seams, with the strap ends extending 4" down from the top of the fold. Be sure the webbing is not twisted.
* Mark the placement of two grommets on each side of the bag. Install the grommets following the manufacturer's instructions, being sure to go through the webbing and all the fabric layers. The grommets secure the webbing strap to the bag.

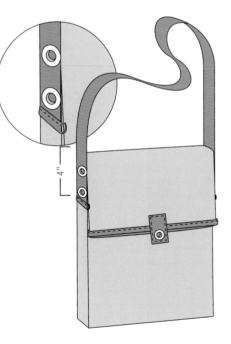

STEP 7

STROLLER TOTE

Designed by Michele Chisholm

This lovely little bag is quite the multitasker! Whether it's for a stroller, shopping cart, or walker, you can alter the pockets to handle the user's specific storage needs, be they a baby bottle and diapers, or grandma's glasses and cell phone. Trim and embellishment can really make this bag special. How about adding some rickrack, an embroidered monogram, or fun appliqué?

MATERIALS

* * 1 yard of 44/45" home decor fabric
* * 1 spool of coordinating thread
* * 3 fabric-covered or decorative buttons, 1" in diameter
* * 25" of trim (optional)

Finished dimensions – 12" tall × 14" wide, excluding straps
Seam allowance – ½" unless otherwise specified

1 Measure, Mark, and Cut

Fold your fabric in half lengthwise with the right sides together, aligning the selvages. Measure and mark the following pattern pieces directly on the wrong side of your fabric, aligning straight edges with the fabric grainline, and cut them out.

* * **Bag body** 13" × 15" (cut 4)
* * **Outside pocket** 8" × 15" (cut 2)
* * **Inside pocket** 5" × 4½" (cut 2)
* * **Straps** 10" × 5½" (cut 3)

2 Mark the Strap and Button Placements

* * On the right side of one bag body, mark three dots along the top raw edge: one at the center, with the other two marks 4" away on both sides. This piece becomes the front exterior.

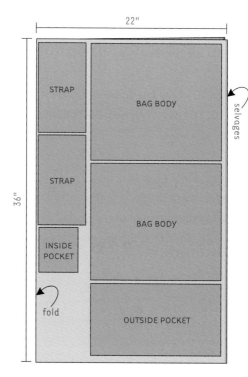

✳ On the right side of the remaining bag body, again mark three dots. Mark the first one in the center and then 4" away on both sides, but this time place them 2" down from the top raw edge. This piece becomes the back exterior.

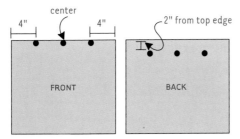

❸ Make and Attach the Straps

✳ Fold each strap in half lengthwise with the right sides together. Stitch the long edge and one short edge, leaving one short edge open for turning. Clip the corners, trim the seam allowances, and turn the straps right side out. Press.

✳ Make a vertical buttonhole (parallel to the long edge) in the center of each strap, 1" from the finished edge. It should accommodate a 1" button.

✳ Center a strap on the right side of the bag front over each of the placement dots, with the raw edges aligned. Baste the straps in place, close to the raw edges.

❹ Sew the Buttons

If you are using fabric-covered buttons, use fabric remnants to cover the button forms, following the manufacturer's instructions. Hand-sew the buttons to the back exterior at the placement marks (see step 2).

❺ Make the Outside Pocket

✳ Pin the outside pocket pieces with the right sides together, aligning the raw edges. Stitch the top edge (15" long) only. Press the seam allowances open and then flip the pocket pieces so the wrong sides are together.

✳ Edgestitch along the top of the pocket. If desired, machine-stitch a piece of decorative trim along the top of the pocket. If the bag is meant for an elderly person with a walker, trim can make the pocket opening more visible.

✳ Pin the outside pocket on the front body with both right sides facing up, aligning the side and bottom raw edges. Mark a vertical line down the center of the pocket and stitch through all layers to create a divided pocket.

❻ Make the Inside Pocket

✳ Pin the inside pocket pieces with the right sides together, aligning all the raw edges. Stitch all around, leaving a 2" opening at the bottom for turning. Clip the corners, trim the seam allowances, and turn the pocket right side out. Press the pocket, pressing the raw edges at the opening to the inside.

✳ Topstitch along the top pocket edge and/or add trim, if desired, as for the outside pocket.

✳ Pin the inside pocket to the right side of one unmarked (lining) bag body piece, centered side to side and at least 3" from the top raw edge. Stitch the sides and bottom, closing the opening as you stitch.

⑦ Stitch the Bag Exterior and Lining

✳ Pin the front exterior and back exterior with the right sides together, aligning all the raw edges. Stitch along the side and bottom edges. Clip the corners, turn the bag right side out, and press.

✳ Pin the remaining (lining) bag body pieces with the right sides together, aligning all the raw edges. Stitch along the side and bottom edges. Press the seams open, but leave the lining wrong side out.

✳ Put the exterior bag inside the lining so the right sides are together and the straps are tucked between them, aligning the top raw edges and side seams. Stitch around the top edge, leaving a 4" opening for turning. Turn the bag right side out, extending the straps outward. Press, turning in the raw edges of the opening. Edgestitch around the top edge, closing the opening as you stitch.

❋ Attaching the Bag

Fold the straps over the top of a stroller or walker handle, and button them to hold the bag in place. Fill the bag with your necessities and be on your way.

BABY OVERALLS

Designed by Sue Kim

Overalls are the ideal pants for little ones just learning to walk, as they allow the perfect freedom of movement. Not only that, but overalls will help keep your little one clean, as the bib helps shield from messy spills.

MATERIALS

* Locate the pattern in the envelope (sheet #4)
* 1 yard of 44/45" home decor fabric
* 1 spool of coordinating thread
* ⅓ yard of 1"-wide elastic

Sizes – 12 months and 24 months

Seam allowance – ½" unless otherwise specified

❶ Determine Your Child's Size

Measure the child's waist and inseam to find the right size. Sometimes the length is more important than waist fit, if child is particularly tall or short.

	12 months	24 months
Waist size	20"	21"
Inseam	8"	10"

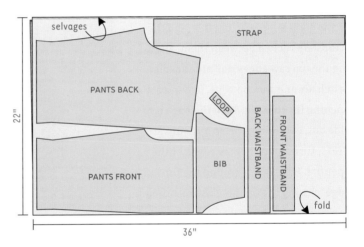

❷ Measure, Mark, and Cut

Fold your fabric in half lengthwise with right sides together, aligning the selvages. Position the pattern pieces, and measure and mark the additional pieces as shown. Cut out the pieces, and transfer the markings from the pattern pieces to the wrong side of fabric.

* **Pants front** (cut 2)
* **Pants back** (cut 2)
* **Bib** (cut 2)

For the 12 months size:

* **Front waistband** 12" × 2½" (cut 2)
* **Back waistband** 15" × 2½" (cut 2)
* **Loop** 3" × 1" (cut 2 on the bias)
* **Strap** 3" × 19½" (cut 2)

For the 24 months size:

* **Front waistband** 12¾" × 2½" (cut 2)
* **Back waistband** 15½" × 2½" (cut 2)
* **Loop** 3" × 1" (cut 2 on the bias)
* **Strap** 3" × 22" (cut 2)

NOTE: *Position the grainline arrow on the pattern pieces along the straight grain of the fabric.*

❸ Construct the Bib

* To make each loop, fold the loop piece in half lengthwise with the wrong sides together and press. Open the loop and press both raw edges to the center crease. Refold along the original center crease and press. Edgestitch the folded edges together.

* Position the loops on one bib piece as indicated on the pattern piece, with the raw edges aligned. Baste the loop edges in place with a ¼" seam allowance.

* Pin both bib pieces with the right sides together, sandwiching the loops between the layers. Stitch along the top and side edges of the bibs, leaving the bottom edge unstitched. Clip the corners, turn the bib right side out, and press. Edgestitch along the three finished edges.

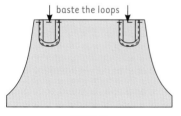

baste the loops

STEP 3

❹ Assemble the Pants

* With the right sides together, stitch a pants front to a pants back along the side seam, then stitch the inside leg seam. Press the seams open. Repeat with the remaining front and back pants pieces.

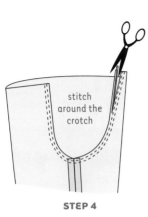

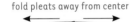

STEP 4

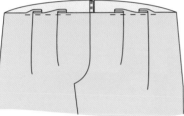

fold pleats away from center

STEP 5

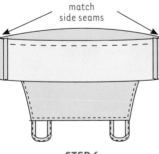

match side seams

STEP 6

* Turn one front/back piece right side out and slip it inside the other so the right sides are together, matching the inner leg seams. Stitch the entire crotch seam from front to back. Stitch again, with a ¼" seam allowance, to reinforce the seam. Trim the seam allowances close to the second stitching line. Turn the pants right side out.

⑤ Make the Pleats

Make the pleats on the front of the pants as indicated on the pattern piece. Fold the pants along each fold line and align it with the placement line, away from the center front of the pants (pleats will point toward the side seam). Pin and baste the pleats in place with a ¼" seam allowance.

⑥ Make the Waistband and Attach the Bib

* Fold each front waistband piece in half so the short ends are together, and mark the center on both long raw edges. Repeat with the back waistband pieces.

* With the right sides together, stitch a front and back waistband piece together along the short ends to create the exterior waistband. Press the seams open. Repeat with remaining front and back waistband pieces to create the waistband facing. Turn the exterior waistband right side out.

* Pin the bib and exterior front waistband with the right sides together, aligning the center fronts. Baste them together with a ¼" seam allowance. Pin the waistband facing to the exterior waistband with the right sides together, sandwiching the bib between the two layers.

* Stitch a seam all the way around. Turn the waistband right side out and press. Edgestitch along the top edge of the waistband.

⑦ Attach the Waistband to the Pants

* Press the bottom raw edge of the waistband facing ½" to the wrong side. With the right sides together, align the raw edges of

the exterior waistband and the top raw edge of the pants, aligning the center front, center back, and side seams. Stitch, taking care to keep the waistband facing out of the stitching.

* Press the waistband and bib up, away from the pants. Pin the waistband facing in place so it conceals the seam allowances. From the right side of the pants, edgestitch along the bottom edge of the exterior waistband, making sure you catch the bottom edge of the waistband facing in the stitching. Leave a 2" break in the stitching at both side seams.

* Insert the elastic into the back waistband facing at the openings left at the side seams. Pin each end of the elastic at the side seams to secure. (You might want to slip the overalls on the child and adjust the length of the elastic to best fit the child.) Stitch the elastic in place along the side seams through all the layers. Complete edgestitching along the bottom edge of the waistband facing, to close the openings.

⑧ Make and Attach the Straps

* Fold and press each short end of the strap ½" to the wrong side. Fold the strap in half lengthwise with the wrong sides together and press. Open the strap and press the raw edges on both long sides in to the center crease. Refold along the original center crease and press. Edgestitch along all four sides of the strap. Repeat with the second strap.

* Pin one short end of each strap onto the back waistband, 1" from each side of the center back seam at a 60-degree angle. Box stitch the straps in place on the back waistband through all the layers.

* Cross the straps in the back, pull them through the front loops, and secure them with a loose knot.

⑨ Hem the Pants

Make a double-fold hem at the bottom of each pant leg, pressing under ½", then another 1". Topstitch close to the folded edge.

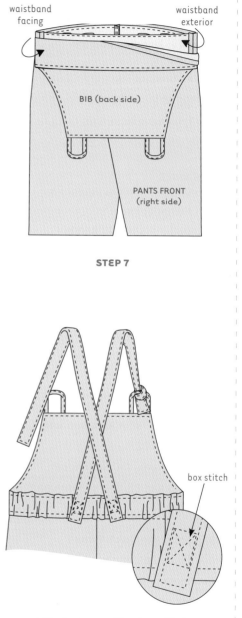

waistband facing   waistband exterior

BIB (back side)

PANTS FRONT
(right side)

STEP 7

box stitch

attach straps with a box stitch
STEP 8

kaleidoscope table runner

Designed by Jenna Lou Odegard

This runner is the perfect accessory to bring some color to your dining table. Although this project calls for a striped fabric, you might also try experimenting with other geometric designs for a variety of interesting kaleidoscopic effects. Whip one up for every season!

MATERIALS

* ✳ 1 yard of 54/55" home decor fabric in a striped pattern
* ✳ 1 spool of coordinating thread
* ✳ ⅝ yard of fusible fleece

Finished dimensions – 52½" long × 11" wide
Seam allowance – ¼" unless otherwise specified

① Measure, Mark, and Cut

Fold your fabric in half lengthwise with the right sides together, aligning the selvages. Measure and mark the following pattern pieces directly on the wrong side of your fabric, as shown in the cutting diagram, and then cut them out. Note that the squares are cut on the bias to use the striped pattern to create the chevron design.

* ✳ **Border** 2¼" × 53" (cut 2 on fold)
* ✳ **Back panel** 27" × 11½" (cut 2)
* ✳ **Bias squares** 4¼" square, cut on bias (cut 28, four of those on fold)

Cut from fusible fleece:

* ✳ **Back panel** 27" × 11½" (cut 2)

② Create the Back Panel

Fuse the fleece to the wrong side of the back panels following the manufacturer's instructions. Pin the panels with the right sides together, aligning all the raw edges. Stitch the panels together along one 11½" edge with ½" seam allowance and press the seam open. Set the back panel aside.

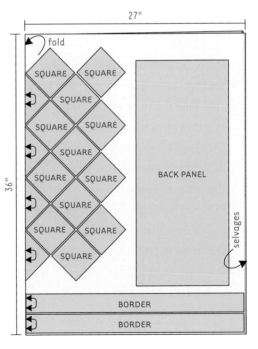

CUTTING LAYOUT

③ Assemble the Front

* Pin two squares with the right sides together, aligning all the raw edges and ensuring that stripes are going in the same direction. Stitch the pieces together along one side and press the seam open. When the pair is opened, the stripes will be going in opposite directions, forming a V pattern.

STEP 3

* Continue to stitch the remaining squares into pairs in the same fashion.
* On a work surface, arrange the pairs in a pattern that you like, so that you have a design that is 2 squares wide by 14 squares long. Stitch the pairs together to create the front, two pairs at a time, pressing the seams open as you stitch.

④ Add the Borders

Pin one border to the assembled front along one long raw edge, with the right sides together. Stitch and press the seam open. Repeat with the remaining border on the opposite side of the front.

⑤ Assemble the Table Runner

* Pin the front and back with the right sides together. Stitch around all the sides, leaving a 4" opening on one long edge for turning. Clip the corners, turn the table runner right side out, and push out the corners.
* Press, turning under the raw edges of the opening. Edgestitch all around, closing the opening in the process.

⑥ Quilt the Table Runner

Quilt the table runner by hand or by machine, as desired. For a simple approach, stitch in the ditch of the existing seamlines. Alternatively, try stitching along selected stripes, or perpendicular to stripes on each piece.

Kitchen Gift Set

Designed by Anna Buchholz

No matter how careful you are removing hot dishes from the oven, you can sometimes burn yourself or scorch your clothes! And no matter how hard you try to bring your reusable shopping bags with you, plastic bags always seem to accumulate. Sound familiar? Well, fret no more! This project consists of a long casserole oven mitt and a plastic grocery bag holder. Make one for yourself, or to give as a great housewarming gift.

MATERIALS

* 1 yard of 44/45" home decor fabric, denim, or similar heavy material
* ¼ yard of insulated batting
* 1 spool of coordinating thread
* 20" of ½"-wide nonroll elastic, cut into two 10" lengths
* Denim needle (optional)
* French curve, 8" plate, or similar for curve template

Finished dimensions — Casserole Mitt: 17" long × 7" wide; Bag Holder: 17" long × 10½" wide, excluding hanging strap

Seam allowance — ½" unless otherwise specified

1 Measure, Mark, and Cut

Fold your fabric in half lengthwise with the right sides together, aligning the selvages. Measure and mark the following pattern pieces directly on the wrong side of your fabric, aligning the straight edges with the fabric grainline, and then cut them out.

* **Main mitt** 8" × 36" (cut 2 on fold)
* **Hand piece** 8" × 9" (cut 2)
* **Bag holder** 20" × 22" (cut 1 on fold)
* **Hanging loop** 20" × 3" (cut 1)

Cut from insulated batting:

* **Main mitt** 8" × 3" (cut 1)

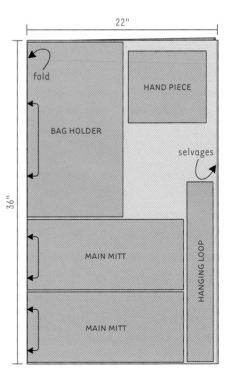

CUTTING LAYOUT

Casserole Mitt

① Round and Hem the Curves

* Using a French curve or a plate, round each 8" end of all the fabric and batting main mitt pieces and one 8" end of both hand pieces. Make sure all resulting curved edges are identical.

* Hem the 8" straight edge of each hand piece (opposite the curved end) with a ½" double-fold hem.

② Lay Out the Pieces

Lay out the pieces in the following order on a work surface and pin them together:

* main mitt batting
* main mitt fabric, right side up
* hand pieces, right side up on each end
* second main mitt fabric, wrong side up

③ Stitch the Mitt

Stitch all around, leaving a 4" opening along one straight edge for turning. Clip the curves, trim the seam allowances, and turn the mitt right side out. Press the mitt, and press the edges at the opening to the inside. Edgestitch all around, closing the opening as you stitch.

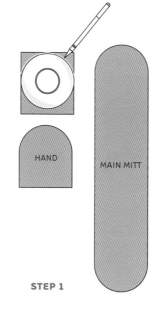

HAND

MAIN MITT

STEP 1

Plastic Bag Holder

① Stitch the Sides

Fold the bag holder in half with the right sides together, aligning the 20" edges. Stitch that edge and press the seam open.

② Make the Casings

Press under both raw edges ¼", then press under another 1". Edgestitch near the first fold to form a casing on each end, leaving a 2" opening in each casing for the elastic.

③ Thread the Elastic

Thread one 10" length of elastic through each casing with a safety pin. Overlap the elastic ends and stitch them together securely, taking care that elastic is not twisted. Slip the elastic ends back in the casings and slipstitch the openings closed.

④ Make and Attach the Loop

* Press all raw edges of the hanging loop ½" to the wrong side. Fold the loop lengthwise with the wrong sides together, and stitch all around.
* Fold the loop in half across the width and pin the ends just inside the top edge, on each side of the vertical seam. Stitch the loop in place with a box stitch (it is okay to stitch through both the casing and the elastic).

PORTABLE PICNIC

Designed by Keri McCarthy

This portable picnic is a blanket with built-in pockets for picnic plates and flatware. Since this doesn't take much time at all to make, you can get going even sooner to the park, zoo, or beach. While this project calls for home decor fabric, try oilcloth or coated cotton for an easy-care version that can be wiped down. The wider the fabric, the larger the blanket, but the instructions work with any fabric width.

MATERIALS

* 1 yard of 44/45", 54/55", or 58/60" nondirectional home decor fabric
* 1 spool of coordinating thread
* 3 buttons, 1" in diameter
* Scraps of interfacing
* 2 yards of twill tape or ribbon

Finished dimensions – Depends on width of fabric; 35" long × 29", 39", or 45" wide

Seam allowance – ¼" unless otherwise specified

① Measure, Mark, and Cut

Trim away the selvages and lay out your fabric in a single layer with the wrong side facing up. Measure and mark the following pattern pieces directly on the wrong side of your fabric, then cut them out.

* **Flap** 36" × 6" (cut 1)
* **Pocket** 36" × 7" (cut 1)
* **Picnic blanket** (remaining fabric)

  44/45" fabric 36" × 30"

  54/55" fabric 36" × 40"

  58/60" fabric 36" × 46"

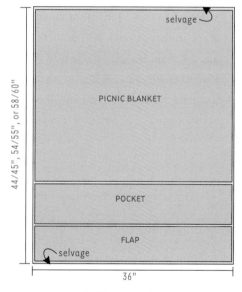

CUTTING LAYOUT

NOTE: *The dimensions of the pocket are meant for 9" dinner or dessert plates. Larger plates will require alterations in pocket cut measurements and divider width (see step 3).*

② Hem the Blanket and Pocket

* Hem three sides of the blanket with a ¼" double-fold hem, leaving one 36" edge unhemmed.

* Hem both short ends and one long side of the pocket in similar fashion, again leaving one 36" edge unhemmed. This unhemmed edge becomes the bottom of the pocket.

③ Attach and Divide the Pocket

* Aligning raw edges, pin the right side of the pocket to the bottom wrong side of the blanket (both pieces have wrong side facing up). Stitch along the raw edge. Fold the pocket over the seam to the right side of the blanket and press the seam.

* Stitch the short sides of the pocket to the blanket by stitching in the "ditch" of the existing hem stitches.

* Mark and stitch vertical lines on the pocket 12", 16", 20", and 24" from one side. If you plan to use plates larger than 9" in diameter, you might want to lay out your picnic plates and flatware on the pocket and draw vertical pocket lines to accommodate your own picnic gear.

④ Prepare the Top Flap

Hem both short ends and one long side of the flap with ¼" double-fold hem, leaving one 36" edge unhemmed. This unhemmed edge becomes the top of the flap. Fold the top raw edge of the flap ¼" to the wrong side, but do not stitch.

⑤ Make the Buttonholes

Fold the flap in half across the width, pressing a light crease to mark the center, then fold in half again and press another light crease to mark the quarter points. Unfold the flap and lay it flat. Make three horizontal buttonholes 1" above the long finished edge of the flap, directly on the center and quarter points.

OPTIONS: *You can install Velcro or snaps instead of buttons if you prefer. Just make sure to attach them on the wrong side of the flap.*

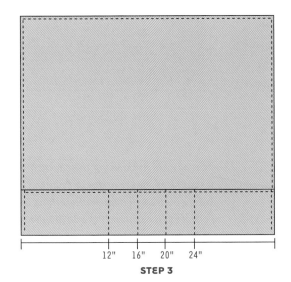

12" 16" 20" 24"

STEP 3

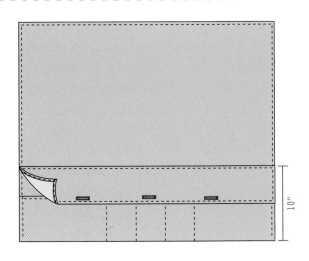

10"

STEP 6

6 Attach the Flap

With right sides facing up, pin the unstitched folded edge of the flap on the blanket, 10" up from, and parallel to, the bottom edge, so that the buttonhole edge of the flap covers the top edge of the pocket. Edgestitch the top of the flap in place.

7 Attach the Buttons

Hand-sew the buttons to the pocket so they align with the button-holes, taking care not to catch the blanket in the stitching. (Or, if you are using Velcro or snaps, install the remaining halves.)

✻ Fold and Go!

Fill the pockets with picnic plates and flatware. Fold the blanket in thirds length-wise, folding at the inner edges of the plate pockets. Then fold the blanket in thirds or in fourths crosswise, depending on the size of the blanket. Wrap and tie the ribbon or twill tape around the blanket like a pack-age, and enjoy!

CHIC CARRYALL

Designed by Sue Kim

Stylish enough to take anywhere and large enough to hold just about anything, this versatile tote can be slung over your shoulder or carried by hand. With its generous size and only a few seams, it's also great for showing off a large bold print that might get lost on a smaller bag.

MATERIALS

* Locate the pattern in the envelope (sheet #4)
* 1 yard of 54/55" heavyweight home decor fabric
* 1 spool of coordinating thread
* 1 yard of 22"-wide medium-weight fusible interfacing
* 1 magnetic snap, ½" or ¾" in diameter

Finished dimensions – 16½" wide × 21" tall (strap included)

Seam allowance – ½" unless otherwise specified

1 Measure, Mark, and Cut

Lay out your fabric in a single layer with the wrong side facing up. You might want to trace the pattern to make four copies, or trace the pattern four times on the wrong side of the fabric as shown. Measure and mark the additional pieces, lining up the straight edges along the fabric grainline. Cut out all the pieces, and transfer the markings from the pattern pieces to the wrong side of fabric.

* **Bag body** (cut 4)
* **Straps** 12½" × 4" (cut 2)
* **Pocket** 6" square (cut 2)

Cut from interfacing:

* **Bag body** (cut 2)

NOTE: *Position the grainline arrow on the pattern pieces along the straight grain of the fabric. Mirror the Bag Body pieces along the indicated line on the pattern.*

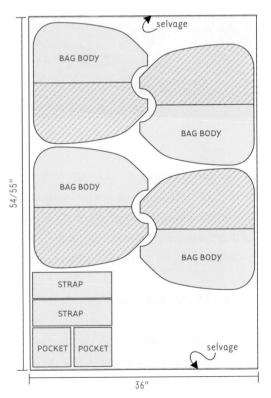

CUTTING LAYOUT

❷ Interface the Fabric

Fuse interfacing to the wrong side of the remaining body pieces (without handles), following the manufacturer's instructions. These interfaced pieces become the lining.

❸ Stitch the Gusset

Stitch the dart openings on the bottom corners of each bag body with the right sides together to form gussets. Backstitch a few times to secure the seams. Trim the seam allowances and press toward the center of the bag.

❹ Make the Straps

* Fold each strap in half lengthwise with the wrong sides together, and press. Open and press the long raw edges to the wrong side to meet the crease. Refold each strap in half lengthwise and edgestitch the long edges of each strap together.

* With the right side of one noninterfaced exterior facing up, pin one end of a strap at the placement mark on the left side, aligning the raw edges. Baste the strap end in place, leaving the opposite end free to be attached later. Repeat with the remaining strap and the second noninterfaced exterior. Set these pieces aside.

❺ Add the Closure

Attach the corresponding pieces of the magnetic snap to the right side of the lining pieces at the placement marks, following the manufacturer's instructions.

FABRIC NOTE

If you cut the pocket from scrap fabric instead, you can fit the bag body and straps into one yard of 44/45" fabric.

⑥ Make the Pocket

* Pin the pocket pieces with the right sides together, aligning the raw edges. Stitch the sides and bottom, leaving the top edge open. Clip the corners and turn the pocket right side out, pushing out corners. Fold the top raw edges ½" to the wrong side. Edgestitch the top edge, to close the opening.
* Pin the pocket to the right side of one lining at the placement marks. Edgestitch along the side and bottom edges to attach the pocket.

⑦ Make the Exterior and Lining

* Pin the two exteriors with the right sides together, aligning the raw edges. Be sure to also align the gusset darts.
* Stitch the side and bottom edges between markings, leaving the top open, taking care not to catch the handles in the stitching line. Clip the curves and turn the exterior right side out.
* Stitch the lining in the same fashion, leaving a 5" opening along the center bottom edge for turning.

start/stop stitching

STEP 7

⑧ Assemble the Bag

* Insert the exterior into the lining so the right sides are together, aligning the side seams and top raw edges. Stitch from the markings on each top edge, leaving the short straight edges at the top unstitched to attach the handle in a later step. Clip the curves and turn the bag right side out.
* Edgestitch the lining opening closed, or hand-sew it closed with a slipstitch.
* Push the lining into the exterior.

⑨ Finish the Straps

* Fold the raw edges at the strap placement openings ½" to the wrong side and press. Insert the free end of each strap at least ½" into its respective opening and pin. Take care that the handle is not twisted.
* Starting at one side seam, edgestitch all around the entire top edge, being sure to catch the straps in the stitching.

SHaken, NOT STiRReD MaRTini SHaDe

Designed by Jamie Halleckson & Carmen Marti

Sometimes a Roman shade is just the thing you're looking for to provide a little respite from bright sunlight. With one yard of fabric, you can brighten or change the mood of any single window. It's about the least expensive and quickest renovation project you can do.

MATERIALS

* 1 yard of 54/55" home decor fabric
* 1 spool of coordinating thread
* ¼"-diameter dowels (exact number depends on the length of the shade; sample used 5)
* Small plastic rings (3 for each dowel)
* 1" × 2" board for the batten
* Screw eyes (exact number depends on width of shade; sample used 3)
* Nylon cording (sample used about 7 yards)
* 2 L-brackets and screws
* 1 small awning cleat

In addition to your standard sewing tools, you'll need:

* Saw for cutting dowels and batten (or have them cut at a hardware store)
* Staple gun or small brads and hammer
* Drill

Finished dimensions – Shown sample is 54" long × 25" wide

Seam allowance – ½" unless otherwise specified

SIZE VARIATIONS

The sample shown here was made with a yard of fabric cut in half lengthwise to make two 36" × 27" panels. These were then pieced and trimmed to fit the finished window dimensions. Using this method, a shade from one yard of 54/55" fabric could fit a window up to 68" long × 25" wide. If left unpieced, a yard of nondirectional print fabric could be turned on its side and used to fit a window up to 51" long × 34" wide.

❶ Measure, Mark, and Cut

Measure the height and width inside the window frame to determine the desired finished size. Add 3" to the length and 2" to the width to determine the cutting dimensions of the fabric. Cut and piece your fabric, as needed, to make a rectangle to the desired cutting dimensions. To save confusion later, label the top, bottom, and sides along the edges within the seam allowance.

❷ Hem the Side and Bottom Edges

Zigzag or serge along all four edges of the shade. Fold the side edges 1" to the wrong side and stitch ¾" from the folded edge to hem the sides. Repeat with the bottom raw edge; this will simultaneously form the bottom dowel casing.

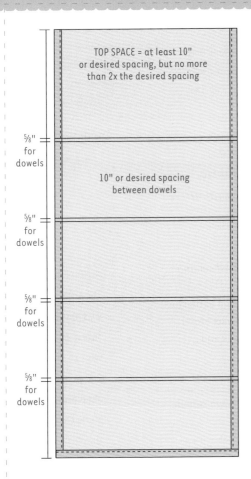

TOP SPACE = at least 10"
or desired spacing, but no more
than 2x the desired spacing

⅝"
for
dowels

10" or desired spacing
between dowels

⅝"
for
dowels

⅝"
for
dowels

⅝"
for
dowels

STEP 3

❸ Determine the Placement of the Dowel Casings

If your fabric has a design, determine the desired look when the shade is drawn up to help you decide on the number and placement of the dowel casings. Keep in mind that casings should be equally spaced, and at least 8" and no more than 14" apart. It is fine for the uppermost dowel casing to be more than 14" from the top edge of the shade. For ours, we placed the casings 10" apart, with the uppermost dowel casing about 16" from the top edge of the shade.

* Place the shade on a work surface with the wrong side up. Measure up from the bottom hem seam and use tailor's chalk or pencil to mark two parallel lines across the width of the fabric. The first line should be drawn the distance you want the dowel casings to be spaced (for our shade, 10"). The second line should be ⅝" above the first.

* Continue working your way up the length of the fabric, marking pairs of horizontal lines in similar fashion (see the illustration). You are done when the space between your uppermost line and the top edge of the fabric is more than your desired spacing distance, but less than two times your spacing distance (for this sample, more than 10" but less than 20").

❹ Stitch the Dowel Casings

To make each casing, fold the fabric with the right sides together at a pair of marked lines, matching up the lines all the way across the width. Press the fold. Stitch along the marked line and press the seam. This will form a channel for the dowel on the wrong side of the fabric.

❺ Make and Insert the Dowels

Cut the dowels so they are 1" shorter than the width of the shade and insert one into each casing. Slipstitch or whipstitch the casing ends closed if desired, or leave the casing open if you want the dowels to be removable for washing the shade.

⑥ Attach the Plastic Rings

Place the shade wrong side up on your work surface. Measure and mark the placement of the small plastic rings as follows:

* On each dowel casing, make a mark 1" in from each side edge.
* If the shade is 26" wide or smaller, make a third mark halfway between the first two marks on each casing.
* If the shade is wider than 26", make two more marks evenly spaced between the first two marks. (Generally you want rings for the cording somewhere between 8" to 12" apart on a Roman shade.)
* Take care that all the ring placement markings line up in perfect vertical columns from casing to casing, to ensure that the shade draws up evenly.
* Hand-sew a ring at each placement mark.

⑦ Attach the Batten and Screw Eyes

* Cut the 1" × 2" batten board to the width of the finished shade.
* Place the top raw edge of the shade, right side up, near the edge of one 2" side of the batten, with the finished side edges aligned with the short ends of the batten.

* Staple to secure the fabric to the batten (you may use small brads if you don't have a staple gun). Turn over the batten so the shade wraps around and covers it completely from the right side.
* On the 1" underside of the batten (no fabric is attached to this edge), attach a screw eye exactly above each vertical column of rings.

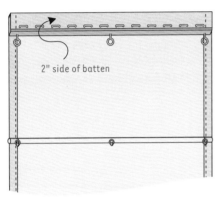

2" side of batten

STEP 7

8 Cut the Cording to Size

* Determine the amount of cording needed. You will need as many cords as you have rings on each dowel casing (ours used three cords). Decide on which side of the shade you want the cords to hang. For reference in the measurements below, the shade shown in the photograph fits a window 25" wide by 54" tall.
* Cord 1 is the cord farthest from the side where all the cords will hang, so it needs to be the width of the window, plus 1½ times the height of the window (for example, 25" + (1.5 × 54") = 106").

* Cord 2 is the cord along the side where all the cords will hang, so it just needs to be 1½ times the height of the window (for example, 1.5 × 54" = 81").
* If you have only **three** rings across, cord 3 needs to be ½ times the width of the window, plus 1½ times the height of the window (for example, (0.5" × 25") + (1.5 × 54") = 93.5").
* If you have **four** rings across, cord 3 needs to be ⅔ times the width of the window, plus 1½ times the height of the window. And cord 4 needs to be ⅓ times the width of the window, plus 1½ times the height of the window.

9 Attach the Cording

* Begin at the bottom ring farthest away from the side of the shade where your cords will hang and attach one end of cord 1 to this ring with a square knot.
* Feed cord 1 through the rings directly above the bottom, anchor ring, then through all the screw eyes on the batten so that the excess will hang down the opposite side.
* Starting at the ring (along the bottom hem) next to the one cord 1 is tied to, attach cord 3 with a square knot and feed it up and over through the rings in a similar fashion.
* If you have a cord 4, attach and feed it in a similar fashion next to cord 3.
* On the last bottom ring, attach and feed cord 2 straight up through the rings in a similar fashion.
* Tie all the cords together just below the screw eye.

10 Install the Completed Shade

* Making sure that the batten is completely level and with the right side of the shade facing out, attach the shade inside the window frame with the L-brackets.
* Attach the awning cleat to the outside of the window frame.
* Adjust your shade cords to raise and lower the shade. Knot the bottom of the cords together and trim as needed.

TUFFET INSPIRED OTTOMAN

Designed by Heather Scrimsher

Little Miss Muffet sat on her tuffet, and now you can too! Who knew that by simply sewing two squares together, you can create an amazingly comfortable ottoman for lounging? Looking for a quick, easy, and fun coffee table? Simply place a tray on top and you've created an instant table.

MATERIALS

* 1 yard of 54" home decor fabric
* 1 spool of coordinating thread
* 8 large buttons, ¾" to 1" in diameter
* 8 small buttons, ½" to ⅝" in diameter
* 5-pound box of polyester fiberfill

Finished dimensions – 20" wide × 20" deep × 11" tall

Seam allowance – ½" unless otherwise specified

① Measure, Mark, and Cut

Fold your fabric in half lengthwise with the right sides together, aligning the selvages. Measure and mark the following pattern piece directly on the wrong side of your fabric, aligning the straight edges with the fabric grainline, and then cut out.

* **Top/bottom** 27" square (cut 2)

NOTE: *If you are unable to cut two perfect 27" squares from your fabric, you may cut the squares slightly smaller. Most important is that the pieces are exact squares.*

② Mark the Top and Bottom Pieces

Find and make a ⅜" notch at the center of each side of both pieces. On the wrong side of both pieces, mark a dot ½" from each corner.

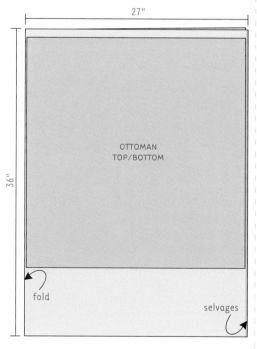

27"

36"

OTTOMAN
TOP/BOTTOM

fold

selvages

CUTTING LAYOUT

❸ Stitch the Top and Bottom Together

To sew the top and bottom pieces together, you will be sewing eight lines, each half the length of one side of the square, then rotating either the top or bottom piece before stitching the next line. Don't worry; it sounds trickier than it actually is:

* With the right sides together, match a dot with a notch. Stitch from the notch/dot connection to the next dot/notch connection with a ½" seam allowance. Leave your needle down in the fabric, lift the presser foot and pivot the corner, lining up the next edges. The notches will help you turn the corners and keep the edges aligned. Repeat this until only one edge remains unstitched.

* When stitching the last edge, leave a 5" opening in the middle for turning and stuffing the ottoman. Clip all the corners and turn the ottoman right side out through the opening.

❹ Stuff the Ottoman

Stuff the ottoman through the opening, taking care that the corners are well stuffed. Continue stuffing the ottoman until it is the desired firmness. Carefully hand-sew the opening closed using a slipstitch.

❺ Embellish the Ottoman

Stack a smaller button on top of a larger one, matching at least two holes. Hand-sew the two buttons together at one of the eight corners of the ottoman. Repeat with the remaining buttons and corners.

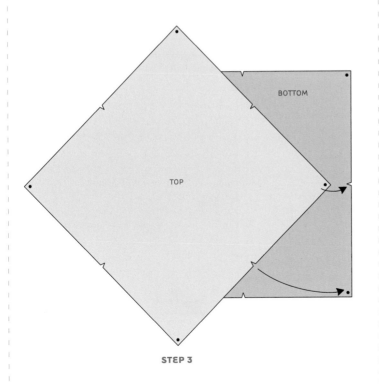

STEP 3

Easy Dining Chair Slipcover

Designed by Cherie Killilea

Using just one yard of home decor fabric, you can create your own tailored slipcover. Give the thrift store side chair new life, or add some pizzazz anywhere in your home with covered chairs. You'll never need to send a side chair out to be reupholstered again!

MATERIALS

* 1 yard of 54/55" home decor fabric
* 1 spool of coordinating thread
* Newsprint, poster board, or similar large-format paper for tracing and making pattern pieces
* Dining room side chair
* Paper scissors

Finished dimensions – custom fit; sample is 24" tall × 13" wide × 17" deep

Seam allowance – ½" unless otherwise specified

① Make the Pattern Pieces

Lay out your pattern paper on a work surface large and sturdy enough to accommodate your chair (perhaps the floor). Place the chair on its side on top of the paper and trace the profile of the chair back and seat as exactly as you can. Note that some measurements, particularly the back and seat width, will need to be measured against the chair, as they will not be captured by your profile tracing. Use the table on the opposite page to record the chair measurements.

TRACING TIP: *Extend the profile tracing as far below the seat as you would like the slipcover to extend over the legs. Keep in mind that a highly cushioned seat may cause the slipcover to slide up the sides a few inches, so extend your tracing farther down the legs to accommodate this movement if necessary. In the shown sample, the pattern profile was extended 3" below the bottom of the seat.*

FABRIC NOTE

One yard of fabric is enough to make a straight slipcover, but not enough to make a slipcover with a full "skirt" that completely covers the chair legs. You can however, use these instructions as the basis for a full slipcover if you want to use more than one yard of fabric.

Inside Back: Length/height measurement includes the top edge of the chair back. Measure the depth of the top edge and on down to where the inside back meets the seat top. (Add 1" for seam allowance.) Width measurement will not come from your profile tracing. Measure the width of the chair back at its widest point. (Add 1" for seam allowance.)

Outside Back: Length measurement is from the top of chair back to the desired bottom hem. (Add 2" for seam allowance and hem.) Width measurement is the same as the inside back. (Add 1" for seam allowance.)

Upper Side: Length/height measurement is from the top of the chair back to the top of the seat. Width measurement is the widest point from the inside back to the outside back. Add 1" for seam allowance to both measurements.

Lower Side: Length/height measurement is from the seat top to the desired bottom hem. Add 2" for seam allowance and hem. Width measurement is from the outside back to the seat front. Add 1" for seam allowance.

Seat: Length measurement is from the inside back, over the seat, and down the seat front to the desired bottom hem. (Add 2" for seam allowance and hem.) Width measurement will not come from your profile tracing. Measure the width of the seat at the back and at the front. If they differ significantly, the seat pattern piece should be shaped as a trapezoid accordingly. The top edge of the seat should be the same width as the bottom edge of the inside back. (Add 1" for seam allowance.)

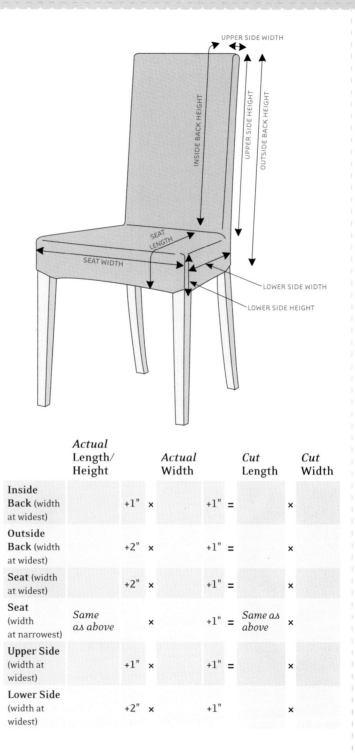

	Actual Length/ Height		Actual Width		Cut Length		Cut Width
Inside Back (width at widest)		+1" ×		+1" =		×	
Outside Back (width at widest)		+2" ×		+1" =		×	
Seat (width at widest)		+2" ×		+1" =		×	
Seat (width at narrowest)	*Same as above*	×		+1" =	*Same as above*	×	
Upper Side (width at widest)		+1" ×		+1" =		×	
Lower Side (width at widest)		+2" ×		+1"		×	

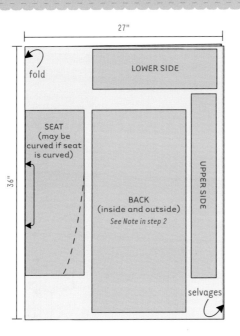

27"

fold

LOWER SIDE

SEAT
(may be
curved if seat
is curved)

36"

BACK
(inside and outside)
See Note in step 2

UPPER SIDE

selvages

CUTTING LAYOUT

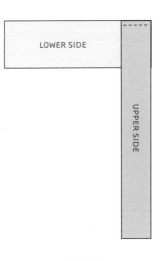

LOWER SIDE

UPPER SIDE

STEP 3

❷ Measure, Mark, and Cut

Fold your fabric in half lengthwise with the right sides together, aligning the selvages. Measure and mark the following pattern pieces directly on the wrong side of your fabric, then cut them out. It is helpful to label each piece and mark the top and bottom edges with a disappearing fabric marker on the wrong side of the cut pieces.

* **Upper side** (cut 2)
* **Lower side** (cut 2)
* **Inside back** (cut 1)
* **Outside back** (cut 1)
* **Seat** (cut 1 on fold)

NOTE: *The outside back is typically longer than the inside back, although the cutting layout suggests they are the same length. Take care to cut accordingly; you may choose to cut two of the larger pieces, and then trim one to fit the smaller dimensions.*

❸ Assemble the Sides

* Pin the bottom raw edge of one upper side with the top raw edge of one lower side with the right sides together and the back raw edges of both aligned. Stitch the pieces together along the upper side bottom edge only.
* Repeat with the remaining upper side and lower side.
* Press the seam allowances toward the upper side, and edgestitch ⅛" from the seams for reinforcement and to hold the seam allowances in place.

❹ Attach the Backs and Seat

* Pin the top edges of the outside back to the inside back with the right sides together. Stitch along this edge.
* Pin the bottom edge of the inside back and the inside (top) edge of the seat with the right sides together. Stitch along this edge.
* Press all the seam allowances toward the inside back and edgestitch ⅛" from the seams for reinforcement and to hold the seam allowances in place.

❺ Attach the Sides

* With the right sides together, pin the seat/back assembly to one side assembly. Align the seam between the two side pieces with the seam joining the seat and inside back.
* Stitch the upper side to the inside back as indicated in the diagram, starting at the seams and stopping ½" from the top of the upper side piece.
* Pivot the lower side pieces so the top raw edge of the lower side aligns with the side raw edge of the seat. Stitch the lower side to the seat as indicated in the diagram, starting at the seams and stopping at the seat front, pivoting at the corner of the lower side.
* Attach the remaining side assembly to the other side of the inside back and seat in similar fashion.

❻ Complete the Slipcover

* Pivot the top edge of the upper side to align with the remaining inside back. Stitch the upper side to the inside back, stopping ½" from the corner. Pivot the upper side again to align the long edge of the side assembly with the outside back piece. Stitch together.
* Attach the remaining side assembly to the opposite side of the inside and outside backs in similar fashion.
* Hem the bottom raw edge with a 1" double-fold hem. Clip the curves and turn the slipcover right side out. Slip it over the chair and forget all about the shabby upholstery underneath!

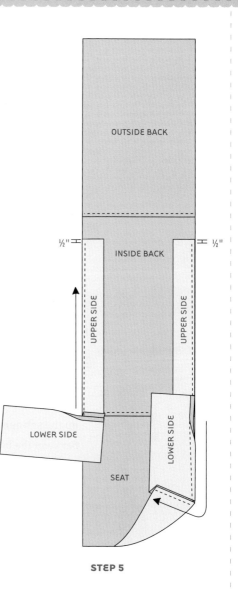

STEP 5

EIGHT-BOTTLE TOTE

Designed by Susan Byrd

Whether you attend a lot of parties or recycle avidly, this tote is a great way to carry up to eight 750 ml wine bottles. Red or white, empty or full, you'll surely find a need for this cute, clever, and functional bag. Replace the cotton batting with insulated batting to keep chilled bottles cool; resize as desired to hold beer or soda bottles instead!

MATERIALS

* 1 yard of 54/60" nondirectional home decor fabric
* 1 spool of coordinating thread
* 1 package (3 yards) of double-fold ¾" bias tape (or make your own)
* Cotton batting, cut to 30" × 36"
* 1⅔ yards of coordinating 1½"-wide webbing
* Heavy-duty sewing needle (optional)
* Walking foot (optional)

Finished dimensions – 17" wide × 12½" tall
Seam allowance – ½" unless otherwise specified

❶ Quilt the Fabric

* With the wrong sides together, fold your fabric in half lengthwise, matching up the selvages. Sandwich the batting between the layers. Pin through all three layers.
* Mark your choice of quilting lines using a disappearing marker, washable fabric pen, or tailor's chalk. (You could try diagonal lines at a 45-degree angle, 2" apart.)
* Machine-quilt the layers together, following your lines. You may want to use a walking foot, if you have one.

❷ Measure, Mark, and Cut

Measure and mark a 25" × 35" rectangle directly onto the wrong side of your fabric and cut it out.

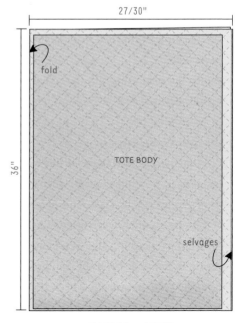

27/30"

fold

36"

TOTE BODY

selvages

CUTTING LAYOUT

❸ Make the Body

* Fold the body in half with the right sides together, aligning the 25" edges. Stitch along the 25" length to form a tube. Trim the seam allowances to ¼" and zigzag or serge the edges to prevent fraying. Turn the "tube" right side out. Press all around, especially along the seam.

* Cut two pieces of bias tape to fit around the ends of the tube with at least 1" of overlap and press the short raw ends to the wrong side for a clean finish. Pin the bias tape around each raw edge, enclosing all the fabric raw edges in the bias tape. Stitch the bias tape in place, making sure to catch back of the bias tape in the stitching.

❹ Add the Handles

* Cut two 30" pieces of webbing. Press under both short ends of each strap ¼" and then under again 1½".

* Flatten the tube slightly, centering the seam on the bottom. On one side of each end of the tube, pin the handles 4" in from each side edge, with the folded edges facing down. Make sure the folded edges of the handles are not visible above the bias tape and baste them in place by hand.

* Stitch each handle end in place with a box stitch, securing the handles just below the bias tape (only stitch through one quilted layer). Remove the basting stitches. The side with the handles will form the outside(s) of the finished bottle tote, while the side with the center seam will form the inside of the tote.

⑤ Make the First Six Compartments

* Measure 5½" from each folded side and mark two horizontal lines with tailor's chalk down the entire length of the bag. Measure and mark the center of the tube from bias tape end to bias tape end.
* Stitch along all marked lines, through all the layers.
* Fold the tote along the stitched center line, making sure the handles are on the outside of the tote. You can now see how pockets for six bottles have been formed.

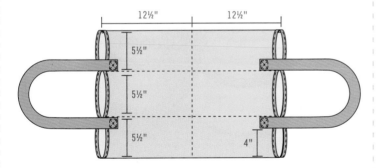

STEP 5

⑥ Make the Final Two Compartments

* Using double or triple strands of thread for strength, whipstitch the center of the inner edges of the opposite pockets together, as shown in the diagram. Be sure that the newly created pockets in the center have a minimum clearance of 5½" to fit the bottles (*see the illustration*).
* Fill up and go! When using the bag, be sure to fill the outer six pockets with bottles before using the inner two. This ensures that the inner two bottles stay secure.

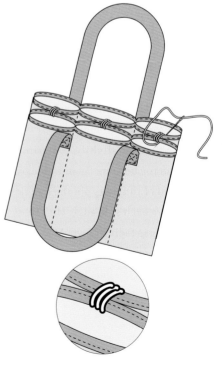

STEP 6

CHAPTER 5

Flannel

When you think of cotton flannel, you might think of baby blankets and cotton pajama pants. The cozy comfort of flannel certainly lends itself to these applications, but why stop there? There are plenty of other items just waiting to be made out of the favorite flannel in your stash.

Fabric Facts

Flannel is a soft, woven fabric. While traditional flan-nel is made from wool, in this chapter we are referring specifically to *cotton* flannel (refer to the wool chapter for working with wool flannels and other wool fabrics). It doesn't have a pile, but does have a light nap, the result of brushing of the woven fabric in the manufacturing pro-cess. It may be brushed on one side, or both. For the most part, flannel can be sewn, handled, and cared for just as you would quilting-weight cotton.

Attributes

100% woven cotton with very soft and minimal nap. The brushed effect may be apparent on just one or both sides.

Needle Type(s)

Use an 80/12 universal needle.

Sewing Machine Accessories

Standard presser foot is fine; other feet may be called for in project construction instructions.

Stitch Types, Tips, and Machine Settings

2-2.5mm stitch length for seams, longer for topstitching.

Marking

Like most cottons, wax-based marking methods are not suitable for flannel; all other marking types are fine.

Cutting

No special equipment required. Depending on the brushed effect on the flannel, you may want to treat it as a napped fabric. Single-layer cutting is preferred; if folding for double-layer cutting, fold with the right sides together and pin the layers to minimize fabric "creep" from the brushed surface.

Interfacing

No particular interfacing requirements; fusible or sew-in is fine.

Seams

Press open to minimize bulk (flat-felled seams are also appropriate). Finish your seam allowances to prevent fraying. Finishing options include pinked edges, zigzag stitching, serged edges, or turned and stitched seam allowances.

Pressing and Ironing

Cotton (hot) setting, with steam. Steam is best for removing wrinkles.

Fabric Care

Preshrink all cottons before cutting and sewing, especially if you are making an item you intend to launder! Other-wise, consult the care instructions as recommended by the manufacturer.

SHAGGY CHIC CHENILLE CLUTCH

Designed by Aimee Doyle Pelletier and Carly Stipe

Chenille is so easy to make! Using flannel just makes it that much more snuggly and fuzzy. Sure, chenille pillows are any stylish home's must-have, but why not take a bit of comfort and style with you on the go? This clutch is just the thing!

MATERIALS

* 1 yard of 44/45" cotton flannel
* 1 spool of coordinating thread
* 2 buttons, 1" in diameter
* 27" of 1"-wide ribbon

Finished dimensions – 5" high × 12" wide (when closed)

Seam allowance – ½" unless otherwise specified

① Measure, Mark, and Cut

Fold your fabric in half lengthwise, with the right sides together, aligning the selvages. Measure and mark the following pieces directly on the wrong side of your fabric with the straight edges along the straight grainline.

* **Bag body** 12" squares (cut 9 pieces with 3 cut on the fold)

② Prepare Bag Body Pieces

* Lay one bag body square on a work surface with the right side facing down.
* Stack the remaining eight squares with the right sides all facing up, aligning all the raw edges.
* Place the eight-layer stack on top of the first square with the wrong sides together, aligning all the raw edges.

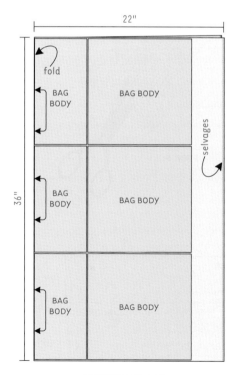

22"

fold

BAG BODY

BAG BODY

BAG BODY

BAG BODY

BAG BODY

BAG BODY

36"

selvages

CUTTING LAYOUT

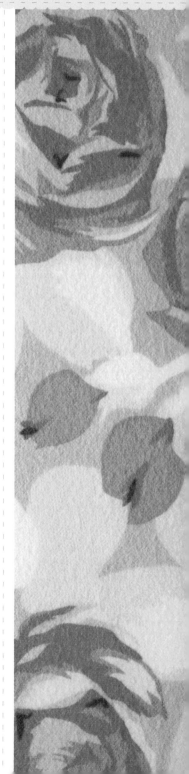

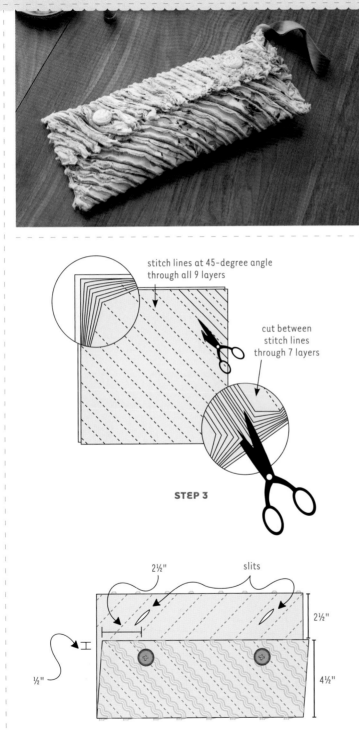

stitch lines at 45-degree angle
through all 9 layers

cut between
stitch lines
through 7 layers

STEP 3

2½"   slits

2½"

½"

4½"

STEP 4

③ Stitch and Cut Chenille Lines

* With tailor's pencil, mark a diagonal
  line on the top fabric layer, from one
  corner to the opposite corner. Stitch
  along the marked line through all nine
  layers.

* Stitch parallel lines approximately
  ¾" apart across the entire surface of
  the fabric layers. Feel free to be free-
  form and arch your stitches slightly.
  This helps the chenille be "shaggier," if
  you like that look.

* Cut the top seven layers between the
  stitching lines, leaving the bottom two
  layers intact (the two layers with the
  wrong sides together).

* Wash and dry the piece.

④ Create Button Closure

* With the fuzzy chenille side facing
  down, fold up 4½" of fabric from the
  bottom to form the clutch body. This
  will leave 2½" of fabric at the top for
  the flap.

* Position one button 2½" from each
  outside edge and ½" from the top edge
  of the clutch body. Sew the buttons in
  place.

* Cut diagonal slits for the buttonholes
  on the purse flap, cutting in between
  the chenille stitching lines, and
  positioning the slits to line up with the
  buttons.

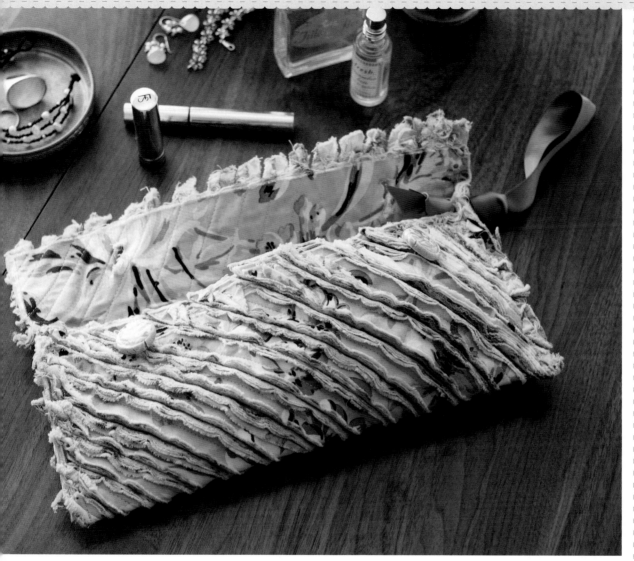

⑤ **Stitch the Sides**

With wrong sides together, stitch the sides ½" from each raw edge of the clutch body.

⑥ **Complete the Clutch**

Cut a small hole with a seam ripper or small scissors on the flap fold, approximately 1" from one side edge, just above the top edge of the folded bottom. Fold the ribbon in half lengthwise and thread both ends through the hole. Knot the ends together on the inside of the bag and tie a second knot on the outside of the flap as close as possible to the clutch.

BOXER SHORTS

Designed by Rebecca Yaker

Boxers or briefs? Well, boxers, of course! Stop hoarding all your beautiful one-yard flannel cuts of fabric for yourself. Share them with the boxer-wearing person in your life. At long last, you can finally stop searching for cute and lively boxer shorts and make your own!

MATERIALS

* Locate the pattern in the envelope (sheet #4)
* 1 yard of flannel; S = 44/45"; M-L = 54"; XL = 60"
* 1 spool of coordinating thread
* ¾"-wide elastic, long enough to fit the waist plus 1"

Sizes – S, M, L, XL
Seam allowance – ½" unless otherwise specified

❶ Determine Your Size

Measure the waist to find the right size.

Inseam for all sizes is 4".

	S	M	L	XL
Waist size	28"–30"	32"–34"	36"–38"	40"–42"

❷ Measure, Mark, and Cut

Fold your fabric in half lengthwise with the right sides together, aligning the selvages. Position the pattern pieces according to the layout and cut them out. Transfer markings from the pattern, including the center front line on the front pattern piece, to the wrong side of fabric.

* **Front** (cut 2)
* **Back** (cut 2)
* **Right facing** (cut 1)

NOTE: *Position the grainline arrow on the pattern pieces along the lengthwise grain of the fabric.*

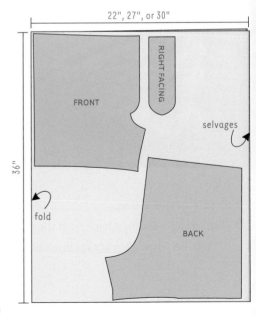

CUTTING LAYOUT

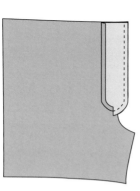

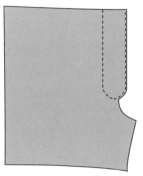

STEP 3

fly extension

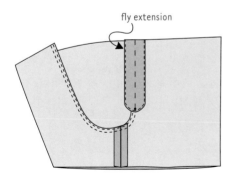

STEP 5

❸ Attach the Right Facing

∗ Staystitch ½" from the curved edge around the right facing piece. Clip from the bottom, up to the dot indicated on the pattern piece. With the right sides together, align the raw edges of the right facing piece with the right front along the fly extension. Stitch around the curve to the clipped dot. Beyond the clipped dot, turn and press the facing seam allowance to the wrong side.

∗ Clip the stitched seam allowance. Turn the facing right side out and press. Edgestitch the facing seam.

∗ Edgestitch the loose side of the facing to the boxer front, using the pressed edge of the facing as a stitching guide.

❹ Stitch the Side Seams and Inseam

With the right sides together, stitch a front piece to a back piece along the side seam. Then stitch the inside leg seam (inseam). Press the seams open. Repeat with the remaining front and back pieces.

❺ Assemble the Pieces

∗ Turn one front/back piece (leg) right side out and slip it inside the other with the right sides together, matching the inner leg seams. Pin the two legs together along the crotch seam.

∗ Stitch the crotch seam starting at the center back, up to the dot indicated on the front piece. At the dot, adjust the stitch length to a basting stitch and continue stitching to the top of the shorts. Stitch again, from the center back to the dot, to reinforce the seam, this time using a ¼" seam allowance. Clip the seam allowances to the dot and trim the seam close to the ¼" stitching line.

∗ Press the right and left fly extensions open. Turn the shorts right side out.

⑥ Finish the Fly Opening

* On the outside of the left front, stitch the left fly extension in place from the top edge of the shorts, down 7½". Do not catch the right fly extension/facing in this stitching line.
* Press the right fly extension toward the left front and baste it in place along the top edge of the shorts with a ¼" seam allowance. Remove the center front basting stitches above the dot from the previous step. Removing these stitches makes the fly opening functional.
* On the outside of the left front, continue the vertical stitching line (from the 7½" point) through all the layers, including the right fly extension/facing. Follow the shape of the facing for a stitching guide so that the stitching mirrors the stitching on the opposite side of the seam.
* Stitch across the fly horizontally at the 7½" point, as shown.

⑦ Make Elastic Casing

Press under the top edge of the shorts ¼", then press under an additional 1". Topstitch close to the folded edge of the casing, leaving a 2" opening at a side seam through which to insert the elastic. Thread a piece of elastic through the casing. Overlap the ends of the elastic by ½", and stitch them together securely. Slip the elastic ends back in the casing and stitch the casing opening closed.

⑧ Hem the Shorts

Press under each short leg ¼", then press under an additional 1". Topstitch close to the folded edge.

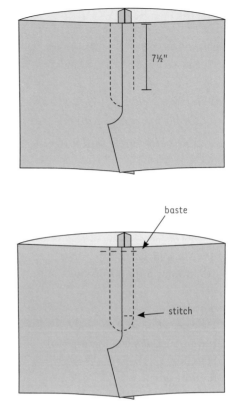

STEP 6

BABY'S ACCESSORY TRIO

Bonnet and Mary Janes designed by Sue Kim

Rattle Ball designed by Atticus Bird

You've found the perfect outfit for your wee one, so, how about the perfect accessories? The baby bonnet and Mary Janes are classic pieces that coordinate well with nearly every ensemble. The rattle ball with the ribbon detailing will certainly keep your little one content.

MATERIALS

* Locate the pattern in the envelope (sheet #3)
* 1 yard of 44/45" flannel fabric
* 1 spool of coordinating thread

For the Mary Janes:

* Two ¾"-long pieces of ¼"-wide Velcro

For Rattle Ball:

* 1¼ yards of ¼"-wide decorative ribbon (such as satin or grosgrain)
* Fiberfill
* Rattle insert

Sizes – Bonnet and Mary Janes are XS, S, M, L; Rattle ball has a 15" circumference

Seam allowance – ¼" unless otherwise specified

❶ Determine Your Child's Size

For bonnet size, measure your baby's head.

	XS	S	M	L
Head circumference	17"	18"	19"	20"

For shoe size, measure your baby's feet.

	XS	S	M	L
Sole length	3¾"	4"	4¼"	4½"

❷ Measure, Mark, and Cut

Fold your fabric in half lengthwise, with the right sides together, aligning the selvages. Position the pattern pieces and measure and mark additional pieces. Cut out the pieces and transfer markings from the pattern to the wrong side of fabric. Separate the pieces by project.

* **Bonnet back** (cut 2)
* **Bonnet crown** (cut 2)
* **Bonnet brim** (cut 2 on fold)
* **Mary Jane sole** (cut 4)
* **Mary Jane upper** (cut 4)
* **Mary Jane strap** (cut 2)
* **Rattle ball** (cut 6)

NOTE: *Position the grainline arrow on the pattern pieces along the lengthwise grain of the fabric.*

In addition to the pattern pieces, measure out the following:

* **Bonnet strap** XS-S = 2" × 16"; M-L = 2" × 18" (cut 2)

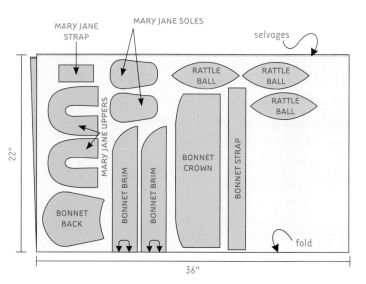

CUTTING LAYOUT

Baby Bonnet

❶ Construct the Crown

* Staystitch along the straight edge of one crown piece. Clip within the seam allowance between the double notches. This will help ease the crown to fit the bonnet back.

* With the right sides together, align the straight edge of the crown with the curved edge of one back piece. Align center points and all notches; pin. Stitch the two pieces together.

* Turn the bonnet right side out and press.

* Repeat these steps with the remaining crown and back pieces to create the lining. Set the lining pieces aside.

❷ Make and Attach the Brim

* With the right sides together, align the raw edges of the two brim pieces and stitch along the curved edge. Leave the straight edge unstitched. Clip the curved seam allowance, turn the brim right side out, and press. Edgestitch the finished edge.

* Use a basting stitch to gather the straight edge of both layers of the brim. Pin the brim to the right side of the exterior crown, aligning centers and double notches. Adjust the gathers so the brim fits evenly, pinning it in place as you go. Stitch the crown and brim together.

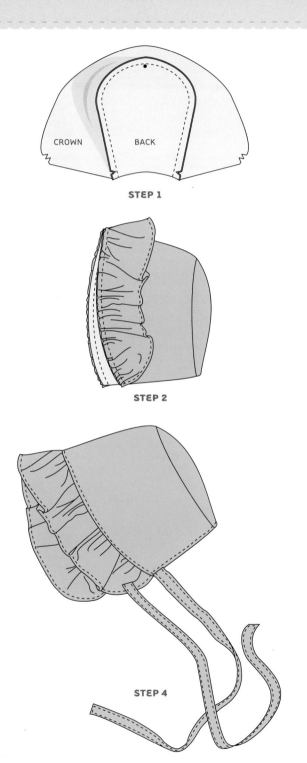

CROWN   BACK

STEP 1

STEP 2

STEP 4

❸ Make the Straps

Press under one short end of the straps ¼". Fold the strap pieces in half lengthwise with the wrong sides together and press. Open the straps, and with the wrong side facing up, press each raw edge to the center crease. Refold the strap in half lengthwise. Edgestitch along all three finished edges of the straps. Pin the straps in place on the wrong side of the bonnet exterior, as indicated on the pattern piece, aligning raw edges. Baste the straps in place using a scant ¼" seam allowance.

❹ Assemble the Bonnet

With the right sides together, pin the lining to the bonnet, aligning all the raw edges and sandwiching the brim and straps in between the two layers. Stitch all the way around, leaving a 3" opening along the bottom back edge. Clip the curved seam allowance and turn the bonnet right side out through the opening. Press the bonnet carefully (avoid pressing the gathers flat) and press the raw edges of the opening to the inside. Topstitch around the entire crown and back piece.

Mary Janes

❶ Prepare the Uppers

* Position the hook piece of Velcro on the right side of one of the upper pieces, following the placement lines on the pattern piece. Stitch the Velcro in place. Repeat with a second upper piece, which should mirror the first, (Velcro placement on opposite side) ensuring that you will have a left and right upper.

* With the right sides together, stitch the heel of each of the four upper pieces. Those with the Velcro will be the exterior uppers, while those without the Velcro will be the lining pieces. Press the seam allowances open.

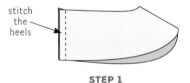

stitch the heels →

STEP 1

❷ Make the Strap

* Press under one short end of each strap ¼". Fold the strap pieces in half lengthwise with wrong sides together, and press. Open the straps with wrong side facing up and press each side to the center crease. Refold the straps in half lengthwise. Edgestitch along all three finished edges of the straps.

* Position a loop piece of Velcro on the end of each strap piece. Stitch it in place. Make sure you have a left and right strap.

∗ Pin each strap with the Velcro facing up on the right side of the upper exterior pieces as indicated on the pattern piece. Baste the straps in place with a scant ¼" seam allowance.

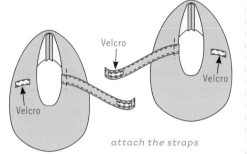

attach the straps

STEP 2

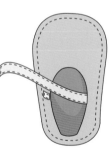

STEP 4

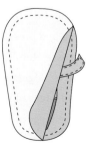

STEP 5

❸ Stitch the Uppers

Pin an upper exterior and lining piece with the right sides together, sandwiching the strap in between the two layers and aligning the center back seams. Stitch the pieces together along the inside edge, catching the strap in the stitching. Clip the seam allowance. Turn the upper right side out and gently press. Repeat with the second set of uppers.

❹ Attach the Uppers to the Soles

Position an upper with the exterior side up and place one sole piece underneath with right side up. Match the heels and toes and pin the sole in place through both the upper exterior and lining. If the upper seems slightly smaller than the sole, carefully clip the upper within the seam allowance at regular intervals, and stretch it to fit the sole piece. Stitch the uppers to the sole piece using a ⅛" seam allowance. Repeat for the second shoe.

❺ Stitch the Bottom Sole

Position an exterior sole on an upper exterior with right sides together. Pin the sole in place, taking care to align the toe and heel. Stitch the sole and upper together using a ¼" seam allowance and leaving a 2" opening along one side edge. Clip and trim the seam allowance and turn the Mary Jane right side out. Turn the seam allowance at the opening to the inside and slipstitch the opening closed. Repeat for the second shoe.

Rattle Ball

❶ Position the Ribbon

Cut the ribbon into fifteen 3" pieces. Fold the ribbon pieces in half with the wrong sides together. Position the folded ribbon strips on the right side of the rattle ball pieces along the left edge, aligning the raw edges. Three rattle ball pieces should have two pieces of ribbon, evenly spaced, and the three remaining rattle ball pieces should have three pieces of ribbon, evenly spaced. Baste the ribbon pieces in place using a scant ¼" seam allowance. Arrange the rattle ball pieces alternating three ribbon pieces and two ribbon pieces, as shown.

❷ Stitch the Sections Together

* With the right sides together, pin and stitch each of the three-ribbon pieces to the two-ribbon pieces. Stop and start the stitching within ¼" of the top and bottom edges.

* Open out the two-section pieces. With the right sides together, pin and stitch the two-section pieces together, until all six pieces have been joined. When sewing the last section together, leave a 2" opening for turning. Turn the ball right side out.

❸ Finish the Rattle Ball

Wrap the rattle piece with fiberfill and place it in the center of the ball through the opening left in the previous step. Continue filling the ball with fiberfill, keeping the rattle positioned in the center, until the ball is filled to your desired firmness. Turn the seam allowance to the inside and hand-sew the opening closed.

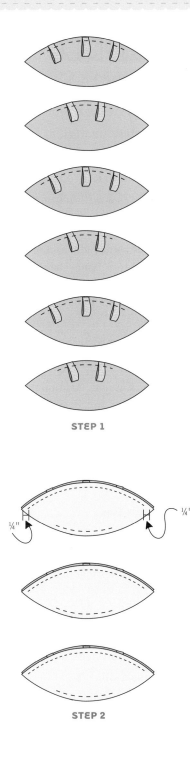

STEP 1

STEP 2

swaddle blanket

Designed by Jaime Morrison Curtis

Swaddling has been practiced for hundreds of years all over the world, likely because swaddling is key for calming a newborn baby. This swaddle blanket helps take the mystery out of folding a traditional square blanket, which, without experience, often comes undone. With this special design, the ties will help hold your little one comfortably and securely.

MATERIALS

* Locate the pattern in the envelope (sheet #5)
* 1 yard of 44/45" flannel fabric
* 1 spool of coordinating thread
* 6½ yards of ¼"-wide double-fold bias tape

Finished dimensions – 42" wide × 35" tall, not including ties

Seam allowance – ½" unless otherwise specified

❶ Measure, Mark, and Cut

Fold your fabric in half lengthwise, with the right sides together, aligning the selvages. Position the pattern pieces according to the layout and cut them out.

* **Blanket** (cut 1 on fold)   * **Swaddle ties** (cut 2)

NOTE: *Position the blanket piece along the lengthwise grain of the fabric and the ties along the bias.*

❷ Make the Ties

Stitch the swaddle ties together with a French seam as follows:

* With the wrong sides together, pin the straight edges of the swaddle ties together. Stitch, using a scant ¼" seam allowance.
* Turn the fabrics wrong side out, so that the right sides are now together, and stitch another ¼" seam to enclose the raw edges of the previous seam (note that your total seam allowance equals ½").
* Press the seam allowance to one side and topstitch the seam in place close to the folded edge.

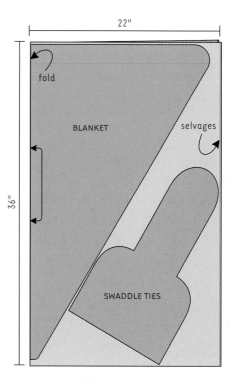

CUTTING LAYOUT

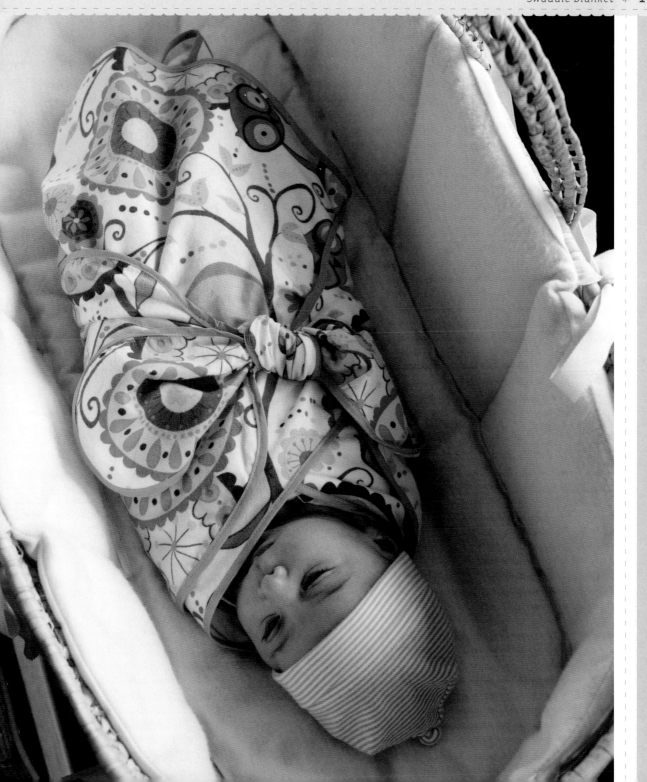

3 Bind the Pieces

Bind the edges of the blanket along all three sides using the double-fold bias tape:

* Unfold one edge of the bias tape and pin it in place along the raw edge of the blanket with the right sides together.
* Stitch using a ¼" seam allowance.
* Refold the bias tape along the original fold line, turning it to the wrong side of the blanket and encasing the unfinished edge.
* Press, pin, and stitch in place close to the folded edge.
* Repeat the above steps to bind the raw edge of the swaddle ties.

4 Attach the Ties to the Blanket

* With both right sides facing up, position the seam of the swaddle ties along the center of the blanket 3" down from the top edge and pin it in place. To make it easier, you might want to mark the center of the blanket with a washable fabric pen.
* Mark with a pin at 6½" down from the top edge of the blanket, and at 10½" down from the top edge along the swaddle ties seam.
* Using a zigzag or other strong decorative stitch, stitch the ties in place down the center of the blanket, leaving an opening between the two marks.

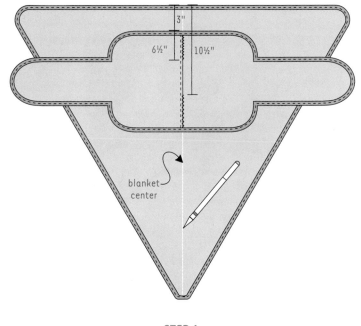

STEP 4

Swaddling Your Little One

Lay the blanket with wrong side facing up. Position your baby with his shoulders below the top edge of the blanket. Fold up the bottom point, and wrap the right and left points of the triangle across his body, tucking the points of the triangle into the opening left in the previous step. Wrap the swaddle ties to the front of his body and tie in place. Finally, enjoy a peaceful night's sleep!

LIBERTY LION & BLANKIE

Designed by Sarah Faix

Liberty Lion is so quick and easy to make that you'll soon have a whole pride of little lion friends. The blanket is a great project for teaching your little one to sew, and can help keep Liberty Lion warm on those cold winter nights! It's large enough to serve as an infant's stroller lap blanket as well.

MATERIALS

* Locate the pattern in the envelope (sheet #3)
* 1 yard of 44/45" flannel fabric
* Scrap of coordinating solid flannel, fleece, felt, velour, or similar fabric for lion face patch
* 1 spool of coordinating thread

For Liberty Lion:
* Embroidery floss in different colors for facial features

* 2 buttons for eyes, ¼" in diameter (optional)
* Polyester fiberfill, enough to stuff the lion

For the Blankie:
* Ribbon, rickrack, or lace trim (optional)

Finished dimensions – Lion is approximately 16" tall × 6½" wide; Blankie is 21" square

Seam allowance – ½" unless otherwise specified

1 Measure, Mark, and Cut

Fold your fabric in half lengthwise with the right sides together, aligning the selvages. Position the pattern pieces according to the layout and cut them out. If you like, you can do some "fussy cutting" (*see the glossary*) with the mane pattern pieces to create a lovely geometric frame for his face. Transfer markings from the pattern to the wrong side of fabric.

* **Liberty Lion head** (cut 2)
* **Liberty Lion body** (cut 2)
* **Liberty Lion leg** (cut 4)
* **Liberty Lion mane** (cut 16)
* **Liberty Lion tail** (cut 2)
* **Liberty Lion ears** (cut 4)
* **Liberty Lion arm** (cut 4)
* **Blankie** 22" square (cut 2)

Cut from coordinating fabric:
* **Liberty Lion face patch** (cut 1)

NOTE: *Position the grainline arrow on the pattern pieces along the lengthwise grain of the fabric.*

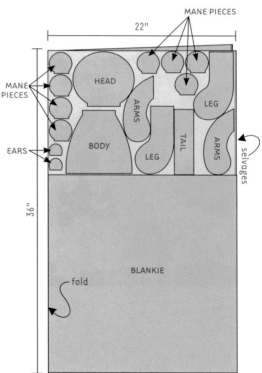

CUTTING LAYOUT

Liberty Lion

1 Make the Arms and Legs

* Pin two arms with the right sides together, aligning all the raw edges. Stitch around the curved edges, leaving the straight edge open for turning. Repeat for the remaining arms.
* Stitch the legs together in the same fashion.
* Notch the curves. Turn all the pieces right side out, using a turning tool if necessary. Press.
* Stuff the arms and legs with fiberfill, leaving 1" unstuffed at the open end. Set them aside.

2 Make the Ears and Mane

* Pin two ears with the right sides together, aligning all the raw edges. Stitch around the curved edges using a ⅛" seam allowance, leaving the straight edge open for turning. Repeat for the remaining ears.
* Stitch eight pairs of manes together in the same fashion.
* Notch the curves. Turn all the pieces right side out, using turning tool if necessary. Press the pieces flat and set them aside.

❸ Make the Tail

Pin the tails with the right sides together, aligning all the raw edges. Stitch around three edges, leaving the short straight edge near the box stitch marking unstitched for turning. Clip the corners and turn the tail right side out. Turn under the raw edges of the opening ¼" to the inside and edgestitch all around.

❹ Attach the Head and Body

With the right sides together, pin one head to the top of one body, aligning the head's bottom straight edge with the body's top straight edge. Stitch along the marked line and press the seam open. Repeat with the remaining head and body pieces.

❺ Assemble the Mane

Starting ½" above the neck seam on the right side of one head (just inside the face patch placement marking), start positioning the manes. Fit the bottom raw edges together to make an octagon shape approximately ¼" smaller than the face patch. The mane pieces should all overlap in the same direction, to form a sort of spiral look. Baste them in place close to the raw edges.

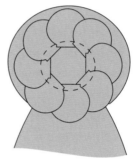

STEP 5

❻ Make and Attach the Face

* Place the face patch right side up on the head, covering the mane raw edges. Stitch it in place with a zigzag or satin stitch.
* If you are using buttons for the eyes, stitch them tightly in place (loose buttons can be a choking hazard). Alternatively, embroider the eyes with a satin stitch.
* Embroider additional facial features as marked.

❼ Attach the Tail, Ears, and Arms

Attach the following pieces to the back head/body:

* Pin the tail horizontally across the right side of the back piece with the end of the tail off to one side. Box stitch the tail in place as indicated at the placement marking.

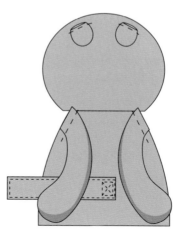

STEP 7

* Pin the ears on the right side of the head/back at the placement markings, aligning the raw edges. Baste them in place close to the raw edges.
* Pin the arms on the right side of the back at the placement markings, aligning the raw edges. The arms should curve away from each other as shown. Baste them in place close to the raw edges.

8 Assemble the Body

* Before pinning the front and back of the lion together, fold the tail and pin it out of the way, safely within the body. Fold the mane pieces toward the middle of the face and pin them out of the way as well.
* Pin the head/body pieces with the right sides together, aligning all the raw edges. Be sure that all the appendages are tucked in between the layers. Stitch around the sides, leaving the bottom straight edge open. Turn under the bottom raw edges ½" to the wrong side and press.
* Notch the curves and turn the body right side out. Stuff firmly, pushing the stuffing up into the body and away from the bottom opening. Add a bit more stuffing than you think is necessary.
* Pin the raw edges of the legs into the bottom opening at the placement marks. Note that Liberty Lion is pigeon-toed, so his toes should point in. Edgestitch the opening closed, making sure to catch the legs in the stitching.

Blankie

1 Stitch the Sides

Pin the squares with the right sides together. Stitch the edges on all sides, leaving a 4" opening for turning. Clip the corners and turn the blanket right side out. Press, turning the seam allowance to the inside at the opening.

2 Topstitch and Embellish

Topstitch around all four sides, closing the opening used for turning. If you like, use a zigzag or other decorative stitch for this step. Embellish with the trim of your choice, if desired.

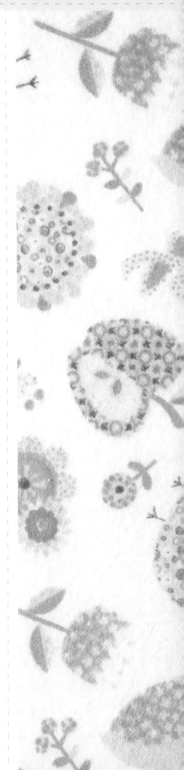

Tatty Duck Cushion

Designed by Clare Carter

Tatty Duck is large and squishy, just right for resting a weary head. She also makes a nice bold accent on a child's bed, a great confidant for talking over the day at school or play. The feather appliqués can be made from the same fabric (right side or wrong side out), or contrasting fabric, whatever you wish, to complete a quirky, quacky friend for the little one in your life!

MATERIALS

* Locate the pattern in the envelope (sheet #4)
* 1 yard of 44/45" nondirectional flannel or quilting-weight cotton fabric
* 1 spool of coordinating thread
* 1⅔ yards of contrasting ⅝" or ⅞" ribbon
* 2 safety eyes

* 24 ounces of fiberfill

Finished dimensions – approximately 17" tall × 18" wide

Seam allowance – ¼" unless otherwise specified

① Measure, Mark, and Cut

With the right sides together, fold your fabric in half lengthwise, aligning the selvages. Pin the pattern pieces in place, cut them out, and transfer the markings from the pattern pieces to the wrong side of fabric.

* **Body** (cut 2)
* **Feathers A–E** (cut 4 of each feather)

Cut from ribbon:

* **18" length for wings** (cut 2)
* **12" length for the eyes** (cut 2)

NOTE: *Note that Tatty Duck is cut sideways, so position the grainline arrow on the straight grain of the fabric. Feel free to fussy cut the feathers (see the glossary) to capture specific design elements of the fabric, if desired.*

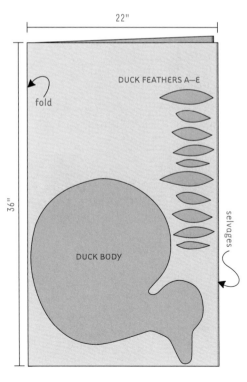

22"

fold

DUCK FEATHERS A—E

36"

DUCK BODY

selvages

CUTTING LAYOUT

❷ Appliqué the Feathers

Separate the feathers into two identical piles (one pile for each side of the duck), with two of each feather shape in each pile. On each side of the duck, do the following:

* Position 10 feathers in the rough shape and location of a wing, overlapping them to create a layered effect. Start with the larger feathers at the base and end with the smaller feathers at the point of the wing near the neck. Don't worry about matching our placement; just suit yourself.
* From one 18" length of ribbon, cut a variety of short lengths of ribbon and tuck them under some of the feathers to add texture. Pin all the feathers and ribbon pieces in place.
* Starting at the top/base of the wing, topstitch the feathers and ribbons in place with straight or zigzag stitches. Be sure to catch every feather and ribbon piece in your stitching. The raw edges of the feather will be loose and start to fray over time, creating a tatty look.

STEP 2

❸ Attach the Eyes

* For each eye, create a rosette out of one 12" length of ribbon by folding it into six to eight loops as shown. Pin as you go to keep the loops even and in place. Stitch an X and then a circle in the center to hold the loops in place.
* Pin a looped ribbon rosette on each side of the head at the placement marks, Stitch around the edge of each rosette and then down each petal to secure it.
* Install one safety eye in the center of each rosette following manufacturer's instructions.

❹ Complete the Duck

* Pin the body pieces with the right sides together, aligning all the raw edges. Stitch around the outer edge, leaving an opening for turning as marked on the pattern.
* Notch the curves, particularly at the beak and neck. Turn the duck right side out at the opening.
* Stuff, starting with smaller pieces of fiberfill in the beak and head. Make sure they are stuffed firmly before moving to the body.
* Once the entire duck is stuffed, turn the open seam allowance to the inside and hand-sew the opening closed with a slipstitch or whipstitch.

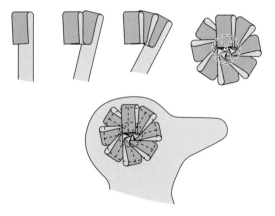

STEP 3

Tic-Tac-Toe Travel Game

Designed by June McCrary Jacobs

This game can go anywhere, quietly! Take it in the car, a plane, a motel, a campground, or just keep it at home in the garden or by the fireplace! It's a great way to spend time as a family, and you can simply slip the pieces in the pocket, tie it closed with ribbon, and go!

MATERIALS

* 1 yard of 44/45" flannel fabric
* 12½" square of cotton batting
* ½ yard of medium-weight sew-in interfacing
* 1 spool of coordinating thread
* 2 metal snaps, ⅝" in diameter (for the pocket)

* 7 decorative buttons, approximately 1" in diameter (for O pieces and pocket decoration)
* 4 small buttons (for the center block of the game board)
* 4 larger buttons (for the corners of game board)

* 1½ yards of medium rickrack
* 1¼ yards of ⅝"-wide striped grosgrain ribbon
* Extra-large yo-yo maker
* Curved edge or cup/saucer for circle template

Finished dimensions – 12" square
Seam allowance – ¼" unless otherwise specified

① Measure, Mark, and Cut

Lay out your fabric in a single layer with the wrong side facing up. Measure and mark the following pieces directly on the wrong side of your fabric as shown in the layout, placing straight edges along the grainline. Cut out the pieces.

* **Game board squares** 4½" square (cut 9)
* **Backing** 12½" square (cut 1)
* **Pocket and lining** 12" × 9" (cut 2)
* **X pieces** 3½" square (cut 10)
* **O pieces** 5" circle (cut 5)

In addition, cut the following pieces from batting:
* **For backing** 12½" square (cut 1)

From medium-weight sew-in interfacing:
* **Pocket** 9" × 12" rectangle (cut 1)
* **X piece** 3½" square (cut 5)
* **From grosgrain ribbon, for ties** Two 21" lengths
* **From medium rickrack** Ten 5" lengths

CUTTING LAYOUT

NOTE: *The white wavy line at the right indicates extra fabric not shown.*

➋ Make the Pocket

* Pin the pocket and pocket lining with the right sides together, aligning all raw edges. Pin the pocket interfacing on top. Round both corners of one 9" (top) edge with a cup or similar circle template.
* Stitch all around, leaving a 4" to 5" opening on the straight (bottom) edge for turning; include the interfacing in the stitching. Clip the corners and turn the pocket right side out, pushing out the corners with a turning tool.
* Turn the seam allowance at the opening to the inside and press the pocket. Stitch ¼" from the edge, around the pocket, closing the opening as you stitch.
* Fold up the bottom edge 4½" and press to form the pocket. Fold the top rounded edge over the bottom edge and press to form the flap. Pin the sides, but don't stitch yet.
* For closures, hand-sew the snaps on the inside of the flap and outside of pocket, 2" from the side edges. To hide the snap stitches, hand-sew buttons on the outer flap.

➌ Attach Pocket and Ties to the Backing

* Center and pin the pocket on the backing, 1" up from the bottom raw edge. Open the pocket flap and stitch the pocket in place along the sides and bottom with an edgestitch. Stitch to just above the pocket top edge on both sides; backstitch to secure. Fold the flap back down.
* Fold each ribbon tie in half to find the center. Pin the ribbon centers 1" above the top of the pocket flap on both sides of the pocket. Attach the ribbons with a box stitch at the center. Tuck the ribbon ties inside the pocket for now and set the backing aside.

➍ Make the Game Board Squares

Note that the game board side is made with four of the squares wrong side up.

* Stack two game board squares, both with the right sides facing up, and align the raw edges. Stitch them together on one side edge and press the seam open. On the square with the wrong side up, place a third square, right side down, and stitch along the opposite side edge. Press the seam open. This is the top row, with two outer squares that are right side facing up.

* Make another strip of three squares in the same fashion, for the bottom row.

* Make the middle row in the opposite fashion, so that the two outer squares will have their wrong side facing up.

* Stitch the three rows together to form the checkerboard, aligning the seams of the squares.

* Hand-sew a small button in each of the corners of the center game board block.

⑤ Stitch the Game Board and Backing

* Pin the game board and backing (with pocket attached) with the right sides together, aligning the raw edges. Pin the batting on top and stitch around all sides, leaving a 5" opening at one edge for turning.

* Clip the corners and turn the game board and backing right side out, pushing out the corners with a turning tool. Press all around, turning the seam allowance at the opening to the inside.

* Edgestitch the outer edges, closing the opening as you stitch. Use a zigzag or other decorative stitch if desired.

* Hand-sew a large decorative button on each game board corner.

⑥ Make the O Game Pieces

Make yo-yos with the five O pieces and the yo-yo maker, following the manufacturer's instructions. Hand-sew a button to each yo-yo center to cover the gathers.

⑦ Make the X Game Pieces

* Topstitch two lengths of rickrack diagonally, forming an X, across five X squares.

* Pin each stitched square to a plain X square with the right sides together. Stitch the outer edges, leaving a 2" opening on one edge for turning. Clip the corners and turn the pieces right side out, pushing out the corners with a turning tool.

* Press each game piece, turning the seam allowance at the openings to the inside. Edgestitch all sides, closing the opening as you stitch.

⭐ Storing the Game

Place the game pieces in the pocket and snap the pocket closed. Fold the game board in half and tie it closed with the ribbon ties.

COZY COMFORT SET

Designed by Jessica Roberts

Being under the weather is a drag! It often leads to feeling miserable, which in turn makes it difficult to get comfortable. Never fear! This cozy comfort trio will help soothe your aches and pains while your body is on the road to recovery. Heat your water bottle, snuggle up with your aromatherapy pillow, and grab your sleep mask for some healing shut-eye. You'll be feeling better in no time!

MATERIALS

* Locate the pattern in the envelope (sheet #4)
* 1 yard of 44/45" flannel fabric
* 1 spool of coordinating thread

For the Hot Water Bottle Cover:
* 1 hot water bottle

For the Aromatherapy Pillowcase:
* 12" × 16" travel pillow form

* 5" × 10" piece of muslin, cotton, or linen for aromatherapy insert
* ½ cup of flaxseed
* 2 tablespoons of herbs, such as peppermint or lavender

For the Sleep Mask:
* 16" of ¼"-wide elastic

Finished dimensions — Hot Water Bottle Cover fits a standard-size hot water bottle; Aromatherapy Pillowcase fits 12" × 16" travel pillow; Sleep Mask is 8" × 3"

Seam allowance — ½" unless otherwise specified

① Measure, Mark, and Cut

Lay out your fabric in a single layer with the right side facing up. Position the pattern pieces according to the layout and measure and mark additional pieces as listed. Cut out the pieces and transfer markings to the wrong side of the fabric.

* **Water Bottle back** (cut 1)
* **Water Bottle front top** (cut 1)
* **Water Bottle front bottom** (cut 1)
* **Pillowcase** 22" × 25" (cut 1)
* **Pocket** 12" × 6" (cut 1)
* **Sleep mask** (cut 2)

NOTE: *Position the grainline arrow on the pattern pieces along the lengthwise grain of the fabric. Mirror the water bottle pieces along the lines indicated on the pattern. The white wavy line indicates extra fabric not shown.*

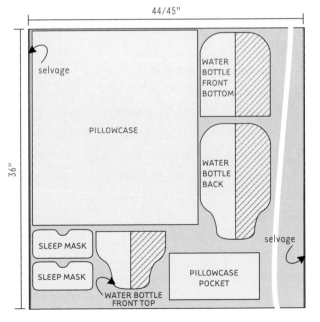

CUTTING LAYOUT

Hot Water Bottle Cover

❶ Make the Front

Create a ½" double-fold hem along the bottom straight edge of the front top piece and the top straight edge of the front bottom piece. With the right sides facing up, position the top front piece on top of the bottom front piece, overlapping the straight edges by 1¼" (together, the pieces will be the same size as the water bottle back piece). Baste the two pieces together along the side edges with a ¼" seam allowance.

❷ Assemble the Cover

With the right sides together, pin the front and back pieces together, aligning the raw edges. Stitch around the outside edge. Clip and notch the curves where necessary. Turn the cover right side out through the overlapped opening on the front and press.

✪ Using the Cover

Fill the water bottle with hot tap water and secure the top tightly. Insert the bottom of the hot water bottle into the cover and pull the top of the cover over the hot water bottle. Ahhhh.

Aromatherapy Pillowcase

❶ Make the Aromatherapy Pocket

With the right sides together, fold the pocket in half to make a 6" square. Stitch around the three raw edges, leaving a 2" opening along one side for turning. Clip the corners and turn the pocket right side out, pushing out the corners with a point turner. Press, turning the seam allowance at the opening to the inside. On the open end, topstitch the opening closed, ¼" from the edge; this edge will be the top edge of the pocket.

❷ Attach the Pocket to the Pillowcase

With both right sides facing up, position the pocket on the pillowcase, 6½" from the top edge and 4" from the right edge. Edgestitch the pocket in place along three sides, leaving the top edge open.

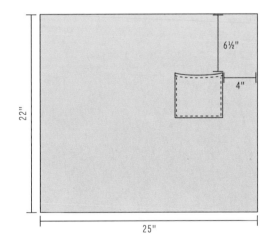

STEP 2

Sleep Mask

③ Assemble the Pillowcase

* With the right sides together, fold the pillowcase in half along the 25" edge. Stitch along the side and bottom edge (the bottom edge is opposite the pocket opening). Clip the corners.

* On the open end of the pillowcase, make a double-fold hem by pressing under the raw edge ½", then another 2". Stitch all the way around, close to the folded edge. Turn the pillowcase right side out, and press.

④ Make the Aromatherapy Insert

* With the right sides together, fold the muslin for the aromatherapy insert in half to make a 5" square. Stitch along two open sides, leaving one end open. Clip the corners, turn the insert right side out, and press.

* Fill the bag with flaxseed and herbs. Turn under the open end ½" to the inside and topstitch it closed ¼" from the edge.

* Heat the aromatherapy insert in the microwave for one to two minutes. Place the warm insert in the pillow pocket, and snuggle with the pillow.

① Attach the Elastic

On the right side of one of the mask pieces, position the ends of the elastic along the raw edges of the mask, according to the placement lines on the pattern piece. Take care that the elastic is not twisted. Baste the ends in place with a ¼" seam allowance.

② Assemble the Mask

Pin the two sleep masks with the right sides together, aligning all the raw edges, and sandwiching the elastic in between the two layers. Stitch around the mask, leaving a 1" opening along the top edge for turning. Clip and notch the curves where necessary. Turn the mask right side out and press, folding in the seam allowance at the opening. Edgestitch around the entire mask, closing the opening used for turning. Now go enjoy some peaceful shut-eye!

CHAPTER 6

woven pile fabrics

Pile fabrics are woven with extra fibers to create a pile (cut or uncut loops) on one or both sides of the fabric. They are made out of a variety of natural or man-made fibers and come in a wide range of weights, from light to heavyweight. Corduroy, velvet, velveteen, chenille, and faux fur are popular examples of pile fabrics. Fleece is also a pile fabric, but it is different enough to warrant a chapter of its own.

Fabric Facts

Corduroy, one of the most popular pile fabrics, is typically made from cotton fibers, and is recognizable by its vertical wales (ribs). It is often labeled by the size of its wales (pinwale, midwale, wide wale), or the number of wales per inch (6 wale, 12 wale, 24 wale). It can be solid, printed, embroidered, stretch, nonstretch, single- or double-sided.

Velveteen, another well-loved pile fabric, should not be confused with velvet, as it is actually closer in structure and content to corduroy. The plush pile of velveteen, with its cut yarn loops, covers the entire surface — unlike corduroy, which has its pattern of pile ribs. Velveteen is typically made from cotton or a cotton blend, has a shorter pile than velvet, and does not drape as well as velvet, but it is easier to sew. By comparison, velvet typically has a backing of silk or another natural fiber, with a rayon or other synthetic pile. Velvet and velveteen come in many forms, including solid colors, printed patterns, stretch, crushed, burnout, and many other variations.

Attributes

Pile fabrics can look very different depending on whether the pile is running up or down on the finished piece. This is also referred to as nap. Typically the fabric will look richer and deeper in color when the pile (nap) runs up, and lighter and shinier when it runs down. Similarly, the fabric tends to feel smooth when you run your hand down the pile, and rough when you run your hand up against it. One catchphrase we've heard is "up for beauty, down for wear." In the end, though, choose whichever look you like best for that particular fabric and project; just be consistent; if one piece is cut with the nap up, all pieces must be cut with the nap up! Since you want the pile to run in the same direction throughout your project, lay out the pattern pieces so the tops of all of them point toward the same end of the fabric. For sewing safety, mark the pile direction on the wrong side of the cut pieces with a fabric marking tool. Some pile fabrics shed quite badly at the raw edges, and can be bulky. Others "creep" during cutting and sewing, so review our tips carefully! Finally, overhandling can crush and mar your fabric, so be gentle.

Needle Type(s)

Use an 80/12 universal needle. 70/10 may work for lighter velvets.

Sewing Machine Accessories

A walking foot and/or a roller foot will help feed the fabric through your machine evenly and minimize crushing the pile. These specialty feet will also help control the fabrics' natural tendency to creep.

Stitch Types, Tips, and Machine Settings

The suggested stitch length is 2.5mm-3mm, but always test your stitching on a scrap first. Experiment with looser tension if necessary for a smooth stitch. Since pile fabrics can be heavy, dense, and thick, help ease the strain on your sewing machine by gently pushing the fabric toward the presser foot; this can also help prevent stretching the fabric. To avoid or minimize fabric creep, try one or more of these techniques: layering tissue paper, lightweight interfacing, or tear-away stabilizer between the fabric layers; lifting the top layer slightly in front of the presser foot; or stopping periodically while stitching and lifting the presser foot with the needle still in the fabric.

Marking

Tailor's tacks, scissor snips, chalk, and fabric pencils are suitable, but mark as little as possible. Never use a tracing wheel on the right side of the fabric, as holes in pile fabric don't close back up and aren't easily hidden. You might also try using drafting tape on the wrong side only of your fabric.

Cutting

Single-layer cutting is preferable so you can pay close attention to the fabric nap. If you are cutting in a double layer, fold the fabric with the wrong sides together so the pile doesn't rub against itself. You'll find it easier to cut in the direction of the pile. We also suggest using very sharp, even newly sharpened, scissors. After cutting, you may find it beneficial to overlock all the cut pieces separately before starting to sew, to help with the shedding pile. If you don't have a serger, you can simply zigzag the cut edges.

Interfacing

Use only sew-in interfacings.

Special Equipment

When laying out the pattern pieces, try using pattern weights rather than pins to avoid permanent holes in the fabric. When you do use pins, place them in the seam allowances only. Fine, new pins are worth the investment. You can also try using clips to hold fabric layers together during stitching.

Seams

Press seam allowances open to minimize bulk. If you did not overlock/serge/zigzag the raw edges of the cut pieces before stitching, serge or pink each edge in the seam allowance individually. Use a pin to pick the pile out of the seams as necessary for flatter seams and edges.

Pressing and Ironing

To help preserve the fabric pile, place a fluffy towel on your ironing board, and then lay the fabric right side down on top of the towel. Press on the wrong side of the fabric only.

Fabric Care

Preshrink all cottons before cutting and sewing, especially if you are making an item you intend to launder! Otherwise, consult the care instructions as recommended by the manufacturer. Launder all pile items inside out. You can freshen and raise the fabric pile with steam and a brush if needed.

FARMERS' MARKET TOTE

Designed by Michelle Fante

Multiple pockets make this a handy shopping bag to stash and separate market produce. It also makes a great craft project bag, or perhaps even an alternative to a traditional diaper bag. This bag has so many uses, you'll likely make more than one!

MATERIALS

* 1 yard of 54/55" nondirectional heavyweight corduroy (*see* Fabric Note)
* 1 spool of coordinating thread
* 6 yards of prepackaged ½"-wide double-fold bias tape, or make your own
* 1⅛ yard of 1¼"-wide webbing for the straps

Finished dimensions — 12½" high × 13½" wide × 7" deep (excluding pockets and handles)

Seam allowance — ½" unless otherwise specified

1 Measure, Mark, and Cut

Lay out your fabric in a single layer with the wrong side facing up. Measure and mark the following pattern pieces directly on the fabric according to the layout, with the straight edges of each piece along the straight grain of the fabric. Mark the top of each piece, so you don't get confused when you start sewing. Cut out the pieces.

* **Exterior front/back** 15" × 17½" (cut 2)
* **Exterior side** 8" × 17½" (cut 2)
* **Facing** 3" × 22" (cut 2)
* **Front/back pocket** 11" × 23" (cut 2)
* **Side pocket** 11" square (cut 2)

Cut from webbing:

* **Straps** 20" long (cut 2)

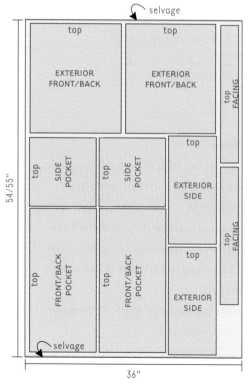

CUTTING LAYOUT

FABRIC NOTE

Stripes or similar geometric patterns look great for this project, but be aware that the pattern on the outside pockets will run perpendicular to the pattern on the main tote body, since the tote panels are cut "sideways." Instead of corduroy, you could use a heavier home decor fabric, as it will help the bag hold its shape.

② Prepare the Front/Back Pockets

* Make a double-fold hem on the top edge of both front/back pockets, pressing under ¼" to the wrong side, and then another 1". Edgestitch close to the inside fold.

* Fold each front/back pocket in half, aligning the 11" edges, and press to mark the center crease. Open the fabric flat.

* Using the illustration as a guide, measure and mark 1¾" on both sides of the center crease and from both side edges (call these marks B).

* Measure and make second marks 2" away from each B mark, as shown (call these marks A).

* Fold each A mark toward each B mark to make box pleats. Press and baste the pleats in place close to the raw edge.

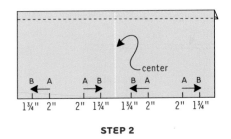

STEP 2

③ Prepare the Side Pockets

* Make a double-fold hem on the top edge of both side pockets, pressing under ¼" to the wrong side, and then another 1". Edgestitch close to the inside fold.

* Working on the right side of each pocket, find and mark the center of the bottom edge. Using a washable fabric pen, measure and mark along the bottom edge 2½" from the center on both sides (call these marks A).

* Measure and mark along the bottom edge again, 4" from the center on both sides (call these marks B).

* Fold A marks toward B marks, creating two pleats that point toward the side raw edges. Press and baste the pleats in place close to the raw edge.

④ Attach the Side Pockets

* Measure and mark a line 5" up from the bottom raw edge of one side exterior piece, on the right side.

* With the right side of the side exterior piece facing up and the wrong side of the side pocket facing up, pin the bottom edge of the pocket along the marked line (the hemmed top edge of the pocket extends away from the top of the exterior piece). The side raw edges should be aligned.

* Stitch the bottom edge in place with ½" seam allowance.

* Flip the pocket up and press. Baste the side raw edges together.

* Repeat with the remaining exterior side and side pocket.

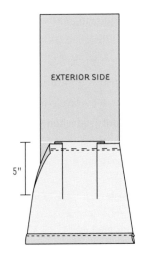

EXTERIOR SIDE

5"

STEP 4

⑤ **Attach the Front/Back Pockets**

* Measure and mark a line 5" up from the bottom raw edge of one exterior front/back piece, on the right side.
* Position and stitch a front/back pocket to an exterior front/back piece the same way as for the side pocket in step 4.
* Repeat with the remaining exterior front/back and front/back pocket.

⑥ **Bind the Raw Edges**

To minimize unraveling and to strengthen the bag, pin double-fold bias tape over the bottom and side raw edges of the exterior front/back and exterior sides. Stitch the bias tape in place, making sure to catch back of bias tape in the stitching. Bind both short edges and the bottom long edge of each facing piece in similar fashion.

⑦ **Attach the Front, Back, and Sides**

* Pin one side edge of a side piece to the side edge of a front/back piece with the right sides together. Stitch and press the seam allowances open.
* Pin and stitch the opposite side of the side piece to one side of the remaining front/back piece in similar fashion. Press the seam allowances open.
* Pin and stitch the remaining side piece to the open side edges of each front/back piece in similar fashion to form a tube or circle (open along the top and bottom edges). Press the seam allowances open.
* With the right sides together, fold and pin the tube in half at the center of both side pieces, aligning the seams and front/back pieces.
* Stitch the bottom edge.

⑧ **Create the Bottom Gusset**

* At both ends of the bottom edge, mark a 3" square. Cut out the squares along the markings.

* Open up the sides at the cutouts and pin the raw edges with the right sides together so they make a straight line. Stitch the raw edges together, forming the bottom gussets that shape the bottom of the bag. Zigzag stitch close to the seam within the seam allowance for reinforcement. (*See illustration on page 238.*) Bind the seam allowances with bias tape.

⑨ **Attach the Straps**

Turn the bag right side out. Pin one strap piece to the right side of each front/back piece with the strap ends 3" in from each side seam and extending above the raw edge by 1". Take care that the strap is not twisted. Baste the straps in place ¼" from the fabric raw edge.

⑩ **Add the Facing**

* Pin the facing pieces with the right sides together, aligning the raw and bound edges. Stitch them together at the short edges to create a ring. Press the seams open and stitch the seam allowances down.
* Pin the facing to the top of the bag with the right sides together and the strap ends sandwiched between them. Align the top raw edges and center the facing seams on the side pieces. Stitch.
* Fold the facing over to the inside of the bag and press. Finish with a row of topstitching ½" from the top edge.

PLAY PANTS

Designed by Lisa Powers

Toddlers need pants that stand up to hours of rough and tumble play. Perfect for girls and boys, these pants feature sturdy pockets and double knee panels that may even outlive the life of the pants. They are so comfortable and durable for your little one; you'll be so pleased with the results, you'll find yourself making more than one pair!

MATERIALS

* Locate the pattern in the envelope (sheet #4)
* 1 yard of 54/60" corduroy fabric
* 1 spool of coordinating thread
* ¾ yard of ¾"-wide elastic (or less, depending on your child's waist size)

Sizes – 2, 3, 4
Seam allowance – ½" unless otherwise specified

① Determine Your Child's Size

Measure the child's waist and inseam to find the right size. If you come up with two different sizes, go with the inseam measurement. You can always make the elastic shorter or longer to fit the waist

	2	3	4
Waist	21"	22"	23"
Finished inseam	13"	14"	15"

② Measure, Mark, and Cut

Fold your fabric in half lengthwise with the wrong sides together, aligning the selvages. Position the pattern pieces according to the layout and cut them out. Transfer markings from the paper pattern pieces to the wrong side of the fabric.

* **Front top** (cut 2)
* **Front knee panel** (cut 4)
* **Front bottom** (cut 2)
* **Back** (cut 2)
* **Pocket** (cut 4)

NOTE: *Position the grainline arrow on the pattern pieces along the straight grain of the fabric.*

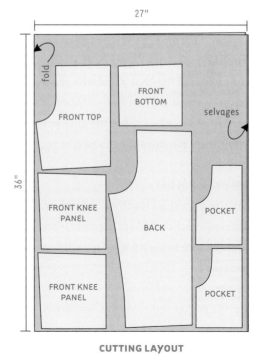

CUTTING LAYOUT

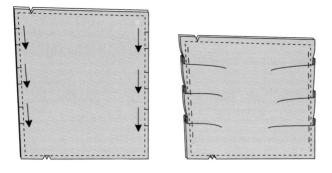

STEP 3

 Stitch and Pleat the Front Knee Panels

With the wrong sides together, stitch together two knee pieces with a ¼" seam allowance. Fold and pin the pleats downward according to the arrows and placement lines as indicated on the pattern piece. Baste the pleats in place.

④ **Assemble the Pants Front**

With the right sides together, align the bottom edge of the front top piece with the top edge of the knee panel, matching notches, and stitch them together. Again, with right sides together, align the bottom edge of the knee panel with the top edge of the front bottom piece, matching notches, and stitch them together. Press the seam allowances away from the knee panel. Repeat with remaining front top, knee panel, and front bottom pieces.

⑤ **Make the Pockets**

* With the right sides together, align the raw edges of two pocket pieces. Stitch them together along the three unnotched edges. Be sure to keep pocket top edge and outer thigh edge unstitched.
* Clip the corner and seam allowances along the curved edge. Turn the pocket right side out, and press. Topstitch ¼" from the finished curved pocket edge. Repeat for second pocket.

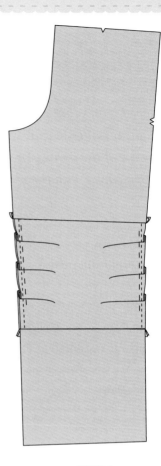

STEP 4

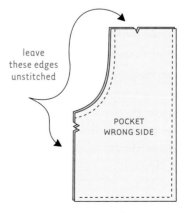

leave these edges unstitched

POCKET WRONG SIDE

STEP 5

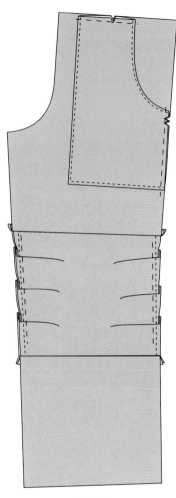

STEP 6

⑥ Attach the Pockets

Pin a pocket on a pant front, aligning the raw edges of the pocket with the raw edges of the pant along the side and top edges, matching the notches. Topstitch the pocket in place with a ¼" seam allowance along the right-angle edges. Baste the pocket in place along the side and top unfinished raw edges. Repeat with the remaining pocket and pant front.

⑦ Stitch the Sides and Legs

* With the right sides together, stitch a front to a back piece at the side seam, and then stitch the inside leg seam. Repeat for remaining front and back pieces.
* Turn one front/back piece right side out and slip it inside the other so the right sides are together, aligning the inner leg seams. Stitch the entire crotch seam from front to back. Stitch again ¼" away in the seam allowance to reinforce the seam. Trim the crotch seam allowance close to the second stitching line.

⑧ Hem the Pants

Stitch a double-fold hem at the bottom of each leg, pressing under ¼", and then another ¾". Topstitch close to the folded edge.

⑨ Make the Waistband Casing

* Make the waistband casing at the top edge of the pants by pressing under ¼", and then another ¾". Edgestitch close to the folded edge of the casing, leaving a 2" opening at the center back seam.
* Cut a length of elastic to fit around your little one's belly, adding an extra 1". Thread the elastic through the waistband casing. Overlap the ends of the elastic ½" and stitch them together securely. Stitch the casing opening closed.

MONSTER BACKPACK

Designed by Pam McFerrin

With this superspooky backpack, your kids can really say a monster ate their homework. Just peek under the flap for a look at the monster mouth ready to gobble! Made of durable corduroy, it's sure to scare off friends and foes alike.

MATERIALS

* Locate the pattern in the envelope (sheets #4 and #6)
* 1 yard of 44/45" wide-wale corduroy
* 1 sheet of white stiffened felt (*see Fabric Note on page 220*)
* Scrap of patterned cotton fabric (red, for mouth background)
* Scrap of solid cotton fabric (red, for mouth appliqués)

* Fusible interfacing
* 1 spool of coordinating thread
* 1 package of ½"-wide double-fold bias tape (or make your own)
* 2 large buttons, 1⅜" in diameter
* 1½ yards of 1"-wide nylon webbing
* One 1" strap adjuster
* Embroidery thread for securing the button eyes

Finished dimensions – 10" wide × 12" high × 4" deep
Seam allowance – ½" unless otherwise specified

❶ Measure, Mark, and Cut

Lay out your fabric in a single layer with the right side facing up. Position the pattern pieces according to the layout and cut them out. Transfer markings from the paper pattern pieces to the wrong side of fabric.

* **Front** (cut 1)
* **Back** (cut 1)
* **Outside flap** (cut 1)
* **Inside flap** (cut 1)
* **Bottom** (cut 1)
* **Sides** (cut 2)

NOTE: *Position the grainline arrow on the pattern pieces along the lengthwise grain of the fabric.*

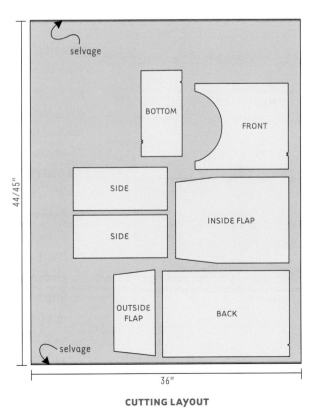

CUTTING LAYOUT

FABRIC NOTE

We suggest using felt that already has a stiffening agent applied. If you cannot find stiffened felt at your local craft shop, you can convert ordinary craft felt with a commercial fabric stiffener.

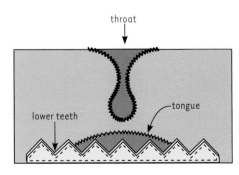

throat

lower teeth — tongue

STEP 2

From white felt, cut:
* **Bottom teeth** (cut 2) * **Top teeth** (cut 2) * **Eyes** (cut 2)

Apply fusible interfacing to the wrong side of both cotton scraps following the manufacturer's instructions, and then cut the following.

From the patterned fabric:
* **Mouth** (cut 1)

From the solid fabric:
* **Tongue** (cut 1)
* **Throat** (cut 1)

② Appliqué the Mouth

* Center the tongue and throat pieces along top and bottom edges of the mouth. Stitch around the inside edges with a narrow, tight zigzag or satin stitch, leaving the outside edges unstitched.
* Stack both bottom teeth pieces together, and appliqué the bottom teeth onto the mouth with a straight stitch.
* Pin the finished mouth onto the front piece, lining up the corners with the placement dots, with right sides facing up. Stitch all around the mouth with a narrow, tight zigzag or satin stitch.

③ Stitch and Bind the Front and Sides

With the right sides together, stitch both sides to the front, stopping each seam ½" from the bottom edge. Pin double-fold bias tape along the top edge, encasing the entire top raw edge and mitering the bias tape at the corners on each side of the front curve. Stitch the bias tape in place, making sure to catch the back of the bias tape in the stitching.

④ Assemble the Backpack

* Cut a 4" piece of the webbing and fold it in half to make a loop. Baste the raw edges of the loop on the right side of the back piece at the placement marks, aligning the raw edges.
* Stitch the bottom to the back with the right sides together, matching the single notches. Start and end the seam ½" from each raw edge. Stitch the opposite edge of the bottom to the front with the right sides together, again starting and ending the seam ½" from each raw edge.

* Stitch the bottom to the sides with the right sides together, starting and ending the seam ½" from each raw edge.
* Stitch the sides to the back, stopping ½" from the bottom raw edge. Note that the back is approximately 4½" longer than the sides, so it will overlap at the top.

⑤ Assemble the Outside Flap

* Center the eye whites on the placement dots on the right side of the outside flap. Stitch around the outer edge with a narrow, tight zigzag or satin stitch.
* Stack and pin the two top teeth pieces together and stitch on all sides with a straight edgestitch. Center them along the bottom edge on the right side of the outside flap, aligning the straight raw edges (teeth will point toward the top of the flap). Baste the teeth in place.
* Cut a 5" piece of webbing. Loop the webbing around the center bar of the strap adjuster and fold it in half, aligning the raw edges. Baste the raw edges together. Place the looped webbing 1½" from one side of outside flap top edge, on the right side of fabric, aligning the raw edges. Baste the webbing loop in place.
* Baste the remaining webbing 1½" from the other side of the outside flap top edge, on the right side of the fabric, with the raw edges aligned.

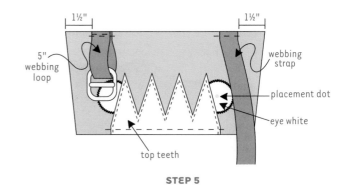

STEP 5

⑥ Attach the Flap to the Backpack

* With the backpack wrong side out, pin the outside flap to the back with the right sides together, aligning the top raw edges. Stitch.
* With the backpack still wrong side out, pin the inside flap to the outside flap/back with the right sides together, aligning the top and side raw edges. Stitch the inside flap to the back within the seam allowance of the existing seam. Be sure not to catch the sides or front of the backpack in the seam.
* Clip the edges and corners close to the seams and turn it all right side out.

⑦ Add the Buttons

Stitch vertical buttonholes to fit your buttons, down the center of the eye whites with contrasting thread. Cut the buttonhole opening with a seam ripper or small scissors. Hand-sew buttons to the front with embroidery thread just above the mouth, aligned with the buttonholes.

⑧ Secure the Straps

Thread the long strap through the loop at the bottom of the backpack. Thread it though the strap adjuster and adjust it to fit with 4" to 5" tail. The bottom loop allows the backpack straps to be fully adjustable with just one adjuster. If you used nylon webbing, seal the ends by melting them briefly with a small flame.

PeTaL PiLLOW

Designed by Pam McFerrin

Grow your own garden and make every day feel like spring with these freshly styled pillows. Whether it's corduroy or double knit, silky sunflowers or dahlias, making these pillows is fun and you'll never get dirty!

MATERIALS

* Locate the pattern in the envelope (sheet #5)
* 1 yard of 44/45" lightweight corduroy (*see* Fabric Note *on page 225*)
* 1 spool of coordinating thread
* 2½ yards of ½"-wide coordinating piping
* 12 ounces of polyester fiberfill
* 4 to 8 decorative buttons
* Zipper foot

Finished dimensions – approximately 12" around × 3" deep

Seam allowance – ½" seam allowance

① Measure, Mark, and Cut

Fold your fabric in half lengthwise with the wrong sides together, aligning the selvages. Position the pattern piece as shown and draw the additional piece. Cut them out. Transfer the markings from the pattern to the right side of one top/bottom piece only.

* **Top/bottom** (cut 2)
* **Side** 4¼" × 23" (cut 2)

Cut the remaining fabric horizontally into 3½"-wide strips. Stack the folded strips to make four layers before cutting the desired petal shape. You can cut as many flower petals you like, depending on the fabric thickness and desired fullness of the pillow. Use any of the petal options provided, or create your own shape (cut approximately 175).

NOTE: *Position the grainline arrow on the side pattern piece along the straight grain of the fabric.*

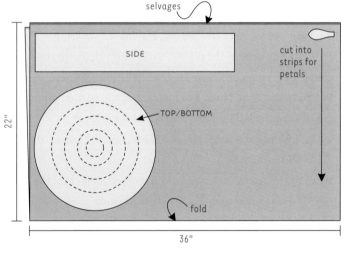

CUTTING LAYOUT

② Stitch Petals to the Pillow Front

* Place two petals side by side and right side down on the right side of the pillow front, aligned with the innermost marked circle.
* Place a third petal, right side down, centered over the first two. Edgestitch the petals in place along their bottom edges. Continue stitching petals around the innermost circle in similar fashion until the circle is filled, taking care not to catch the top edges of previously stitched petals in your stitching.

* Flip the petals right side up to see if there are any gaps. If so, fill the gaps with more petals.
* Stitch petals around each marked circle in similar fashion, working from the center to the outermost circle. Check for any gaps before moving on to the next circle.
* Flip the petals right side up and hand-sew buttons in the center of the pillow top to make a flower center.

③ Make the Pillow Side

* Pin the side pieces with the right sides together and stitch both short ends to make a ring.
* It is best to attach piping using a zipper presser foot. Baste piping to the right side of the side piece along both long edges, ½" from the raw edge, leaving the first 2" and last 2" of the piping free. Cut off any extra piping, leaving a 1" overlap.
* To finish the ends of the piping, use a seam ripper to remove a couple of stitches on each side of all four piping ends.
* Pull back the loose fabric on one top and one bottom piping end (on the same side). Trim the cord ½" so the ends of the cording will abut. Once you have cut both cords, fold the fabric edges ¼" to the wrong side.
* Wrap the folded fabric edges over the opposite ends of the piping for a smooth joining. Finish stitching both pieces of piping in place.

④ Make the Pillow Base

* Pin one piped edge of the side to the pillow bottom with the right sides together, aligning the raw edges. Stitch close to the piping so the piping tape is caught in the seam and does not show on the right side.

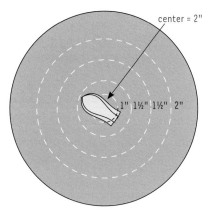

center = 2"

1" 1½" 1½" 2"

STEP 2

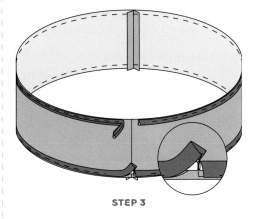

STEP 3

⑤ Complete the Pillow

* Pin the other piped edge of the pillow side to the pillow top in similar fashion. Stitch the seam, leaving a 4" opening for turning and taking care that the petals aren't caught in the stitching.
* Turn the pillow right side out and stuff it to the desired firmness with fiberfill.
* Hand-sew the opening with a slipstitch or whipstitch, adding more fiberfill if necessary.

FABRIC NOTE

Instead of corduroy, you
can try other fabrics such
as double knit or silk.
Look for fabric that has a
good texture, looks good
on the reverse side, keeps
fraying to a minimum, or
creates visual interest
when frayed.

BarnaBy BeaR

Designed by Fiona Tully

Fuzzy, fluffy, cuddly corduroys or chenilles make a perfect pal for snuggling. Barnaby is a sweet addition to any child's menagerie. If you have more than one child to please, you can easily make two bears from one yard of fabric.

MATERIALS

* Locate the pattern in the envelope (sheet #5)
* 1 yard of 44/45" corduroy, chenille, or similar fabric
* 1 spool of coordinating thread
* 8" square remnant of solid fleece, felt, or similar fabric for face
* 2 safety eyes, ¼" in diameter
* Embroidery thread
* 12 ounces of polyester fiberfill
* Turning tool, chopstick or similar (optional)

Finished dimensions – 17" tall × 7" wide excluding arms

Seam allowance – ¼" unless otherwise specified

① Measure, Mark, and Cut

With the wrong sides together, fold your fabric in half lengthwise, aligning the selvages. Position the pattern pieces as shown and cut them out. Transfer the placement markings and facial features from the pattern pieces to the right side of the fabric.

* **Body** (cut 2)
* **Arms** (cut 4)
* **Legs** (cut 4)
* **Ears** (cut 4)

Cut from felt/fleece scrap:

* **Face** (cut 1)

NOTE: *Position the grainline arrow on the pattern pieces along the straight grain of the fabric.*

② Make the Arms and Legs

* Pin two arms with the right sides together, aligning all the raw edges. Stitch around the curved sides, leaving the short straight edge open for turning. Repeat with the remaining arm pieces.
* Stitch the legs together in the same fashion.
* Notch the curves on all pieces, then turn them right side out, using a turning tool if necessary. Press.
* Stuff the arms and legs firmly with the fiberfill, leaving 1" unstuffed at the open ends. Set them aside.

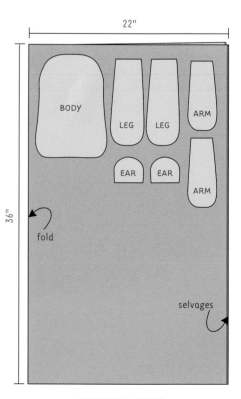

CUTTING LAYOUT

③ Make the Ears

* Pin two ears with the right sides together, aligning all the raw edges. Stitch around the curved sides, leaving the straight edge open for turning. Repeat with the remaining ear pieces.
* Notch the curves, and then turn the ears right side out, using a turning tool if necessary. Press.
* Stuff the ears lightly with the fiberfill and set them aside.

④ Make the Face

* Embroider the nose and mouth on the face piece with embroidery thread. Barnaby was made with a satin stitch for the nose, and a backstitch for the mouth.
* Pin the wrong side of the face on the right side of one body at the placement marks. Edgestitch, zigzag, or satin stitch around the face to attach it to the body.
* Install the safety eyes following the manufacturer's instructions. This becomes the front body.

⑤ Complete the Bear

* Baste the ears onto the right side of the front body at the placement markings, aligning the raw edges.
* Baste the arms and legs onto the right side of the front body at the placement markings, aligning the raw edges.
* Pin the front and back with the right sides together, aligning all the raw edges, and with the arms, legs, and ears tucked inside. Stitch around the body, catching the open ends of the ears, arms, and legs in the stitching. Leave an opening for turning as indicated on the pattern.
* Clip the curves and turn the bear right side out. Stuff the body firmly. Hand-sew the opening closed with a slipstitch or whipstitch.

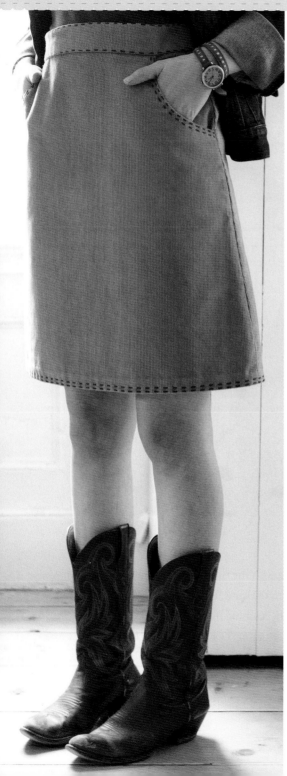

A-Line Skirt with Saddle Stitching

Designed by Lorraine Teigland

Looking for the perfect skirt that is casual enough to wear with a polo shirt, yet formal enough to team with a pretty white blouse and jacket for a dressier occasion? This A-line corduroy skirt fits the ticket! It washes well and looks crisp and stylish even with minimal embellishment. It has scooped pockets and a waistline that sits just below the natural waist. Simple saddle stitching along the waistband, pockets, and hem give it an extra special touch.

MATERIALS

* Locate the pattern in the envelope (sheet #5)
* 1 yard of corduroy fabric (XS–S: 44/45" wide; M–XL: 54/60" wide)
* ¼ yard of coordinating cotton fabric for waistband facing and pocket lining
* 1 spool of coordinating thread
* 7"–9" invisible zipper
* 1 hook and eye fastener
* Embroidery thread in contrasting color for saddle stitching
* Invisible zipper foot (optional)

Sizes – XS, S, M, L, XL

Seam allowance – ½" unless otherwise specified

🟤 Determine Your Size

Measure your waist to find the right size. The finished length for all sizes is 17¾".

	XS	S	M	L	XL
Waist	23"	25"	27"	29"	31"

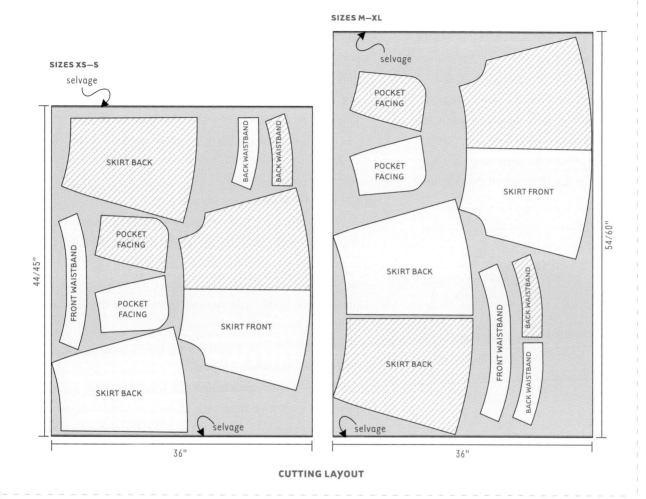

CUTTING LAYOUT

2 Measure, Mark, and Cut

Lay out your fabric in a single layer with the right side facing up. Position the pattern pieces (except for the pocket lining) according to the layout, and cut them out. Transfer markings from the pattern to the wrong side of fabric.

* **Front** (cut 1)
* **Back** (cut 2)
* **Front waistband** (cut 1)
* **Back waistband** (cut 2)
* **Pocket facing** (cut 2)

In addition, cut the following from the coordinating cotton fabric:

* **Front waistband** (Facing) (cut 1)
* **Back waistband** (Facing) (cut 2)
* **Pocket lining** (cut 2)

NOTE: *Position the grainline arrow on the pattern pieces along the straight grain of the fabric. Reverse one of the skirt back, pocket, and back waistband pieces as shown. Mirror the skirt front along the line indicated on the pattern.*

③ Stitch the Pocket Linings

* With the right sides together, pin a pocket lining to the front piece along one of the curved edges. Stitch.
* Notch the seam allowance and press the pocket lining to the wrong side of the skirt so the wrong sides are together. Repeat with the remaining pocket lining on the other side of the skirt front.

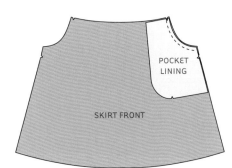

STEP 3

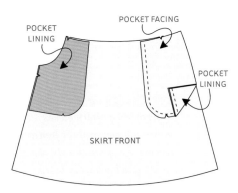

STEP 4

④ Stitch the Pockets

* With the right sides together, pin the pocket facings to the pocket linings, matching the notches and curved edges. Stitch only the curved edges to join the facings to the linings, keeping the skirt front free of the stitching.
* Press the pocket pieces to ensure that they lay smoothly under the skirt front. Pin and baste the upper and side pocket edges to the skirt front with ¼" seam allowances.

⑤ Attach the Waistband Pieces

* With the right sides together, pin and stitch the bottom edge of the front waistband to the top edge of the skirt front. Press the seam allowances up, toward the waistband.
* Do the same with each skirt back and each waistband back piece, pressing the seam allowances up toward the waistband each time.

⑥ Install the Invisible Zipper

Install the invisible zipper at the center back of the skirt according to the manufacturer's instructions. Make sure that the zipper extends up into the back waistband, but that the zipper teeth stop approximately ⅝" below the top raw edge of the waistband. Once the zipper is successfully installed, finish sewing the center back seam of the back skirt pieces. Press the seam allowances open.

⑦ Stitch the Side Seams

With the right sides together, pin and stitch the skirt front to the skirt back, aligning the waistband seams. Press the seam allowances toward the back of the skirt.

⑧ Make and Attach the Waistband Facings

* With the right sides together, pin the side seams of the front and back waistband facing pieces. Stitch and press the seam allowances open, making one complete waistband facing with an opening at the center back.

* Press the bottom edge of the entire waistband facing ½" to the wrong side.

* Unzip the skirt. With the right sides together, pin the top edge of the waistband to the top edge of the waistband facing, matching the center fronts, side seams, and center back. Stitch up one center back, pivot and stitch across the top edge and then down the opposite center back edge.

* Clip the corners. Understitch the top edge of the waistband facing through the seam allowance and the facing fabric. Press the waistband facing to the inside of the skirt. Slipstitch the bottom edge of the waistband facing in place, to conceal the seam allowances.

* Hand-sew a hook and eye set to close the top edge of the center back waistband on the inside of the skirt, just above the zipper.

⑨ Hem the Skirt

Press and hand-sew a ½" double-fold hem along the bottom edge of the skirt.

⑩ Embellish the Skirt

Using all six strands of embroidery floss, hand-sew an evenly spaced running stitch as follows:

* a double row of running stitches, ⅜" apart, around the bottom hem.

* a double row of running stitches, ⅜" apart, along the curved edges of the pockets.

* a single row of running stitches around the top edge of the waistband.

* a single row of running stitches around the bottom edge of the waistband.

As an option, you can use the width of the corduroy wale to determine your running stitch length and help keep the running stitches evenly spaced. For example, if you are working with medium-wale corduroy, each running stitch will span approximately three ridges/wales, which are about ⅜".

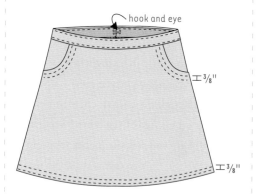

STEP 10

KID'S COMFY CHAIR

Designed by Katherine Donaldson

This design started out as a chair for a dollhouse, but then the question was asked, "What if it was scaled up a bit?" And, yes, the pattern pieces for this chair, large enough for a small child, actually fit within one yard of fabric. We can still hardly believe it ourselves!

MATERIALS

* Locate the pattern in the envelope (sheets #5 and #6)
* 1 yard of 56/60" corduroy
* 1 spool of coordinating thread
* 11 yards of ⅛"-wide ribbon
* 5"-long doll needle
* 64 to 96 ounces of polyester fiberfill (depending on how firmly you stuff it and the stretchiness of the fabric)

Finished dimensions – 16" high × 20" wide × 14" deep

Seam allowance – ½" unless otherwise specified

Seam specific – always begin and end each seam ½" from the edge

① Measure, Mark, and Cut

Lay out your fabric in a single layer with the right side facing up. Position the pattern pieces as shown and cut them out. Transfer all the corner, curve, and placement markings onto the wrong side of the fabric. Accurate placement markings will help you sew the pieces together quickly and easily, so take the time to transfer all the markings and keep the pattern pieces handy to refer to during sewing. The grid of tufting marks on the front, back, and arm pieces, however, needs to be transferred onto the right side of the fabric with a marking method that won't rub off before you start sewing. A good choice is tailor's tacks (see box).

* **Chair back/bottom** (cut 1)
* **Chair front** (cut 1)
* **Chair top** (cut 1)
* **Arm top** (cut 2)
* **Arm inside** (cut 2 as mirror images)
* **Arm outside** (cut 2 as mirror images)

NOTE: *Position the grainline arrow on the pattern pieces along the straight grain of the fabric.*

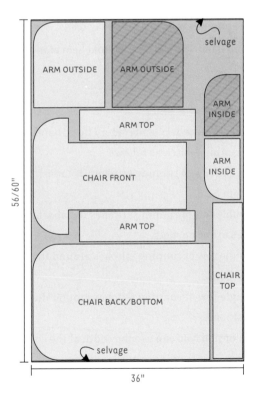

CUTTING LAYOUT

TAILOR'S TACKS

Tailor's tacks are made on cut fabric before removing the paper pattern pieces. Use a doubled contrasting thread and a hand-sewing needle. Take a single stitch at each tufting placement mark, leaving at least a 1" length of thread on either side of the stitch. Carefully pull off the paper pattern, and then loosely tie the thread ends at each stitch to keep the thread from pulling out until you are done with the tufting. To do this quickly, you can take a series of tufting stitches with one length of thread, making sure to leave enough thread between the stitches for tying. Then, cut the threads between the stitches, pull off the pattern, and tie off the thread ends.

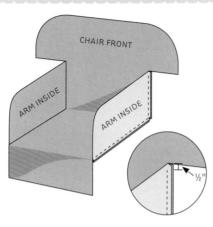

STEP 2

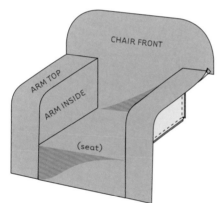

STEP 3

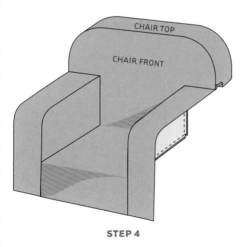

STEP 4

② Attach the Arm Insides

* Pin one arm inside piece to the chair front with the right sides together, matching up the first placement marks.
* Stitch from the first placement mark to the middle placement mark, starting ½" from the edge.
* Pivot the arm inside piece at the middle placement mark and stitch to the last placement mark, stopping ½" from the end. Clip the corner seam allowance.
* Repeat with the remaining arm inside piece.

③ Attach the Arm Tops

* Pin the top edge of one arm top piece to the chair front with the right sides together, matching the placement marks. Stitch between the marks, starting and stopping ½" from each end.
* Pin the inside edge of the arm top piece to the curved edge of the arm inside piece with the right sides together, matching the placement marks. Stitch between the placement marks, starting and stopping ½" from each edge. Notch the curved seam allowances as necessary.
* Match the remaining placement marks on the inside of the arm top piece with the chair front, with the right sides together. Stitch, stopping ½" from the edge.
* Repeat with the remaining arm top piece.

④ Attach the Chair Top

Pin the chair top piece to the chair front with the right sides together, matching the placement marks. Stitch the pieces together, starting and stopping ½" from each edge. Notch the curved seam allowances.

⑤ Attach the Arm Outsides

* Starting at the bottom of the chair, pin one arm outside piece to the free long edge of the arm top with the right sides together, matching the placement marks.

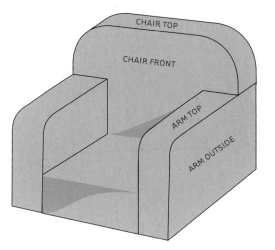

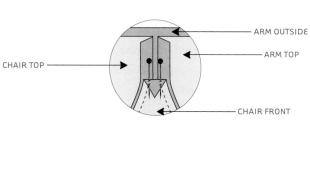

STEP 5

* At the mark where the chair top, chair front, and arm top pieces all meet, press and pin open the seam allowances so they are smooth against the arm outside piece.
* Stitch the pieces together, starting and stopping ½" from each edge. Notch the curved seam allowances.
* Repeat with the remaining arm outside piece.

⑥ Attach the Chair Back/Bottom

* Pin and stitch the chair back/bottom piece to the bottom edge of the chair front, the arm outside, and the chair top pieces, with the right sides together, matching all the placement marks, curves, and corners. Start and stop the stitching at the marked turning gap opening on the bottom edge of the chair front.
* Clip the corners and turn the chair right side out.

⑦ Tuft the Chair

* Loosely stuff the top of the chair back. (It will puff up like a balloon, but don't worry. The tufting will give the chair some structure.)
* Cut a 68" length of ribbon and thread it onto the doll needle.

* Start the tufting at the top row of tufting marks along the back of the chair. Insert the threaded needle into the cavity of the chair through the opening. Bring it to the outside of the chair at the first tufting mark on the chair back/bottom. Continue pulling the needle until there is just 2" of ribbon remaining as a tail inside the chair. Take a few stitches and then knot the ribbon end to the first stitch, or make a strong single knot in the tail. Knot the ribbon ends securely, so they don't pop through once the tufting process begins.
* Sew back and forth from the chair back to the chair front in an S pattern. At each tufting mark, leave a ¼" length of ribbon on the outside of the fabric. Keep a 4" length of ribbon between each mark within the chair cavity.

* At the end of the row, reach inside and tie the ribbon in a knot around the last stitch. If you have extra ribbon when you get to the end, pull it back through the stitches with your fingers or a crochet hook, spreading it out.

* Stuff the space above the row of stitches with small handfuls of fiberfill, being sure to get into the spaces between the ribbon. Continue stuffing until it is firmly stuffed and feels stiff. Add small clumps of stuffing all along the seams at the top of the chair to square them up.

* Remove that row of tailor's tacks.

* Tuft the remaining rows on the chair back and chair arms in similar fashion. First, lightly stuff the area to be tufted. Then, thread the ribbon along a single row of tufting marks, from back to front, tying off the ribbon at the beginning and end of the row. Then, firmly stuff above the tufting, keeping the shape consistent and removing the tailor's tacks as you go. You will need the following lengths of ribbon for each row of tufting (and tuft in this order):

    Chair back, first/top row, 68"

    Chair back, second row, 60"

    Chair back, third row, 52"

    Chair arms, top rows, 36"

    Chair back, fourth/bottom row, 60"

    Chair arms, bottom rows, 40"

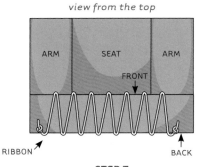

view from the top

ARM   SEAT   ARM

FRONT

RIBBON   BACK

STEP 7

* Remember, the first tied stitch of each row is always at the back of the chair, or, when you are tufting the arms, at the outside back corner.

NOTE: *As you work down the chair from top to bottom, be sure to stuff into the corners between the arm and the back. Once you finish the last row of tufting stitches tying the front and back together, it will be very difficult to get stuffing all the way up to the top of the chair, so make sure the top is even before you get too far down.*

8 Finish the Chair

* After stuffing the tufted section of the chair, begin stuffing the bottom. One large handful at a time, starting at the back corners, stuff the bottom firmly and evenly. Be sure to stuff the back corners particularly stiff to keep the chair from rolling over backward.

* Hand-sew the opening closed with a slipstitch or whipstitch, continuing to stuff the chair with small amounts of fiberfill as you sew. The chair can always accommodate more fiberfill.

MULTI-USE BUCKET

Designed by Brie Jensen

Do you need more storage baskets for your sewing room, office, or playroom? This fast and easy-to-make bucket is a great way to add some stylish storage for all those bits and pieces that seem to build up in your home. Tailor it to suit your needs with a pocket or pocket channels for pencils, knitting needles, paintbrushes, or just about any precious project stash.

MATERIALS

* 1 yard of 44/45" corduroy or home decor fabric
* 1 spool of coordinating thread
* 2 yards of 20"-wide heavyweight interfacing or 1 yard of canvas

* ½ yard of 60"-wide cotton batting
* ½ yard of webbing
* Walking foot (optional)

Finished dimensions – approximately 9" high × 15" wide (at base) × 7" deep
Seam allowance – ½" unless otherwise specified

1 Measure, Mark, and Cut

Fold your fabric in half lengthwise with the wrong sides together, aligning the selvages. Measure and mark the following pieces directly on your fabric as shown, making sure the straight edges are parallel to the grainline. Cut out the pieces.

* **Exterior/interior** 14" × 20" (cut 4)

Cut from batting and interfacing:

* **Batting** 14" × 20" (cut 2)

* **Interfacing or canvas** 14" × 20" (cut 4)

Cut from webbing:

* **Handles** 9" long (cut 2)

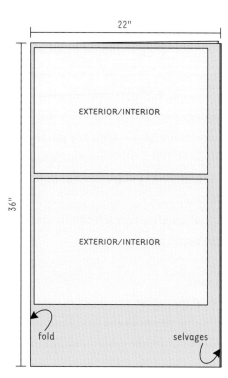

22"

36"

EXTERIOR/INTERIOR

EXTERIOR/INTERIOR

fold

selvages

CUTTING LAYOUT

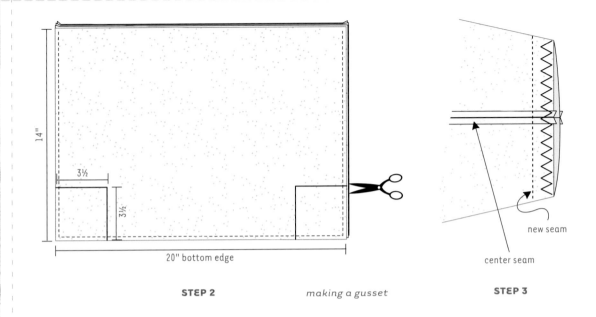

14"

3½

3½

20" bottom edge

new seam

center seam

STEP 2 *making a gusset* **STEP 3**

② Make the Exterior

* On a flat work surface, arrange the cut pieces in the following order: one batting piece, two interfacing pieces, one exterior/interior right side up, one exterior/interior right side down, two interfacing pieces, one batting piece. Align and pin all the corners and raw edges.
* Stitch the short sides and bottom long edge, leaving the top 20" edge unstitched.
* Measure and cut away a 3½" square from each bottom corner. Press the side and bottom seams open.

③ Make the Bottom Gusset

Spread open the bucket sides at the cutout, and then pin the side and bottom seams together, lining up seams and newly cut raw edges. Stitch across the corner to create the gusset. Zigzag stitch within the seam allowance to reinforce the seam. Leave the bucket wrong side out.

④ Make the Interior

* Pin the remaining fabric rectangles with the right sides together. Stitch the sides and long bottom edge, leaving the top 20" edge unstitched.
* Measure and cut away a 3½" square from each bottom corner and make gussets in the corners just as for the exterior piece (*see* step 3). Turn the interior right side out.

⑤ Assemble the Bucket

* Place the interior inside the exterior so the right sides are together, aligning the seams and raw edges.
* Measure 1" from each side of both side seams and mark for webbing placement.

* Sandwich the webbing between the interior and exterior fabric layers, so that the ends of each piece of webbing are positioned at the placement marks on either side of the seams. Align the raw edges of the webbing and the fabric layers, taking care that the webbing is not twisted. Pin the webbing in place.

* Stitch around the top edge, backstitching over each webbing end, and leaving a 5" opening for turning anywhere between the ends of the webbing.

* Turn the bucket right side out, extend the webbing handles, and push the interior into the exterior. Edgestitch around the top, closing the opening as you stitch.

SUGAR & SPICE RUFFLED SKIRT

Designed by Christine Lindh

Everyone loves quick sewing projects for their cute little ones, especially when the finished project is absolutely adorable! This skirt is the perfect project to satisfy a quick sewing fix and can be made in four different sizes. This skirt is everything nice, it flares just enough for a princess look and it's simple enough for play and everyday wear!

MATERIALS

* 1 yard of 44/45" corduroy fabric
* 1 spool of coordinating thread
* 1"-wide elastic (*see step* 2 *for required length*)

Sizes – 2, 3, 4, 5

Seam allowance – ½" unless otherwise specified

❶ Determine Your Child's Size

Measure the waist of the child to find the right size.

	2	3	4	5
Waist size	22"	23½"	25"	26½"
Finished length	11"	12"	13"	14"

❷ Measure, Mark, and Cut

Fold your fabric in half lengthwise with the wrong sides together, aligning the selvages. Using a ruler and washable fabric pen or tailor's chalk, measure and mark the following pattern pieces directly on the fabric, following the cutting layout.

	2	3	4	5
Tier 1 (cut 1 on fold)	10"×42"	11"×42"	12"×42"	13"×42"
Tier 2 (cut 1 on fold)	7½"×42"	8½"×42"	9½"×42"	10½"×42"
Tier 3 (cut 1 on fold)	5"×42"	6"×42"	7"×42"	8"×42"
Waistband (cut 1 on fold)	4"×26¼"	4"×27½"	4"×28¾"	4"×30"
Elastic (cut 1)	22"	23½"	25"	26½"

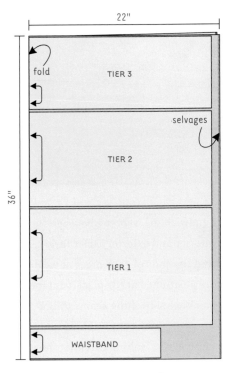

22"

fold

TIER 3

selvages

TIER 2

36"

TIER 1

WAISTBAND

CUTTING LAYOUT

GATHERING THICK LAYERS

Sometimes it can be difficult to gather multiple layers of fabric. If you don't have luck with the basting stitch on your sewing machine, try this tip using a piece of dental floss. Place a length of dental floss just inside the seamline across the area to be gathered; allow the floss to extend slightly beyond the gathered area. Run a zigzag stitch over the floss, being careful not to sew directly on the floss or you will not be able to pull it. Knot one end of the floss and simply pull the other end to gather the fabric. Once you get your fabric pieces sewn together, be sure to remove the dental floss. If the zigzag stitches are visible, remove them with a seam ripper.

❸ Create and Hem the Tiers

With the right sides together and the raw edges aligned, pin and stitch the short edges of each of the tiers to create the center back seams. Press the seams open. Fold, press, and stitch a ½" double-fold hem along the bottom edge of each tier.

❹ Layer the Tiers

Position all three tiers with the right sides facing up and the top edges aligned, with tier 1 on the bottom, tier 2 in the middle, and tier 3 on the top. Take care to align the center back seams. Baste the tiers together along the top raw edge with a scant ¼" seam. Within the seam allowance, mark the center front (directly opposite the center back) using a fabric pen. Use a basting stitch to gather the top edge of the skirt ½" from the top edge.

❺ Prepare the Waistband

* With the right sides together, stitch the short ends of the waistband to create the center back seam. Press the seam open.
* Fold the top raw edge of the waistband ½" to the wrong side and then another 1" to the wrong side to create the elastic casing. Stitch close to the folded edge; leave a 2" opening at the center back seam for inserting the elastic.
* Within the seam allowance on the raw edge of the waistband, mark the center front (directly opposite the center back) with a fabric pen.

❻ Attach the Waistband

With the right sides together, align the raw edge of the waistband with the top of the skirt, matching the center back seams and center front marks. Adjust the skirt gathers to fit the waistband, pinning the skirt and waistband together once the gathers are evenly distributed. Stitch and press the seam allowances toward the waistband. Topstitch ¼" from the seam on the waistband.

❼ Insert the Elastic into the Casing

Cut a length of elastic to comfortably fit around your little one's belly, adding an extra 1" (*see step* 2 *for length guidelines*). Insert the elastic into the waistband casing; be sure to secure the other edge of the elastic to the skirt before you begin pulling the elastic through. Join the two ends of the elastic by overlapping the ends ½" and stitching them together securely. Slip the elastic ends back into the casing and sew the casing opening closed.

CHAPTER 7

coated Fabrics

In the coated fabrics category, we have included just about any material that has a vinyl or rubbery feel and finish, including oilcloth, laminated cottons, and vinyl to name a few. You can also apply much of the information and sewing tips that pertain to coated fabric to sewing with leather. Oilcloth, in some form or another, has been around for ages, but what we call oilcloth today is quite different from the original version!

Fabric Facts

Originally, oilcloth was a sturdy cotton or linen fabric, coated with linseed oil to make it somewhat waterproof. Sometime in the 1950s, modern day oilcloth was born through a process of bonding PVC vinyl to a cotton or poly/cotton background. Tablecloths were then, as now, arguably the most popular use for the material, but we hope to break this trend!

Laminated cotton is thinner and more supple than most other fabrics in the coated category. The wrong side of laminated cotton is quite obviously fabric, by its look and feel. It is the one type of coated fabric that you can most successfully substitute for quilting-weight cotton in apparel or other projects when you want a laminated, semiwaterproof finish. You can even make your own custom laminated cotton with some quilting cotton and iron-on vinyl!

Vinyl can be thick or thin, matte or shiny (like patent leather), smooth or textured. Most of all, it is fun! It can definitely be a challenge for an amateur sewer to stitch vinyl with a standard sewing machine, but it can be done with a little patience. However, a few words of warning: If you fall in love with the fabric and envision a glorious future of vinyl upholstery, bags, clothes, and such, consider investing in a basic straight-stitch, industrial-grade sewing machine.

Attributes

Coated fabrics have at least one smooth, nonporous side and can be easily damaged by pins, needles, and heat. Machine stitches have a tendency to skip, and the fabric can easily stick to the presser foot and throat plate. Coated fabrics can dull your scissors and machine needles quickly (so replace your needle frequently). And, given the solid nature of these materials, they don't breath; so keep that in mind when making clothing out of coated materials.

Needle Type(s)

70/10 universal sharps work on laminated cottons and nylons; larger needles, up to 140/16 universal sharps, may be necessary for thicker oilcloths and vinyl. For the heaviest coated fabrics, you will find that a leather needle works best.

Sewing Machine Accessories

The main problem with stitching coated fabrics is their tendency to stick to your machine throat plate and foot; a Teflon foot is our favorite accessory for combating this problem, but you can also try a roller foot. If you only have your standard (metal) presser foot, try sewing with tissue paper or drafting tape on both sides of the fabric to separate it from the machine.

Stitch Types, Tips, and Machine Settings

Since the holes caused by needles and pins are permanent, use a longer stitch length, about 3-3.5mm, so as not to perforate the fabric as frequently. It's always a good idea to do a test on a fabric scrap first to determine the best stitch length and ensure that the machine will not skip stitches.

Marking

Chalk, drafting tape, and clips, all nonpuncturing and removable marking methods, are most suitable for coated fabrics.

Cutting

Try to use heavy-duty scissors for cutting vinyl and other heavier-weight coated materials. Grainline, by the way, is usually not an important consideration, unless of course the print/pattern is directional.

Interfacing

Interfacing is typically not needed, and rarely used. Most coated materials have enough body of their own! Thinner nylons and laminated cottons are one exception. If interfacing is called for, use sew-in, because coated fabrics can't withstand the high heat required for applying fusible interfacings.

Special Equipment

Use weights to hold pattern pieces in place, since pins can easily mar the fabric. Use binder clips or paper clips to hold pieces together during sewing. If you do use pins, position them within the seam allowances.

Seams

Most coated materials don't fray, so seam allowances can be left unfinished. Pinking shears or seam binding are attractive finishing options.

Pressing and Ironing

Some coated fabrics can't be pressed with any heat, so be sure to test on a scrap fabric. If you do need to press, use low heat and a pressing cloth. We've had success in some instances using parchment or freezer paper as a pressing cloth. In many cases, finger-pressing is sufficient.

Fabric Care

Some coated fabrics can be machine-washed; just be sure to follow the manufacturer's care instructions. Otherwise, simply wipe the coated side of the fabric down with a damp cloth as necessary to clean.

TODDLER SMOCK

Designed by Danielle Wilson

Mealtime and playtime will no longer wreak havoc on your toddler's clothes with this clever cover-all! The water-resistant fabric protects what's underneath, and is easy to spray off or wipe clean. The pocket protects pants from the "trickle-down" effect, and provides handy access to art materials for messy play. The elastic at the wrists offers an extra level of protection for long sleeves. While sized for a 2T, the pattern has sizing lines so you can make the smock bigger or smaller, as necessary.

MATERIALS

* Locate the pattern in the envelope (sheet #6)
* 1 yard of 54/55" oilcloth, coated cotton, or ripstop nylon
* 1 spool of coordinating thread
* ½ yard of ⅜"-wide elastic

Finished dimensions – 15" long from neckline to bottom hem; fits a size 2T as is. Lengthen arms and body for larger sizes. Shorten arms and body for smaller sizes.

Seam allowance – ¼" unless otherwise specified

① Measure, Mark, and Cut

Lay out your fabric in a single layer with the right side facing up. Position the pattern pieces, and measure and mark the additional pieces as shown. To make the smock larger, cut the pattern piece along the sizing lines on the body and underam (or overlap them to make the smock smaller). With a piece of drafting paper underneath the sizing lines, spread the pattern pieces as much as desired, taking care to keep the cut lines parallel. Tape the spread pattern pieces in place and redraw new straight lines to connect the cut lines. Cut out the pieces.

* <u>Smock</u> (cut 1)
* <u>Bib pocket</u> (cut 1)
* <u>Bias strips:</u> 2"-wide strips cut on the bias, enough to make a total of at least 3½ yards of bias binding (optionally, you can use purchased bias binding)

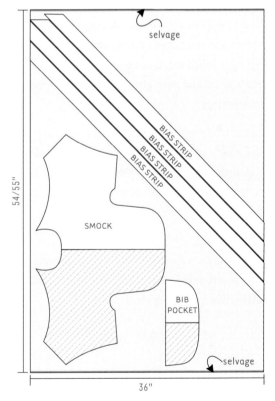

CUTTING LAYOUT

NOTE: *Position the grainline arrow on the pattern pieces along the straight grain of the fabric. Mirror the smock and bib pocket along the line indicated on the pattern.*

❷ Make the Bias Binding

Fold each bias strip in half lengthwise with the wrong sides together and press (with a pressing cloth). Open each strip, and then fold the long raw edges to the wrong side so they meet at the crease. Fold the strips in half again lengthwise and press once more. Cut the bias strips to the following lengths (you might have to piece two strips to obtain the neck/binding tie strip):

* **Neck binding/tie** 36" long (cut 1) (make longer, for longer ties or larger sizes)
* **Bottom binding** 32" long or longer for larger sizes (cut 1)
* **Back shoulder edge binding** 12" long (cut 2)
* **Pocket binding** 14" long (cut 1)
* **Wrist binding** 9" long (cut 2)

❸ Bind and Attach the Bib Pocket

Bind the top edge of the bib pocket with the pocket binding by encasing the top pocket edge between the folds of the binding. Stitch close to the inside binding edge, making sure to catch the back of the binding in the stitching. Trim the binding if it's longer than the bib pocket. Place the pocket right side up on the right side of the smock, aligning the bottom edges. Baste the pocket to the bib along the curved raw edge with an edgestitch, leaving the bound top edge open.

❹ Bind the Smock Edges

* Bind the bottom edge of the smock with the bottom binding in the same manner as the bib pocket in step 3. Start at one underarm, continue down and around the bottom, and then finish at the other underarm (do not bind the straight underarm edge).
* Bind each sleeve opening with the wrist bias bindings, and bind each shoulder edge with the shoulder edge bindings, as in step 3 (again, do not bind straight underarm edges).
* Open the neck/tie binding and press the short raw edges ¼" to the wrong side; refold the neck binding.
* Bind the neck opening with neck binding/tie, aligning the center of the binding with the center of neckline so the binding extends beyond the neck edge on both sides to make the ties. Attach the binding as in step 3, and continue edgestitching the entire length (including the short ends) of the binding to close the ties.

❺ Stitch the Sleeves

* Cut two 7" lengths of elastic (adjust as necessary to fit the child's wrist). Thread the elastic through the sleeve binding with a safety pin and baste each end to the raw edge of the sleeve opening. The wrist opening will gather slightly.
* Fold each smock sleeve with the right sides together, aligning the underarm edges on each side. Stitch from the armpit to the wrist. Turn right side out and commence messy play!

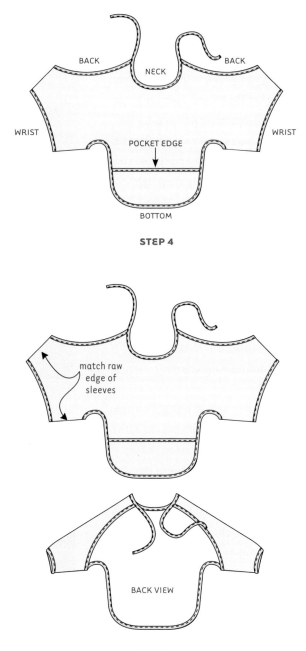

STEP 4

match raw edge of sleeves

BACK VIEW

STEP 5

Airliner Bag

Designed by Nate Van Hofwegen

This roomy, retro-styled airline bag takes travel up a notch with its hot-rod pinstripe detail! This bag is perfect for your favorite 50s or 60s classic car or rockabilly enthusiast. Although an industrial-strength machine is more suitable for sewing very heavy vinyl, lightweight vinyl or other coated material usually works with your trusty home machine.

MATERIALS

* Locate the quilting guide pattern in the envelope (sheet #6)
* 1 yard of 54/55" vinyl
* ⅛ yard of contrasting 54/55" vinyl (optional, for piping)
* 1 spool of coordinating (or contrasting) thread
* Spray adhesive
* ⅓ yard of upholstery foam no thicker than ¼", cut into two 12" squares
* ⅓ yard of muslin, cut into two 12" squares
* 2 O-rings, 1⅞" or 2" in diameter
* Self-adhesive seam tape
* One 24" or 26" heavy-duty/sport polyester zipper
* 7 yards of 1"-wide polyester webbing
* Six ½"-diameter rivets (⅜" or ⅝" also suitable) (optional)
* Heavy-duty sewing machine needle
* Zipper foot
* Cup, glass, or other circle template

Finished dimensions – 11" high × 11" wide × 3" deep
Seam allowance – ½" unless otherwise specified

① Measure, Mark, and Cut

Lay out your fabric in a single layer with the wrong side facing up.

Measure and mark the following pattern pieces directly on the fabric.

* **Body** 12" square (cut 4)
* **Side** 4" × 28" (cut 2)
* **Inside pocket** 8" × 16" (cut 1)
* **Small inside pocket** 5" × 14" (cut 1)
* **Zipper band** 3" × 26" (cut 2)
* **Strap loop** 2½" × 10" (cut 2)
* **Strap** 2½" × 54" (cut 1)
* **Piping** 1½" × 54" (cut 2)

NOTE: *The cutting layout shows piping fabric cut out of the main fabric, though the sample shown uses a contrasting vinyl for these pieces. The choice is yours.*

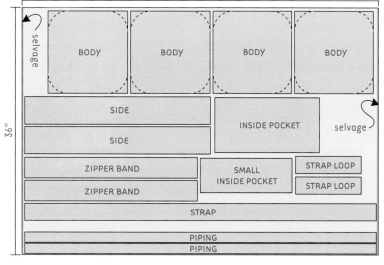

CUTTING LAYOUT

❷ Shape and Quilt the Body Panels

* Round off the corners of the body, muslin, and foam squares with a circle template, taking care that all the corners are rounded identically and the body pieces remain symmetrical side to side and top to bottom (shown as dashed lines in the cutting layout).
* On each body piece, make a mark on each side 4" down from the top edge.
* Determine if you want a quilted, topstitched design on just one or both exterior sides of the bag. If you want both sides of the bag quilted, repeat the following steps twice, once for each side.
* Trace the quilting pattern provided, or any design of your choice, onto the 12" muslin squares with a pen or marker. Note that the image on the finished bag will be the reverse (mirror image) of what you draw on the muslin, so reverse any lettering.
* Using spray adhesive, adhere a foam square to the wrong side of a body piece.
* Adhere the muslin square to the exposed side of the foam in the same fashion, so the quilting design faces you and is centered on the foam/body exterior piece.
* With the muslin side on top, stitch along the markings with a long stitch length. This will create the topstitching on the vinyl, which is facing down.
* These quilted, topstitched body panels become the bag exteriors.

❸ Add Pockets to the Lining

* Fold each pocket in half widthwise with the wrong sides together, aligning the short edges, to form a finished pocket. The folded edge becomes the top edge of each pocket.
* Round the bottom corners of each pocket (if desired) using a circle template. Baste the layers together, close to the raw edges (alternatively, use seam tape to adhere the layers).
* Fold the webbing in half lengthwise, and bind all four sides of each pocket with webbing, being sure to catch the back of the webbing in the stitching.
* Center each pocket on the right side of an unquilted body piece and attach with an edgestitch along the two sides and bottom, leaving the top open. These pieces become the lining.

❹ Line the Exterior and Make the Sides

* Pin one lining to an exterior piece with the wrong sides together, aligning all the raw edges (foam and muslin is sandwiched between). Baste around all four sides, close to the raw edges (alternatively, use seam tape to adhere the layers). Repeat with the remaining lining and exterior.
* Pin the two side pieces with the wrong sides together, aligning all the raw edges. Baste all the edges together, close to the raw edges (alternatively, use seam tape to adhere the layers).
* Fold both short ends of the side 1" to the wrong side and topstitch ¼" from the folds. Add a second, parallel line of stitching ¼" away from first stitch line.

❺ Make the Piping

* Stitch the short ends of one piping piece with the right sides together to form a loop. Finger-press the seam open.
* Repeat for other piping piece.
* Fold each piping loop in half lengthwise with the wrong sides together, and stitch it to the right side of each exterior, with the raw edges aligned.

⑥ Attach the Side to the Exteriors

* Mark the center of each long edge of the side. Also mark the center of the bottom edge of both exterior pieces.
* Matching the marked center points, stitch the side to one exterior piece with the right sides together and the piping sandwiched between them. Starting at the center bottom, stitch out and around to finish the seam on one side, and then repeat from the center in the opposite direction. Leave the second exterior unattached for the time being.

⑦ Make the Zippered Panel

* Close the zipper and lay it on one zipper band with the right sides together, aligning the raw edges. Center the zipper lengthwise if it is shorter than the band.
* Using a zipper foot, stitch the zipper tape and band together, close to the raw edge. Stitch a second row, close to the first, for extra strength.
* Fold the zipper band back on itself close to the zipper coil, so both right sides are facing up. Topstitch ¼" from the fold. Add a second, parallel line of stitching ⅛" away from the first stitch line.
* Repeat to attach the remaining zipper band to the opposite side of the zipper tape.

⑧ Attach the Zippered Panel to One Exterior

* Mark the center of each long side of the zippered panel. Also mark the center of the top edge of both exterior pieces.
* Matching the marked center points, stitch the zippered panel to the exterior/side piece with the right sides together and the ends of the zipper panel extending slightly beyond the finished ends of the side. It may help to start stitching at the center top and work your way out to each side. There will be a lot of layers to stitch through, so take it slowly and carefully.

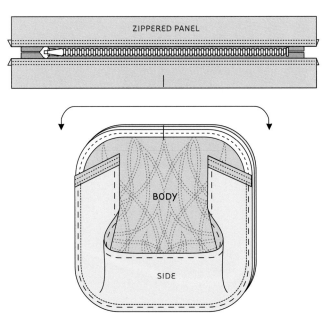

STEP 8

⑨ Make the Straps and Strap Loops

✳ Cut the webbing into one 54" and two 10" pieces. Center each piece of webbing on the wrong side of a corresponding strap loop and strap piece, and adhere them with seam tape.

✳ On each piece, wrap the vinyl around to the exposed side of the webbing and adhere the edges with seam tape so they meet in the center of the webbing. Note that the webbing is no longer visible and will make the strap and strap loops extra sturdy.

✳ Topstitch along the length of the strap and strap loops to secure the layers. The sample features four lines of stitching on each piece, with two stitching lines, ⅛" apart, centered on each half of the strap.

✳ Thread each strap loop through one O-ring. Fold the loops in half over the O-ring and baste the edges together.

⑩ Attach the Strap Loops to the Side

✳ Center the ends of each strap loop on the wrong side of each finished end of the side so that the raw edges of the loops extend at least 2" below the hemmed edges of the side.

✳ Attach a strap loop to each side with two rivets, following the manufacturer's instructions. Attach the first one ½" down from hemmed edge and the other 1" below the first rivet. (Alternatively, you may attach the strap loops with a box stitch.)

⑪ Attach the Remaining Exterior

Attach the side/zippered panel to the remaining exterior as in steps 6 and 8.

⑫ Bind the Raw Edges

Fold the remaining webbing in half lengthwise and bind the remaining interior raw edges with the webbing, making sure to catch the back of the webbing and all the vinyl layers in the stitching. Turn the bag right side out.

⑬ Attach the Straps

Thread one short end of the 54" strap through one O-ring, from the outside to the inside. Fold the end 1" to the wrong side, and then another 1½" over the O-ring. Use rivets or a box stitch to attach the folded end to the strap and secure the O-ring within the fold. Repeat for the other end of the strap and O-ring, being sure the strap is not twisted.

STEP 10

5-GALLON GARDEN BUCKET CADDY

Designed by Rachel Knoblich

This perfect project for the avid gardener solves two problems: how to make the ubiquitous tool bucket pretty, and how to store your well-used garden tools!

MATERIALS

* Locate the pattern in the envelope (sheets #6 and #7)
* 1 yard of 54/55" laminated fabric, oilcloth, or similar material (nondirectional or bidirectional print)
* 1 spool of coordinating thread
* 12 yards of ½"-wide double-fold bias tape.
* One 5-gallon bucket with handle

Finished dimensions – Each piece is 24" tall × 18" wide before folding over the bucket. Together they fit a standard 5-gallon bucket.

Seam allowance – ½" unless otherwise specified

① Measure, Mark, and Cut

Fold your fabric in half lengthwise with the right sides together, aligning the selvages. Position the pattern pieces on the fabric, cut out the pieces, and transfer the markings from the pattern pieces to the wrong side of the fabric.

* **Side panel** (cut 2)
* **Exterior pocket** (cut 2)
* **Interior pocket** (cut 2)

Cut from bias tape:

* **Ties** 14" long (cut 8) (remaining bias tape is used to bind the edges as instructed)

NOTE: *Position the grainline arrow on the pattern pieces along the straight grain of the fabric. Mirror the pieces along the indicated line on the pattern.*

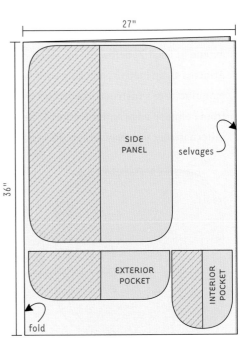

CUTTING LAYOUT

② Bind and Attach the Exterior Pocket

* Bind the top edge of each exterior pocket with bias tape. Edgestitch close to the open edge of the bias tape, catching the back of the tape in the stitching.
* Position one exterior pocket, right side up, on the right side of one side panel, aligning the bottom raw edges. Baste along the sides and bottom close to the raw edges. Repeat for the remaining exterior pocket and side panel.
* Topstitch vertical lines on each exterior pocket at the placement marks to form smaller divided pockets.

③ Bind and Attach the Interior Pocket

* Bind all the edges of each interior pocket with bias tape, as in step 2.
* Position one interior pocket, right side up, on the right side of one side panel at the placement marks. (The interior pocket will appear upside down. This is because the side panel will be folded over the top edge of the bucket.)
* Stitch around the curved side and bottom edges, leaving the top straight edge of the interior pocket open. Repeat for the remaining interior pocket and side panel.

④ Add the Finishing Touches

* Bind all the edges of each side panel with bias tape, as in step 2.
* Open each tie piece and fold both short ends ¼" to the wrong side. Press and refold each tie. Edgestitch along all three open sides of each tie.
* Stitch one end of each tie to the wrong side of each side panel at the placement dots, backstitching for extra strength.
* Place each finished side panel on the opposite side of a 5-gallon garden bucket so that the interior pockets are on the inside, and the exterior pockets are on the outside. The edges of the side panels should align with the bucket handle. Tie the corresponding top ties together just above the bucket handle, and tie the corresponding lower ties below the bucket handle. Fill the caddy with garden gloves, trowels, spades, pruning shears, and all your gardening paraphernalia, and get to work in the garden!

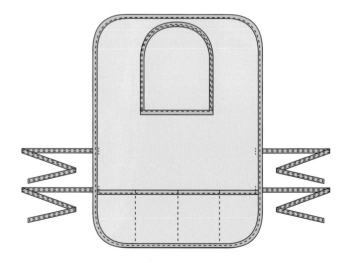

STEP 4

Gym Bag Set

Designed by Lauren Booth

Here's an easy way to carry everything you need for your active lifestyle!
This gym bag is big enough for your workout clothes, snacks, and shoes.
Keep your shoes or dirty clothes separate with the accompanying mini bag.

MATERIALS

* ✳ 1 yard of 44/45" oilcloth, coated cotton, ripstop nylon, or similar material
* ✳ 1 spool of coordinating thread
* ✳ 1½ yards of 2"-wide nylon webbing
* ✳ 1½ yards of 1½"-wide nylon webbing
* ✳ One 1½"-wide plastic slide
* ✳ One 1½"-wide plastic rectangular ring
* ✳ One 22" nonseparating zipper
* ✳ Zipper foot
* ✳ 1 yard of ¼"-diameter cording
* ✳ 1 cord stop
* ✳ Dinner plate, 9" in diameter, or similar circle template
* ✳ 1 heavyweight machine sewing needle, such as a denim needle (optional)
* ✳ Lighter or match (optional)

Finished dimensions – Gym Bag is 8" high × 22" long; Mini Bag is 10½" wide × 14" tall
Seam allowance – ½" unless otherwise specified

TIP: *You can prevent nylon webbing from fraying by fusing the fibers at the cut end. To do this, carefully melt the ends with a lighter or match.*

① Measure, Mark, and Cut

Lay out your fabric in a single layer with the wrong side facing up. Measure and mark the following pattern pieces directly on the wrong side of your fabric. Use a 9"-diameter plate or circle template to trace the two gym bag ends.

* ✳ **Gym Bag body** 26" × 23" (cut 1)
* ✳ **Gym Bag ends** 9" diameter circles (cut 2)
* ✳ **Outer pocket** 9" × 14" (cut 1)
* ✳ **Mini bag** 22" × 16" (cut 1)

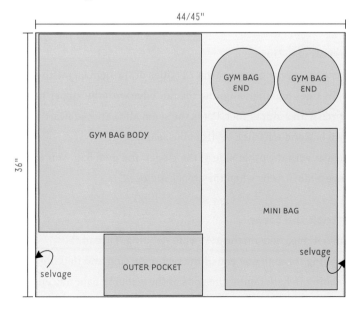

CUTTING LAYOUT

Gym Bag

① Make the Outer Pocket

Fold the pocket in half with the right sides together, aligning the 9" sides, so the folded piece is 7" × 9". Stitch the 9" edge closed. Turn the pocket right side out and press so that the seam forms the top edge of the pocket. Both sides remain unstitched. Edgestitch along the top edge of pocket, close to the seam.

② Attach the Outer Pocket and Webbing

* Place the gym bag body on a work surface with the right side up and one 23" edge at the top. Center the outer pocket on the body, 4" from the top edge. Edgestitch the bottom edge of the pocket to the body.
* Cut the 2"-wide webbing into two pieces of equal length. Pin the webbing onto the gym bag as shown, covering the raw edges of the pocket. Edgestitch both long edges of the webbing, catching the pocket edges in the stitching.

③ Install the Zipper

* Place the zipper on one of the 23" sides of the gym bag with the right sides together, aligning the raw edge with the zipper tape. Stitch with a zipper foot. Press the seam allowances toward the gym bag and topstitch ¼" from the seam.
* Repeat with the other side of the zipper and gym bag. You will have a fabric tube when the zipper is closed.

④ Attach the Strap

* Cut a 4" length from the 1½"-wide webbing. Thread the webbing through one end of the rectangle ring and fold the webbing in half. Center the ends of the webbing over one end of the zipper on one side of the body, aligning the raw edges, and stitch the webbing in place. Do not stitch through any metal parts of the zipper.

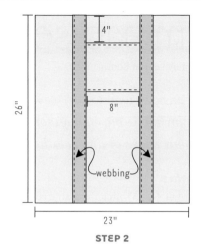

STEP 2

* Center one end of the remaining webbing over the other zipper end, aligning the raw edges, and stitch the webbing place.

⑤ Assemble the Bag

Pin one bag end to an open raw edge of the fabric tube with the right sides together, aligning the raw edges all around. Stitch, catching the stitched ends of the webbing in the seam, but take care to keep the loose end of the webbing out of the seam. Open the zipper slightly and repeat with the remaining bag end.

⑥ Finish the Strap

* Thread the loose end of the long strap onto the slide, and then through the rectangle ring, being careful not to twist the strap.
* Thread the strap back through the slide and fold the raw edge under. Stitch the folded edge to the strap, close to the slide.

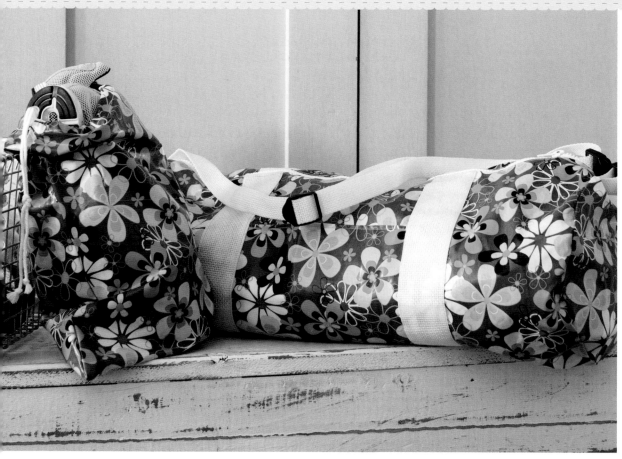

Mini Bag

① Hem the Sides

Hem both short sides of the mini bag with a ½" double-fold hem. This finishes the side raw edges inside the completed bag.

② Make the Casing

Make the casing for the cording by folding one long edge ¼" to the wrong side and then again another ¾". Stitch close to the folded edge.

③ Stitch the Bottom

Fold the fabric in half with the right sides together, aligning the short, hemmed edges. Stitch across the bottom and up the sides, stopping the stitching just below the casing. Backstitch at the beginning and end of the seam.

④ Insert the Cording

Run the cording through the casing, attach the cord stop, and knot the ends.

UMBRELLA REDO

Designed by Katie Steuernagle

Make a "perfect storm" with your favorite coated fabric and an old umbrella! As long as the frame is in great shape, you can give that worn, torn old umbrella a new life with this easy project. You'll never let a little rip keep you indoors again!

MATERIALS

* 1 yard of 54/55" oilcloth or other laminated fabric
* 1 spool of coordinating thread
* Umbrella, 36" in diameter or smaller (make sure the ferrule piece at the top can be unscrewed and removed easily)
* Posterboard or other large-format paper or interfacing for making a pattern
* 3" circle template
* Beeswax (optional)

Finished dimensions – depending on umbrella; no wider than 36" wide when opened
Seam allowance – ¼" unless otherwise specified

① Remove the Fabric from the Old Umbrella

Open the umbrella and unscrew the ferrule. Make note of how and where the fabric is attached to the ribs and to the ball tips at the end of each rib. You will be attaching the new fabric to the ribs and ball tips in the same places and in the same fashion. Carefully snip the stitches where the fabric is attached to the ribs and where they run through the ball tips. Take care to keep the ball tips in a safe place, as you will need them to complete the umbrella.

② Make a Pattern from the Old Fabric

Cut one of the original triangular pieces from the old fabric along the seam. Trace the piece on the pattern paper, and add ¼" around all the sides for the seam allowance. Cut out the pattern.

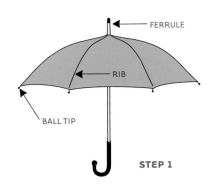

FERRULE

RIB

BALL TIP

STEP 1

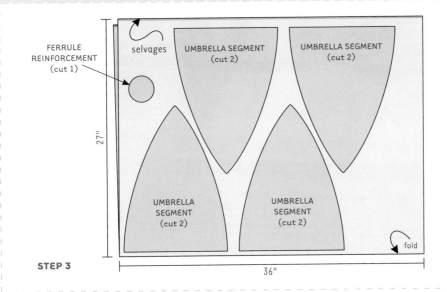

FERRULE REINFORCEMENT (cut 1)

selvages

UMBRELLA SEGMENT (cut 2)

UMBRELLA SEGMENT (cut 2)

UMBRELLA SEGMENT (cut 2)

UMBRELLA SEGMENT (cut 2)

27"

fold

STEP 3

36"

③ Measure, Mark, and Cut

Fold your fabric in half lengthwise with the right sides together, aligning the selvages. Trace around the pattern four times on the wrong side of the fabric so you can cut eight umbrella segments. Also trace a 3"-diameter circle for the ferrule reinforcement. Cut out the pattern pieces.

④ Stitch the Segments

Position two umbrella segments with the right sides together, aligning all the raw edges. Stitch along one side, stopping ¼" from the end point. Add additional umbrella segments in similar fashion, finally joining the first and last segments together to form a big circle. For extra protection from the elements, rub beeswax on the stitching to coat the thread and prevent rain leaks.

⑤ Attach the Fabric to the Frame

With right side up, drape the joined segments over the ribs, lining up the seams with the ribs. Hand-stitch the ball tips at the end of each seam, and slip the ball tips over the corresponding ribs. Once all eight ball tips are in place and attached, hand-stitch the new shade in place within the seam allowance to the ribs in the same places where the old fabric was attached.

⑥ Complete the Umbrella

* Trim around the ferrule reinforcement piece with pinking shears, if desired.
* Punch or cut a small hole in the center of this piece, so you can place the piece at the top of the umbrella and allow the ferrule to be screwed back into the umbrella frame through the fabric.
* Open the umbrella and slip the ferrule reinforcement onto the center top of the umbrella. Reattach the ferrule to hold the pieces in place.

Sit-Upon-a-Saurus

Designed by Chelsey Mona

Remember those old school sit-upons you made as a scout out of wallpaper and newspaper? They were a great idea, though not very durable when made out of newspaper. This sit-upon-a-saurus has renewed longevity when made of oilcloth or laminated fabric, and it has carrying handles and a pocket for your book, trail guide, or field guide! While sized for a toddler, it can easily be enlarged for an older child or adult with a single yard of fabric.

MATERIALS

* 1 yard of 44/45" oilcloth or laminated fabric
* 1 spool of coordinating thread
* 15" square of 2"-thick upholstery foam

Finished dimensions – 15" square × 2" deep

Seam allowance – ¼" unless otherwise specified

① Measure, Mark, and Cut

Fold your fabric in half lengthwise with the right sides together, aligning the selvages. Measure and mark the following pattern pieces directly on the wrong side of your fabric.

* **Top/bottom panel** 15½" square (cut 2)
* **Side panel** 2½" × 15½" (cut 4)
* **Strap** 20" × 3½" (cut 2)

Open up fabric and cut:

* **Pocket** 13" × 15½" (cut 1)
* **Handle** 8" × 3" (cut 1)

② Make the Straps

Press both long raw edges of one strap ¼" to the wrong side. Fold the strap in half lengthwise with the wrong sides together so the folded edges align. Press, and edgestitch the long edges together. Repeat with the remaining strap. Set the straps aside.

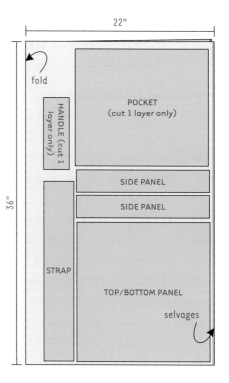

CUTTING LAYOUT

❸ Make and Attach the Handle

* Press all four raw edges of the handle ¼" to the wrong side. Fold the handle in half lengthwise with the wrong sides together, and the pressed edges aligned. Press and edgestitch around all four sides.

* On the right side of one side panel, measure and make handle placement marks 5" in from each short end. Stitch the handle ends at the placement marks with a box stitch. There will be slack in the handle for easy carrying. This piece becomes the top side panel.

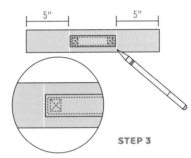

STEP 3

❹ Make and Attach the Pocket

Hem the top edge of the pocket with a ¼" double-fold hem. Pin the pocket, right side up, onto the right side of one top/bottom panel, aligning the bottom and side raw edges. Baste the pocket in place close to the raw edges. This becomes the top panel.

❺ Attach the Side Panels to the Top Panel

* Pin the top side panel along the top edge of the top panel with the right sides together, aligning the top and side raw edges. Starting and stopping ¼" from each end, stitch the two pieces together along the top edge.

* Stitch the remaining three side panels to the top panel in similar fashion. All seams should meet but not cross.

* Stitch the short ends of the side panels together where they meet, starting and stopping ¼" from each end.

❻ Attach Straps to the Bottom Panel

* On the remaining bottom panel, find and mark the center of the top edge. Pin one short raw edge of each strap on either side of this center point, and baste the straps in place close to the raw edge. This becomes the bottom panel.

* Along the bottom edge of the bottom panel, measure and make strap placement marks 3" in from each side. Pin the bottom outside edge of each strap at each placement mark and baste them in place close to the raw edge.

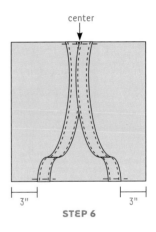

STEP 6

❼ Complete the Cushion

With the right sides together, stitch the bottom panel to the side panels, pivoting at the corner points. Leave an 8" opening for turning along one side. Turn the cover right side out. Insert the foam into the opening and then sew it closed with a slipstitch or whipstitch.

DAY OF THE WEEK PLANNER

Designed by Patricia Hoskins

In a busy household, it's difficult to keep track of who needs what, and when! This wall hanging lets you keep track of those odds and ends, papers, and other items needed on a day-to-day basis. Scribble the weekdays or dates on the chalk cloth labels, erase, and relabel as often as necessary.

MATERIALS

* 1 yard of 58/60" oilcloth, laminated cotton, or similar coated material
* ⅛ yard of 48" chalk cloth
* 1 spool of coordinating thread
* 12 yards of ½"-wide double-fold bias tape
* 3 grommets, ⅜" in diameter or larger
* Three 1" squares of Velcro (optional, for tab loops)

Finished dimensions – 36" tall × 40" wide

Seam allowance – ½" unless otherwise specified

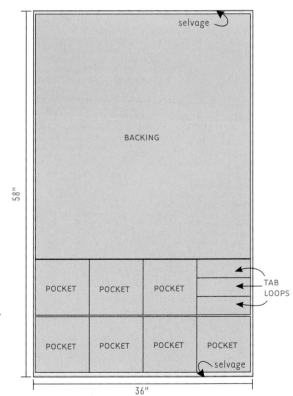

① Measure, Mark, and Cut

Lay out your fabric in a single layer with the wrong side facing up. Measure and mark the following pattern pieces directly on the wrong side of your fabric.

* **Backing** 36" × 40" (cut 1)
* **Pockets** 9" square (cut 7)
* **Tab loops** 9" × 3" (cut 3; optional)

Cut from chalk cloth:
* **Labels** 4½" × 6" (cut 7)

② Bind All the Pieces

Encase all the edges of the backing between the folds of the bias tape. Stitch close to the inside edge of the bias tape, mitering the bias tape at the corners and catching the back of bias tape in the stitching. Repeat for all the pocket pieces.

③ Label the Pockets

Center one label on one pocket. Zigzag the label in place. Repeat with the remaining labels and pockets.

CUTTING LAYOUT

④ Attach the Pockets

Arrange the pockets on the backing as desired. In our sample, the pockets are arranged in three rows, with two pockets on the top and bottom, and three pockets in the middle, all slightly angled. Edgestitch the pockets in place along the sides and bottom, leaving the top edge open.

⑤ Complete the Organizer

Following the manufacturer's instructions, install the grommets slightly down from the top edge, at each corner, and in the center.

⑥ Make the Tab Loops (Optional)

If you want to hang your organizer from a horizontal pole or rope, you may want to create tab loops to run through the grommets:

* Fold all the raw edges of one tab loop piece ¼" to the wrong side and press. Fold the tab loop in half lengthwise, press, and edgestitch all around. Stitch one Velcro half at one short end and the other Velcro half on the reverse side of the other end.
* Repeat with the remaining two tab loops.
* Thread each tab loop through one grommet and secure the Velcro ends.

BICYCLE PANNIERS

Designed by Matt DeVries

These bags, designed to fit a bicycle's rear rack, are just the thing for cycling storage! The profiled design reduces heel-strike, while the carrying handle allows for easy portability. The straps provide a little extra carrying capacity; slip in a rolled up newspaper or magazine on your way to a favorite sidewalk café.

MATERIALS

* Locate the pattern in the envelope (sheets #6 and #7)
* 1 yard of 44/45" laminated cotton, oilcloth, vinyl, or similar fabric
* 1 spool of coordinating thread
* 3⅓ yards of 1"- to 1½"-wide webbing

* ⅔ yard of 1"-wide double-faced Velcro or standard sew-on Velcro
* 4 parachute buckles of appropriate width to accommodate webbing
* Reflective 3M stripe (optional)

Finished dimensions – each pannier bag is 11" high × 11" wide × 5" deep
Seam allowance – ½" unless otherwise specified

① Measure, Mark, and Cut

Lay out your fabric in a single layer with right side facing up. You might want to make copies of each pattern piece or trace around them because you are cutting multiple fabric pieces from each pattern. Position the patterns on the fabric according to the layout and cut them out. Transfer markings from the pattern pieces to the wrong side of the fabric. Measure and mark the bottom/handle piece.

* **Front** (cut 2)
* **Back** (cut 2)
* **Flap** (cut 2)
* **Side** (cut 4)
* **Bottom/handle** 4" × 8" (cut 3)

NOTE: *Position the grainline arrow on the pattern pieces along the straight grain of the fabric. Mirror the front, flap, and back along the line indicated on the pattern.*

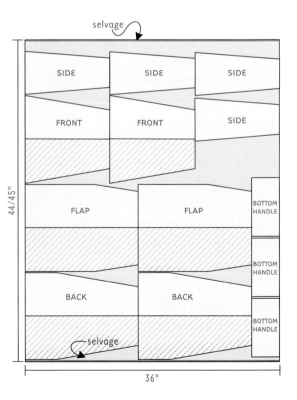

CUTTING LAYOUT

DESIGN NOTE

This bag is made without a lining because the two panniers take up the entire yard of fabric. A waterproof lining could be added if desired (if using a lightweight material).

② **Attach the Webbing and Buckles to the Front**

* Cut four 4" pieces from the webbing. Thread one piece through the female half of a parachute buckle and fold it in half, aligning the ends. Baste the ends together. Repeat with the remaining pieces of webbing and parachute buckles.

* Pin two webbing/buckle pieces on the bottom raw edge of each front piece at the placement marks, aligning the raw edges. Edgestitch the webbing ends in place.

③ **Assemble the Back**

* Pin the back pieces with the right sides together, and stitch across the top wide edge.

* The pannier will be attached to the bicycle with four double-faced Velcro straps. To custom-fit the straps to your bicycle, lay the back pieces across the rear carrier rack with the right side facing up and the seam centered on the rack. At least 2" from each side raw edge, feel for the rack below the fabric and mark where the center of the four straps should be positioned. (When this piece is facedown later on, the loops will wrap around the side poles of the rack.)

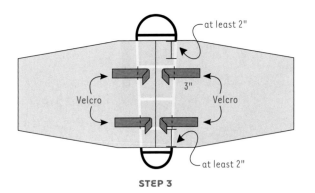

STEP 3

* If you are using standard sew-on Velcro, create double-sided Velcro by placing the wrong sides of the hook and loop pieces together (hooks and loops facing away from each other), and stitch along the long edges.

* Cut the Velcro into four 6" pieces and mark a straight line across the center of each.

* Center the Velcro pieces on the placement marks and stitch along the center line, leaving 3" straps on each side of the center line loose, so they can be wrapped around the bicycle rack.

④ **Make the Handle**

Fold the short ends of the handle ½" to the wrong side and press. With the wrong sides facing, press the handle in half lengthwise. Unfold, and then press both long raw edges 1" to the wrong side, toward the crease. Refold the handle in half lengthwise, press, and edgestitch all around.

⑤ **Make the Flaps**

Pin the flap pieces with the right sides together, and stitch across the top wide edge. Press seam allowance open. Fold all the raw edges of seamed flaps ½" to the wrong side and press. Topstitch to hem the flaps.

NOTE: *If the fabric is flexible and thin enough, you may choose to create a ¼" double-fold hem rather than the indicated ½" single-fold hem.*

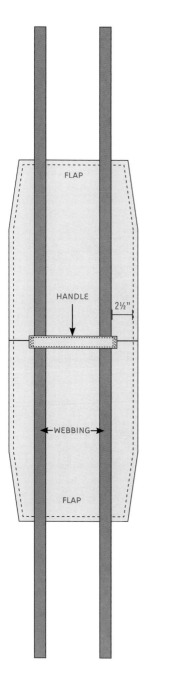

FLAP

HANDLE

2½"

←WEBBING→

FLAP

STEP 6

⑥ **Attach the Webbing and Handle to the Flaps**

* Cut the remaining webbing into two 1½-yard pieces and mark a line across the center of each piece. Pin the webbing pieces to the flaps so the marked (center) lines of the webbing are positioned directly over the seam, and 2½" from each hemmed edge. Stitch on the marked center lines to attach each webbing piece to the flaps.

* Center the handle, right side up, over the right side of the flap seam; the handle should extend ½" beyond the webbing pieces. Stitch the handle to the flaps along the short edges, just outside the webbing. Stitch again close to the first stitch line for added security.

⑦ **Assemble the Panniers**

* Stitch two sides to each front with the right sides together, stopping ½" from each top and bottom corner.

* Stitch one bottom to each front with the right sides together, starting and stopping ½" from each bottom corner.

* Stitch the sides to each bottom with the right sides together, stopping ½" from each bottom corner.

* Stitch one back to each bottom with the right sides together, starting and stopping ½" from each bottom corner.

* Stitch the backs to the sides with the right sides together, starting and stopping ½" from each side corner.

* Turn the pannier set right side out.

* Fold the top raw edge of the panniers and the sides of the seamed back ½" or ¼" to the wrong side and press. Topstitch to hem.

⑧ Attach the Flaps to the Panniers

* Pin the flap to the pannier with the wrong sides together, aligning the center seams and side edges. Edgestitch the flap to the back along the side edges, stopping short of the pannier bag openings.

* Keeping the webbing and Velcro straps pinned out of the way, mark stitch lines across each flap approximately 3½" from the center seam. Make sure the marked lines are below the Velcro straps (on the back) and above the pannier bodies. Topstitch the flaps to the back along the marked lines.

⑨ Complete the Pannier Webbing

* Run the webbing down each flap and stitch it in place at the bottom (hemmed) edge, 1½" from each side edge.

* Secure the webbing to the flap at any desired points. The webbing on the sample shown is only stitched once, halfway between the top center seam and bottom edge. You can instead tack it twice, breaking the webbing into thirds; or stitch it down the entire length of the flap. If the webbing is left unattached in segments, you can slide newspapers, maps, craft projects, or other items through for even more storage!

* Thread the flap webbing through the male half of the parachute buckle and trim it to the desired length, being sure to leave it long enough to accommodate a fully stuffed pannier. Hem the loose raw edge of webbing with a double-fold hem.

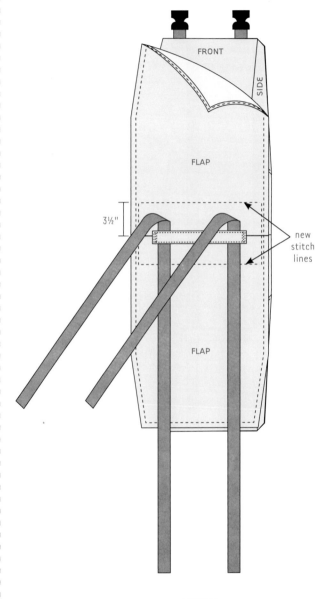

STEP 8

SUPERHERO Cape & SHORTS

Designed by Rachael Theis

The imagination of young children is astounding; they love to daydream that they can be anyone: one day a knight, and the next a superhero. Help your little one truly get into character with this superhero cape and shorts. He or she will be saving the world in no time!

MATERIALS

* Locate the pattern in the envelope (sheet #7)
* 1 yard of 58/60" coated cotton, or similar fabric
* 1 spool of coordinating thread

Sizes – Cape is one size with a finished length of 31"; Shorts are one size to fit children approximately ages 3 to 7. Adjust the elastic to customize the fit.

Seam allowance – ½" unless otherwise specified

For the Superhero Cape:
* 4 yards of ½"-wide double-fold bias tape

For the Shorts:
* 2 yards of piping
* ⅔ yard of ¾"-wide elastic
* ⅓ yard of cotton lining fabric
* Zipper or piping foot

① **Measure, Mark, and Cut**

Fold your fabric in half lengthwise with the right sides together, aligning the selvages. Position the pattern pieces according to the layout and cut them out. Transfer markings from the paper pattern pieces to the wrong side of the fabric.

* **Cape** (cut 1 on fold)
* **Shorts front** (cut 2)
* **Shorts back** (cut 2)

In addition, cut the following from the lining fabric:

* **Shorts front** (cut 2)
* **Shorts back** (cut 2)

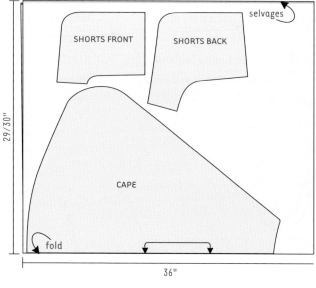

CUTTING LAYOUT

NOTE: *Position the grainline arrow on the pattern pieces along the straight grain of the fabric.*

Shorts

① Attach the Right Facing

With the right sides together, stitch one shorts front to a shorts back along the inseam. Repeat with the remaining front and back and with the lining pieces. Set the shorts lining aside.

② Pipe the Shorts

On the right side of one of the shorts exterior, pin the piping along the raw edge of the shorts back, starting at the top of the side seam. Continue pinning the piping in place down the side seam, across the leg opening, and ending at the placement mark as indicated on the shorts front pattern piece. At this mark, taper the cut end of the piping off the edge of the seam allowance. Use a zipper foot to baste the piping in place. Repeat with the remaining shorts exterior pieces.

③ Attach the Lining

* With the right sides together, align the raw edges of the lining and the corresponding exterior. Using a zipper foot, stitch the lining and shorts together between the placement marks indicated on the pattern piece. Clip the seam allowance at the placement marks and around curved edges.

* Turn the pieces right side out, and gently press the shorts from the lining side. Baste both exterior and lining raw edges together above the placement marks.

* Repeat with the remaining shorts and lining pieces.

④ Assemble the Shorts

* With the right sides together, stitch the front piece to the back piece along the side seam, from the top edge to the placement mark. Press the seams open. Repeat with the remaining front and back pieces.

* Turn one front/back piece right side out and slip it inside the other so the right sides are together, matching the inner leg seams.

* Stitch the entire crotch seam from front to back. Stitch again, this time with a ¼" seam allowance, to reinforce the seam.

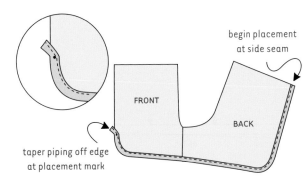

begin placement
at side seam

FRONT

BACK

taper piping off edge
at placement mark

STEP 2

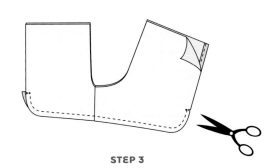

STEP 3

⑤ Make the Elastic Casing

Press the top edge of the shorts ¼" to the wrong side. Turn and press an additional 1". Topstitch close to the folded edge of the casing, leaving a 2" opening at a side seam through which to insert the elastic. Cut the elastic the appropriate length to fit comfortably snug around your little one's belly, adding an extra 1". Thread the elastic through the casing with a safety pin, overlap the ends by ½", and stitch the ends together securely. Slip the elastic ends back inside the casing and stitch the casing closed.

Superhero Cape

① Bind the Edge of the Cape

Pin the bias tape along the outside raw edge, fully encasing the outside edge of the cape between the folds of the bias tape. Edgestitch the bias tape in place, catching the back of the bias tape in the stitching.

② Make the Neck Ties

Cut a 32" length of bias tape and mark the center. Match the center of the bias tape to the center of the neck edge and pin the bias tape along the neckline, fully encasing the raw edge (it will extend off the cape on both ends to form ties). On each of the short ends, turn the bias tape ½" to the wrong side. Edgestitch the entire length of the bias tape, including the short ends.

BREEZY KITE

Designed by Rachael Theis

A fun idea for a large or panel print, this project, designed by a long-time kite aficionado, will take your creativity and favorite fabric soaring to new heights! It's also easy to clean after crash landings!

MATERIALS

* Locate the pattern in the envelope (sheet #6)
* 1 yard of 54/55" oilcloth or laminated cotton
* 1 spool of coordinating thread
* Grommet, 1¼" in diameter
* 6 yards of ⅞" double-fold bias tape (if buying packaged, it may be called quilt binding)
* Four 36"-long wooden dowels, ¼" in diameter
* Kite string
* Kite string reel (typically sold packaged with kite string)

Finished dimensions – 28" from nose to tail, 38" from nose to wingtip, and 50" from wingtip to wingtip

Seam allowance – ¼" unless otherwise specified

① Measure, Mark, and Cut

Lay out your fabric in a single layer with the right side facing up. Cut out the pieces, and transfer the markings from the pattern pieces to the wrong side of the fabric.

* **Kite body** (cut 2, one reversed)
* **Open up the fabric and cut the center flag** (cut 1)

NOTE: *Position the grainline arrows on the pattern along the straight grain of the fabric.*

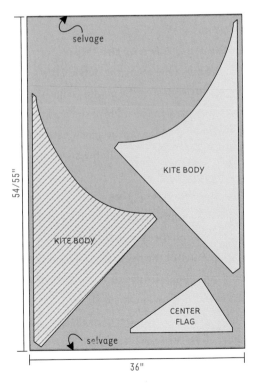

CUTTING LAYOUT

②Attach the Center Flag

* Install the grommet on the center flag at the placement mark, following the manufacturer's instructions.

* With the right sides together, pin the body panels along the center of the kite, aligning all the raw edges. Insert the center flag between the layers, matching the placement dots so the nose and tail are in the correct position and all the raw edges are aligned.

* Stitch the center seam of the kite, from the nose to the tail, being sure to catch all the layers in the stitching.

③Bind the Kite Wings

* Cut two 3" lengths of bias tape. Fold each in half to make 1½" loops and pin the raw edges to the wrong side of the kite body at the support bar placement marks, at a slight angle. The fold of the bias tape should point toward the tail, and the loop openings should be parallel to the center seam. These are the support bar placement loops.

* Cut two lengths of bias tape, each 2 yards and 6" long (the bias tape will form the channels for the dowels). Starting at the nose of the kite, use each length to bind a side of the kite, letting the excess binding hang off of each wingtip for the kite tails. As you stitch along the edge of the bias tape, be sure to catch the raw edges of the support bar loops in the stitching, leaving the loop free to support the wooden dowel later.

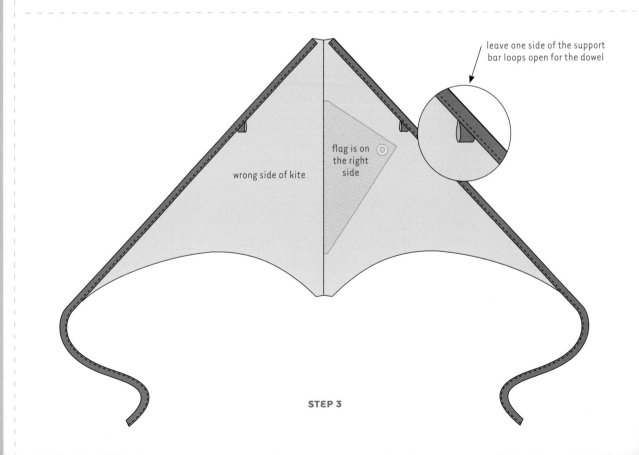

leave one side of the support bar loops open for the dowel

flag is on the right side

wrong side of kite

STEP 3

* From the nose of the kite, insert a dowel into the bias binding channel on both bound edges of the kite. Topstitch across the binding at the wingtips, to close the channels and hold the dowels in place.
* Fold the raw edge of each tail ¼" to the wrong side and press.
* Edgestitch along the open edges of the extra binding at each wingtip to make the tails.

④ Insert the Center Dowel

* Fold the kite in half with the right sides together, and stitch the ends of the binding together at the nose.
* Fold the kite in half with the wrong sides together, and topstitch a 1" channel for the center wooden dowel from the nose to the tail parallel to the center seam. Take care not to catch the center flag in the stitching.
* Cut one wooden dowel to fit within the channel (approximately 27" long) and insert it into the channel.
* Cut one 36" length of binding and topstitch the long open side closed. Insert one short end into the end of the center channel to form the center tail.
* Stitch the center tail in place, closing the channel opening as you stitch.

⑤ Attach Support Bar and String

* Lay the kite flat on your work surface with the wrong side facing up. Measure the distance between the far sides of each support bar loop. Cut the remaining dowel to fit (approximately 16"–17") and insert it into loops. This should make the kite fairly taut.
* Thread the kite string through the grommet and tie a knot to secure it. Wind the string on the reel. Find a grassy field on a windy day and let it fly!

COUPON WALLET

Designed by Patricia Hoskins

Keep those pesky, but oh-so worthwhile, clipped coupons corralled with this easy-to-clean compact organizer. It's a must-have for any frugal shopper, and it certainly makes the weekly chore a little cheerier when it's made in a bright fabric of your choice! The coated fabric makes it easy to wipe down.

MATERIALS

* 1 yard of 54/55" lightweight laminated cotton, oilcloth, or similar fabric
* ¼ yard of lightweight clear vinyl
* 1 spool of coordinating thread
* 12" length of elastic cord
* Small plate or cup for rounding the corners
* Unlined note card or cardstock for labels

Finished dimensions – 4" tall × 7½" wide × 2" deep
Seam allowance – ¼" unless otherwise specified

① Measure, Mark, and Cut

Fold your fabric in half lengthwise with the right sides together, aligning the selvages. Measure and mark the following pattern pieces directly on the wrong side of your fabric.

* **Top/bottom panel** 2½" × 8" (cut 4)
* **Flap** 4" × 8" (cut 2)
* **Front/back panel** 5" × 8" (cut 4)
* **Side panel** 5" × 16" (cut 4)
* **Divider** 4½" × 7" (cut 16)

Cut from clear vinyl:

* **Interlining** 7" × 14" (cut 1)
* **Tab** 1½" square (cut 8)

Cut from cardstock:

* **Label** ⅜" × 1½" (cut 8)

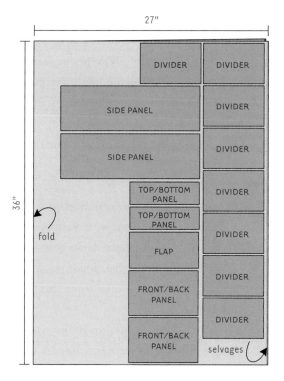

CUTTING LAYOUT

➋ Form the Dividers

* Pin two divider pieces with the right sides together, aligning all the raw edges. Fold one clear vinyl tab in half and insert it between the top edges of the dividers, 1" from the left edge, with the raw edges aligned. Stitch across the top and bottom edges with a ¼" seam allowance. Leave the short sides unstitched. Clip corners, turn the divider right side out, and press. Edgestitch along the top and bottom edges.

* Repeat the process for another divider piece, but this time position the vinyl tab 2½" from the left edge.

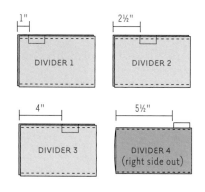

STEP 2

* For the third divider, position the tab 4" from the left edge.
* For the fourth divider, position the tab 5½" from the left edge. You now have a set of four dividers with staggered tabs.
* Repeat the above step to make four more dividers with the same tab positions as the first four.

❸ Stitch the Cover

* Round the two top corners of both flap pieces.
* Assemble one flap, two top/bottoms, and two front/backs as shown, with the rounded edges on the outside of the joined pieces. Stitch them with the right sides together.

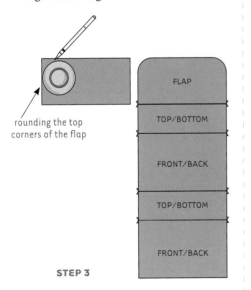

rounding the top corners of the flap

STEP 3

* Assemble another identical set of pieces.
* Pin the two assembled covers with the right sides together, aligning all the raw edges. Stitch all around, leaving a 4" opening centered along the flap. Notch the curves, clip the corners, and turn the cover right side out. Press.
* Round the corners of one short edge of the vinyl interlining so the interlining matches the shape of the finished cover.
* Insert the interlining into the cover through the opening, so the corners are aligned.
* Fold the elastic cord in half and insert the ends into the center of the flap opening.
* Edgestitch around the cover, closing the opening and catching the elastic loop in the stitching.

❹ Make the Side Panels

* With the right sides together and the raw edges aligned, stitch two side panels together, leaving a 4" opening on the bottom long edge for turning. Clip the corners and turn the side panel right side out and press. Edgestitch along the top and bottom edges, closing the opening in the stitching. Repeat for the remaining side panel pieces.
* Test your fabric marking pen or chalk on a fabric scrap to make sure the markings can be removed. On each side panel, draw a vertical line 1" from the left edge, followed by another line ¾" away from the first line. Repeat these measurements all the way across the panel as shown. The last line will be 1½" from the right edge.

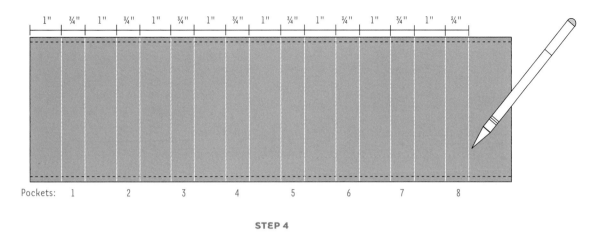

| 1" | ¾" | 1" | ¾" | 1" | ¾" | 1" | ¾" | 1" | ¾" | 1" | ¾" | 1" | ¾" | 1" | ¾" |

Pockets: 1   2   3   4   5   6   7   8

STEP 4

⑤ **Attach the Dividers to the Side Panels**

* Fold one side panel between the first line and the second line
  (a ¾" slot), so that the two lines match up. Insert the first
  divider into the fold, aligning the bottom raw edges, and pin
  the fold in place. Continue inserting dividers into the ¾" slots
  in the same way, all the way across.

* Repeat for second side panel on the opposite end of the dividers. Stitch along the marked lines on both side panels.

* Hand-sew the accordion pleats together at the bottom, leaving
  the ends of the side panels free.

⑥ **Attach the Cover**

* Stitch the free ends of the side panels to the sides of the front
  and back cover, with the finished edges aligned.

* Print your desired categories on the cardstock labels. Ours
  are labeled: Bread/Grains, Frozen, Refrigerated, Personal/Pet,
  Canned/Boxed, Baking/Snack, Cleaning/Other, Condiments/
  Jars. But feel free to choose your own! Slip the labels into the
  clear vinyl tabs, load up on coupons, and don't forget to take it
  with you to the grocery store!

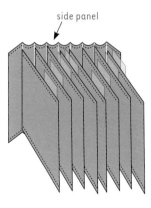

side panel

STEP 5

under-the-sink cleaning stash

Designed by Michelle Fante

Keep a cleaning kit handy with this organizer that hangs on an inner cabinet door and fits neatly underneath your kitchen or bathroom sink. The oilcloth wipes down easily, making it perfect for the grungiest of utility cabinets! Grommets allow for easy hanging from nails or hooks.

MATERIALS

* 1 yard of 48" oilcloth, laminated cotton, or similar coated fabric
* 1 spool of coordinating thread
* 2½ yards of ½"-wide double-fold bias tape
* 3 grommets, ½" inside diameter (or approximately 1" outer diameter)

Finished dimensions – 19" high × 13" wide
Seam allowance – ½" unless otherwise specified

 Measure, Mark, and Cut

Lay out your fabric in a single layer with the wrong side facing up. Measure and mark the following pattern pieces directly on the wrong side of your fabric.

* **Organizer exterior** 20" × 13" (cut 2)
* **Top pocket** 6" × 17" (cut 2)
* **Bottom pocket** 8" × 29" (cut 2)
* **Facing** 2" × 13" (cut 2)

 Make the Exterior

* Position the exterior pieces with the right sides together, and the raw edges aligned. Position the facing pieces with the right sides together, and the raw edges aligned. Pin one long edge of the facings to the top edge of the exterior pieces. Stitch the top edge through all four layers and the bottom edge through the two exterior layers.

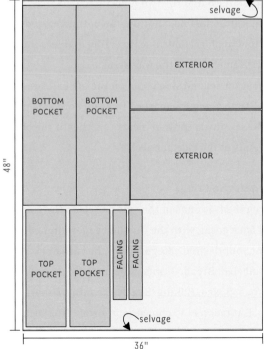

CUTTING LAYOUT

* Turn the exterior right side out, with the facing pieces sandwiched on the inside, and press. Edgestitch along the top and bottom edges of the exterior.
* Topstitch across the exterior, 1½" down from the top edge, catching the bottom edge of hidden facing pieces in the stitching.

③ Make the Top Pockets

* With the wrong sides together, baste around the edges of the top pocket pieces.
* Bind the top edge of the top pocket by encasing it between the folds of the bias binding. Stitch close to the inside binding edge, making sure to catch the back of the binding in the stitching. Measure in 6" from the right raw edge and mark a vertical line. This will become the stitching line dividing the right and left top pockets. Find the center point between this line and the left raw edge and mark; this becomes the center of the left top pocket.
* Make and label two marks on each side of the left pocket center: one 2" on each side of the center (label these A), and a second mark 4" on each side of the center (label these B). Fold each A mark toward each B mark to create pleats that point toward the side edges. Press and pin, or baste the pleats in place close to the raw edge.

④ Make the Bottom Pockets

* With the wrong sides together and the raw edges aligned, baste around the bottom pocket pieces close to the raw edges.
* Bind the top edge of the bottom pocket with bias tape, the same as for the top pocket in step 3.
* Working on the right side, find the center (14½" from either side) and draw a vertical line. This will become the stitching line dividing the right and left bottom pockets.
* Find and mark the center points of each divided bottom pocket.
* Make two marks on each side of each bottom pocket center: one 2" on each side of the center (label these A), and a second mark 6" on each side of the center (label these B). Fold each A mark toward each B mark to create pleats that point toward the side edges. Press and pin, or baste the pleats in place close to the raw edge.

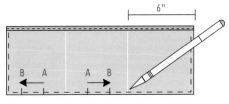

STEP 3

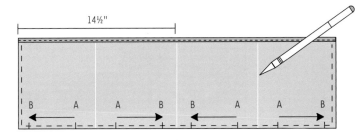

STEP 4

⑤ Attach the Top Pocket

* Position the top pocket with the wrong side up, on the exterior. The top edge of pocket should face toward the bottom edge of the exterior, and the bottom edge of pocket should lay 8" down from the top edge of the exterior.

* Stitch along the bottom edge of the pocket. Flip the pocket up so the right sides face up and press the seam. Baste the side edges of the top pocket and exterior together, close to the raw edges. Topstitch along the marked (center) vertical line.

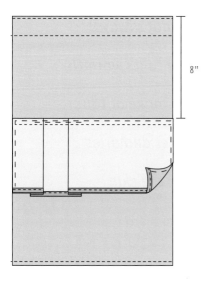

8"

STEP 5

⑥ Attach the Bottom Pocket

* Position the bottom pocket with the wrong side up, on the exterior. The top of the pocket should extend off the bottom of the exterior, and the bottom edge of pocket should lay 1½" up from bottom edge of the exterior.

* Stitch along the bottom edge of the pocket. Flip the pocket up so the right sides are facing up and press the seam. Baste the side edges of bottom pocket and exterior together, close to the raw edges.

* Topstitch two vertical lines 1" on either side of the center marked line to create a narrow 2" channel at the center of the bottom pocket. Take care not to catch the pleats in the stitching. This creates a cleaning brush pocket.

* Topstitch one vertical line 1" from the right raw edge of the bottom pocket to create a narrower pencil pocket.

⑦ Add the Finishing Touches

* Bind the side edges of the exterior with bias tape, the same way as for the top edge of the top pocket in step 3, but fold the top and bottom raw edges of the bias tape in ¼" to the wrong side before stitching.

* Install grommets across the faced top edge of the exterior following the manufacturer's instructions. The first grommet should be centered from side to side and between the upper stitching lines. The remaining grommets should be placed no closer than 1" from the side edges, also centered between the upper stitching lines.

CHAPTER 8

Fleece

Fleece is a knitted fabric with a light, strong pile that mimics wool at a much lighter weight. Typically made from synthetic fibers such as polyester, fleece is usually (but not always) a reversible fabric with great shape retention. Due to its warmth, weight, and softness, fleece is frequently used to make outdoor and winter apparel. After all, it helps repel water and dries quickly. Fleece is quite comfortable against the skin and also makes great cuddly toys.

Fabric Facts

Fleece comes in a variety of weights and pile thicknesses, and you can even find it double-sided. Faux fur has some of the same attributes as fleece, but with a much thicker/higher pile. Although solid fleece is ubiquitous, there are also plenty of intriguing prints.

Attributes

Fleece has the attributes of both knits and pile fabrics. It stretches primarily along the crossgrain. To determine the right side, stretch the cut edge and the cut edge will curl toward the wrong side. That said, use the side you like best! There will definitely be times you like the look of the "wrong" side better. You may find it necessary to mark the right/wrong side of the fabric before cutting so you don't get confused when you are sewing and to keep the project consistent. Fleece does not retain pressed creases or pleats.

Needle Type(s)

Use 70/10 for light fleece and up to 80/12 or 90/14 for heavier fleece. Either universal sharp or ballpoint needles are appropriate.

Sewing Machine Accessories

The satin stitch foot or walking foot is preferred, primarily due to the thickness and springiness of the fabric.

Stitch Types, Tips, and Machine Settings

You will likely achieve the most success with longer stitches, such as 3mm for seam construction.

Marking

Most marking methods are appropriate, including chalk and fabric markers. Label the right or wrong side of each cut piece with safety pins or drafting tape when it's hard to tell which is which.

Cutting

Since fleece moves and stretches, make sure all the fabric is on a level work surface and not hanging off, to avoid stretching and distorting.

Interfacing

Interfacing is rarely needed since fleece has plenty of its own body, and its stretchability is typically important in a fleece project. If interfacing is used, it's to stabilize closures such as zippers; and in these cases, only use sew-in interfacing, as pressing a fusible can crush the fleece pile.

Special Equipment

Fleece can dull your scissors quickly, so it's best to work with newly sharpened scissors. Although fleece typically resists creases and pleats, you can use a 1:1 vinegar/water spray solution when pressing to try to sharpen and set such details, at least temporarily.

Seams

There is no need to finish seam allowances, since fleece does not unravel. However, stretching at seams can be a problem. You can stabilize seams with clear elastic if you want to retain stretch at the seam, or use seam tape or twill tape for more rigid seams.

Pressing and Ironing

Avoid pressing, as you can crush the pile. Instead, finger-press.

Fabric Care

No preshrinking is necessary. Launder inside out, and dry on low or no heat. In general, follow manufacturer's care instructions.

ON-THE-STRAP CAMERA CASE

Designed by Sue Walsh

Tired of bulky, cumbersome, traditional camera bags? This superlightweight case uses the camera's own strap for carrying, and can stay on the strap while you are taking pictures. It's so easy to carry along! As an added bonus, a small interior pocket holds your lens cap, USB cable, or SD cards.

MATERIALS

* ✳ Locate the pattern in the envelope (sheets #5 and #6) or create your own pattern following the instructions in step 1
* ✳ 1 yard of 58/60" light- to medium-weight fleece
* ✳ 1 spool of coordinating thread
* ✳ 3" of ⅞"-wide sew-on Velcro, cut into three 1" squares

* ✳ Embellishments as desired (sample uses three 1"-diameter buttons)
* ✳ 3" square of firm but flexible, transparent plastic sheeting
* ✳ ¼ yard of ⅞"-wide ribbon or webbing for tabs
* ✳ Paper for creating pattern pieces (optional)

Finished dimensions — 8" long × 7" wide × 3" deep

Seam allowance — ¼" unless otherwise specified

① Create Custom Pattern Pieces

If your camera is larger or smaller than a standard SLR camera and zoom lens (approximately 3½" high × 7" wide, with lens height 2½"), you may choose not to use the pattern pieces provided for this project and instead draft your own pattern. Simply follow the basic shapes of the pattern pieces provided and trace around your camera. You will draft three customizable pattern pieces: body panel, quilting panel, and side panel.

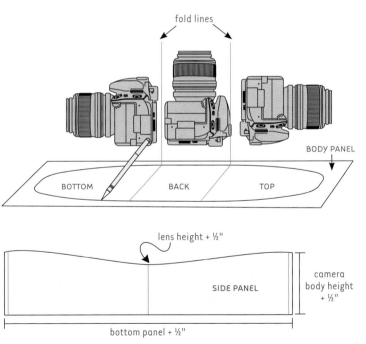

fold lines

BODY PANEL

BOTTOM BACK TOP

lens height + ½"

SIDE PANEL

camera body height + ½"

bottom panel + ½"

STEP 1

To make your own **body panel**:

* For the bottom section of the body panel, place the camera on pattern paper or interfacing with the lens front 1" from the paper edge. Trace around the camera, ⅝" away from the outer edge (for ease and seam allowance).

* For the back section, roll the camera onto its back and trace along the sides, extending the bottom panel and maintaining the ⅝" allowance on all sides.

* Create the top section by retracing the bottom panel. You should have one long body panel that includes all three sections. Draw lines to mark these sections, just as they are marked on the pattern. You will want to refer to them later.

To make your own **quilting panel**, trace a pattern piece the same shape as the body panel, but ½" smaller all the way around.

To make your own **side panel**:

* Determine the length by measuring around the curve of the bottom section of the body panel, from one end to the other. Add ½" for seam allowances (¼" at each end).

* For the width, make the ends the height of your camera's body plus ½". Make the center the height at the end of your camera lens plus ½". Trace a smooth line from the outer points to the inner points.

CUSTOM-FITTING YOUR CAMERA CASE

* Although this project comes with pattern pieces designed to fit most common digital SLR/DSLR cameras with a standard zoom lens, instructions are also provided to design your own pattern to fit your personal camera.

* Because camera lenses are typically positioned slightly off-center on the body, the pattern pieces are shaped to accommodate this. The pieces are *not* symmetrical side to side. Take care when pinning and stitching the body pattern pieces to make sure you are attaching the correct body piece to the correct panel piece!

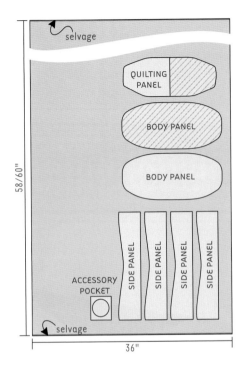

CUTTING LAYOUT

❷ Measure, Mark, and Cut

Whether you've decided to use the existing pattern pieces or have drawn your own, lay out your fabric in a single layer with the right side facing up. Position the pattern pieces as shown and cut out the pieces. Transfer markings from the pattern pieces to the wrong side of fabric.

* **Body panel** (inner and outer) (cut 2, one reverse)
* **Side panel** (cut 4)
* **Quilting panel** (cut 1)
* **Accessory pocket** (cut 1)

Cut from plastic sheeting:
* **3½"-diameter circle** (cut 1)

NOTE: *There is a 3"-diameter circle cutout in the center of this piece.*

NOTE: *Position the grainline arrow on the pattern pieces along the straight grain of the fabric. Mirror the quilting panel along the line indicated on the pattern. The wavy white line indicates extra fabric not shown.*

❸ Quilt the Outer Body Panel

Pin the quilting panel to the wrong side of one body panel, centering it ½" in from the raw edges. This will become the outer body panel. Quilt with free-motion stitching as desired, covering the panel evenly. You can stitch circles, squiggles, zigzags, or even add eyes and teeth to make an animal case. The possibilities are endless!

❹ Make the Pocket

* Place the plastic circle on the wrong side of the accessory pocket, centering it over the cut-out hole. Edgestitch it in place.
* Center and pin the pocket on the right side of the remaining (inner) body panel. Edgestitch the pocket in place on three sides, leaving the top edge (the edge facing the top section) unstitched.

❺ Mark the Inner Body Panel

Check the shape and size of the bottom, back, and top sections as drawn on the pattern by placing the camera on the inner body panel (the nonquilted one) and wrapping it over the top of the camera just as it will wrap when the case is finished. Pin or baste across the top and bottom fold lines so you can see exactly where the top, back, and bottom sections meet. This will be an important guide in the next step.

6 Attach the Side Panels to the Inner Body Panel

* With the right sides together, pin the bottom (long straight edge) of one side panel to the bottom section of the inner body panel, starting and ending at the basted markings you made in step 5. Stitch the seam, starting and stopping ¼" from each end and pivoting at the corners.

* Pivot the back section of the inner body panel so you can pin the short ends of the side panel to the inner body panel as shown. The side panel should reach the other basted markings from step 5. Stitch the seam, stopping ¼" from each end.

* Stitch the bottom (long straight edge) of a second side panel to the top section of the inner body the same way as you stitched the bottom section, but *do not* stitch the short edges of the side panel to the back panel. This side panel will function as the top flap.

7 Attach the Side Panels to the Outer Body Panel

Attach the remaining two side panels to the outer body as in step 6. Turn right side out.

8 Assemble the Inner and Outer Body Pieces

With the right sides together, pin the outer body to the inner body, along the side panels with all the raw edges aligned. Stitch the seam, with ¼" seam allowance, leaving a 3" opening along one edge for turning. Clip the corners, trim any excess fabric and seam allowances, and turn the camera case right side out. Push out the corners with a point turner and hand press all the seams to flatten them. Edgestitch along all the outer edges closing the opening.

9 Add the Tabs, Closures, and Embellishments

* Cut the ribbon into three 3" lengths. Fold each piece in half and baste the raw edges together to create tabs. Baste the raw edge of each tab to the wrong side of one Velcro hook square half.

* Pin these tabbed hook Velcro squares to the inside of the top flap, at the center front and ½" in from the corners, as shown. Allow about ½" of the folded end of each tab to extend past

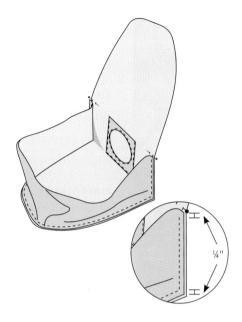

STEP 6

the bottom edge of the flap, so they are accessible on the outside.

* Stitch the loop half of each Velcro square to the outside of the bottom side panel, at the center front and ½" in from each side seam, aligning them with the stitched hook Velcro tabs.

* Add button, beads, or appliqués on the outside of the top flap to hide the Velcro stitching lines, if desired.

* To use your new on-the-strap camera cover, simply pull the front tab to undo the Velcro (leaving the back Velcro pieces fastened). Slide the bag along the strap, take your photos, slide the camera back into the case, and refasten the Velcro.

pajama BOOTS

Designed by Sue Kim

Cute PJs are a necessity, but what about cute PJs for your feet? These pajama boots fit the bill! Whether cozying up by the fire with a mug of hot cocoa or kicking back and relaxing with your favorite book this winter, your toes will be toasty and very cute in these stylish, indoor, comfy boots.

MATERIALS

* Locate the pattern in the envelope (sheet #8)
* 1 yard of 58/60" fleece (outer fabric and lining)
* 1 spool of coordinating thread

Sizes – 5, 6, 7, 8, 9, 10
Seam allowance – ¼" unless otherwise specified

① Determine Your Size

Sizing is determined according to the length of your sole. Note that there are also two calf size options. Measure around your calf at the largest point to determine which calf size to use.

	5	6	7	8	9	10
Sole Length	9"	9¼"	9½"	9¾"	10"	10¼"
Regular calf is less than these measurements; larger calf is greater than.	15¼"	15½"	16"	16½"	16¾"	17¼"

② Measure, Mark, and Cut

Lay out your fabric in a single layer with the right side facing up. Position and pin the paper pattern pieces according to the diagram. Make sure the grainline arrows are on the straight grain of the fabric, so the pieces stretch as needed to fit over the foot and calf. Transfer markings from the pattern pieces to the wrong side of the fabric before removing the paper pattern pieces.

* <u>Sole</u> (cut 4)
* <u>Upper shoe</u> (cut 4)
* <u>Calf</u> (cut 4)

Also measure, mark, and cut the following piece:

* <u>Tassel block</u> 10½" × 6" (cut 2)

NOTE: *Position the grainline arrow on the pattern pieces along the straight grain of the fabric.*

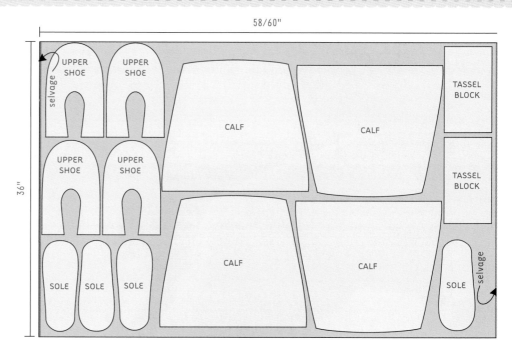

CUTTING LAYOUT

❸ Attach the Upper Shoe to the Calf

* With the right sides together, align the raw edge of the inside curve of the upper shoe piece with the lower raw edge of the calf piece, matching centers and side edges. Pin the pieces together at the notches first and then along the rest of the seam, gently stretching the upper shoe piece to match the calf piece. Stitch the pieces together.

* Carefully clip the curved seam allowance where necessary. Fold the piece in half lengthwise with the right sides together and stitch a seam along the back of the calf and ankle.

* Repeat with remaining upper shoe and calf pieces.

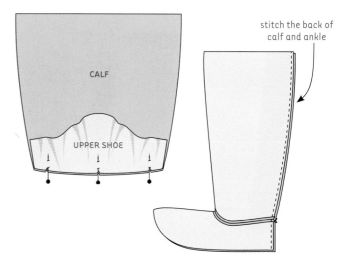

stitch the back of calf and ankle

STEP 3

④ Attach the Sole

* Pin the sole and the upper shoe with the right sides together, aligning all the raw edges. Begin by pinning the center fronts and center backs together. Continue pinning between the center points. If the upper shoe seems slightly smaller than the sole, carefully clip the upper shoe within the seam allowance at regular intervals, and stretch it to fit the sole.

* Stitch the sole and upper shoe together and clip the seam allowances so the seam is smooth. Repeat with the remaining sole and upper shoe pieces.

* Turn two sets of completed boots right side out; these are the exterior boot pieces. Keep the remaining two sets of complete boots wrong side out to act as the linings.

pin the center front and back first

STEP 4

⑤ Assemble the Exterior and Lining

* Insert the exterior boot inside the lining boot with the right sides together. Finger-press the center back seams open and pin both pieces together around the top edge of the boot. Stitch the exterior and lining together along the top edge, leaving a 3" opening for turning.

* Turn the boot right side out through the opening, tucking the lining inside the exterior boot. Topstitch around the top edge of the boot, closing the opening as you stitch. Repeat with the remaining exterior and lining.

⑥ Make and Attach the Tassel

* From each tassel block (one for each boot), cut 21 pieces measuring ½" × 6".

* Neatly stack the 21 tassel pieces on top of each other. Hand-sew across the center of the tassels, securely binding all the pieces together. Wind the thread around the center of the tassels three or four times. Sew the center one final time and make a knot to secure the stitches.

* Pin the center of the tassel on the center back seam, 1" down from the top edge of the boot. Sew through the center of the tassel to attach it firmly. Repeat with the second set of tassel pieces and second boot. Fluff the tassels!

MONSTER-WEAR HAT & MITTENS

Designed by Erin Currie

Have fun this winter with a whimsical hat and mittens set! Great for young and old, it's sure to bring a smile to the face of all passersby on the bleakest of winter days. Not right for you this winter? Well, Halloween always seems to be right around the corner. Use this monster-wear hat and mittens set as the cornerstone of an outrageous Halloween costume!

MATERIALS

* Locate the pattern in the envelope (sheets #2 and #8)
* 1 yard of 58/60" double-sided reversible (two color) fleece
* scraps of coordinating fleece for ears and claws (optional, if you are unable to find double-sided fleece; see Fabric Note on opposite page)
* 1 spool of coordinating thread

For the hat:

* ½ yard of coordinating narrow ribbon or cording

Size: hat and mittens are one size, fitting up to a medium man's hand

Seam allowance: ¼" unless otherwise specified

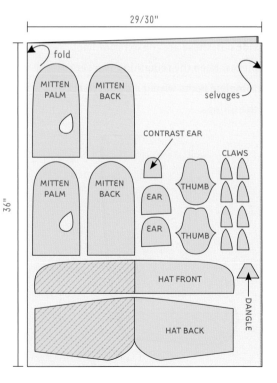

29/30"

fold

MITTEN PALM

MITTEN BACK

selvages

CONTRAST EAR

CLAWS

MITTEN PALM

MITTEN BACK

EAR

THUMB

EAR

THUMB

36"

HAT FRONT

DANGLE

HAT BACK

CUTTING LAYOUT

① Measure, Mark, and Cut

Fold the fabric in half lengthwise with the right sides together, aligning the selvages. Position the paper pattern pieces according to the diagram. Make sure the grainline arrows on the pattern pieces are on the straight grain of the fabric so the pieces will stretch to fit the head and hands. Transfer the markings (center front/back, ear, and ribbon placement) to the wrong side of the fabric.

* **Hat back** (cut 2)
* **Hat front** (cut 2)
* **Ear** (cut 4)
* **Dangle** (cut 2)
* **Contrast ear** (cut 2 or cut from contrast fabric)

* **Mitten palm** (cut 4)
* **Mitten back** same piece as palm, but don't cut the thumb hole (cut 4)
* **Thumb** (cut 4)

To match Contrast Ear:

* **Claws** (cut 16 or cut from contrasting fabric)

NOTE: *Mirror the hat front and back along the line indicated on the pattern pieces.*

FABRIC NOTE

When working with a double-sided fleece, the terms "right side" and "wrong side" are relative. It is up to you to determine which side of the fabric to use as your right and wrong side, or which side to use as the primary color and which to use for the details. If you are unable to locate two-color reversible fleece, you can use scraps of another color to bring contrast to the ears and claws.

Monster-Wear Hat

1 Stitch the Ears

* Center and pin the wrong side of a contrast ear onto the right side of an ear with the bottom edges aligned. Zigzag around the curved raw edge of the contrast ear to join the two layers. Repeat with the other contrast ear and one more ear piece.
* With the right sides together, pin a stitched ear to one of the remaining ear pieces, aligning the raw edges. Stitch them together along the curved edge, leaving the straight edge open for turning. Repeat with the remaining pieces. Turn both ears right side out.
* Pin the ears onto the right side of the back hat at the placement marks, with the contrast ears facing up. Edgestitch them in place.

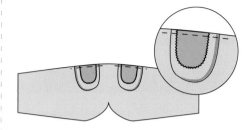

STEP 1

2 Attach the Hat Front and Hat Back

* With the right sides together, pin the long straight raw edges of the hat front and hat back, sandwiching the ears between the two layers. Stitch the pieces together to form the hat exterior.
* With the right sides together, fold the hat in half, aligning the curved raw edges at the back. Stitch the center back seam.
* Repeat with the remaining hat front and back pieces (no ears on the lining pieces) to create the lining.

ears tucked inside

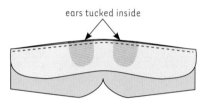

STEP 2

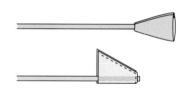

STEP 3

3 Make the Dangles and Ties

Cut two 8" pieces of ribbon or cording. With the right sides together, fold one dangle piece in half, aligning all raw edges and sandwiching the ribbon in between the two layers. Stitch along the outer edges while catching the end of the ribbon, leaving the bottom edge unstitched. Trim the seam allowance and turn the dangle right side out. Repeat with the other dangle and ribbon piece.

4 Attach the Ties

Tack the raw end of each ribbon onto the hat front at the placement marks.

5 Assemble the Exterior and Lining

Pin the hat and lining with the right sides together, aligning all raw edges and tucking the ties between the layers. Stitch around the outer edges, leaving a 3" opening along the back bottom edge for turning. Clip the seam allowance as needed. Turn the hat right side out. Topstitch around the edge of the hat with a ¼" seam allowance, closing the opening as you stitch.

Monster-Wear Mittens

① Make the Claws

* Pin the claw pieces in pairs with the right sides together. Stitch the curved edges, leaving the bottom straight edges open. Turn the eight claws right side out.

* To attach the claws, you'll need two palm pieces (thumb holes cut out) and two thumb pieces. Pin three claws on the placement lines on the right side of a palm piece, aligning the raw edges. Pin a fourth claw on the right side of the thumb piece placement line, aligning the raw edges. Do the same with the remaining claws, palm, and thumb. Edgestitch all the claws in place.

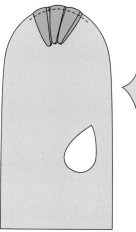

STEP 1

② Make and Attach the Thumb

* With the right sides together, fold a thumb in half along the center line. Two of the thumbs will have claws, which should be tucked toward the inside of the thumb. Stitch around the curved edge from the top to the dot; backstitch. Repeat with the remaining thumb pieces. Turn all the thumbs right side out.

* With the right sides together, position the raw edge of a thumb with a claw along the thumb hole of a palm piece with claws. Align the center marks and dot markings. Stitch the thumb and palm together. Repeat with the remaining thumb and palm with claws; these are the exterior palm pieces. Then repeat with the remaining palms and thumbs (without claws); they become the lining pieces.

③ Assemble the Mittens

* With the right sides together, align and pin the raw edges of an exterior palm piece and exterior back piece, with the claws and thumb sandwiched between. Stitch the pieces together along the curved edges, leaving the straight bottom edge open. Clip the seam allowances as needed and turn the mitten right side out. Repeat with remaining exterior pieces, and then with the lining pieces; do not turn the linings right side out.

* Insert a mitten exterior into a mitten lining (right sides together), aligning the side seams, thumbs, and raw edges. Stitch the pieces together around the raw edge, leaving a 3" opening for turning. Trim and clip the seam allowances as needed and turn the mitten right side out. Topstitch around the cuff edge at a ¼" seam allowance, closing the opening used for turning. Repeat to make the second mitten.

PIG & PIGLETS

Designed by Lorraine Teigland

This big pig has a zippered pocket containing six (or more, if you like) little piglets that look just like her! The piglets have Velcro snouts allowing them to "nurse" at the matching Velcro dots on Mama Pig's belly. Let her loose in your play pigsty and let your little farmer have at it. Mama is even big and sturdy enough for little tykes to "ride" her for a fun change of pace. At the end of a long day of farming, prop your feet on her for a bit of rest.

MATERIALS

* Locate the pattern in the envelope (sheets #7 and #9)
* 1 yard of 58/60" pink fleece
* 1 spool of coordinating thread
* Scraps of pink, black, white, and brown felt for eyes, ears, feet, nostrils
* ¼ yard (or fat eighth) of quilting-weight cotton or muslin for pocket
* 10" pink zipper
* Black embroidery floss
* 12" of pink yarn, cut into six 2" lengths, for piglet tails
* 6" length of Velcro, ⅝"- or ¾"-wide, cut into 6 circles; or 6 Velcro dots (preferably pink)
* 3" of ¼"-wide elastic for tail
* Two 12-ounce bags of fiberfill

Finished dimensions – Mama Pig is 12" tall × 20" long × 14" wide; Baby Pigs are 3" tall × 4½" long × 3½" wide

Seam allowance – ½" unless otherwise specified

① Measure, Mark, and Cut

Fold the fabric in half lengthwise with the right sides together, aligning the selvages. Position and pin the paper pattern pieces according to the diagram. Cut them out and transfer the markings from the pattern pieces to the wrong side of fabric. Then cut the additional pieces as listed.

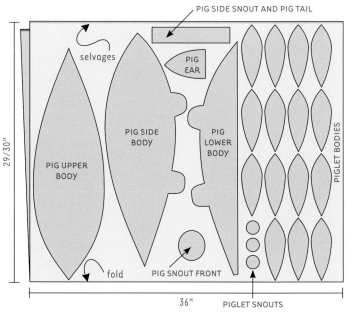

CUTTING LAYOUT

* **Pig side snout and pig tail** (cut 2)
* **Pig upper body** (cut 2)
* **Pig side body** (cut 2)
* **Pig lower body** (cut 2)
* **Pig ear** (cut 2)
* **Pig snout front** (cut 1)
* **Piglet body** 5 per piglet (cut 30)
* **Piglet snout** 1 per piglet (cut 6)

Cut from white felt:

* **Pig ear** (cut 2)
* **Piglet ear** 2 per piglet (cut 12)

Cut from darker pink felt:

* **Piglet ear** 2 per piglet (cut 12)
* **Piglet foot** 4 per piglet, (cut 24)
* **Pig nostrils** (cut 2, trace from pig snout front)

Cut from brown felt:

* **Piglet foot** 4 per piglet (cut 24)

Cut from black felt:

* **Pig eye** (cut 2, trace eye placement circle on upper body pattern)

Cut from cotton:

* **Inside pocket** 9" × 20" rectangle (cut 1)

NOTE: *Position the grainline arrow on the pattern pieces along the straight grain of the fabric. The smaller pieces, such as the ear and snout, can be fit in between the larger pieces.*

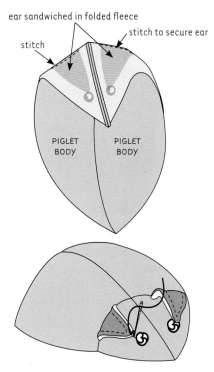

ear sandwiched in folded fleece

stitch to secure ear

stitch

PIGLET
BODY

PIGLET
BODY

STEP 3

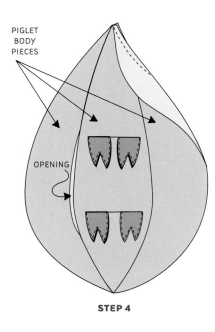

PIGLET
BODY
PIECES

OPENING

STEP 4

② Make Piglet Ears and Feet

* Pin the white piglet ears to the pink piglet ears. Edgestitch around all the sides.
* Pin the brown piglet feet to the pink piglet feet. Edgestitch around all the sides.

③ Make Piglet Upper Body

For each piglet body, do the following:

* Pin two piglet body pieces with the right sides together, and stitch along one curved edge.
* Using black floss, embroider two French knots for eyes on the front of the piglet body at the placement marks, one on each body piece.
* With the white side facing up, baste the straight edge of one piglet ear behind each eye at the placement marks. Fold the upper body at the fold marks with the right sides together, catching the straight edge of the ears in the fold. Stitch or hand-sew ⅛" from the fold to secure the bottom edge of the ear in the shallow fold of fabric.
* If you want the piglets to match their mama, tack the tips of the ears to the upper body.

④ Make Piglet Lower Body

For each piglet body, do the following:

* Baste the straight edge of four piglet feet to one piglet body at the placement marks (shaped end pointing toward back of piglet), with the pink side facing up. Fold the upper body at the fold marks with the right sides together, catching the straight edge of the feet in the fold. Stitch or hand-sew ⅛" from the fold (as for the ears). This becomes the piglet bottom.
* Pin the piglet bottom to a plain piglet body piece with the right sides together, and stitch along one curved edge. Stitch another piglet body piece to the other side of the piglet bottom, leaving a 2½" opening for turning and stuffing.

⑤ Complete the Piglets

For each piglet body, do the following:

* For the tail, knot one 2" length of yarn at both ends. Pin the upper body to the lower body, right sides together, and insert the yarn between layers at the piglet rear, letting one knotted end hang out. Stitch all around, catching the yarn in the stitching.

* Turn the piglet right side out through the opening and stuff. Hand-sew the opening closed with a slipstitch or whipstitch.

* Stitch the loop half of a Velcro circle in the center of the piglet snout. Hand-sew a running stitch close to the edge of the snout and pull the thread to gather and shape the snout. Stuff the snout lightly and then sew the gathered edges closed.

* Hand-sew the snout onto the piglet's face using a slipstitch or whipstitch.

STEP 5

⑥ Stitch the Pig Top Body

* Pin two upper body pieces together and stitch along the top edge. Stitch the pig eyes to the upper body at the placement marks.

* Pin the white pig ears to the pink pig ears with the right sides together. Stitch along the curved side edges, leaving the bottom edge open. Clip the seam allowance and turn the ears right side out. Attach the ears to the pig top body at fold placement marks, as you did for the piglet ears. Hand-tack the tip of each ear to the body at the placement marks.

⑦ Make the Pig Tail

* Fold the tail in half lengthwise with the right sides together. Pin a 3" length of elastic to one short edge so the elastic extends away from the tail. Stitch the long edge and the short edge with the elastic, catching the edge of the elastic in the seam. Leave the opposite short end open for turning.

* Turn the tail right side out (the elastic is now inside the tail) and pull the elastic tight to make the tail coil. Stitch the opening closed, catching the free end of the elastic in the stitching.

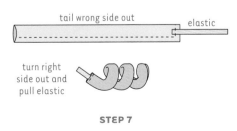

STEP 7

8 Create the Inner Pocket

* Open the zipper. With the right sides together, pin the zipper tape along the straight raw edge of one lower body at the zipper placement markings.
* Baste the zipper in place, using a zipper presser foot.
* With the right sides together, align one short edge of the pocket with the same lower body at the zipper placement markings, sandwiching the zipper between the fleece and pocket layers. The zipper pull should extend beyond the zipper placement markings.
* Stitch the layers together, using a zipper foot.
* Pin and stitch the opposite side of the zipper to opposite short edge of the pocket and remaining lower body in similar fashion.
* Fold the pocket in half widthwise with the right sides together, aligning the two lower body pieces at the same time. Stitch the side edges of the pocket.
* Stitch the lower body pieces together from the front tip to the zipper and from the zipper to the back tip, leaving an opening as marked on the pattern for stuffing and turning.

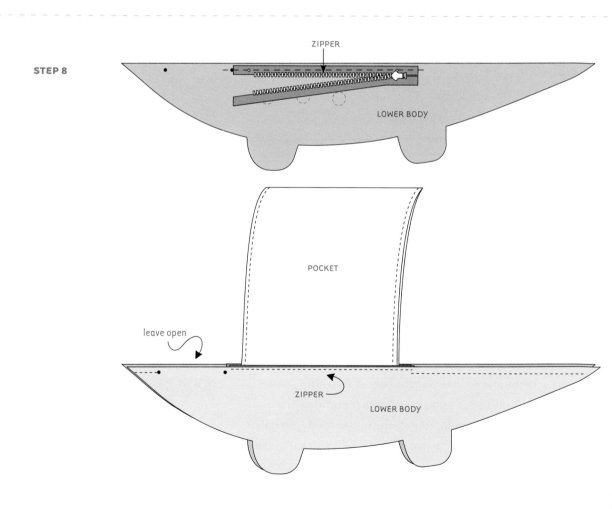

STEP 8

ZIPPER

LOWER BODY

POCKET

leave open

ZIPPER

LOWER BODY

⑨ Complete the Pig Body

* Stitch the hook half of the Velcro dots to the lower body, three on each side of the zipper at the placement marks.
* Pin a side body to one side of the lower body, aligning the feet and bottom raw edges. Stitch along the bottom edge. Repeat, stitching the remaining side body to the other side of the lower body.
* Pin the lower/side body and upper body with the right sides together, aligning the raw edges. Sandwich the tail between the layers at the rear and stitch the side seams.
* Turn the pig right side out through the opening. Stuff the pig, filling the feet firmly before stuffing the body. Insert all the piglets into the pocket about halfway through stuffing to ensure that you leave enough room for them inside the pig.
* Finish stuffing the pig firmly. Hand-sew the opening closed.

⑩ Attach the Snout

* Stitch the nostrils onto the pig snout.
* With the right sides together, fold the snout side in half across the width, aligning the short ends. Stitch the short edges to form a ring.
* Stitch the snout side to the snout with the right sides together. Stuff the snout, turn the raw edges to the inside, and hand-sew the snout to the pig face, centering it over the point where the seams all join.

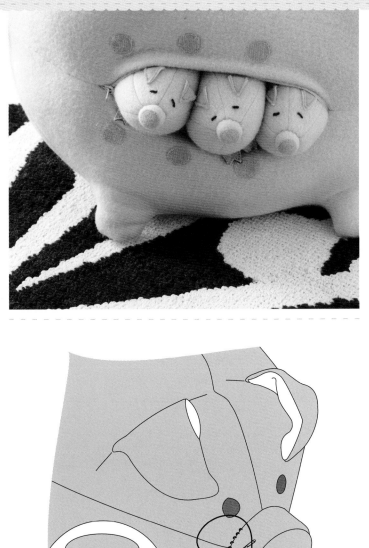

SNOUT SIDE

SNOUT FRONT

hand-sew to face

turn right side out and stuff

STEP 10

HUGH ManaTee

Designed by Lindsay Conner

With the marvelous manatee climbing up on the endangered species list, here's a way you can add to their soft, cuddly number. Create a new friend, pillow, or seat and raise environmental awareness at the same time. Careful attention to eyebrow placement can lend your manatee his (or her) own unique expression!

MATERIALS

* Locate the pattern in the envelope (sheet #8)
* 1 yard of 58/60" fleece
* 1 spool of coordinating thread
* Dark felt scraps for facial features
* Small piece of paper for face template
* Matching thread for felt
* 12 ounces of fiberfill

Finished dimensions – approximately 23" inches long × 6" tall
Seam allowance – ¼" unless otherwise specified

① Measure, Mark, and Cut

Lay out your fabric in a single layer with the right side facing up. Position the pattern pieces as shown, mirroring both along the indicated line on the pattern. There are no grainline arrows, so you can position the pieces as they fit best on the fabric. Cut them out and transfer the facial feature placement markings from the pattern pieces to the fabric.

Cut from fleece:

* **Top** (cut 1)
* **Bottom** (cut 1)

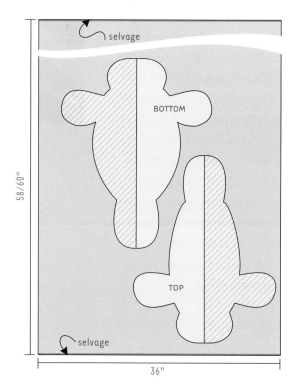

CUTTING LAYOUT

NOTE: *The white wavy line at the top indicates extra fabric not shown.*

② Make the Face

Trace the shapes of the facial features from the pattern onto a piece of paper to provide a template for the eyes, nostrils, and eyebrows. Cut out bits of dark felt for these pieces and hand-sew them to the right side of the top at the markings.

❸ Pin the Body Pieces

Pin the top and bottom pieces with the right sides together. Start by aligning and pinning the raw edges of the fins, tail, and head. Then, starting at the tail, pin the sides; as you near the fins, you'll notice about 1" of excess fabric on each side of the top piece. Pinch and fold the extra fabric toward the tail end to add shape to the body. Baste across the folds to hold them in place.

❹ Stitch the Manatee

* Starting on one side, stitch around all the edges, leaving a 3" opening for turning and stuffing at the tail. Stitch a reinforcing seam along the inner side of both fins.
* Turn the body right side out and stuff it with the fiberfill to the desired thickness and firmness. Stuff the face and fins well before moving to other areas of the manatee. The tail should contain less filling than the rest of the body. Hand-sew the opening closed with a slipstitch or whipstitch.
* Flip the manatee belly up. On each end of the mouth, fold the mouth flaps ½" toward belly, so mouth appears to downturn slightly. Hand-sew to secure.

BUTTON-UP BOLERO

Designed by Caroline Critchfield

With the exception of some simple hand-finishing techniques, you won't believe how easy this project is to complete without your sewing machine! *A bit like origami, once folded, your fabric becomes a little jacket with a fold-back collar and cuffs. The bolero simply folds together and is secured with buttons all along the front and the back of the sleeves. Adorable blanket stitching along the edges gives it a perfect finished look.*

MATERIALS

* Locate the pattern in the envelope (sheet #7)
* 1 yard of 58/60" fleece
* Embroidery floss or pearl cotton in a coordinating color
* 15 buttons, 1" to 1½" in diameter
* 1 spool of coordinating thread

Sizes – 12-18 mo, 2T, 4T, 6, 8

① Determine Your Child's Size

Measure your child's chest to find the size.

	12-18 months	2T	4T	6	8
Chest size	19"	21"	23"	25"	26½"

② Measure, Mark, and Cut

Lay out the fabric in a single layer with the right side facing up. Pin the pattern piece directly onto the fabric and cut it out. Transfer the markings for button placement before removing the paper pattern piece. Then cut along the five solid lines per the pattern.

* <u>Bolero</u> (cut 1)

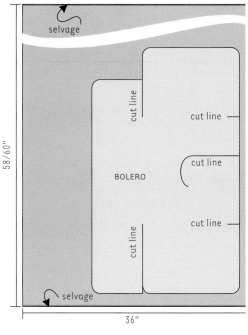

CUTTING LAYOUT

NOTES: *Position the grainline arrow on the pattern piece along the straight grain of the fabric. The white wavy line at the top indicates extra fabric not shown.*

❸ Finish All the Raw Edges

Thread an embroidery needle with embroidery floss (or pearl cotton) and choose a point along the edge of the jacket where you wish to begin stitching. A good location is the bottom edge of the sleeve, as this location will be least visible on your finished bolero. Stitch all the raw edges all the way around the bolero with a blanket stitch (*see the glossary*).

❹ Fold and Button the Bolero

* Lay out the jacket with the wrong side facing up. Fold the right upper sleeve section down and the front lapel over, as shown. Fold the lower right section to the center, overlapping the upper front section by a few inches. Ensure that the corner fits snugly and that the bottom edge is straight. Place four pins at the button placement marks as indicated on the pattern piece.

* Turn the jacket over and fold the front of the sleeve so that it overlaps the back by a few inches. Fold the cuff back about 1¾" and place three pins on the back of the sleeve as indicated on the pattern piece. One pin should be close to the armpit to tightly close up any hole there, the second pin should be over the cuff, and the last pin should be halfway in between.

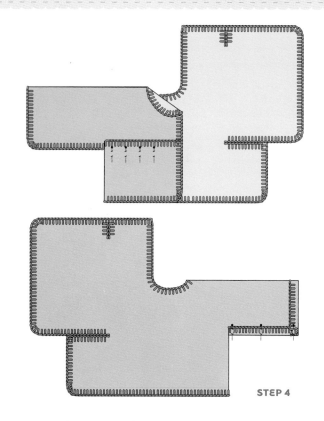

STEP 4

* Repeat the previous folding steps with the left side of the jacket, noting that you will only need three pins to secure the left front pieces. Sew buttons on at each designated position, through the layers of overlapped fabric, to hold the shape of the jacket body and sleeves. For closure, stitch on two more buttons, evenly spaced, along the left center front edge as shown in the photograph.

❺ Make Buttonholes

Mark three vertical buttonholes on the right front edge of the garment as they correspond to the three center front buttons. Carefully cut the buttonholes on the right front, long enough to accommodate the diameter of the buttons. Note that the center buttonhole will be cut through two layers of fabric. Hand-sew around the buttonholes with a small blanket stitch.

BUNNY PILLOW

Designed by Marlene Gaige

A great floor cushion or a perfect pillow pal, this bunny is a huggable ball of fluff!
Using a doll joint allows you to swivel the head, adding even more to its already
abundant personality. But you can skip that for simplicity's sake if you like!

MATERIALS

* Locate the pattern in the envelope (sheets #5 and #6)
* 1 yard of 58/60" polar fleece or knit fake fur
* Scrap of pink or other contrasting fleece (for ears, nose, and paw pads)
* Scrap of white fleece (for tail)
* 1 spool of coordinating thread
* Small saucer or plate (about 7" in diameter) for use as circle template
* 30mm safety eyes (other options: glass eyes, buttons, or felt/fleece scraps)
* Small amount of fiberfill
* 4 long pipe cleaners
* Embroidery floss or pearl cotton for nose and mouth (pink, black, or other color of your choice)
* 24" × 24" pillow form
* 65mm plastic doll joint (optional)

Finished dimensions – approximately 22" square × 9" high, including head

Seam allowance – ½" unless otherwise specified

① Measure, Mark, and Cut

With the right sides together, fold your fabric in half lengthwise, aligning the selvages. On the main fabric, mark a 23" square for the bunny body and position the head and ear pattern pieces as shown. Cut out the pieces, and transfer the markings from the pattern pieces to the fabric. From the pink (or other color) contrasting fleece, use the patterns to cut out two ears, one nose, two back paws with four toes, and two front paws with four toes. From the white fleece, use the pattern to cut out one tail.

TIP: *When working with thick fleece or faux fur, it helps to trace the paper patterns onto thin cardboard, boxboard, or template plastic.*

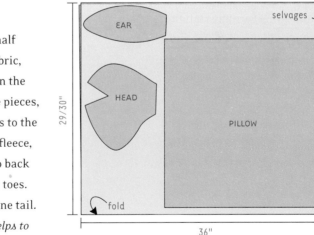

CUTTING LAYOUT

Cut from main fabric:
* **Head** (cut 2)
* **Ear** (cut 2)
* **Pillow** 23" square (cut 2)

Cut from pink (contrasting) fleece:
* **Front paw** (cut 2)
* **Back paw** (cut 2)
* **Ear** (cut 2)
* **Nose** (cut 1)

Cut from white fleece:
* **Tail** (cut 1, mirror along lines indicated on the pattern)

NOTE: *Position the grainline arrow on pattern pieces along the straight grain of the fabric.*

➋ Make the Pillow Base

* Use the small plate or saucer (or the tail pattern piece) as a template to round off the corners on both pillow pieces.
* On the right side of one pillow piece, position and appliqué (*see the glossary*) the paw prints on all four corners, keeping them at least 1½" from the raw edge for seam allowance. Toes should face the corner edges. This piece becomes the pillow bottom.
* Pin the two pillow pieces with the right sides together, and stitch around the outer edges, leaving a 10" opening along one straight edge for turning and stuffing.
* Turn the pillow right side out through the opening. Partially stuff the rounded corners with fiberfill, using just a handful of fiberfill for each corner. Set the pillow aside.

➌ Make and Attach the Head

* Pin the dart openings on each head piece closed with the right sides together and stitch with a scant ¼" seam allowance.
* Pin the heads with the right sides together and stitch around the outer curve, leaving the bottom straight edge open. Notch the curves and turn the head right side out.

* Install safety eyes at the placement marks on each side of the head, following the manufacturer's instructions. (If you are using something other than safety eyes, stitch them in place.)
* Stuff the head firmly. If you are using a plastic doll joint, insert the male side into the head. Gather the head bottom closed, turning the raw edge to the inside as you go.
* Mark the head placement on the pillow top: 5" from the top seam and centered side to side. If you are using a doll joint, insert the 6" plastic circle inside the pillow before adding the washer and locking the disc. If you are not using a doll joint, hand-sew the head securely at the placement mark.

➍ Make and Attach the Ears

* With the right sides together, pin one ear from the main fabric to one ear from the contrasting fabric. Stitch around the outer curved edge, leaving the bottom straight edge open. Trim the seam allowances and turn the ear right side out. Repeat with the remaining ear pieces.
* Twist two pipe cleaners together at each end, and make a rough ear shape. Repeat with the two remaining pipe cleaners. Turn the bottom edges of the ears to the inside. One at a time, insert the pipe cleaners into the ears and baste across the bottom of the ears to secure the pipe cleaners.
* Fold the bottom of each ear in half lengthwise with the pink/contrasting fabric on the inside. Hand-sew the ears onto the head, with each one centered on a dart, 2" below the center seam and the contrasting part of the ear facing toward the eyes.

➎ Stitch the Nose

Hand-sew the nose onto the point of the head, over the seam. Embroider the mouth and outline around the nose as shown with an outline stitch and embroidery floss.

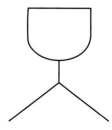

⑥ Add Finishing Touches

* Insert the pillow form into the pillow and hand-sew the opening closed with a slipstitch or whipstitch.

* With knotted thread, sew a running stitch around the outer edge of the tail circle. Pull the thread to gather the circle and stuff it with fiberfill before pulling it closed and tying it off. Hand-sew the tail to the pillow top, just above the back seam and centered side to side.

TIP: *If you are using very fluffy fleece or faux fur, you may want to pick the fur out of the seams for a more polished look.*

"WORK in COMFORT" TRAVEL SET

Neck Pillow designed by Jennifer Blum

Lap Desk designed by Patricia Hoskins

The soft and comfy neck pillow provides support for snoozes in the car, plane, train, or bus. Whether it's time to eat or to work, the lap desk provides the perfect surface, complete with shallow storage pockets on each side. An envelope closure and Velcro attachments mean that you can take the tray off and the stuffing out for laundering. If you want to take the lap desk on a flight, save packing room and weight by removing the pillow form and stuffing the lap desk with some of your packed clothes instead!

VELCRO OPTIONS

Home decor Velcro has adhesive on one half for adhering to hard surfaces, while the other half is a traditional sew-on variety. Since one side of the Velcro will be attached to the tray, this type of Velcro is ideal. However, an alternate solution is to use sew-on Velcro and strong, permanent glue to adhere to the tray.

MATERIALS

* Locate the pattern in the envelope (sheet #8)
* 1 yard of 58/60" fleece
* 1 spool of coordinating thread
* 12 ounces of polyester fiberfill (divided in half for each project)

For the Neck Pillow:

* Carabiner or similar clip (optional)

For the Lap Desk:

* ½ yard of 44/45" muslin for the pillow form
* Two to three 2-pound bags of poly pellets or similar pellet (beanbag) stuffing material
* ⅓ yard of NU-Foam, thick batting, or upholstery foam (optional)
* 12" × 16" melamine tray
* ⅓ yard of home decor Velcro

Finished dimensions – Neck Pillow is 14" across; Lap Desk is 16" × 12" × 3" high

Seam allowance – ½" unless otherwise specified

NOTE: *Keep in mind that the neck pillow and lap desk are cut from the same yard of fabric. Place your pattern pieces economically, following the cutting layout. See each project for details.*

1 Measure, Mark, and Cut

Lay out your fabric in a single layer with the wrong side facing up. Position and pin the paper pattern pieces according to the diagram. Cut them out and transfer the markings from the pattern pieces to the wrong side of fabric. Then cut the additional pieces as listed.

* **Neck Pillow** (cut 2)
* **Clip loop** 4" × 1" (cut 1) (optional)
* **Lap Desk top** 13" × 17" (cut 1)
* **Lap Desk bottom** 13" × 12" (cut 2)
* **Long side** 4" × 17" (cut 2)
* **Short side** 4" × 13" (cut 2)
* **Pocket** 4" × 9" (cut 2)

Cut from muslin:

* **Lap Desk top/bottom** 17" × 13" (cut 2)
* **Long side** 17" × 4" (cut 2)
* **Short side** 13" × 4" (cut 2)

Cut from foam/batting (optional):

* **Lap Desk top** 12" × 16" (cut 1)

NOTE: *Position the grainline arrow on the pattern piece along the straight grain of the fabric. Mirror the Neck Pillow along the line indiated on the pattern.*

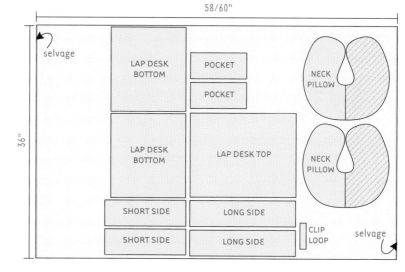

58/60"

selvage

LAP DESK BOTTOM	POCKET	NECK PILLOW
LAP DESK BOTTOM	LAP DESK TOP	NECK PILLOW
SHORT SIDE	LONG SIDE	
SHORT SIDE	LONG SIDE	CLIP LOOP

POCKET

36"

selvage

CUTTING LAYOUT

Neck Pillow

❶ Create the Clip Loop

Fold the clip loop piece in half with the wrong sides together, aligning short ends. Baste the short ends together.

❷ Stitch the Pillow

Pin the two pillow pieces with the right sides together, aligning the raw edges. Insert the clip loop between the layers, with the basted raw edges extending slightly past the pillow raw edges (anywhere along the outside edge is fine for the clip loop). Stitch around the edges, leaving a 3" opening for turning and stuffing. Notch the curves and turn the pillow right side out. Stuff the pillow with fiberfill and hand-sew the opening closed with a slipstitch. You can clip a carabiner through the loop so you can clip the pillow to your luggage.

Lap Desk

❶ Make the Pillow Form

* Starting and stopping ½" in from each corner, stitch both muslin short sides to one muslin top/bottom with the right sides together. Then stitch both long sides to the same top/bottom in the same fashion. The seams should meet but not cross.

* Stitch all four sides to the remaining top/bottom in the same fashion, leaving a 6" opening in the center of one side for turning and stuffing.

* Starting and stopping ½" in from each corner, stitch all four side seams. Clip the corners. Turn the pillow form right side out, pushing out all corners.

* If you are using foam or batting, insert it into the pillow form, aligning the corners. Stuff the corners and sides with fiberfill. Finish stuffing with pellets to the desired firmness. Slipstitch the opening closed and set the pillow form aside. If you aren't using foam or batting, stuff the entire form with fiberfill and pellets and slipstitch the opening closed.

❷ Make the Envelope Back

* Hem each fleece bottom piece along one 13" edge by pressing under ¼", then another ¾". Edgestitch close to the inner fold.

* Place both bottom pieces right side up and overlap the hemmed edges approximately 2½". Use the top piece as a template so that the overlapped pieces together measure the same length and width as the top piece. Baste the bottom pieces together with an edgestitch along the overlapped side raw edges.

③ Make and Attach the Side Pockets

* Make a ¼" double-fold hem along the top edge of each pocket, then fold and press each side edge ½" to the wrong side.
* Position each pocket on one short side so the pocket is centered from side to side, and the bottom edges are aligned. The hemmed pocket top edge should be ½" below the top edge of the side piece. Edgestitch the pockets in place along the sides and bottom edges.
* If you wish, create narrow channels on one or both pockets with vertical lines of topstitching. For instance, create channels just wide enough for a box of crayons or digital devices.

④ Attach Velcro to the Top

Cut the Velcro into four 3" lengths. Stitch the loop halves to the right side of the fleece top, 3" in from each corner.

⑤ Make the Lap Desk Base

* Starting and stopping ½" in from each corner and with the right sides together, stitch both fleece short sides to the top as you did for the pillow form. Take care not to catch the top of the pockets in the stitching. Stitch both long sides to the top in similar fashion.
* Stitch all four sides to the pieced envelope bottom with the right sides together and in the same fashion. You do not need to leave an opening for turning and stuffing.
* Starting and stopping ½" in from each corner, stitch all four side seams. Clip the corners and turn the lap desk base right side out, pushing out all the corners.
* Insert the pillow form through the envelope closure.

⑥ Complete the Lap Desk

Attach the Velcro hook halves to the bottom of the tray to align with the loop halves sewn to the fleece top. If you are using home decor Velcro, the hook halves already have adhesive on them. If you are using sew-on Velcro, adhere the hook halves to the tray with a permanent adhesive, following the manufacturer's instructions.

CHAPTER 9

Knits

Knits are typically quite stretchy and flexible, although the amount and direction of stretch varies widely from one type of knit to the next. A knit may stretch in one direction or both directions, and may stretch very little, or over 50 percent! This is an important consideration when choosing fabric for a specific project. Pay attention to instructions that call for "stretch knits only" and don't try to substitute a woven fabric, or you'll be very disappointed in the results! That said, you can use knits in projects designed for woven fabrics, but choose a stable knit fabric with minimal stretch.

Fabric Facts

Knitted fabrics can be made from just about any fiber, including cotton, wool, rayon, and more. While woven fabrics are produced by interlacing threads in two directions (warp and weft), knits are made with a series of interlocking loops. Lengthwise columns of stitches are called ribs; crosswise rows are called courses. The designations "ribs" and "courses" for knits correspond to "straight grainline" and "crossgrain."

Jersey knit is the most basic and common knit fabric. Jersey stretches crosswise and has little lengthwise stretch. It is soft with great drape and the vertical ribs are visible on the right side, while the horizontal courses (loops) are visible on the wrong side. Your favorite comfy T-shirt is a great example of a basic cotton jersey knit.

Double knits, as the name implies, are double the thickness. The fabric surface looks the same on both sides and appears finely ribbed. Double knit fabric is stable; it stretches only a little bit and has great shape retention. While 1970s polyester double knit is probably the first thing that comes to mind when you hear the term, rest assured there are many double knit fabrics out there that are lovely!

Interlock is also a double-sided fabric with a fine rib on both sides, but it is much lighter in weight than double knit, and has better drape and moderate crosswise stretch. Interlock is made by interlocking two ribbed fabrics, each made with a single yarn. They are commonly found in solids, yarn-dyed stripes, and prints.

Other knits you might be familiar with include ribbing, sweatshirt fleece, terrycloth, and velour.

Attributes

When used in garment construction, knits need much less wearing ease than wovens, so you need less fabric and the fit is easier. Knits are also resistant to wrinkles and do not crease well. To determine the right side, stretch the cut edge and it will curl toward the right side. That said, regardless of the "right" side, use the side you like best as the "right" side! There are definitely fabrics where you'll like the look of the "wrong" side best.

Needle Type(s)

Use ballpoint needles, which slip between the fibers rather than piercing the fibers. 70/10 or 80/12 are suitable sizes for most knits.

Sewing Machine Accessories

Sergers are awesome, but not necessary for sewing with knits. When using a sewing machine, try a walking foot to minimize unwanted stretching during stitching (double knits, however, stitch up well with a standard presser foot). Polyester or poly-blend thread has inherent stretch, so it is the preferred thread for sewing with knits. Don't wind your bobbin at a high speed, because that can stretch the thread and cause puckering at your seams.

Stitch Types, Tips, and Machine Settings

When using a sewing machine, stitch most seams with a small zigzag or stretch stitch. Alternatively, you can sew with a straight (nonstretch) stitch, if you use a "stretch-as-you-sew" technique. Make the stitch length longer, between 3mm or 4mm, and manually stretch the fabric as you feed it through the machine. When the knit fabric relaxes to its original state after stitching, the stitches will "bunch up" and appear much shorter; however the stitches will stretch as the fabric stretches while the garment is being worn. An additional hint: If your seams are wavy, lengthen the stitch setting. Conversely, shorten the stitch length if your seams are puckering. When stitching a lightweight knit, the fabric may have a tendency to bunch at the beginning of the seam, or get caught in the throat plate. To avoid this, instead of backstitching, leave your thread tails long and tie off in a knot at the beginning and end of each seam.

Marking

Soap slivers, fabric markers, or chalk are good marking tools for knits, though you should avoid using wax-marking methods on cotton fabrics.

Cutting

Make sure the entire length of fabric is on the work surface and not hanging off, to avoid stretching and distorting. Pins may also stretch and distort the fabric, so consider using pattern weights to hold the pattern pieces in place. Scissors may stretch the fabric during cutting, so you might have better success with a rotary cutter. Treat knits as a napped fabric, even though they may not have nap, because the knit stitch has a visible direction that may show up through subtle shading. Mark the direction on the wrong side of the fabric.

Interfacing

Interfacing is not frequently used with knitted fabrics, since the finished project is typically meant to be less structured than an item made from woven material. When necessary, use a fusible knit interfacing, which has crosswise stretch.

Special Equipment

Use hem clips, binder clips, or similar tools to keep raw edges from curling during stitching.

Seams

Knits do not typically unravel; however, they can stretch out of shape. You may want to stabilize seams that will be under a lot of stress with clear elastic, which helps maintain stretch in the seam but prevents the garment from losing shape at shoulders and necklines. Stabilize seams that do not need to retain their stretch with seam tape.

Pressing and Ironing

When pressing, be sure to lift the iron when you move it; if you drag the iron across the fabric, you can stretch it out of shape. Press in the direction of the lengthwise ribs. Choose a heat setting appropriate to the fiber composition (cotton, wool, polyester).

Fabric Care

Care depends on fiber content. Prewash (if appropriate because of shrinkage) using the same care method you intend to use for the finished item. Some cotton knits have progressive shrinkage, meaning that they continue to shrink slightly with each wash. To minimize this problem in your finished project, prewash and machine dry two or three times before cutting.

CHEEKY PANTY & CAMI SET

Designed by Sarah Seitz

Every girl needs a comfortable and cute camisole and panty set. The problem is, they can be difficult to find in colorful and whimsical prints and patterns. Look no further! This adorable, sexy pair of knickers is a cinch to make.

MATERIALS

* Locate the pattern in the envelope (sheet #8)
* 1 yard of 54/60" knit fabric
* 1 spool of coordinating thread
* 4 yards of stretch lace
* 1¼ yards of ½"-wide elastic

For the cami only:

* ⅛ yard of ⅜"-wide clear elastic

Sizes – camisole is S, M, L; panty is XS, S, M, L, XL

Seam allowance – ½" and should be sewn with a zigzag or stretch stitch, unless otherwise specified

① Determine Your Size

Measure your bust to find the right size for the camisole.

	S	M	L
Bust size	34"	36"	38"

Measure your hips to find the right size for the panties.

	XS	S	M	L	XL
Hip size	35"	37"	39"	42"	44"

② Measure, Mark, and Cut

Lay out your fabric in a single layer with the right side facing up, then fold the selvages 11" and 13" toward the center, as shown. Position the pattern pieces according to the layout, along the fabric folds where indicated, and cut them out.

* **Cami bodice front** (cut 1 on fold)
* **Cami bodice back** (cut 1 on fold)
* **Cami skirt front/back** (cut 2 on fold)
* **Panty front** (cut 1 on fold)
* **Panty back** (cut 1 on fold)
* **Panty lining** (cut 1)

In addition to the paper pattern pieces, measure and mark the following:
* **Cami binding/shoulder straps** 30½" × 2" (cut 2)

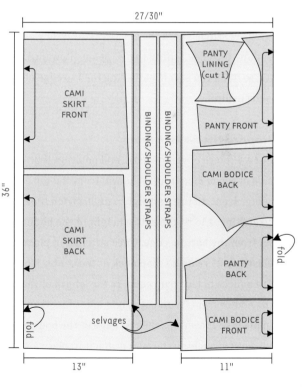

CUTTING LAYOUT

NOTE: *Position the grainline arrow on the pattern pieces along the straight grain of the fabric.*

Camisole

① Stitch the Sides

With the right sides together, stitch the side seams of the cami skirt front and back. Press the seams open and turn the skirt right side out. Mark the center point on the top edge of both front and back.

② Gather the Top Edge of the Skirt

Cut a length of ¼" elastic equal to your chest measurement, just underneath your bust. Divide the elastic into quarters and mark it accordingly. Starting at one side seam, pin the elastic to the top edge of the skirt, matching the markings on the elastic with the center front, opposite side seams and center back markings. This should help distribute the elastic evenly across the skirt. Using a wide zigzag stitch, stitch the elastic to the wrong side of the skirt around the top edge, within the ½" seam allowance. Stretch the elastic to fit as you stitch, gathering the top edge of the skirt. Set the skirt aside.

③ Prepare the Bodice Front

* Cut a 4" piece of clear elastic and position it on the wrong side of the bodice front, ½" down from the top edge, along the center front. Using a straight stitch, stitch the elastic in place, stretching it to fit the entire height of the bodice, stopping ½" from the bottom edge. Once stitched in place, the relaxed elastic will create a scoop neck at the center front.
* Cut a piece of lace trim equal to the length of the top edge of the bodice front. With both right sides facing up, pin the lace in place so it overlaps the raw edge of the bodice front by ½". Without stretching the lace, stitch it in place along the bottom edge of the lace, curving it naturally with the top edge of the bodice front. Stitch again, this time where the lace overlaps the raw edge of the fabric.

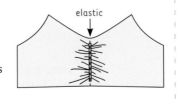

elastic

④ Stitch the Bodice Front and Back

With the right sides together, pin the bodice front and back together and stitch the side seams. Press the seams open.

⑤ Attach the Skirt

With the right sides together, pin the skirt to the bodice, aligning the bottom edge of the bodice with the top edge of the skirt and matching the side seams. Stitch along the bottom edge of the elastic, stretching the skirt to fit the bodice. Press the seam allowance up toward the bodice.

⑥ Bind the Cami

* With the right sides together, stitch the short ends of the binding pieces together to create one 60" long piece. Press seam open. Fold and press the binding in half lengthwise with the wrong sides together. Open the binding and, with the wrong side facing up, fold and press each long edge to the center crease. Refold the binding in half length-wise along the original fold line.
* Pin the seam in the binding to the center back of the bodice, encasing the raw edge of the bodice between the layers of the binding. Continue pinning the binding to the bodice, working from the center back in both directions, past the side seams and up the front underarm, fully encasing the raw edge. Extra bind-ing will extend off both front edges of the bodice.

＊ Using a straight stitch, edgestitch the binding to the bodice along both long edges. Continue stitching along the binding that extends off the edge of the bodice.

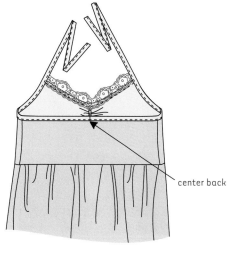

center back

STEP 6

🔟 **Hem the Cami**

＊ With both right sides facing up and starting at a side seam, pin the lace trim along the bottom edge of the cami, so it overlaps the raw edge of the skirt by ½". Without stretching the lace or the skirt, stitch it in place along the edge of the lace. Stitch again, this time where the lace overlaps the raw edge of the fabric. Alternatively, you may finish the bottom edge of the cami with a double-fold hem.

🔟 **Position the Shoulder Straps**

Try on the cami and, with some assistance, pin the ends of the straps to the bodice back, approximately 3" from each side seam, or wherever they feel most comfortable. Make sure that the straps are not twisted. Note that you may need to shorten the straps. Remove the cami and stitch the straps to the wrong side of the bodice back binding.

Panties

❶ Attach the Lining

* Fold the short end of the lining piece ¼" to the wrong side and stitch. As an option, you may also serge this edge.
* With both wrong sides facing up, pin the lining to the panty back along the straight edge. With the right sides together, pin the panty front and back (including the lining) along the same straight edge. Stitch all three layers together, as pinned.
* Fold and press the lining toward the front piece, covering the seam allowance. Edgestitch the lining in place along the two curved leg edges.

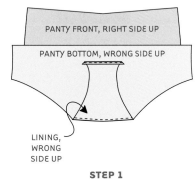

PANTY FRONT, RIGHT SIDE UP

PANTY BOTTOM, WRONG SIDE UP

LINING, WRONG SIDE UP

STEP 1

❷ Apply Lace to the Leg Openings

* Cut a piece of lace trim the length of the leg edge, minus 3". With both right sides facing up, pin the ends of the lace to each end of the leg opening, overlapping the raw edge of the panty by ½". Pin the center of the lace at the crotch seam.
* Stitch along the edge of the lace, stretching it to fit the leg opening between the pins. Stitch again, this time where the lace overlaps the raw edge of the fabric.
* Repeat with the second leg opening.

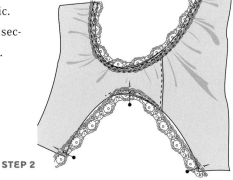

STEP 2

❸ Apply Lace to the Waist

Cut a piece of lace trim the length of the front waist edge, minus 3". With both right sides facing up, pin the ends of the lace to each end of the front waist, overlapping the raw edge of the panty with the lace by ½". Pin the center of the lace to the center front of the front piece. Stitch the lace in place following the technique as described in step 2. Repeat, to stitch lace trim along the back waist edge.

❹ Stitch the Front and Back

Position the front and back pieces with the right sides together, and stitch along both side seams. Press the seams open. Turn the panties right side out and press with a warm iron to loosen any wrinkles.

HOODED WRAP SHIRT

Designed by Annelie Hervi

Knits are so soft, and your little one will certainly enjoy the comfort of this hooded wrap shirt. This unique top has great layering potential and works well for both girls and boys. As an added bonus, it doesn't require any buttons, zippers, snaps, or other trim; a yard of fabric and some thread are all you need!

MATERIALS

* Locate the pattern in the envelope (sheet #9)
* 1 yard of 44/45" knit fabric
* 1 spool of coordinating thread

Sizes – 18-24 months and 2/3T
Seam allowance – ½" unless otherwise specified

1 Determine Your Child's Size

Measure the child's chest to find the right size.

	18-24 mo	**2-3T**
Chest size	19"-20"	21"-22"

2 Measure, Mark, and Cut

Fold your fabric in half lengthwise with the right sides together, aligning the selvages. Position the pattern pieces according to the layout, and draw the additional piece listed. Cut out the pieces and transfer markings from the pattern pieces to the wrong side of fabric.

* **Front** (cut 2)
* **Back** (cut 1 on fold)
* **Sleeve** (cut 2)
* **Hood** (cut 2)
* **Tie** 2¾" × 24"(cut 2)

NOTE: *Position the grainline arrow on the pattern pieces along the straight grain of the fabric.*

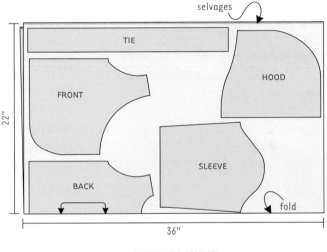

CUTTING LAYOUT

3 Attach the Front, Back, and Sleeves

With the right sides together, pin the front to the back at the shoulder seams; stitch. Press the seam allowances open. With the right sides together, pin the top edge of a sleeve to each armhole opening, aligning the raw edges. Stitch the shirt and sleeves together and press the seam allowances away from the sleeves, toward the shirt.

④ Stitch the Side Seams

With the right sides together, stitch the left side seam and underarm seam in one continuous seam. Repeat for the right side seam, taking care to leave a 1" opening as indicated on the pattern piece. Press the seam allowances open. Edgestitch around the side seam opening.

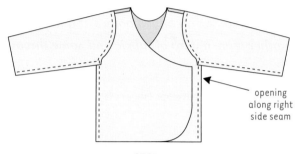

opening along right side seam

STEP 4

⑤ Make and Attach the Hood

* With the right sides together, stitch the hood pieces together along the center back seam. Press the seam allowances open.
* Press under the front edge of the hood ½" to the wrong side, then press under another ½". Topstitch close to the folded edge.
* With right sides together, position the hood along the neck edge, aligning the center back seam of the hood with the center back of the shirt. Stitch the hood to the shirt. Note that the front edges of the hood will extend to where the right and left front overlap.

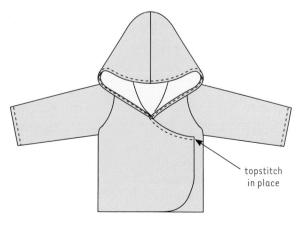

topstitch in place

STEP 5

* Press the seam allowances away from the hood, toward the shirt. In doing so, note that the remaining raw edge that extends beyond the hood on the shirt front will also be turned ½" to the wrong side. Topstitch in place.

⑥ Hem the Shirt Edges

Turn and press the sleeve openings ½" to the wrong side and topstitch them in place. Turn and press the remaining side and bottom curved raw edges of the shirt ½" to the wrong side and topstitch in place.

⑦ Make and Attach the Ties

* Fold each tie in half lengthwise with the right sides together and stitch along the three unfinished edges, leaving a 2" opening along the long side for turning. Clip the corners, turn the ties right side out and press. Edgestitch along all four edges of both ties.
* Pin the ties on the wrong side of the shirt front edges as indicated on the pattern piece so the ties extend off the shirt. Box stitch the tie ends in place.

ROLLER SKATE ROMPER

Designed by Katie Varela

Get ready for some roller boogie, toddler style! This fun, vintage, 80s-inspired romper is perfect for knit fabrics. It looks great made all in one print, or you can try fun variations like adding a contrasting fabric for the shoulder ties and waistband. Have some fun, strap on the roller skates, and go, go, GO!

MATERIALS

* Locate the pattern in the envelope (sheet #8)
* 1 yard of 44/45" knit fabric
* 1 spool of coordinating thread
* ⅔ yard of ¾"-wide elastic

Sizes – 0-6 months, 6-12 months, 12-18 months, 2T
Seam allowance – ½" unless otherwise specified

① Determine Your Child's Size

Measure the child's waist to find the right size.

	0-6 months	6-12 months	12-18 months	2T
Waist size	19"	20"	20½"	21"

② Measure, Mark, and Cut

Fold your fabric in half lengthwise with the right sides together, aligning the selvages. Position the pattern pieces according to the layout, and draw the additional pieces listed below. Cut out the pieces and transfer markings from the pattern to the wrong side of the fabric.

* **Shirt front** (cut 1 on fold)
* **Shirt back** (cut 1 on fold)
* **Shorts front** (cut 2)
* **Shorts back** (cut 2)
* **Waistband** (cut 1 on fold)

In addition to the paper pattern pieces, measure and mark the following:

* **Front/back binding** 1½" × 5" (cut 2)
* **Armhole binding/shoulder ties** 1½" × 30" (cut 2 on fold)

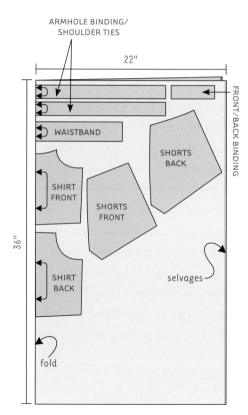

CUTTING LAYOUT

NOTE: *Position the grainline arrow on the pattern pieces along the straight grain of the fabric.*

③ Stitch the Shorts

* With the right sides together, pin and stitch the shorts front pieces along the center front. Press the seam allowances open.

* With the right sides together, pin and stitch the shorts back pieces along the center back. Press the seam allowances open.

* Pin and stitch the shorts front and shorts back, with the right sides together, along the side seams and inseam. Press all the seam allowances open and turn the shorts right side out.

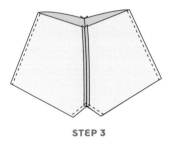

STEP 3

④ Stitch the Shirt

Pin the shirt front and shirt back with the right sides together along the side seams; stitch. Press open the seam allowances.

⑤ Attach the Shirt and Shorts

With the right sides together, pin the bottom edge of the shirt to the top edge of the shorts, matching the side seams and aligning the raw edges. Stitch the shirt and shorts together along the waist seam.

6 Attach the Waistband

* Stitch the short ends of the waistband with the right sides together, creating a circle. Press the seam allowances open. Fold and press both long edges of the waistband ½" to the wrong side.
* With both right sides facing up, center and pin the waistband over the waist seam of the romper, aligning the waistband seam with one of the side seams of the romper.
* Using a zigzag stitch, sew the waistband to the romper along the top edge of the waistband. Sew along the bottom edge of the waistband, leaving a 2" opening at one side seam.
* Cut the elastic to the appropriate length to comfortably fit around the child's belly, adding an extra 1". Slide the elastic through the waistband casing, overlap the ends by ½", and stitch the ends together securely. Slide the elastic ends back into the casing and stitch the opening closed.

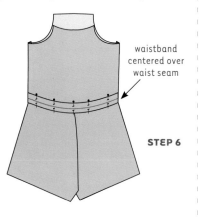

waistband centered over waist seam

STEP 6

7 Attach Binding and Straps

* Fold the front/back binding pieces and the armhole binding/ shoulder tie pieces in half lengthwise with the wrong sides together and press. Open the binding pieces with the wrong sides facing up and fold and press each long edge to the center crease. Refold the binding in half lengthwise along the original fold line.
* Pin the front and back binding strips along the top straight edges of the romper front and back, fully encasing the raw edges. Edgestitch the binding strips in place and trim away any binding that extends beyond the edges of the front and back.
* Mark the halfway point on each armhole binding/shoulder tie piece.

* Pin the halfway point of the armhole binding/shoulder tie piece, matching the halfway point with the armhole side seam. Continue pinning the binding to the romper, from the side seam around the armhole in both directions to encase the raw armhole edges. The armhole binding/shoulder tie piece will extend beyond the edge of the romper in both the front and back to make the tie ends. Stitch the binding to the romper and continue stitching the entire length of the ties, stitching the ends closed. Repeat for the other armhole.
* Try on the romper and tie the shoulder ties in bows over the shoulders. Trim the shoulder ties to the desired length and knot the ends.

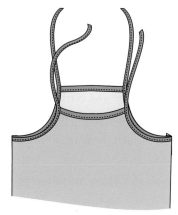

STEP 7

8 Hem the Shorts

Stitch a ½" double-fold hem in each of the leg openings. Try it on a cutie pie and enjoy!

Last-Minute Tunic

Designed by Heidi Massingill

This top can be made in a wardrobe pinch, using your favorite knit fabric. It's easy fitting and flattering, and can be worn with leggings, jeans, and skirts. The versatility of this top is going to make it one of your favorite go-to items in your wardrobe!

MATERIALS

* Locate the pattern in the envelope (sheet #8)
* 1 yard of 54" knit fabric
* ¼ yard of contrasting 54" knit fabric
* 1 spool of coordinating thread

Sizes — S, M, L, XL
Seam allowance — ½" unless otherwise specified

① Determine Your Size

Sizing is determined according to your bust and waist measurements.

	S	M	L	XL
Bust size	34"	36"	38"	40"
Waist size	30"	32"	34"	36"

② Measure, Mark, and Cut

Fold your fabric in half lengthwise with the right sides together, aligning the selvages. Position the pattern piece according to the layout and cut it out. Transfer markings from the pattern to the wrong side of fabric before removing it. See the chart on the next page for more information on the binding and contrasting hem.

* **Front/back** (cut 2)

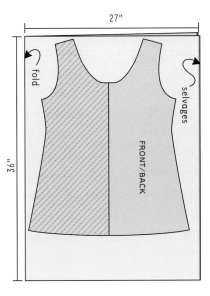

CUTTING LAYOUT

NOTE: *Place the arrow on the pattern piece along the straight grain of your fabric. Mirror the front/back along the line indicated in the pattern.*

OPTION

If you choose not to use a contrasting fabric to finish the bottom edge of the tunic, you may instead make a ½" double-fold hem.

BINDING WITH KNIT FABRIC

The binding technique described in step 4 differs from the way traditional double-fold binding is usually stitched — the inside binding edge is left raw. Knits do not unravel, or fray, which makes this technique possible. In addition, knits can be very bulky, especially when working with multiple layers. Eliminating the need to turn under the edge eliminates bulk.

Cut the following rectangular pieces from the contrasting fabric or from your primary fabric if you prefer:

	S	M	L	XL
Armhole binding (cut 2)	2¼" × 13"	2¼" × 14¼"	2¼" × 15¾"	2¼" × 17"
Neck binding (cut 1)	2¼" × 33"	2¼" × 34"	2¼" × 35"	2¼" × 36"
Hem contrast band (cut 1)	4½" × 42"	4½" × 44"	4½" × 46"	4½" × 48"

③ Attach the Front and Back

Pin the front and back pieces with the right sides together. Stitch the shoulder seams and side seams with a ½" seam allowance. Reinforce all the seams by stitching again with a ¼" seam allowance. Press all the seam allowances toward the back of the tunic.

④ Bind the Neck Edge

* With the right sides together, stitch the short ends of the neck binding strip to form a circle. Press the seam open.
* Mark the binding into fourths. Pin the neck binding along the neck edge with the right sides together, matching the marks on the binding with the shoulder seams, center front, and center back. Stitch the binding to the neck edge with a ¾" seam allowance.
* Press the binding up and over the edge of the seam allowance to the inside of the tunic. Pin the binding in place so the loose edge covers the seam allowance inside the tunic. From the right side, edgestitch close to the seam, catching the loose binding edge in the stitching. Stitch again ½" away.

⑤ Bind the Armholes

* With the right sides together, stitch the short ends of each armhole binding strip to form a circle. Press the seams open.
* Mark the binding into fourths as before. Position each armhole binding along the tunic's armhole edges with the right sides together, matching the marks on the binding with the shoulder seam, side seam, and quarter marks on the tunic. Stitch the bindings to the tunic, following the directions in the previous step.

⑥ Attach the Contrast Hem

* With the right sides together, stitch the short ends of the hem band to form a circle. Press the seam open.
* With the right sides together, pin one raw edge of the hem band to the bottom raw edge of the tunic, matching the side seams. Stitch with a ½" seam allowance.
* Press the hem band and seam allowance down, away from the tunic. Fold the hem band in half, with the wrong sides together, to the inside of the tunic (the edge of the hem will cover seam allowance inside the tunic). Pin it in place and, from the outside of the tunic, stitch close to the seam, catching the loose edge of the contrast hem in the stitching. Stitch again ½" away.

SPEEDY RUFFLE SCARF

Designed by Jenna Lou Odegard

Make your favorite outfit pop with any old yard of jersey knit you have lying around. You will not believe the professional results you can accomplish in just one afternoon, before heading out on the town!

MATERIALS

* 1 yard of 44/45" knit jersey fabric
* 1 spool of coordinating thread
* 1 spool of contrasting thread (optional)

Finished dimensions – 65" long × 6" wide
Seam allowance – ¼" unless otherwise specified

① Measure, Mark, and Cut

With the right sides together, fold your fabric in half lengthwise, aligning the selvages. Measure and mark the following pattern pieces directly on the wrong side of your fabric as shown in the cutting layout, then cut them out.

* **Main panel** 6" × 44" (cut 3 on fold)
* **Ruffle panel** 4" × 44" (cut 4 on fold)

② Create Main Panel and Ruffles

* Pin two main panels with the right sides together, and stitch along one short end. Attach the remaining main panel to a free short end of the two panels to make one long strip.
* Stitch all four ruffle panels together end to end in similar fashion.

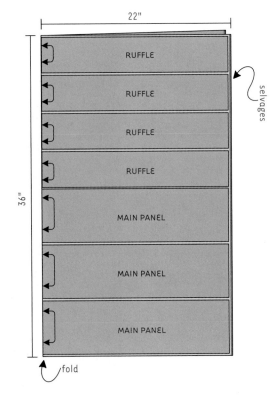

CUTTING LAYOUT

③ Gather the Main Panel

* Lay out the main panel flat on your work surface with the right side up. Thread a hand-sewing needle with a 65"-long thread, knotting one end. This thread will be removed once the scarf is completed, so consider using a high contrasting thread.

* Starting in the center of one short end, bring the needle and thread through the fabric so the knot is on the wrong side. Stitch along the center of the entire length of fabric using a 1" long running stitch, gathering the fabric as you stitch. Tie off the thread on the wrong side of the opposite end.

* Arrange the gathers so they are evenly distributed along the length of the panel.

④ Gather and Attach the Ruffle

* Gather the ruffle strip in a similar fashion, again using a 65"-long thread. Since this panel is longer than the main panel, there will be more gathers.

* Center and pin the ruffle onto the main panel, aligning the short ends. Take care that the panels are not twisted. Pin frequently to distribute the gathers evenly.

* Machine-stitch through both layers along the center of the panels and ruffles. Carefully remove the knot from one end of each running stitch thread, and pull out the threads.

REVERSE APPLIQUÉ BABY ROMPER

Designed by Stephanie Sterling

Have you ever wondered how to create a reverse appliqué embellishment? This project presents the perfect opportunity. Not only that, you end up with a functional and darling baby romper in your favorite stashed knit fabric. Now go customize your baby romper!

MATERIALS

* Locate the pattern in the envelope (sheet #9)
* 1 yard of 44/45" knit fabric
* 1 spool of coordinating thread
* 9 sew-in snaps for size 0-6 months; 11 sew-in snaps for size 6-12 months
* 5" square of coordinating knit fabric for reverse appliqué tree
* Embroidery thread (optional)

Sizes – 0-6 months, 6-12 months

Seam allowance – ½" unless otherwise specified

① Determine Your Child's Size

Measure the child's chest and inseam to find the right size. (Sometimes length is a better determining factor for size than chest measurement.)

	0-6 months	6-12 months
Chest size	Up to 17"	Up to 18"
Finished inseam	6½"	8"

② Measure, Mark, and Cut

Fold your fabric in half lengthwise with the right sides together, aligning the selvages. Position the romper pattern piece according to the layout and draw the binding strips as indicated. Cut out the pieces. Do not trace the tree template onto the fabric. Keep the pattern available for placement reference for the appliqué and sew-in snaps.

* **Romper** (cut 2)
* **Binding strips** 1½" × 44" (cut 3 on fold)

NOTE: *Position the grainline arrow on the pattern piece along the straight grain of the fabric. Mirror the romper along the line indicated in the pattern. The binding strips are positioned on the crossgrain, as shown, so they will stretch less.*

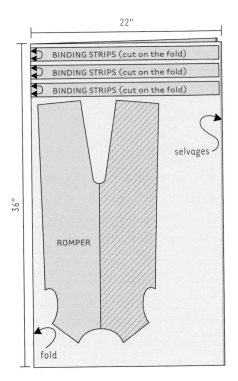

CUTTING LAYOUT

**APPLIQUÉ
OPTIONS**

The reverse appliqué image can be made with the tree template provided or you can create a simple graphic shape of your own. Once you play with this technique, you can start adding multiple colors and layers to your design. Whatever design you choose, please note that you must use a scrap of fabric slightly larger than your appliqué design.

③ Make the Reverse Appliqué

* Trace the tree shape appliqué template onto a separate, thin sheet of paper. Center the contrasting fabric square underneath the romper front, ¾" down from the top edge, with both right sides facing up. Center the appliqué template on top and pin all three layers together. From the right side, neatly machine-stitch around the template, following the outline of the tree as close as possible; then remove the paper template. On the wrong side, trim away the excess contrasting fabric that falls outside of the stitching line.

* On the right side of the romper, cut away the romper fabric inside the stitching line, leaving the contrasting fabric in place. Trim as close to the stitching as possible, so the contrasting fabric shows through. Feel free to add any additional embellishment, such as embroidery.

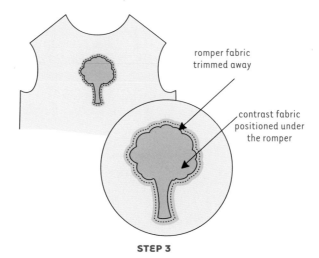

romper fabric trimmed away

contrast fabric positioned under the romper

STEP 3

④ Stitch the Shoulders

Pin the romper front and back pieces with the right sides together at the shoulder seams. Stitch the left shoulder seam all the way across. Stitch the right shoulder seam 1", from the armhole edge toward the neck edge, then backstitch, leaving the rest of the right shoulder open. Trim both seam allowances close to the stitching line.

5 Apply the Binding

* Pin one binding strip along the neck edge from one side of the shoulder opening to the other side, with the right sides together. Stitch with a ½" seam allowance and trim off any excess binding. Press the binding up and over the edge of the romper to the inside. Pin it in place and, from the outside of the romper, stitch close to the folded edge. Because knits do not unravel, the inside raw edge doesn't need to be clean finished. (*See* Binding with Knit Fabric *on page* 334.)

* Repeat this binding technique to bind both armholes, as well as both the front and back inside leg edges.

6 Bind the Right Shoulder

* Spread open the front and back raw edges of the right shoulder seam and measure the total length. Cut a piece of binding this measurement plus 1".

* Fold and press both short ends of this binding piece ½" to the wrong side. With the right sides together, pin this binding strip along the shoulder edge. Stitch with a ½" seam allowance. Complete the binding application as in step 5.

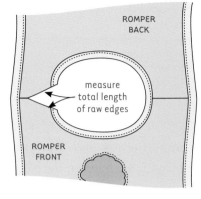

ROMPER
BACK

measure total length of raw edges

ROMPER
FRONT

STEP 6

7 Stitch the Side Seams

With the right sides together, stitch the romper front to the romper back along both side seams. Trim the seam allowance close to the stitching line.

8 Hem the Romper

Hem the leg openings with a ½" double-fold hem.

9 Add the Snaps

Refer back to the pattern piece for snap placement. Hand-sew three snaps along the binding of the right shoulder and the remaining snaps along the inside leg openings, making sure the two snap halves line up.

sassy dress

Designed by Lisa Powers

Dresses are easy, fun, and carefree, especially when they're made out of comfy knit fabrics. This playful dress is no different, with its A-line shape that offers comfortable fluidity. The contrast trimming adds just a bit of sass, making sure that this dress will be a favorite, fun choice for your little girl. And, if you're working with a striped contrasting fabric, consider cutting the binding strips on the bias for some fun diagonal stripes.

MATERIALS

* Locate the pattern in the envelope (sheet #9)
* 1 yard of 44/45" knit fabric
* 1 spool of coordinating thread
* 1 button, ¾" to 1" in diameter
* ⅛ yard of contrasting knit fabric for bindings (optional)

Sizes – 18-24 months, 2T, 3T

Seam allowance – ½" unless otherwise specified

① **Determine Your Child's Size**

Measure the child's chest to find the right size.

	18-24 mo	2T	3T
Chest size	20"	21"	22"

② **Measure, Mark, and Cut**

Lay out your fabric in a single layer with the right side facing up. Position the pattern pieces according to the layout, draw the back facing using the measurements listed below, and cut out the pieces. Transfer markings from the pattern to the wrong side of fabric.

* **Dress front** (cut 1)
* **Dress back** (cut 1)
* **Sleeves** (cut 2, one reversed)
* **Pocket** (cut 2)

In addition to the paper pattern pieces, measure and mark the following:

* **Back facing** 4" × 2" (cut 1)

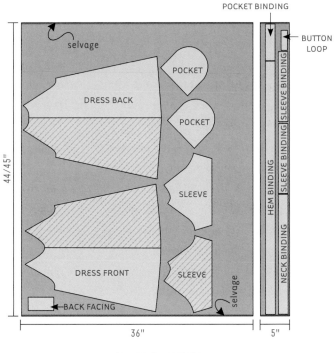

CUTTING LAYOUT

NOTE: *Mirror the front and back along the line indicated on the pattern.*

Cut the following pieces from the contrasting fabric (or from the main fabric, if you prefer):

* **Button loop** 1" × 3" (cut 1)
* **Pocket binding** 1½" × 5½" (cut 1)
* **Sleeve binding** 1½" × 10½" (cut 2)
* **Neck binding** 1½" × 18" (cut 1)
* **Hem binding** 1½" × 38" (cut 1)

NOTE: *Position the grainline arrow on the pattern pieces along the straight grain of the fabric, which means the pocket pieces will be cut on the bias.*

❸ Make and Attach the Pocket

* Pin the two pocket pieces with the right sides together. Stitch around all sides, leaving a 2" opening along the top edge for turning. Clip the corners and curved seam allowances. Turn the pocket right side out and tuck the seam allowance into the opening; press.

* Pin and stitch the pocket binding strip to the top edge of the pocket, with the right sides together. The binding strip will extend beyond the edges of the pocket on both sides. Press the binding up and then fold it over the seam allowance to the wrong side, so that ½" of the binding is visible. Edgestitch the binding strip to the pocket, catching the loose edge of the binding on the inside of the pocket in the stitching. Pin the extra binding extending from each side to the wrong side of the pocket. (*See* Binding with Knit Fabric *on page* 334.)

* Pin the pocket on the right side of the dress front at the placement marks. Edgestitch the pocket along the side and bottom edges, starting and finishing at the binding strip.

④ Make the Front Pleat

Fold the dress front in half, with the right sides together, along the center front line. Stitch along the pleat line as indicated on the pattern piece, through both layers. Unfold the dress front and press to create a reverse pleat at the center front. Stitch a ¼" seam at the top edge to hold the pleat in place.

STEP 4

⑤ Make the Back Button Loop

Fold the loop piece as you would double-fold binding (in half along its length with the long edges pressed in to the center). Edgestitch along the long open edge, through all the layers.

⑥ Make the Back Opening

* Fold the loop in half and position it on the right side of the back piece along the center back, ½" down from the neck edge. Pin it in place.
* With the right sides together, center the back facing on the back piece, aligning the top raw edges, and sandwiching the loop between the two layers. Pin it in place.
* Stitch the layers together along the back marked lines (it might help to transfer the markings from the back pattern piece onto the facing), pivoting at the corners. Using sharp scissors, cut through all the layers in the center of the stitched lines. Make angular cuts toward the bottom two corners; be very careful to clip right up to, but not through, the stitching lines.

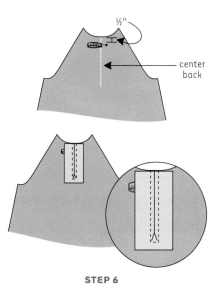

STEP 6

✳ Turn the back facing through the opening to the wrong side of the back piece and press. The loop will extend out from the seam. Edgestitch along the finished edges of the back opening.

7 Bind and Attach the Sleeves

Attach the sleeve binding pieces to the bottom edges of both sleeves the same way you attached it to the top of the pocket in step 3. With the right sides together, stitch the front sleeve edge to the dress front, matching notches. Press the seam allowance toward the dress front. Repeat, stitching the back sleeve edge to the dress back, matching notches. Press the seam allowance toward the dress back. Repeat to attach the second sleeve.

8 Stitch the Side Seams

With the right sides together, pin the dress front/sleeve to the dress back/sleeve, matching the underarm seams. With the right sides together, stitch the left side seam and underarm seam in one continuous seam. Repeat for the right side seam. Press the seam allowances toward the back of the dress.

9 Bind the Hem

Attach the hem binding to the bottom edge of the dress in the same way as the pocket and sleeve edges. Start attaching the binding near a side seam (so the overlapping ends are inconspicuous). Trim the binding so it only overlaps the starting edge by ½".

10 Bind the Neck Edge

Pin the neck binding strip along the neck edge of the dress, the same way as for the hem, pocket, and sleeves. Trim the excess binding that extends beyond the back neck opening to ½" and fold the extra binding to the wrong side to make a clean finish at the back neck opening. Edgestitch the binding in place. Hand-sew a button on the right edge of back opening, opposite the loop.

space beans target toss

Designed by Archer DeHoskins

This beanbag toss game can be customized for the theme of your choice, but templates are provided for the space theme shown. Vary the size of the holes for different point values, to make the game that much more challenging. Covering a purchased artist's stretched canvas makes it super easy to put together. Prop it up at an angle by leaning it against a chair or wall, and put a few beanbags or other small weights in front of the game board for stability.

MATERIALS

* 1 yard of 58/60" knit fabric with minimal or moderate stretch
* 1 spool of coordinating thread
* 24" × 30" stretched framed artist's canvas with ¾" depth (*see* Size Variations *on page* 348)
* Craft knife
* 3 yards of ¼"-wide elastic
* Safety pin

* 9 craft felt squares in colors of choice
* 2 to 3 pounds of dried beans, seed corn, or popcorn kernals
* Fabric glue (optional)
* Circle template and spacecraft templates (pattern sheet #2)

Finished dimensions – 22" × 28" game board; beanbags are 4" square
Seam allowance – ¼" unless otherwise specified

①　Measure, Mark, and Cut

Lay out your fabric in a single layer with the wrong side facing up. Measure and mark the following pattern pieces directly on the wrong side of the fabric, and cut them out.

* **Game board** 36"x 30" (cut 1)
* **10 Beanbags** 4½" squares (cut 20)
* **Pocket strip** 6" × 17¾" (cut 1)
* **Pocket strip** 6" × 17" (cut 1)
* **Pocket strip** 6" × 16¼" (cut 1)
* **Pocket strip** 6" × 15½" (cut 1)
* **Pocket strip** 6" × 14¾" (cut 1)

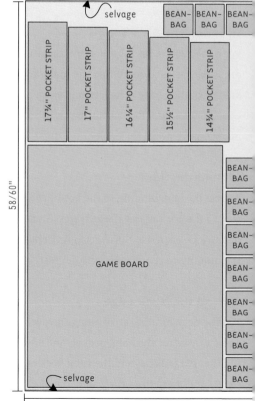

CUTTING LAYOUT

SIZE VARIATIONS

The instructions are written for a 24" × 30" canvas. If you can't find that exact size, a slightly smaller canvas with similar dimensions can be used. The minimum suggested size is 18" × 24". Just keep in mind that the fabric covering the game board should measure 6" longer and wider than the canvas frame, so adjust as necessary to fit your frame.

2 Prep the Canvas Frame

Use the five circle templates to trace five circles on the back of the canvas. Follow our general plan by referencing the photograph, or make up your own. We placed the smallest circle roughly in the center, while avoiding the frame's crossbeam. Cut out the circles from the canvas with a craft knife. Keep the canvas circle cutouts as templates for later steps with felt appliqué.

3 Make the Game Board Cover

* In each corner of the game board fabric, cut out a 3" square. Fold each corner diagonally, with the right sides together, so the outer corners meet. Stitch each corner.
* Fold all the raw edges of the cover ½" to the wrong side and edgestitch to form a casing, leaving a 2" opening. Thread the elastic through the opening and all the way through the casing. Temporarily secure the elastic ends together with a safety pin.
* Slip the fabric over the front of the canvas screen and draw the elastic tight until you are satisfied with the fit. It should be tight enough for a snug fit, but loose enough that you can remove it easily.
* Repin and trim the elastic to the proper length. Overlap and stitch the ends together, tuck the elastic into the casing, and stitch the opening closed. Place the fabric over the canvas frame once more, taking care to align the corners and adjust the gathers in the elastic casing so they are evenly distributed.

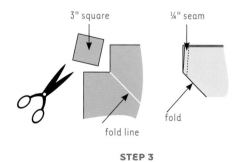

STEP 3

④ Make the Target Holes

With the cover in place over the canvas, and working from the back, trace the circle cutouts onto the wrong side of the game board fabric with marking pencil or chalk. These lines will be your stitching lines, not your cutting lines. Remove the game board cover from the canvas and mark a cutting line ¼" inside each of the marked stitching lines.

⑤ Make the Pockets

Fold the 17¾" pocket strip in half across the width with the right sides together, aligning the short raw edges. Stitch along the short edge to form a 6" tube. Turn the tube right side out. Pin one raw edge to the cutout for the 5½" circle with the right sides together, and stitch. Turn the pocket right side out and push it to the back of the game board fabric. From the wrong side, stitch across the bottom of the remaining raw edge, flattening it slightly to form the bottom of the pocket. Repeat for the remaining pocket strips and circles:

* Use the 17" pocket strip for the 5¼" circle.
* Use the 16¼" pocket strip for the 5" circle.
* Use the 15½" pocket strip for the 4¾" circle.
* Use the 14¾" pocket strip for the 4½" circle.

⑥ Make the Circle Appliqués

Select the felt colors you want to encircle the targets on the game board. With the game board fabric still off the canvas, center each felt square on the canvas behind a different cutout, and trace around the cut-out circle. Remove the felt squares from the canvas and draw whatever shape you like around the first circles (another circle, star shape, wavy lines); you might want to practice on a sheet of paper first. Cut out the inner circle and the outer shape. Stitch or glue each felt appliqué around its target on the game board cover. If you are gluing, place the fabric back on the canvas for a level, firm surface.

⑦ Make the Number Appliqués

Using a bold graphic font, print out the numbers 1, 2, 3, 4, 5, and 0, each approximately 2" tall. Cut the numbers from the printer paper to use as pattern pieces. Trace around the patterns onto the felt and cut out one of each number and five zeros. Place whichever felt numbers you wish above each target and stitch or glue them in place.

⑧ Make the Beanbags

Find the spacecraft templates (pattern sheet #2). Choose two felt colors and trace five matching shapes onto each color; cut them out. Center each felt piece on the right side of a beanbag fabric square and stitch or glue in place. Pin each appliquéd square to a remaining square with the right sides together. Stitch on all sides, leaving a 2" to 3" opening for turning and stuffing. Turn each bag right side out and stuff them with dried beans or corn. Hand-sew the openings closed with slipstitch or whipstitch. Prop up your game board at the desired angle and try to get your spaceship or rocket ship to land and score the most points!

FLaT-screen TV cover

Designed by Melissa Haworth

Who really likes the look of the TV screen looming on the living room wall? Disguise it when it's not in use with this easy-to-make, easy-to-store screen cover! A dust-free screen is merely an added bonus to the lovely decor. Don't have a flat-screen television? Follow the same basic instructions to make a computer monitor screen cover instead.

MATERIALS

* 1 yard of 54/60" knit fabric
* 1 spool of coordinating thread
* ¼"-wide elastic, long enough to go around the perimeter of the TV with some stretch (for our sample, approximately 3½ yards)

Finished dimensions – custom fit to your TV
Seam allowance – ½" unless otherwise specified

① Measure the TV

Measure the full height, width, and depth of the television. Add 1" to the depth measurement. Double the depth + 1" measurement and add it to the height and width measurements. This extra amount will allow the cover to wrap around the TV on all four sides.

Example: For a 26" × 40" × 3" television:
3" depth + 1" = 4" then 4" × 2 = 8"
Add 8" to the height and width for cutting measurements = 34" × 48"

② Cut the Fabric

Lay out your fabric in a single layer with the wrong side facing up. Measure and mark a rectangle according to the dimensions from step 1, and cut it out.

NOTE: *Cut the piece so the long edges are on the straight grainline of your fabric.*

③ Cut Out the Corners

Measure and mark a square that is equal to the depth of the television + 1" at each corner. Cut out the marked corners. In our example that measurement was 4", but use your own TV measurements. The measurements between the inside corners of each cutout should equal the original dimensions of your television.

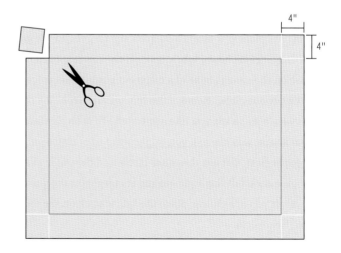

4"

4"

STEP 3

④ Stitch the Corners

Fold each corner diagonally, so the cut edges are right sides together, and the outer corners of each cutout meet. Stitch each corner (*see the illustration on page* 348).

⑤ Add the Elastic

* Fold the raw edge of the cover ½" to the wrong side and edgestitch to form a casing, leaving a 2" opening. Thread the elastic through the opening and all the way through the casing. Temporarily secure the ends together with a safety pin.

* Slip the cover over the TV and draw the elastic tight until you are satisfied with the fit. It should be tight enough for a snug fit, but loose enough that you can take it off and put it on easily.

* Trim the elastic to the desired length. Overlap and stitch the ends together, tuck the elastic back into the casing, and stitch the opening closed.

MONKEY LEGGINGS

Designed by Yasuko Solbes

Baby and toddler leggings have long been a ubiquitous clothing staple in Japan. This pair is incredibly comfy and cute, as well as very functional with its diaper-size gusset. Easy to make and fun to wear, these leggings are perfect for both girls and boys!

MATERIALS

* Locate the pattern in the envelope (sheet #9)
* 1 yard of 44/45" knit fabric
* 1 spool of coordinating thread
* ⅔ yard of ¾"-wide elastic
* 7" square of contrasting knit fabric for gusset (optional)
* Purchased star appliqué or fabric scrap for appliqué

Sizes – 6 months, 12 months, 2T

Seam allowance – ½" unless otherwise specified

① Determine Your Child's Size

Measure the child's waist and inseam to find the right size. If these measurements indicate two different sizes, go with the inseam; it's easier to adjust the elastic than to add length.

Length	6 months	12 months	2T
Waist size	19"	20"	21"
Finished inseam	12"	13"	15"

② Measure, Mark, and Cut

Lay out your fabric in a single layer with the right side facing up. Position the pattern pieces according to the layout and cut them out. If you prefer, cut the gusset pattern piece from contrasting fabric. Transfer markings from the pattern pieces to the wrong side of fabric before removing the paper pattern pieces.

* **Front leggings** (cut 1)
* **Back leggings** (cut 1)
* **Cuffs** (cut 2)
* **Gusset** cut from contrasting fabric if you prefer (cut 1)

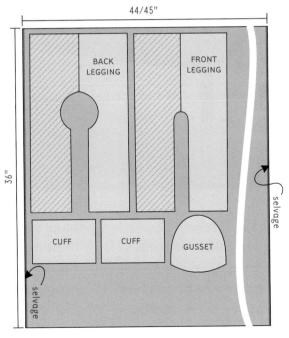

CUTTING LAYOUT

NOTE: *Position the grainline arrow on the pattern pieces along the straight grain of the fabric. Mirror the leggings along the line indicated on the pattern. The white wavy line indicates extra fabric not shown.*

❸ Attach the Gusset

With the right sides together, align the curved edge of the gusset with the curved opening on the back legging piece, matching all the placement numbers except number 4 (the bottom edge of the gusset is left loose). Carefully stitch along the curve with a zigzag or stretch stitch. Press the seam allowances toward the leggings.

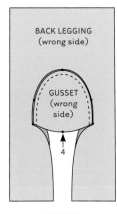

BACK LEGGING
(wrong side)

GUSSET
(wrong side)

4

STEP 3

❹ Attach the Front and Back

With the right sides together, align the side seams of the front and back pieces and stitch them together. Press the seam allowances toward the back. Align the front and back inseams, matching the number 4 on the gusset with the center front on the leggings, and stitch them together. Turn the leggings right side out.

❺ Make and Attach the Cuffs

* Fold the cuff in half crosswise with the right sides together, aligning the shorter edges, and stitch along shorter edge. Press the seam allowances open.
* Fold the stitched cuff in half along the fold line as indicated on the pattern piece, with the wrong sides together. Baste the raw edges together.
* Pin the cuff to the leg opening with the right sides together, aligning the raw edges and positioning the cuff seam with the legging inseam. Stretch the cuff as needed to fit the leg opening, and stitch. Press the seam allowances toward the legging.
* Repeat with second cuff and leg opening.

❻ Make the Waistline Casing

* Press the top edge of the leggings ¼" to the wrong side, then press under another 1". Topstitch close to the inside folded edge of the casing, leaving a 2" opening at one side seam.
* Cut the elastic to the appropriate length to comfortably fit around the child's belly, adding an extra 1". Slide the elastic through the waistband casing, overlap the ends by ½", and stitch the ends together securely. Slide the elastic ends back into the casing and stitch the opening closed.

❼ Attach the Appliqué

* With the right sides together, fuse or stitch a purchased appliqué or fabric embellishment (cut into any shape) onto the leggings, over the gusset seam.

CHAPTER 10

WOOL

Wool, a natural animal fiber with great antimicrobial qualities, is made into a tremendous assortment of fabrics in a variety of weights and constructions. Generally speaking, wool has fabulous attributes: it absorbs moisture and retains heat when wet, it is lighter weight than comparably sized cotton fibers, and it is naturally water repellent and flame retardant. Wool fabrics can be woven or knit, smooth or textured, soft or crisp, and sheer or opaque. Your choice of wool fabrics is endless. Here is some basic information and a fabulous selection of projects to get you started.

Fabric Facts

Wool is easy to shape and mold, making it a great option for tailoring. Simply use steam to help shape darts and curved seams, and ease fullness when setting in sleeves. There are two basic categories of wool fabrics: woolens and worsteds.

The term *woolen* is often considered a generic name for all wool fabrics, but it is a specific type of woven wool fabric. Woolen refers to a wool fabric that is thick, soft, fuzzy, and somewhat "spongy." Woolens generally have a nap, don't hold a crease well, and have a bit of body. Typical uses include coats, blankets, and casual wear. For the amateur sewer, woolens are often the easiest wools to sew, as minor sewing imperfections are naturally concealed.

Worsteds, by contrast, are smooth and lustrous in both appearance and feel. They have a prominent weave, are stronger and lighter in weight than woolens, and hold a crease well. Worsteds also tend to drape better than woolens and are a great choice for tailored clothing. Worsteds tend to spot and stain easily, and when pressed, will pick up a shine quickly, so take care to use your pressing cloth!

Other wool fabrics that are enjoyable to work with include boiled and felted wool, which are formed though a combination of heat, moisture, pressure, and abrasion. They are easy to sew and don't fray. Note that you do not need to use wool felt for the projects in this book that call for felt; in many cases craft felt (which is not wool) will certainly do!

Attributes

Any wool, other than superwash wool, tends to felt when it is exposed to moisture and/or heat, which is why most wool fabrics are dry cleaned or hand washed in cold water. Lighter color wools (white, off-white) are most resistant to felting. Wool is not commonly printed; rather, color variations in a finished fabric are usually achieved through a yarn-dye process. Wools have inherent elasticity and are stronger than most cotton fabrics.

Needle Type(s)

The most appropriate needle size and type varies depending on the construction and weight of the fabric. 80/12 and 90/14 universal needles work well for all but the lightest or heaviest of weights. If the wool fabric is a knit, refer to the knits chapter.

Sewing Machine Accessories

While a standard presser foot is usually suitable, you may find that heavier, "spongier" fabrics feed better with a walking foot.

Stitch Types, Tips, and Machine Settings

The best stitch length setting varies depending on the construction and weight of the fabric. A 2-3mm stitch length works well for most wools, except for very light or very heavyweights. If the wool fabric is a knit, refer to the knits chapter.

Marking

Tailor's tacks, drafting tape, and scissor snips are the best marking method for most wool fabrics. Chalk may work well for wools with no or low nap. With many wool fabrics, you may need to mark the right/wrong side of the cut pieces so you aren't confused when you start sewing.

Cutting

Since wool has natural elasticity, and many wool fabrics are medium to heavyweight, make sure all the fabric is on the work surface and not hanging off to avoid stretching and distorting during cutting.

Interfacing

Sew-in interfacings are preferred for tailored projects. Fusible interfacings may not always fuse well at the heat setting required for wool.

Special Equipment

Use pure soap (such as Ivory) to rub on the wrong side of seams and creases while pressing, for a sharper look.

Seams

To reduce bulk, trim the seam allowances and press them open. Finish the seam allowances with an overlock or zigzag on any wools that fray. Binding is also an attractive option, particularly for unlined jackets.

Pressing and Ironing

Set your iron on the wool setting and always use steam. Ideally you will use two pressing cloths, both made of wool, one underneath, between the fabric and ironing board, and one on top, between the fabric and iron. If you touch the iron directly to the fabric, the fabric will become shiny, and the 4-H ladies will not be pleased. You can buy official pressing cloths at the fabric store, but in a pinch, a thin dish towel or a wool scrap works just fine.

Fabric Care

Closely follow the manufacturer's care instructions printed on the fabric bolt. Machine and/or hand washing may be possible, though most wool items should generally not be machine dried. Dry cleaning might be your best option depending on the fabrication and construction of the item.

cool season clutch

Designed by Leigh Ann Tennant

This clutch is begging to cozy up by your side! Perfectly paired with nubby sweaters and leather boots, this casual-chic wool bag will carry all your "must-haves" through the cold weather months. For a twist, try making it in fun tweed!

MATERIALS

* ✳ Locate the pattern in the envelope (sheet #4)
* ✳ 1 yard of 44/45" wool or similar cool weather fabric
* ✳ ½ yard of medium-weight fusible interfacing
* ✳ 1 spool of coordinating thread
* ✳ Leftover yarn in coordinating color (or one hank of crewel yarn)
* ✳ Fabric-covered-button kit, 1½" in diameter
* ✳ 1 magnetic snap closure

Finished dimensions – 7" tall × 16" wide
Seam allowance – ⅜" unless otherwise specified

❶ Measure, Mark, and Cut

Lay out your fabric in a single layer with the right side facing up. Position the pattern pieces according to the layout, and measure and mark the additional pieces. Cut out the pieces and transfer the markings from the pattern to the wrong side of the fabric.

* ✳ **Front/back** (cut 4, mirror along indicated line)
* ✳ **Side accents** (cut 4, two reversed)
* ✳ **Leaves** (cut 4)

Also cut from fabric:

* ✳ **Button cover** 2½"-diameter circle (cut 1)
* ✳ **Binding strip** 36" × 3" (cut 1)

Cut from interfacing:

* ✳ **Front/back** (cut 4)

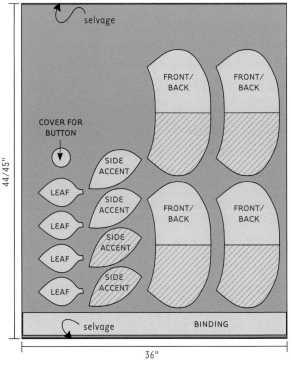

CUTTING LAYOUT

❷ Make the Leaves

Pin two leaf pieces with the right sides together, and stitch around, leaving the stem area unstitched, as marked on the pattern. Trim the seam allowances to ⅛". Turn the leaf right side out and press. Repeat with the remaining pair of leaves. Hand-sew a running stitch along the edges of the leaves using yarn.

③ Make the Side Accents

Pin two side accents with the right sides together, and stitch along the inside curve. Trim the seam allowances to ⅛". Turn the side accent right side out and press. Repeat with the remaining side accent panels.

④ Attach the Side Accents

* Fuse interfacing to the wrong side of each front/back piece, following the manufacturer's instructions.
* Pin the side accents to the right side of one front/back piece, with one on each side as marked on the pattern. This becomes the front of your bag.
* Hand-sew a running stitch along the finished edge of each side accent with yarn, attaching the accent to the bag front. Also hand-sew two parallel rows of running stitches down the center of the bag front.

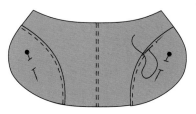

STEP 4

⑤ Assemble the Bag

* Pin the bag front to another front/back piece with the right sides together, and stitch along the sides and bottom, leaving the top edge open. Trim the seam allowances to ⅛". Turn the front right side out, and press.

* Pin the remaining two front/backs with the right sides together, and stitch along the sides and bottom with ⅝" seam allowance, leaving the top edge open. Trim the seam allowances to ⅛" and press. This will become the lining of the bag; the larger seam allowances allow the lining to fit well within the bag exterior even if you are using a thick, stiff fabric.
* Install the corresponding halves of the magnetic snap closure 1" from the top edge, centered on the right side of each lining section, following the manufacturer's instructions.
* Carefully fit the lining inside the exterior so the wrong sides are together, stretching to fit if necessary, and hand-baste the exterior and lining together close to the raw edges.

⑥ Bind the Top Edge

* Fold one short end of the binding strip ½" to wrong side and press. Fold the binding strip in half lengthwise with the wrong sides together, and press. Starting with the folded end and aligning the raw edges, stitch both layers of the binding to the top edge of the bag lining. When you come all the way around to the beginning, overlap the binding 1" and trim off the excess.
* Fold the binding over to the front side of the bag, press, and pin it in place. Hand-sew the bottom folded edge of the binding to the front of the bag.

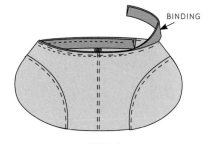

BINDING

STEP 6

⑦ Add the Leaf Detail

* Hand-sew the leaves to the top left corner of the bag.
* Cover the button with the fabric circle, following the manufacturer's instructions, and hand-sew it over the stems of the leaves onto the bag.

SLIP STRAP BaG

Designed by Alyce Dyer-Hall

This conversation piece is worn like a cuff. Slip one strap through the other and around your wrist. Pull the overlapped strap down along the side to close the purse. Making this bag is a bit like origami, and once you get the gist you can customize it to suit your own taste and creativity, with patchwork or perhaps zippered pockets. A layer of fleece interfacing gives the bag some body, providing a cushion for fragile items.

MATERIALS

* 1 yard of 44/45" nondirectional wool or home decor fabric
* 1 spool of coordinating thread
* ¾ yard of fusible fleece
* 2 decorative pins or buttons (optional)

Finished dimensions – 17" tall × 13" wide

Seam allowance – ½" unless otherwise specified

1 Measure, Mark, and Cut

Fold your fabric in half with the right sides together, aligning the selvages. Measure and mark the following pattern pieces directly on the wrong side of your fabric.

* **Bag body** 35½" × 7½" (cut 4)
* **Pocket** 7½" × 14" (cut 4 on fold)

Cut from fusible fleece:

* **Pocket** 7½" × 14" (cut 2)

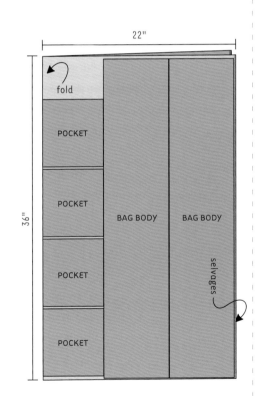

CUTTING LAYOUT

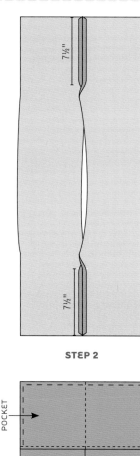

STEP 2

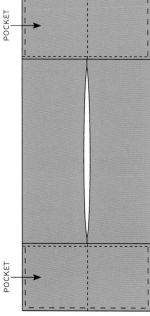

STEP 3

② Make the Bag Body

* Along one long edge of each body piece, make a mark 7½" in from both short ends. This is both a stitching stop point and a pocket placement indicator.

* Pin two body pieces, right sides together, aligning the marked long edges. Stitch from each short edge to the markings, leaving the middle between the markings unstitched. The new piece will be 35½" long × 14" wide, with a long unstitched opening in the middle.

* Press the seam allowances open. Repeat with the two remaining body pieces.

③ Create the Pockets

* Fuse a piece of fleece to the wrong side of one pocket, following the manufacturer's instructions. (If it has a hard time fusing to the wool, you can also baste together with edgestitch.) Pin this pocket to another pocket with the right sides together, aligning all the raw edges. Stitch the pockets together across one long raw edge (this edge becomes the top of the pocket). Press and turn the pockets at the seam so the wrong sides are together. Edgestitch along the top edge.

* Repeat with the remaining fusible fleece and pocket pieces.

* Pin each seamed pocket onto the right side of one bag body at opposite ends, aligning the side and bottom raw edges. The top of each pocket should face toward the middle opening, and sit ½" from the opening. Baste the pockets to the body close to the sides and bottom raw edges.

* Stitch a line in the center of each pocket, from the finished top edge to the bottom raw edge of the pocket, to create divided pockets. This piece becomes the bag lining. The other body piece is the bag exterior.

Wool felt flower brooch courtesy of Kelly Hanson Handmade (www.kellyjhanson.etsy.com)

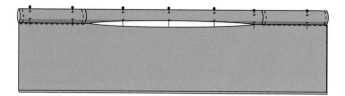

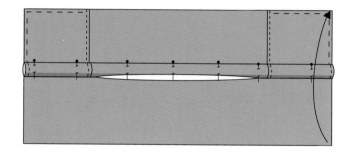

❹ Stitch the Center Opening

* Pin the lining and exterior with the right sides together, aligning the raw edges. Stitch the pieces together on each side of the center opening, taking care not to catch any seam allowances in the stitching. Clip the seam allowances at all the seam intersections.

* Pull the lining through the opening so that the wrong sides are together.

❺ Stitch Half the Slip Straps

* Lay the bag flat on your work surface with the exterior facing up. Starting at one long side, roll all the layers up to the center of the bag and pin it to keep the roll temporarily secured.

* Open the exterior and lining layers on the other half of the bag, and fold them over the roll so their right sides are together and the roll is encased between them.

* Stitch the top raw edges together, starting and stopping ½" from the top of each pocket, leaving 7½" unstitched at each end.

* Remove the pins and turn your work right side out through the tube.

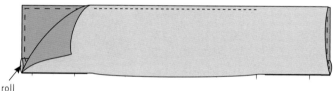

roll
between
layers

STEP 5

❻ Stitch the Remaining Slip Straps

* Lay the bag flat on your work surface once again, with the exterior facing up. Open up the rolled half of the bag. Roll up the two layers you just sewed, to keep them out of the way as in step 5. Pin to keep the roll temporarily secured.

* Bring the layers that were rolled up in step 5, but are now flat, over and around the roll, so that the right sides are together, the roll is encased between them, and the pieces form a tube once again.

* Stitch the top raw edges together, starting and stopping ½" from the top of each pocket, leaving 7½" unstitched at each end.

* Remove the pins and turn the bag right side out through the tube. Press.

⑦ Complete the Bag

* Fold the bag in half across the width
  so that the right sides of the lining
  (with the pockets) are on the outside.
  This positions the right sides of the
  two exterior pieces together between
  the two lining layers. Align all the raw
  edges. Move the lining layers out of the
  way and pin the exterior layers, with
  the right sides together.

* Stitch along the sides and bottom raw
  edges of the exterior. Clip the corners.
  Roll up the slip straps toward the
  lining to keep them out of the way (as
  in step 5). Bring the lining layers over
  and around the rolled-up straps, so that
  the right sides are together and the raw
  edges and corners are aligned.

* Stitch along the sides and bottom raw
  edges of the lining, leaving a 9" opening
  along the bottom edge for turning. Clip
  the corners. Carefully turn the bag right
  side out through the opening.

* Hand-sew the opening closed. Reinsert
  the lining back into the bag. Hand-sew
  decorative buttons or attach pins onto
  the body and strap, as desired.

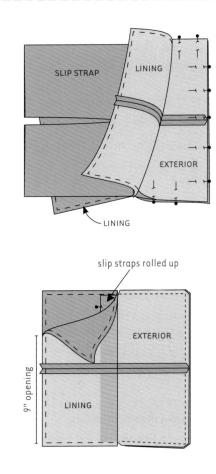

STEP 7

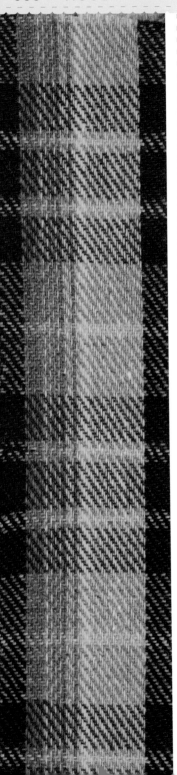

OBI BELT

Designed by Kathy Stowell

As practical as it is glamorous, this obi belt is a delightful accessory that will complement any ensemble. Try tying it different ways for different occasions. As an added bonus, this project is quick and easy to sew!

MATERIALS

* Locate the pattern in the envelope (sheets #4 and #5)
* 1 yard of 44/45" wool fabric
* 1 spool of coordinating thread
* 1 yard of medium-weight fusible interfacing

Sizes – S, M, L, XL

Seam allowance – ½" unless otherwise specified

❶ Determine Your Size

Measure your waist to find your size.

	S	M	L	XL
Waist	28½"	30"	32"	34"

❷ Measure, Mark, and Cut

Lay out your fabric in a single layer with the right side facing up. Position the pattern pieces according to the layout, and cut them out. Cut the same pieces from interfacing.

* **Obi body** (cut 2)
* **Obi belt strap** (cut 4)

NOTE: *Position the grainline arrow on the pattern pieces along the straight grain of the fabric. Mirror the obi body along the line indicated on the pattern.*

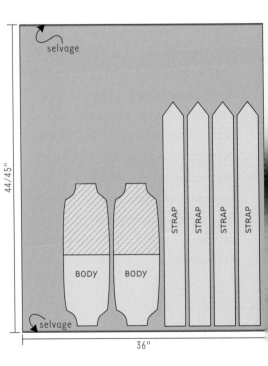

CUTTING LAYOUT

③ Apply the Interfacing

Fuse interfacing to the wrong side of each of the fabric pieces following the manufacturer's instructions.

④ Attach the Body and Strap Pieces

With the right sides together, align the short straight end of one obi strap piece with one straight end of one obi body piece. Stitch the pieces together and press the seam allowances open. Repeat, sewing another obi strap to the opposite side of the obi body. Repeat with the remaining straps and body piece. You should now have two obi belts.

⑤ Finish the Belt

* Pin the obi belts with the right sides together, aligning all the raw edges. Stitch, leaving a 4" opening along the bottom edge of the body piece for turning. Trim the seam allowances, clipping and notching the curves where necessary. Turn the obi right side out and press. Press the seam allowances at the opening to the inside.

* Topstitch around the entire perimeter of the belt (straps included), stitching the opening closed as you stitch.

LITTLE GIRL'S CAPELET

Designed by Danielle Wilson

You've seen vintage-inspired capelets here and there, and now you can make one for your little girl! It's simple, darling, unique, and uses a yard of fabric perfectly. This self-lined capelet is totally finished inside and out. The Peter Pan collar gives it a polished finishing touch. It is ideally suited for the beautiful drapability of a wool suiting fabric.

MATERIALS

* Locate the pattern in the envelope (sheets #7 and #9)
* 1 yard of 54/55" wool fabric
* 1 spool of coordinating thread
* ⅔ yard of ¼"-wide grosgrain, velvet, or satin ribbon

Sizes – One size fits many little girls (2-6)
Seam allowance – ½" unless otherwise specified

❶ Measure, Mark, and Cut

Fold your fabric in half lengthwise with the right sides together, aligning the selvages. Position the pattern pieces according to the layout, and cut them out.

* **Capelet front** (cut 4)
* **Capelet back** (cut 2 on fold)
* **Collar** (cut 2)

NOTE: *Position the grainline arrow on the pattern pieces along the straight grain of the fabric.*

❷ Assemble the Exterior and Lining

Pin the shoulder edges of two fronts to one back with the right sides together, from the neck edge to the bottom of the capelet. Stitch and press the seam allowances open. Repeat with the remaining pieces until you have two capelets, one exterior and one lining.

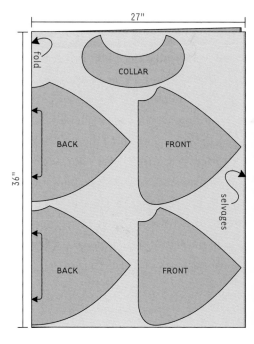

CUTTING LAYOUT

❸ Make the Collar

* On one of the collar pieces, trim ⅛" from the outer curved edge (not the neck edge). This trimmed piece will be the collar lining, and trimming it slightly will ensure that the finished collar lies flat.
* Pin the outer collar and the collar lining with the right sides together along the outer curved edge (you will need to slightly stretch the trimmed collar lining piece for both pieces to line up). Stitch along the outer curved edge, and clip the seam allowances as necessary. Turn the collar right side out and press so that the outside edge rolls slightly toward the lining. Press and edgestitch ⅛" from the finished collar edge. Baste the neck edges together ¼" from the raw edges.

❹ Attach the Collar and Ties

* Mark the center of the collar and the center of the back capelet at the necklines.
* Pin the lining side of the collar to the right side of the exterior capelet, aligning the raw neck edges and the center back markings. The ends of the collar should be ½" from each front edge of the capelet. Baste the collar and capelet together with a ¼" seam allowance.
* Cut the ribbon into two 12" pieces. Pin each ribbon piece to the front edge of the capelet, ⅝" below the neck edge, and so the raw edges of the ribbon and body align. Tack the edge of the ribbons in place. Hem the opposite ends of the ribbons, or simply tie them in little knots.

NOTE: *If you are working with synthetic ribbon, you may choose to melt the ends using a lighter to keep the ends from fraying.*

❺ Finish the Capelet

* Pin the capelet exterior and lining with the right sides together, aligning all the raw edges, and sandwiching the collar and ties between the two layers. Stitch, leaving a 4" opening along the bottom edge of the capelet for turning.
* Trim the seam allowances and clip the curves and corners, as necessary. Turn the capelet right side out and carefully press. Press the seam allowances at the opening to the wrong side.
* Starting at the middle of the neck, on the body of the capelet, edgestitch ⅛" from the seam, around the entire perimeter or the capelet, closing the opening in the stitching. Edgestitch the capelet with the exterior facing up to ensure a neater finish. Give your garment a final press.

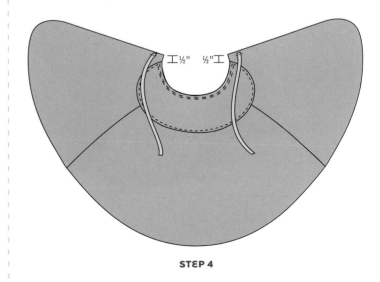

STEP 4

URBAN WABBIT HUNTING CAP

Designed by Carolyn M. Lipke

This lined wool cap has an earflap piece that can be buttoned up or worn down when it is really cold. The pattern can be easily altered for different head sizes. Make a few, in different fabrics, so you have choices that are cozy enough for a walk in the woods and chic enough for city streets!

MATERIALS

* Locate the pattern in the envelope (sheets #8 and #9)
* 1 yard of 44/45" wool fabric
* 1 spool of coordinating thread
* 2 buttons, ¾" in diameter

* Two 8" × 10" pieces of heavyweight fusible interfacing
* Small plate or drinking glass (to round earflaps)

Finished dimensions – head circumference 22" to 24" (*see* Resizing the Hat *on page* 373)

Seam allowance – ½" unless otherwise specified

① Measure, Mark, and Cut

Lay out your fabric in a single layer with the right side facing up. Position the pattern pieces according to the layout, and cut them out. Transfer the markings from the patterns to the wrong side of the fabric.

* **Brim** (cut 2)
* **Crown** (cut 1)

Also cut from fabric:

* **Earflap:** 15½" × 4" (cut 2)
* **Side band:** 24½" × 4¾" (cut 2)

Cut from interfacing:

* **Brim** (cut 2)

NOTE: *Position the grainline arrow on the pattern pieces along the straight grain of the fabric. The cutting layout shows pieces cut out on a single layer of fabric to allow for accurate plaid matching, if necessary. The white wavy line indicates extra fabric not shown.*

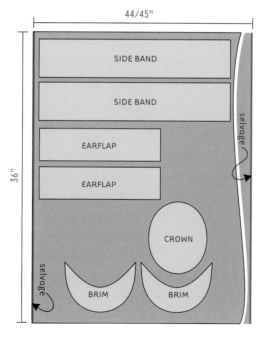

CUTTING LAYOUT

② Make the Brim

Fuse interfacing to the wrong side of both brim pieces following the manufacturer's instructions. With the right sides together, sew the brim pieces along the outside curve. Trim and notch the seam allowances, turn the brim right side out, and press. Topstitch ¼" from the outside curved edge. Baste the raw edges together. Set the brim aside.

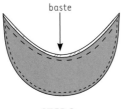

baste

STEP 2

③ Make the Earflap

* Round the two bottom corners on one long edge of the earflap pieces by tracing a small drinking glass or plate, starting the curve 1½" from each corner. Make sure all rounded corners are the same shape and cut around the marked lines.
* Make the earflap the same way as the brim, stitching the two pieces with the right sides together along the side and bottom curved edges. Trim and notch the seam allowances, turn the earflap right side out, and press. Topstitch ¼" from the outside curved edge. Baste the top, straight raw edges together.

④ Make the Side Band Exterior and Lining

* Fold each side band piece in half, right sides together, so the piece is 12¼" × 4¾", and mark the center at the fold. Stitch the short edges together to make a complete circle for the exterior. Repeat with the remaining side band to create the lining. Press the seam allowances open.
* Turn and press the bottom raw edge of the lining ½" to the wrong side.
* Pin the side bands with the wrong sides together, aligning the center back seams and top raw edges. Baste them together ½" from top edge.

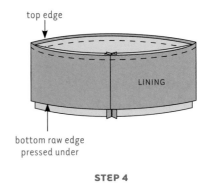

top edge

LINING

bottom raw edge
pressed under

STEP 4

⑤ Attach the Crown

Pin the right sides of the crown and side band exterior together, matching the single notch with the center back seam and the double notch with the center front marking. Stitch the crown in place through both the side band exterior and lining layers, being careful to smooth and realign the fabric as you stitch around the curves. Trim the seam allowances to ¼" and zigzag the edges together for a clean finish. Press the seam allowances toward the side band and topstitch ⅛" from the seam on the side band, through all the layers.

RESIZING THE HAT

The pattern is written for a finished head circumference of 23½". If you wish to make the cap larger or smaller, follow these easy steps:

1. Measure your head circumference and determine the desired finished circumference of your cap.

2. Calculate the difference between the pattern circumference (23½") and yours. Add or subtract this amount from the length of the side band and earflap pieces.

3. To resize the crown, use a measuring tape to draft a new pattern. Trace the existing crown pattern piece without ½" seam allowance onto a larger piece of drafting paper. Form the tape measure into an oval that is the desired hat circumference measurement, and position it around the existing crown pattern equidistant from the pattern piece's seamline at all points to ensure a perfect oval. Trace around the tape measure to mark your new seamline. Add ½" for seam allowance to the seamline that you just drew to make a new cutting line.

NOTE: *You can also enlarge the crown piece the desired amount with a photocopy machine.*

6 Attach the Brim and Earflap

Aligning the center front markings, pin and stitch the brim to the right side of the side band exterior, taking care not to catch the side band lining in the stitching. Mark the center back on the earflap and align the marking with the center back seam of the side band exterior, with the raw edges together. Stitch the earflap to the right side of the side band exterior, taking care not to catch the side band lining in the stitching. Press the seam allowances toward the side band.

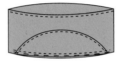

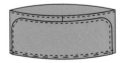

STEP 6

7 Secure the Side Band Lining

Carefully align and pin the folded edge of the side band lining to cover the brim/earflap/side band seam allowance. Neatly topstitch ⅛" from the folded edge of the lining, through all the layers, making sure that both the brim and earflap are not caught in the stitching.

8 Add Buttons and Buttonholes

Make diagonal buttonholes near the curved edges of the earflap, as shown. Fold the brim up to mark button locations on the cap side to correspond to the buttonholes. Remember that the earflap is a bit thick, so take care to sew the buttons on relatively loosely, with a thread shank, if necessary.

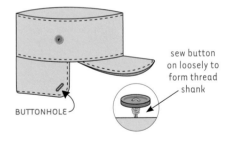

BUTTONHOLE

sew button on loosely to form thread shank

STEP 8

seafarer's tricorn Hat

Designed by Becka Rahn

The best costumes usually need just one perfect accessory to bring them to life. This fabulous hat works for a soldier, pirate, or historical figure and is great for Halloween, Renaissance festivals, history day, and school plays.

MATERIALS

* Locate the pattern in the envelope (sheet #9)
* 1 yard of 36" or 44/45" wool fabric or felt
* 1 spool of coordinating thread

Sizes – small (youth) has a 22" circumference; large (adult) has a 23½" circumference
Seam allowance – ½" unless otherwise specified

* 1 yard of medium to heavyweight fusible interfacing (optional)
* 1 package of ⅝" rickrack trim
* 1 large decorative button
* Buttonhole or embroidery thread

① Measure, Mark, and Cut

Fold your fabric in half lengthwise with the right sides together, aligning the selvages. Position the pattern pieces according to the layout. Cut out the first two pieces listed, then unfold your fabric and cut only one of the remaining two pieces (measure and mark the rosette). Transfer the markings from the patterns to the wrong side of the fabric.

* **Brim** (cut 2)
* **Side band** (cut 1 on fold)
* **Crown** (cut 1)
* **Rosette** 5" × 12" (cut 1)

Cut from interfacing (optional):
* **Brim** (cut 2)
* **Crown** (cut 1)
* **Side band** (cut 1)

NOTE: *Fuse interfacing to the felt before you cut the pieces, following the manufacturer's instructions. The interfaced side will be the wrong side of the pieces. Do not interface the rectangle for the rosette. Mirror the crown and brim along lines indicated on the pattern.*

② Attach the Side Band and Crown

* Fold the side band piece with the right sides together, aligning the center back short raw edges, and stitch the center back seam.

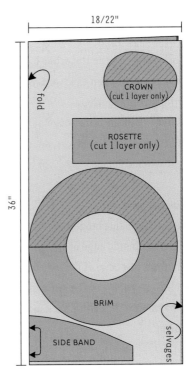

18/22"

fold

CROWN
(cut 1 layer only)

ROSETTE
(cut 1 layer only)

36"

BRIM

SIDE BAND

selvages

CUTTING LAYOUT

* With the right sides together, match and pin the center front of the crown with the center front of the side band. Repeat, matching the center back of the crown with the center back seam of the side band. Continue pinning the crown and side band pieces together at regular intervals, easing the crown to fit, as necessary.
* Stitch the crown to the side band.

❸ Make the Brim

* Pin the brim pieces with the wrong sides together, along the inside circle.
* Sandwich the rickrack between the outer edge of the brim pieces so that half of the rickrack is visible beyond the brim edge, while the other half is sandwiched between the two layers. Pin the layers together.
* Stitch close to the outer edge of the brim, through all the layers, securing the rickrack in place.

❹ Attach the Brim

* With the right sides together, match and pin the inside edge of the brim to the bottom raw edge of the side band, matching the center back seam of the side band with the center back mark on the brim.

* Baste the brim and side band together ¼" from the raw edges. Try on the hat or measure the head circumference of the tricorn recipient. If you need to adjust the fit of the hat, you can sew with a slightly smaller or larger seam allowance. A smaller seam allowance will make the hat slightly larger, a larger seam allowance will make it slightly smaller.
* If necessary, remove the basting stitches and baste again with the desired seam allowance width. Once satisfied with the fit, stitch the brim and side band together the desired distance from the raw edges, as previously determined. Reinforce this seam by stitching a second time within the seam allowance, close to the first stitching. Trim the seam allowances.

❺ Make the Rosette

* Fold the 5" × 12" rectangle in half with the wrong sides together, aligning the long edges. With a hand-sewing needle and a long piece of heavy thread, stitch through both layers along the 12" edge, with a gathering stitch. At ½" intervals, cut from the folded edge to ¼" from the gathering stitches.
* Pull both ends of the gathering thread very tightly to form a fabric ring. (There will be an opening in the center.) Tie the ends of the thread together securely.

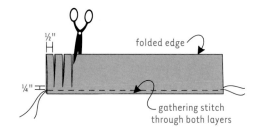

½"

folded edge

¼"

gathering stitch through both layers

STEP 5

6 Finish the Hat

* Fold up the edges of the brim at the placement dots (center back and one on each side) and invisibly tack the brim to the side band, taking care not to crease the brim.
* Position the rosette on one side of the hat brim and hand-sew it in place. Finish the rosette by sewing a large decorative button in the center. Ahoy, Matey!

KNIGHT IN SHINING ARMOR

Designed by Becka Rahn

It can be hard to find truly cool costumes for boys, whether for Halloween or just for pretend play. This simple, inexpensive, and eye-catching costume is great for boys or girls, both little ones and grown ones.

MATERIALS

* Locate the pattern in the envelope (sheet #9)
* 1 yard of 72"-wide wool or acrylic felt
* 1 spool of coordinating thread
* 8" square of contrasting colored felt
* 2 large buttons, or two 1" squares of Velcro

Finished dimensions – S (child size 5-10), L (small/medium adult)

Seam allowance – ½" unless otherwise specified

① Measure, Mark, and Cut

Fold your fabric in half with the right sides together, aligning the selvages. Position the pattern pieces according to the layout, and measure and mark the helmet band. Cut out the pieces, and transfer the center front marking on the yoke pattern piece to the wrong side of the fabric. Transfer the outline of the shield to the wrong side of one armor piece.

* **Front/back** (cut 4)
* **Side tabs** (cut 4)
* **Yoke** (cut 2)
* **Helmet** (cut 2)
* **Wing** (cut 4, 2 reversed)
* **Cheek** (cut 4, 2 reversed)
* **Nose** (cut 2)

Unfold the remaining felt and cut:

* **Dragon** (cut 1)
* **Helmet band** 4" × 22" (small) or
  4" × 24" (large) (cut 1)

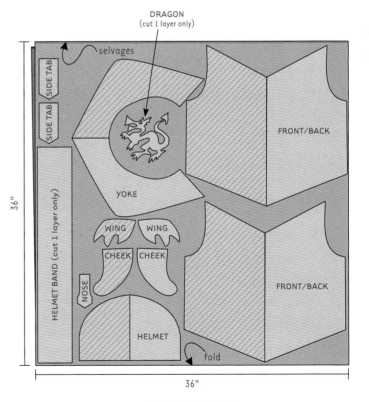

CUTTING LAYOUT

NOTE: *Mirror the front/back, yoke, and helmet along the line indicated on the pattern.*

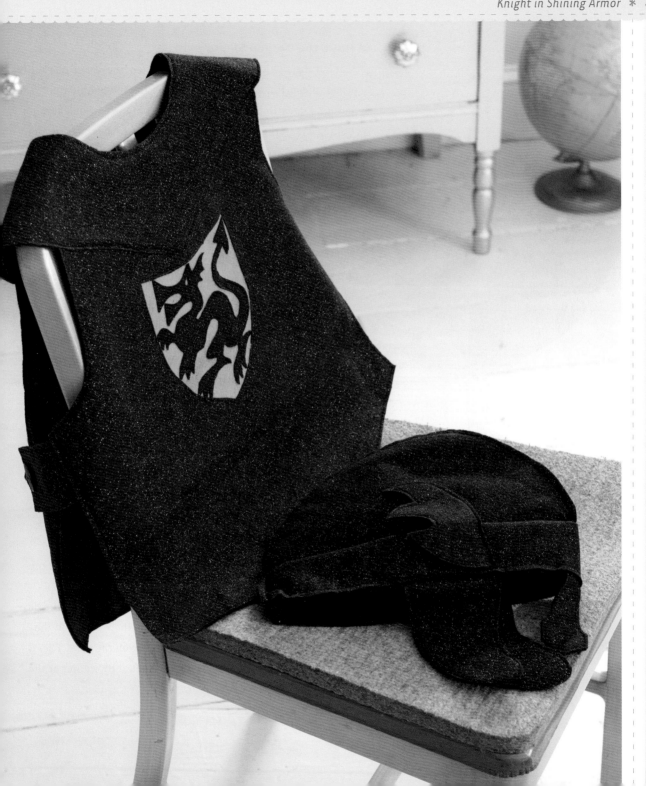

STEP 3

② Make the Dragon Shield

* Cut out the shield shape along the marked line of one marked armor piece. Pin the square of contrasting felt behind the cutout. Edgestitch around the raw edge of the cutout, catching both layers in the stitching. Trim away the excess contrasting felt from the wrong side close to the stitching line.
* Center the dragon on the shield, and edgestitch or hand-sew it in place.

③ Stitch the Front and Back

* Pin two side tabs with the wrong sides together. Edgestitch around all four sides. Repeat with remaining side tab pieces.
* Make a large buttonhole in each stitched tab, approximately ½" from the pointed end. If you are using Velcro instead of buttons, stitch one half of one Velcro piece to the wrong side of each tab at the same location.
* Pin the armor piece with the shield to another armor piece with the wrong sides together, aligning the raw edges. Tuck the side tabs between the layers just underneath each armhole so the straight short end of each tab is ½" inside the raw edges. Edgestitch all around. This becomes the armor front.
* Pin the remaining armor pieces with the wrong sides together and edgestitch all around them to make the armor back.

④ Attach the Armor Yoke

* Pin the two yokes with the wrong sides together along the top (neck) edge.
* Slip the top edge of the front and back armor pieces ¼" inside the bottom edge of the yoke layers. Match the V shape on the armor front with the center front marking on the yoke. The center back edges of the yoke should meet at the center of the armor back. Pin the yoke to the armor.

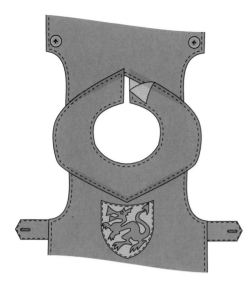

STEP 4

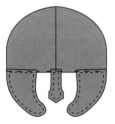

STEP 5

* Edgestitch all around the yoke, being sure to catch all the layers in the stitching to secure the armor front and back.
* Hand-sew the buttons on the armor back, so they align with the side tab buttonholes. Or, stitch the remaining Velcro half in place.

⑤ Make the Helmet

* Pin the helmet pieces with the wrong sides together, aligning the raw edges. Stitch along the top curved edge, leaving the straight bottom edge open.
* Pin two wings with the wrong sides together, aligning the raw edges. Edgestitch all around. Repeat with the remaining wings. Stitch the nose and cheek pieces in the same way.
* Overlap the top edge of the nose ¼" over the bottom edge on the right side of the helmet at one end of the seam and baste it in place.
* Measure and mark 2½" from each side of the nose. Overlap the top edge of the cheek pieces ¼" over the bottom edge on the right side of the helmet at the markings, with the curved sides facing toward the nose. Baste the cheeks in place.

⑥ Attach the Helmet Band and Wings

* Fold the helmet band in half widthwise, and stitch the short edges together. Fold the helmet band in half lengthwise, wrong sides together. Pin the band to the right side of the helmet so the raw edges of the band are aligned with the bottom raw edge of the helmet, covering the overlapped ends of the nose and cheek. Edgestitch the band in place, being sure to catch all the layers in the stitching.
* Pin the straight edges of the wings on each side of the helmet band, just above the cheeks. The wing points should face toward the back of the helmet. Hand-sew or machine-stitch them in place.

pretend sewing machine

Designed by Caitlin Betsy Bell

Do you have a little helper who wishes she were big enough for her own sewing machine? This plush toy is outfitted with interactive features like buttons for dials, a spool of "thread," and threading loops. Give your wee one some fabric scraps and she can be just like mom (or dad) with this toy!

MATERIALS

* Locate the pattern in the envelope (sheet #9)
* 1 yard of 44/45" wool or acrylic felt
* 1 spool of coordinating thread
* 6" × 3" scrap fabric for appliqué
* ⅜ yard of ½" rickrack, ribbon, or other trim
* 6" length of ½" ribbon for thread loops
* 2 buttons, ⅞" or 1" in diameter
* 1 to 2 bags of polyester fiberfill

* Scrap of gray or other contrasting felt (presser foot, other parts)
* Two 2½" lengths of pipe cleaner or chenille stems
* Grommet, ¼" in diameter (optional)
* 1 small empty thread spool
* 60" (or longer) length of shoelace or ⅛" cording for pretend "thread"
* Glue (optional)

Finished dimensions — 11½" high × 13" wide × 4" deep
Seam allowance — ¼" unless otherwise specified

① Measure, Mark, and Cut

Fold your fabric in half with the right sides together, aligning the selvages. Position the pattern piece, and measure and mark the additional pieces as shown. Cut out the pieces, and transfer the markings from the pattern piece to the wrong side of fabric.

* **Front/back** (cut 2)
* **Sides** 4½" × 34" (cut 2)
* **Thread loops** 3" × ½" (cut 2)

Cut from contrasting felt:
* **Presser foot** (cut 2)
* **Presser foot ankle** ¾" × 1¾" (cut 1)
* **Shank/thread holder** 2½" × 1" (cut 2)
* **Shank base** 1" × 2" (cut 2)

NOTE: *Position the grainline arrow on the pattern piece along the straight grain of the fabric.*

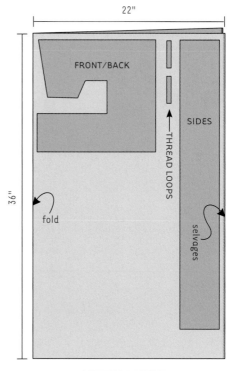

CUTTING LAYOUT

② Embellish the Sewing Machine Front

* Zigzag or satin stitch the 6" × 3" fabric scrap onto the right side of one front/back as indicated on the pattern. Hand-sew the buttons in place. This becomes the sewing machine front.
* Stitch the rickrack, ribbon, or other trim on the front as indicated on the pattern.

* Fold the thread loops in half across the width, aligning the short edges. Pin these on the right side of the sewing machine front where indicated on pattern, aligning the raw edges. Baste in place with edgestitch.

③ Make and Attach the Sides

* Pin the sides, right sides together, aligning all raw edges. Stitch the sides together at both short ends with ½" seam allowance, to form a ring.
* Pin the side and front with the right sides together and the raw edges aligned, starting and finishing at the inside curve (under the arm) of the sewing machine. Stitch the pieces together, easing around the corners and clipping as necessary.
* Stitch the side to the remaining front/back in similar fashion, leaving a 4" opening at the bottom edge for turning and stuffing.
* Turn the sewing machine right side out and stuff it firmly, starting with all the corners. Sew the opening closed with a slipstitch or whipstitch.

④ Make the Thread Holder and Shank

* Wrap one shank/thread holder piece completely around one pipe cleaner and stitch the loose end in place to hold the felt closed. Fold a shank base in half lengthwise to form a ½" × 2" piece. Wrap it around one end of the shank/thread holder and stitch it in place. Repeat with the remaining pieces to make one shank and one thread holder. Set the shank aside.
* Hand-sew the thread holder to the top of the sewing machine, 3" in from the right side and centered front to back.

⑤ Make and Attach the Presser Foot

* Pin the presser foot pieces with the wrong sides together, and stitch all around. Hand-sew the presser foot to the narrower end of the shank.
* Fold the ankle in half across the width with the wrong sides together, to make a roughly square shape. Punch a small hole or install a small grommet, following the manufacturer's instructions, in the center of the ankle. Hand-sew the ankle to the back of the shank. Stitch the wider end of the shank to the machine, at the marking.

⑥ Make and Attach the Thread Spool

Wrap one end of the cording or shoelace around the empty spool and stitch or glue it in place, leaving at least 24" of lacing dangling free. Place the thread spool on the thread holder, and thread the cording through the loops and through the hole in the ankle.

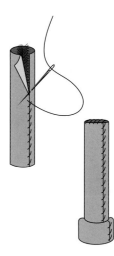

STEP 4

STEP 5

wave illusions pillow

Designed by Caroline Sanchez

Have you ever created texture on a flat fabric simply by sewing it a certain way? This pillow cover showcases a geometric design with an illusion of curves. Shadows created by the tucks give it an elegant dimension that you won't be able to help but run your fingers over!

MATERIALS

* 1 yard of 44/45" wool fabric
* 1 spool of coordinating thread
* 16" square pillow form

Finished dimensions – 16" square
Seam allowance – ½" unless otherwise specified

1 Measure, Mark, and Cut

Lay out your fabric in a single layer with the wrong side facing up. Using a ruler and washable fabric pen or tailor's chalk, measure and mark the following pattern pieces directly onto the fabric, aligning the straight edges with the straight grain of the fabric.

* **Front** 18" × 24" (cut 1)
* **Front facing** 17" × 17" (cut 1)
* **Back** 17" × 12" (cut 2)

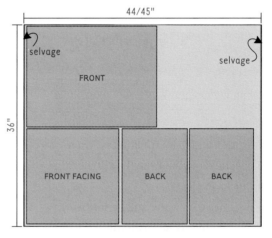

CUTTING LAYOUT

2 Mark the Wave Lines

Lay the front piece right side up on a flat surface. Starting 4" from the left side, using a disappearing ink fabric pen, mark 24 vertical lines in ½" increments.

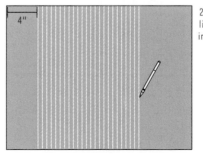

24 vertical lines at ½" increments

STEP 2

❸ Stitch the Vertical Tucks

* The tucks are made on the right side of the fabric. Fold the fabric with the wrong sides together, lining up the first two marked lines. Stitch on the marked lines to create a tuck. Repeat with the subsequent lines to create a total of 12 tucks.
* Trim your pillow top to 17" square, taking care *not* to trim any fabric from the left side of the front piece.

❹ Create the Waves

* Measure down 2½" from the top edge and mark a horizontal line across the tucks. Below that first marked line, continue marking six more lines in 2" increments. The top and bottom lines will each be 2½" from the respective edges to allow for ½" seam allowances.
* Stitch from left to right ¼" from the top edge, so that all the tucks fold toward the right.
* Stitch from right to left along the first marked line so that all the tucks fold toward the left.
* Repeat on each subsequent marked line, each time alternating the direction you sew the tucks. Finish by stitching ¼" from the bottom edge in the opposite direction from the stitched line just above it to keep your tucks in place.
* Spritz the disappearing ink lines with water and be sure they are completely gone before pressing, as heat can cause the lines to become permanent. Allow the pillow top to air-dry as much as possible.
* Press the pillow top on both sides of the tucks, steaming away any excess water. Then, using the very edge of your iron, press the tucks out from each horizontally sewn line to give them a crisp edge. Be careful not to crush the tucks.

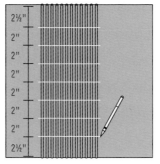

2½"
2"
2"
2"
2"
2"
2"
2½"

STEP 4

❺ Create the Pillow Envelope Back

* Press one long edge of a back piece ¼" to the wrong side and again another ¾", and stitch close to the folded edge. Repeat along one long edge of the remaining back piece.
* Layer the two hemmed back pieces with the right sides facing up, overlapping the hemmed edges by 5", to create a 17" square. Baste the layers together at the overlaps, a scant ¼" from the raw edges (*see the glossary*).

❻ Assemble the Pillow

* Pin the front and front facing pieces with the wrong sides together, aligning all the raw edges. Baste them together ¼" from the raw edges.
* Pin the front and back with the right sides together. Stitch them together around all four sides. Turn the pillow cover right side out and check that all the tucks are in the correct direction at the outside edges, and adjust if needed (by pulling out the pillow cover assembly stitches).
* Turn the pillow cover inside out, clip the corners, trim the seam allowance to ¼" and zigzag over the raw edges.
* Turn the pillow cover right side out, stuff your pillow form inside, and enjoy your elegant new pillow!

BartHolomew Bookends

Designed by Emily Steffen

Fun and functional, these hedgehog bookends do an admirable job corralling your books while lending an aura of cuteness to your room and bookshelves. Although not just for kids, don't be surprised if these become a modern nursery must-have!

MATERIALS

* Locate the pattern in the envelope (sheets #6 and #8)
* 1 yard of 44/45" wool, tweed, or similar fabric
* ¼ yard of coordinating solid fabric for the head (optional)
* 1 spool of coordinating thread
* 2 quart-size plastic freezer bags
* 6 cups of poly pellets, dried beans, rice, seeds, or similar stuffing material
* 12 ounces of polyester fiberfill
* Leftover yarn or embroidery floss
* 4 buttons, ½" diameter, or embroidery floss, for eyes
* Tapestry needle

Finished dimensions – 9" high × 13" wide
Seam allowance – ¼" unless otherwise specified

① Measure, Mark, and Cut

Fold your fabric in half lengthwise with the right sides together, aligning the selvages. Position the pattern pieces according to the layout and cut them out. Transfer the placement markings from the pattern pieces to the wrong side of fabric. Instructions are for making two hedgehogs, but you can easily make four from one yard of fabric if using contrasting fabric for the heads.

* **Body** (cut 4)
* **Bottom gusset** (cut 2)

Cut out of coordinating solid fabric, or remaining main fabric:

* **Head** (cut 4)

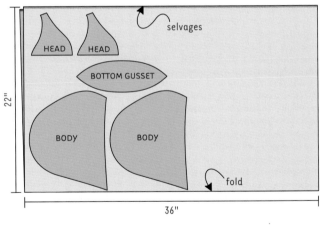

CUTTING LAYOUT

② Attach the Bottom Gusset

* With the wrong sides together, stitch one body to one side of a bottom gusset, starting and stopping ¼" from the raw edge as marked.
* With the wrong sides together, stitch a second body to the other side of the same bottom gusset in similar fashion.
* With the wrong sides together, stitch the body pieces together around the top curve, leaving a 3" opening for stuffing.
* Repeat with the remaining bottom gusset and body pieces.

③ Assemble and Stuff the Hedgehogs

Fill each freezer bag with three cups of pellets, beans, or rice and secure it tightly. Insert each stuffed freezer bag into a hedgehog body, letting it rest completely at the bottom. Stuff the rest of each body firmly with the fiberfill. Hand-sew the opening closed with a slipstitch or whipstitch.

④ Create the Heads

* Pin the two head pieces with the right sides together, and stitch around, leaving the straight edge open. Turn the head right side out and press the straight raw edges ⅛" to the wrong side. Stuff the head with fiberfill, leaving enough space at the opening so you can attach the head to the body.

* Pin the head to the body at the placement marks and hand-sew it in place with a slipstitch or whipstitch. Repeat with the remaining body and head pieces.

⑤ Add the Finishing Touches

* Hand-sew buttons on the head for eyes, or embroider eyes with the satin stitch.

* To create yarn "spikes" on the hedgehog body, thread a tapestry needle with yarn. Take a very small stitch through the fabric, and trim the yarn so that 1½" of yarn sticks up on each side of the stitch. Twist the yarn tightly. Tie the yarn ends into a knot to secure the stitch and the twists. Repeat to create spikes all over the body, as desired.

GLOSSARY

Appliqué. Any technique that adheres one fabric piece to another in a decorative fashion. An appliqué may be applied with double-sided fusible interfacing, a zigzag/satin topstitch along the edges of the top fabric, or a slipstitch with the top fabric's raw edges turned under, among other techniques. Hand embroidery is also often incorporated.

Backstitch. Used to secure and reinforce your stitching at the beginning and end of a seam to keep it from unraveling. See chapter 1, page 11.

Ballpoint needle. Available for both machine and hand-sewing, this needle has a rounded point so it slides between the yarns of knitted fabrics, instead of piercing them.

Basting. Long stitches, done by hand or by machine, to temporarily hold fabric sections together. The stitches are removed once the final seaming is complete, so do not backstitch at the beginning or end of the seam. Basting is also used to gather an area of fabric. Leave the beginning and ending thread tails long since they are used to draw up the fabric and create a gathered effect.

Batten. A thin strip of wood used to fasten down edges of material, such as in a roman shade.

Bias. The diagonal grain of the fabric, it accents the natural stretch of the fabric. True bias is found at an exact 45-degree angle from both the straight and crossgrain of the fabric.

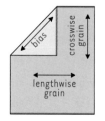

Bias tape. Made from a strip of fabric that has been cut along the bias grain of the fabric. You can buy it pre-packaged with a single or double fold, or make it yourself. It is often used to finish or encase garment edges.

Binding. Encasing the raw edges of a project with another piece of fabric, often bias tape. Purchased bias tape is narrower on top, so that as long as you sew with the narrower side facing up, you will be sure to catch the back of the binding in the stitching.

Blanket stitch. A decorative stitch, used for edge finishing, appliqué, and buttonholes. The blanket stitch is worked the same as the buttonhole stitch, only with space between the stitches. Working from left to right, insert the needle the desired stitch length from the edge and bring it out below the fabric edge, and over the thread as shown. Carry the thread to the right of the previous stitch to form a loop for the next stitch.

Blindstitch. Available on many sewing machines, this stitch is most commonly used for creating blind hems. For blindstitching by hand, see Slipstitch.

Box stitch. Often used to secure handles and straps to bags. Using a short, straight stitch, stitch a square or rectangle, typically 1" or 1½" in size, close to three finished edges. Then, stitch an X between the stitched corners.

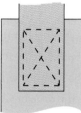

Casing. A channel created by sewing a line of stitching parallel to a finished edge, or by sewing two lines of stitching parallel to each other, through two layers of fabric to allow elastic, cording, ribbon, or other material to pass through. Casings are a popular finishing technique for elastic and drawstring waistbands.

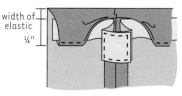

Clipping curves. Used to reduce tension on concave seams (inward curves). Clip within the seam allowance to, but not through, the stitching line. Sharper curves require more clipping, and corners are typically clipped at a 45-degree angle. For outer curves, see Notching.

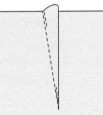

Crosswise grainline. The direction of the fabric threads that are perpendicular to the selvage and parallel to the cut end of the fabric. It is the opposite of lengthwise grain, and there is a little bit of stretch when the fabric is pulled in this direction.

Darts. Small seams that take in fullness and add shaping to a project. They are wide at the seam edge and taper to a point.

Directional fabrics. Fabric prints may be unidirectional (one-way), bidirectional (two-way), or nondirectional (tossed). With a unidirectional print, there is a definite top and bottom to the print, most frequently because objects in the design all face the same direction, top to bottom. Bidirectional prints may be symmetrical, top to bottom (if there are characters or objects, half face "up" and half face "down"), but are not symmetrical side to side. Nondirectional prints allow you to place the fabric any direction without changing the look of the finished project.

Doll needle. A very long, thin needle that can completely pierce a three-dimensional stuffed sewn object such as a doll or plush animal.

Double-fold hem. A hem that has been folded and pressed twice to the wrong side of the fabric before being topstitched. The first fold is typically ¼"; the second fold can vary.

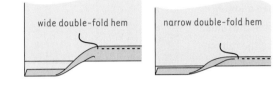

wide double-fold hem   narrow double-fold hem

Drafting tape. A sticky tape that resembles masking tape but is easily removable from delicate surfaces and does not leave a sticky residue. Used for marking difficult-to-mark fabrics such as fleece and woolens.

Edgestitch. A style of topstitching that is typically stitched ⅛" away from an edge, with a slightly longer stitch length than what is used for structural seams. Edgestitching may be used to close an open seam after turning, or may simply be a decorative touch.

Embroidery. A hand-sewing technique that adds an extra-special touch to any project. Some popular embroidery stitches are French knots, stem stitch, chain stitch, satin stitch, and blanket stitch.

Facing. A shaped pattern piece that is used to finish shaped garment edges, such as the neckline, armhole, or button placket. Facings are typically 2" to 3" wide, but the width can depend on the application, placement, and size of the garment.

Finger-press. To manually crease a seam allowance, fold, or other part of a fabric piece with your fingers. Frequently used when needing to press fabric out of the way during stitching, when it would be impractical or inconvenient to remove the fabric from the sewing machine in order to press with an iron before sewing the rest of the seam.

Flat-felled seam. A very strong seam that hides raw edges and is sewn in multiple steps. First, stitch a ½" or ⅝" seam with the wrong sides together. Trim one layer of the seam allowance in half, to ¼". Fold and press the longer seam allowance in half, encasing the other, trimmed allowance. Topstitch the folded edge to the fabric, encasing all the raw edges.

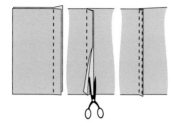

Free-motion stitching. A form of machine embroidery that is done by manipulating the fabric, held taut in an embroidery hoop, to create a thread design. This technique can also be used for quilting multiple fabric layers together. Sometimes a special presser foot is needed, such as a darning foot, that allows you to move the fabric in all directions. It also requires a machine that allows the feed dogs to be dropped.

French curve. This sewing tool is used to connect two (or more) points with a smooth curve. Especially useful for drawing neck and armholes edges as well as truing seams.

French seam. Often used for durability and tidiness to hide raw edges of seams in unlined and sheer fabric projects. Stitch a scant ¼" seam with the wrong sides together. Then, turn the fabrics wrong side out (right sides together) at the seam and stitch another ¼" seam to enclose the raw edges.

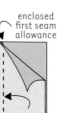

scant ¼"

enclosed first seam allowance

first row of stitches

second row of stitches

Fussy cutting. Cutting a specific motif from printed fabric rather than randomly cutting yardage. Often used in appliqué.

Gathering. Used decoratively and functionally to draw up a larger piece of fabric by pulling basting stitches (see Basting) so it can be sewn to a smaller piece. To adjust gathers evenly, mark the halfway, quarter-length, and even eighth-length distances on both the main fabric and the piece that is to be gathered before beginning the gathering process. Match the marks as you pull the gathering threads to ensure that you join the pieces evenly. The piece to be gathered is typically about twice as long as the main fabric, so these marks will be farther apart on the gathering piece.

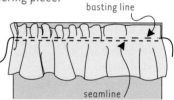

basting line

seamline

Grainline. The direction of the fabric threads that runs parallel to the selvage edges. Sewing patterns usually have a double-ended arrow printed on the pattern piece indicating grainline. When laying out your pattern pieces, make sure that the arrow lines up with the straight grainline. It is the opposite of the "crosswise" grainline. See also Crosswise grainline.

Hand-sewing. A sewing machine can't do everything! Hand-sewing is often the only way to stitch a button or other closure onto a completed item, or to ensure that you only stitch through one layer of fabric. A few other finishing techniques, such as slipstitching and whipstitching, are only accomplished by hand.

Interfacing. Used to provide shape, stiffness, and support; it is typically found in collars, cuffs, lapels, waistbands, and bags. It is available in either iron-on/fusible or sew-in versions.

Lengthwise grainline. This is the edge parallel to the selvage. See also Grainline.

Markings. A variety of notations typically found on pattern pieces that help with the construction of a project. Examples include darts, pleat lines, dots, notches, pocket placements. Be sure to transfer all markings to the wrong side of the fabric before removing the paper pattern pieces.

Nap. See Woven Pile Fabrics, page 209.

Notching. Used to make convex seams (outward curves) lie flat, notches are cut at regular intervals within the seam allowance to, but not through, the stitching line. Sharper curves require more notches.

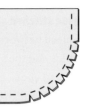

Pile. The yarns that stand up from the woven backing of a fabric, such as on corduroy, velvet or velveteen, creating nap or surface texture. See chapter 6.

Pinking. Cutting a zigzag edge using pinking shears or a pinking rotary cutter.

Pintucks. Often decorative and sometimes used for shaping, pintucks are formed by matching two lines (typically ⅛" apart), wrong sides together, stitching close to the fold, thereby creating a folded tuck. Most commonly, tucks are stitched along the grainline and are equal distances apart.

Piping. A decorative detail inserted between two seams. One edge has welting, while the other has a raw edge to attach, called a flange. Buy prepackaged piping or make your own with a bias strip of fabric and small cording.

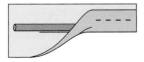

Pivot. A great way to stitch a corner. Stop short of the fabric raw edge, the same width as the seam allowance. Leaving the needle down in the fabric, lift the presser foot up and turn the fabric 90 degrees to continue stitching the seam.

Plain weave. The simplest and most common weave. The warp and fill (weft) threads are uniform. Plain-weave fabrics are easy to sew and provide optimum printing results. They can be yarn-dyed (woven stripe and/or plaid). Voile, quilting cotton, and flannel are examples of plain-weave fabrics.

Pleats. Folds or pleats can be either inverted or extroverted, and stitched in a variety of widths. They are common in skirts, but also appear in a variety of other items. Pleats provide both decorative and functional fullness and are typically found in four variations: box, knife, inverted, and accordion.

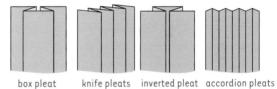

box pleat   knife pleats   inverted pleat   accordion pleats

Quilting. Quilted fabric generally has batting sandwiched between two layers of fabric and is decoratively stitched through all the layers. If you are quilting your own fabric, you should generally do so before cutting out your pattern pieces, as quilting draws fabric in and makes it smaller.

Right side. The right side of the fabric is the side on which the design is printed, and is almost always used for the outside of your garment or accessory. If you are working with a solid piece of fabric where the right side is not readily obvious, determine which side you want to call the right side, and then be consistent. You may want to designate and mark the same side of each cut fabric piece as the wrong side to avoid a sewing mistake.

Scant seam. A seam with slightly narrow seam allowances. For example, to sew a scant ¼" seam, move your fabric over a bit to sew a slightly smaller than ¼" seam (somewhere between ¼" and ⅛").

Seam allowance. The distance between the seamline (stitching line) that joins two or more pieces of fabric together and the cut edge of the fabric. Standard seam allowances are frequently ⅝" wide, but it is becoming increasingly common for seam allowances to be ½" wide.

Seamline. This is your basic stitching line for joining two (or more) pieces of fabric together.

Selvage. The selvage is a finished fabric edge and it does not fray. The selvages are parallel to the straight grainline and perpendicular to the cut fabric edges. Most pattern pieces are positioned on the fabric parallel to the selvages.

Slipstitch. An invisible hand stitch that joins two fabrics together, also called a blindstitch. Bring the needle out of one fabric, and pierce the other fabric directly opposite, then run the needle under the fabric (or between the fold if you are sewing a folded edge) about ¼". Bring the needle out and repeat for the other fabric layer. Continue so that you are forming straight stitches between the two fabrics, with the thread running under or between the fabric layers between the straight stitches. After a few stitches, pull the thread gently to tighten and hide the stitches.

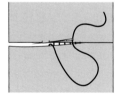

Smocking. Decorative pleating and stitching techniques used to control fullness. The width of the fabric required for a smocked project is often three times the width of the finished piece. (See examples of smocking on page 36.)

Stabilizer. A temporary fabric designed to support fabric, most commonly used for embroidery. Available in four varieties: cut-away, tear-away, iron-away, wash-away. Tear-away is the most appropriate for the applications in this book.

Staystitch. A straight, longer than usual stitch, used to stabilize a bias or curved fabric edge to prevent it from stretching or becoming distorted. It is typically done through a single fabric layer, just within the seam allowance.

Stitch in the ditch. A stitch through multiple layers of fabric, used when you don't want topstitching to show. On the right side of the fabric, stitch through all the layers directly over the existing seam, or in the "ditch" of the existing seamline. Be precise!

Tissue stitched seam. A seam in which tissue paper is inserted between the layers of fabric, or between the fabrics and the sewing machine and/or presser foot, then removed upon completion of stitching.

Topstitch. Visible stitching on the right side of a project, which can be purely decorative or can provide reinforcement. It can be a single straight stitch, a double stitch created with a twin needle, a shell stitch, or a zigzag. A straight stitch looks best with a slightly longer stitch length than the one used for seams. If your topstitching is slightly irregular, use it on printed fabrics and the print will conceal the irregularities.

Trimming corners. Cut corner seam allowances at a 45-degree angle close to where the two stitching lines meet. This will ensure a sharp corner once the fabric is turned right side out.

Tucks. Like darts, tucks are used to help eliminate fullness. They can be both functional and decorative. For a variation on a decorative tuck, *see* Pintucks.

Twill weave. The most durable fabric weave with better drapability than a plain-weave fabric. Typically a solid fabric, you may also find printed twills and yarn-dyes (woven stripes and/or plaids). It is distinguishable by its diagonal lines woven into the fabric. The most common twill fabric is denim.

Warp. The lengthwise yarns.

Weft. The crosswise yarns used in creating woven fabrics, inserted at a right angle to the warp.

Whipstitch. Unlike a slipstitch, a whipstitch is not invisible but is used similarly to stitch two pieces of fabric together. In a whipstitch you always come out of the same piece of fabric and stitch in the same direction into the second piece of fabric. If the whipstitch is done at a raw edge, it will overcast that edge.

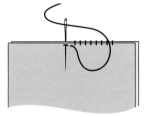

Wrong side. The side of the fabric on which the design is *not* printed, and is almost always the inside of your garment or accessory. See Right side.

Yarn-dye. Fabric woven or knit of yarns that were dyed before weaving (or knitting) to create stripe and/or plaid patterns.

Zigzag. A basic sewing-machine stitch that looks like a zigzag. Typically, it can vary in length and width. A very close zigzag stitch may be called a satin stitch, and can be used for buttonholes. Zigzag stitches within a seam allowance can also be used to finish seams when no serger is on hand, and is also frequently used to provide a bit of reinforcement at a stressed seam.

The photo stylist would like to thank:

MODELS:
Ruby Focarino
Hudson Burckhard
Stella Cornillon
Romi Butscher
Maeve Butscher
Iris Larson
Britta Storey Zeff
Julia Bullock
Lily Kramer
Zoe Ewing

LOCATIONS:
Waddle n Swaddle, Rhinebeck, New York
Wing & Clover, Rhinebeck, New York
Home of Joanna and Evan Smith-Rakoff
Bard College
The Fisher Center for the Performing Arts @ Bard College

PROPS:
Michelle Varian
Ferm Living
Canvas Home
Sawkille
D. Bryant Archie
Um
Waddle n Swaddle
Wing & Clover
No Sugar

resources

More Fabric Facts

Betzina, Sandra. *More Fabric Savvy: A Quick Resource Guide to Selecting and Sewing Fabric.* Taunton Press, 2004.

Dan River Mills Inc. *Dan River's Dictionary of Textile Terms, 3rd ed.* Dan River Cotton Mills, 1945.

Long, Connie. *Sewing with Knits.* Taunton Press, 2000.

Shaeffer, Claire. *Claire Shaeffer's Fabric Sewing Guide, 2nd ed.* Krause Publications, 2008.

Fabric

Crafty Planet
612-788-1180
www.craftyplanet.com

Funky Fabrix
61-07-38-558479
www.funkyfabrix.com.au

Pink Chalk Fabrics
888-894-0658
www.pinkchalkfabrics.com

Sew, Mama, Sew!
503-380-3584
www.sewmamasew.com

superbuzzy
805-644-4143
www.superbuzzy.com

Buttons

AccessoriesOfOld.com
301-279-7595
www.accessoriesofold.com

As Cute As a Button
619-223-2555
www.ascuteasabutton.com

Hushco Buttons
877-487-4262
www.hushcobuttons.com

Trims and Other Details

BeadWarehouse
802-775-3082
www.beadwarehouse.com

Cheeptrims.com
877-288-8746
www.cheeptrims.com

JKM Products Corporation
800-767-3635
www.jkmribbon.com

Les' Bon Ribbon
225-262-1921
www.lesbonribbon.com

M&J Trimming
800-965-8746
www.mjtrim.com

Rochford Supply
866-681-7401
www.rochfordsupply.com

ZipperStop
888-947-7872
www.zipperstop.com

Inspiration and Forums

BurdaStyle
www.burdastyle.com

Craft
www.craftzine.com

Craftster
www.craftster.org

Etsy
www.etsy.com

GetCrafty
www.getcrafty.com

ThreadBanger
www.threadbanger.com

And of course, the blogs and sites of our amazing contributors!

Our Featured Fabrics

Most of the fabrics featured in this book come from the following manufacturers and/or designers. Visit their websites or your favorite fabric sources to view their current collections of fabric prints, which change regularly.

Rowan (Westminster Fibers)
www.westminsterfabrics.com

* **Amy Butler**
  www.amybutlerdesign.com

* **Free Spirit**
  www.freespiritfabric.com

* **Heather Bailey**
  www.heatherbaileystore.com

* **Joel Dewberry**
  www.joeldewberry.com

* **Anna Maria Horner**
  www.website.com

* **Denyse Schmidt**
  www.dsquilts.com

* **Annette Tatum**
  www.annettetatum.com

* **Valori Wells**
  http://valoriwells.com

* **Jay McCarroll**
  www.website.com

Alexander Henry Fabrics
www.ahfabrics.com

Michael Miller Fabrics
www.michaelmillerfabrics.com

* **Sandi Henderson**
  http://sandihendersondesign.com

* **Patti Young**
  www.website.com

Robert Kaufman Fabrics
www.robertkaufman.com

* **Laurie Wisbrun**
  http://lauriewisbrun.com

* **Ann Kelle**
  www.annkelle.com

MODA
www.unitednotions.com

Riley Blake Designs
http://www.rileyblakedesigns.com/

Oilcloth International
http://oilcloth.com

Hoffman Fabrics
www.hoffmanfabrics.com

JAPANESE IMPORTS:

Kokka
www.kokka.co.jp

* **Etsuko Furuya**
  www.f-echino.com

Lecien
www.lecien.co.jp

CONTRIBUTOR BIOS

Aimee Doyle Pelletier and Carly Stipe

✳ *Shaggy Chic Chenille Clutch, page 177*

Aimee and Carly are crafty cousins who were taught to knit and sew by their English grandmother, Nanny Jean. Many years later, these artists and moms opened a yarn and fabric shop in historic downtown Stillwater, Minnesota. Darn Knit Anyway is a source for education, unique yarns, textiles, handmade gifts, and craft accessories. Aimee and Carly have created a place their Nanny Jean is proud of, a place that is dedicated to providing a creative outlet for novice and experienced crafters and local artists.
www.darnknitanyway.com

Alexis Meschi

✳ *Tuxedo Dress, page 68*

Alexis of Santa Cruz, California, is a stay-at-home mother to three wonderful daughters and the wife of a fantastic husband. She loves designing and sewing and is constantly inspired to push herself to try new things. Inspired by textures, tone-on-tone colors, and classic looks with a twist, you can find Alexis' designs, tutorials, and ideas at her website. You don't need money, status, or influence to create something of beauty or substance; you need heart.
www.madebylex.com

Alyce Dyer-Hall

✳ *Slip Strap Bag, page 361*

For Alyce, the pattern always comes last. She creates her pieces with love, improvising from the inside out to find creative uses for everyday items. Alyce's admiration of the fine arts is infused in the custom care she takes creating unique, sustainable, storied pieces. She enjoys working with clients and the challenge of designing one-of-a-kind, practical products. In particular, Alyce loves to machine quilt; she puts the feed dogs down and draws with colorful quality threads.

Anna Buchholz

✳ *Kitchen Gift Set, page 152*

Anna is a second-time contributor to the One-Yard Wonders series. She learned how to sew at a young age by watching her mother and grandmother. When she's not in front of the sewing machine, Anna enjoys baking, knitting, playing Rock Band with her husband, and throwing tennis balls for her dog to chase. See more of Ann's work at her blog.
http://sewsewetc.blogspot.com

Anna Graham

✳ *Fold Over Bag, page 140*

Like many sewists, Anna grew up sewing with her mom. Although sewing was not her favorite activity, she loved being able to create something on her own. Her two daughters inspired her to start sewing more and after discovering the blogging world, Anna never turned back. She takes great pleasure in creating, improvising, discovering new techniques, and making her house a home.
www.noodle-head.com

Annelie Hervi

✳ *Hooded Wrap Shirt, page 327*

Annelie, a stay-at-home mother, loves designing and creating. With a degree in architectural drafting, she uses the computer to create new patterns for fabric and clothing. You can find her original fabric designs, buy her creations, and read about her many projects at her blog.
www.craftandcackle.blogspot.com

Archer DeHoskins

✳ *Space Beans Target Toss, page 346*

Archer is a crafting and publishing prodigy, having been in utero during the writing and editing of the first *One-Yard Wonders* book. He enjoys eating, reading, playing, and interacting with various stuffed and real animals. The inspiration for his Space Beans Target Toss came from a wooden vintage clown beanbag game board in his parents' basement, and the plethora of robots and rocket ships that decorate his room.

Atticus Bird

✳ *Rattle Ball (Baby's Accessory Trio), page 184*

Atticus lives in Minneapolis, Minnesota. He's fairly new to crafting, and is honored to have had his project selected for inclusion in this book. This has been his greatest craft accomplishment, and it has given Atticus the confidence to keep on crafting!
http://anewhuman.wordpress.com

Becka Rahn

* *Knight in Shining Armor, page 378*
* *Seafarer's Tricorn Hat, page 375*

Becka is a geek for fiber art and technology. She grew up in Rapid City, South Dakota, and used her very first paycheck from a summer theater job to purchase a new sewing machine. She works as the education manager at the Textile Center of Minnesota, where she teaches sewing, felting, digital design, and technology skills to crafters of all ages.
www.beckarahn.com

Brie Jensen

* *Multi-Use Bucket, page 237*

Brie is a registered nurse living in Hudson, Wisconsin, with her husband and two children. Two incredibly creative and talented parents raised her. Brie enjoys sewing and crafting and especially enjoys making children's clothing, bags, accessories, home decor, and baby items. She also enjoys woodworking projects and cooking.
www.iammamab.blogspot.com

Caitlin Betsy Bell

* *Pretend Sewing Machine, page 382*

Caitlin was raised all across the United States and grew up elbow deep in the dirt and the craft drawer. Her business, Nifty Kidstuff, started on a whim when she was just 15 years old. Since then, her crafty endeavors have led her to the Savannah College of Art and Design with a major in fibers. She has a passion for making authentic, quality toys from natural fibers and with love.
www.niftykidstuff.typepad.com

Candace Davis

* *Bees Knees Pocket Bag, page 105*

Candace taught herself to sew at the age of 12 when she became frustrated with everything in her closet. She still loves to sew her own clothing, but spends much more time creating new bags for her business, Wonder Stitching. Candace also teaches sewing classes at her favorite local independent craft shop, Crafty Planet. She spends her spare time, on the rare occasion she finds it, knitting and embroidering.
www.wonderstitching.com

Caroline Critchfield

* *Button-Up Bolero, page 310*
* *Pretty Pinafore, page 72*

Caroline lives in Palm Bay, Florida, and started Carolina Fair Designs as an excuse to stay crafty. She has a degree in Russian language and literature, and has four children, two boys and two girls. She started sewing before she could remember, and loves creating without patterns. She especially likes finding easier, more creative ways to sew the things her family uses and wears.
www.carolinafair.blogspot.com

Caroline Sanchez

* *Gazillions of Gathers Pillow, page 25*
* *Wave Illusions Pillow, page 385*

Caroline (a.k.a. Care) has been an avid sewist ever since her mom taught her the basics when she was just six years old. When she wasn't rummaging through her mom's scrap bins, you could find her stitching away at the sewing machine. Care owes much to her incredibly supportive husband, who enables her to be an at-home mommy to their three children, and never rolls his eyes at the scads of fabric she brings home!
www.obsessivelystitching.blogspot.com

Carolyn Lipke

* *Urban Wabbit Hunting Cap, page 371*

Carolyn has been sewing since she had enough hand-eye coordination to safely wield fabric shears. She enrolled in 4-H at age eight and grew up with a healthy love for all things fabric, especially wool! After grad school, Carolyn went to work in the wilds of Alaska. She then sailed the high seas with the Sea Education Association, sewing the whole time. Under the label Immer Designs, she now focuses on crafts made from found objects.
www.immerdesigns.etsy.com

Chelsey Mona

* *Sit-Upon-a-Saurus, page 263*

Chelsey is a St. Paul, Minnesota, artist who creates jewelry and other handmade goods under the name Silverbug Studio. You can find her pieces at I Like You in Minneapolis or online at the site listed below. Chelsey is the creator of Craft Support, an online question and answer blog that helps you make your next project a craft winner.
www.silverbugstudio.com

Cherie Killilea

* *Easy Dining Chair Slipcover, page 168*

StudioCherie is Cherie's sewing pattern and design company. Her most popular patterns were inspired by her own personal needs. From re-covering chairs to re-envisioning ubiquitous items like a duffle bag or a sunglass case, Cherie has a solution for a variety of needs. Look for printed versions of StudioCherie patterns in the Simplicity Pattern catalog, and PDF versions are available directly from Cherie's web location.

www.studiocherie.etsy.com

Christine Lindh

* *Sugar & Spice Ruffled Skirt, page 240*

Christine is a mom to three amazing children and wife to an equally amazing husband, Carl. She likes to sew and craft in her spare time and loves to share her projects with others. Christine has a crafty/sewing blog where you can find many how-tos and project tutorials meant to inspire you to make something handmade.

www.fromanigloo.blogspot.com

Cindy Hopper

* *Child's Chef Hat & Apron, page 97*

Cindy blogs at Skip to My Lou, a website where you can find everything from sewing gifts and throwing parties to cooking delicious food. The site is full of free patterns, downloads, and tons of inspiration. Cindy loves sharing ideas to help inspire people to make memories with their families and friends and hopes to help others experience the satisfaction of creating and the joy of celebrating.

www.skiptomylou.org

Clare Carter

* *Tatty Duck Cushion, page 197*

Australian Clare loves to create magic with a needle and thread. She is a textile artist with a background in fashion and costume design. Clare blogs, laughs, observes, and grows on her website. Join her on the journey!

www.lulucarter.typepad.com

Daljeet Kaur

* *Mandarin Dress, page 89*

Daljeet has been a waitress, stewardess, ODAC instructor, and teacher. Throughout all her careers, the only constant was her preoccupation with sewing and all things related. Daljeet finally made the plunge to set up a tailoring studio in her own home and has been happy ever since! She loves writing patterns, as it is very simpatico with her compulsive need for order! She has a two-year-old daughter who inspires her children's patterns.

www.themeasuringtape.etsy.com

Danielle Wilson

* *Toddler Smock, page 246*
* *Little Girl's Capelet, page 368*

Danielle loves playing with fabric, making messes, and all things crafty. She delved into pattern making in order to create things she'd imagined but couldn't find for her two children, or outfit her obnoxiously long torso in dresses that actually fit. She resides happily with her husband, children, and chickens in Alpine, Utah, and is so excited to be a part of this great book!

www.mysparkle.blogspot.com

Destri Bufmack

* *Hot Pad Apron, page 53*

Destri is a stay-at-home mom who recently decided to dig out her sewing machine. Now addicted to fabric, Destri can't buy anything for her little girl to wear, because she is determined to make it herself! Destri's website, The Mother Huddle, is a place where mothers gather and share all the things they would if they were huddled up on a blanket in the park. You are invited to join their huddle, have a seat on the blanket, and share your talents and ideas as well.

www.themotherhuddle.com

Don Morin

* *Halter Wrap, page 17*

Don is a clothing designer, patternmaker, and educator living and working in Toronto, Canada. He writes a pattern making/design blog called Bag'n-telle that provides expert ideas and tutorials about creative fashion bag design and construction techniques. It has a do-it-yourself approach for the home sewer.

http://bagntell.wordpress.com

Elizabeth Dronen

* *Organizer Wallet, page 56*

Elizabeth's mother taught her how to sew when she was young, but Elizabeth never took much interest until recently. Today, Elizabeth mostly sews clothing for herself, and loves making wallets for her friends and family. She works as an industrial engineer and finds those skills come in handy when altering and constructing garments, her favorite part of sewing. Learn more about Elizabeth on her blog.

http://elily00.wordpress.com

Emily Steffen

* *Bartholomew Bookends, page 388*

Emily grew up with sewing machines and handmade crafts, and her love for them runs deep and long. She currently is a photographer by day and lover of sewing machines and knitting needles by night. Constantly doodling and dreaming, Emily has lofty goals of living on a hobby farm in Wisconsin surrounded by rolling hills, chickens, her pugs, and a giant front porch for her crafty juices to run wild.

www.emilysteffenphoto.com/blog

Erin Currie

* *Monster-Wear Hat & Mittens, page 298*

Erin is a mad scientist by day and seamstress by night. During the day you can find her working on her PhD at the University of California, San Francisco, in biochemistry. Nights and weekends Erin is sewing for herself, her friends, and her store, Seamstress Erin's Stuff to Make You Smile.

www.seamstresserin.com

Fiona Tully

* *Barnaby Bear, page 226*

Australian Fiona is the stay-at-home mum of two gorgeous girls and a designer of textile craft patterns. Fiona believes she was genetically wired to craft and that crafting runs through her veins! In a previous life Fiona was a preschool teacher. This combined with memories of her childhood and playing with her little girls inspires Fiona to create projects with a colorful, child-like quality.

www.twobrownbirds.typepad.com

Gene Pittman

* *Hi-Fi Habitat, page 45*

Gene's appreciation for craft was instilled when he was an undergraduate in North Carolina. Constantly surrounded by makers of things, he grew to understand the "craft of craft" and applied it to his own work. Trained as a sculptor, he now spends most of his time behind a camera or playing with his one-year-old son.

www.genepittman.com

Heather Scrimsher

* *Tuffet Inspired Ottoman, page 165*

Heather often tells her husband not to worry, that her obsession with creating things is cheaper than therapy. As a teen, Heather learned how to alter patterns to make her wardrobe. After the birth of her first daughter, she started sewing for children. She has been a 4-H leader and taught sewing professionally, specializing in serger sewing. Heather blogs about how to use a serger and other items in the sewing studio.

www.fiberosity.com

Heidi Massingill

* *Last-Minute Tunic, page 333*

Heidi and her daughter Megan are co-owners of Stitch Cleveland in Lakewood, Ohio, where they share their fun ideas and excitement for sewing in private and group sewing lessons. They also offer a colorful array of fabrics and patterns that seem to motivate everyone who enters the store. When they are not busy with students, you will find them — usually with thread clinging to their clothes — sewing, of course!

www.stitchcleveland.com

Jaime Morrison Curtis

* *Swaddle Blanket, page 190*

Jaime is author of the bestselling book *Prudent Advice: Lessons for My Baby Daughter (A Life List for Every Woman)*, founding editor of *Prudent Baby: DIYs for Small Fries*, editor of DailyCandy Kids Los Angeles, and mother to two-year-old Scarlet Jane. A former marketing executive, Jaime spent her single years exercising her passport with a backpack, a notebook, and a ticket to the local art museums before settling down to start her family.

www.prudentbaby.com

Jamie Halleckson and Carmen Marti

* *Shaken, Not Stirred Martini Shade, page 161*

Mother-daughter team Jamie and Carmen make up City Chic Country Mouse. Jamie (City Chic) lives in Saint Paul, Minnesota, with her husband and their fur-babies. Her day job is at the University of Minnesota, but she spends her free time designing for City Chic Country Mouse. Carmen (Country Mouse) lives in Cloquet, Minnesota, with her husband and their fur-babies. She has been sewing since she was a little girl and has tried many different crafts, but always comes back to her first love, sewing.
www.citychiccountrymouse.etsy.com

Jenna Lou Odegard

* *Kaleidoscope Table Runner, page 150*
* *Speedy Ruffle Scarf, page 336*

Jenna Lou is a self-taught designer, fabric hoarder, and Jill-of-all-trades living in southern Minnesota with her husband and pets. She has run her business, Jenna Lou Designs, since 2006, featuring handmade handbags, wallets, and accessories. In 2008 she expanded to include original sewing patterns, hoping to inspire others to learn her beloved craft of sewing.
www.jennalou.com

Jennifer Blum

* *Neck Pillow ("Work in Comfort" Travel Set), page 316*

Growing up an only child, Jennifer kept herself entertained by making things. Jennifer's childhood creativity transgressed into her adult career as a graphic designer. She holds a BS in design, but to escape the glow of her computer, Jennifer turns to her passion for color and texture, which she combines with her attention to detail to fashion a treasure trove of handmade creations.
www.urbansparrow.etsy.com

Jess Durrant

* *Logan's Guitar, page 84*

As a child, Jess traveled to craft and art fairs with her mother, a weaver, knitter, sewer, and maker of many homemade things. But it wasn't until she joined the Minnesota RollerGirls that sewing became an integral part of her life. In that very first season, her entire team had to make their own uniforms. Using her vintage Singer 221, yards of black and pink broadcloth, a Bo-Peep pattern, and a lot of help from her mom, Jess rediscovered the fun of sewing.

Jessica Roberts

* *Cozy Comfort Set, page 204*

Jessica lives in Columbus, Ohio, where she sews, crochets, embroiders, gardens, and does whatever other crafty endeavors she can add to her "regular" job. Her husband, dogs, parrot, and chickens tolerate the benign neglect this causes. You can find more about Jessica at her blog.
www.kusine.com/blog

Jolene Lightfoot

* *Convertible Diaper Clutch, page 64*

Jolene is fortunate that her husband Carl loves her enough to pretend the mid-project messes, which tend to spill out of her sewing room, do not exist. She is a stay-at-home mom to young son, Mason, with a second child born in June of 2011. Jolene stocks a variety of treasures, quilts, bags, convertible diaper clutches, aprons, covered journals, and whatever she is inspired to sew at any given moment in her online shop.
www.nthnbutmoonshine.etsy.com

June McCrary Jacobs

* *Tic-Tac-Toe Travel Game, page 200*

June considers herself fortunate to have had many of her original sewing, quilt, and stitchery designs and sewing-related articles published in nationwide magazines, including *Sew News* and *Crafts 'n things*. June openly admits that she enjoys hand-sewing and embroidery even more than she enjoys sewing on her sewing machines! During her nonsewing time, she enjoys spending time with her family, reading, and visiting museums and historic homes.

Katherine Donaldson

* *Hanging Book Display, page 135*
* *Kanzashi Clock, page 80*
* *Kid's Comfy Chair, page 232*

Katherine loves to make things, any things, including robots, quilts, her own wedding dress, and dinner! These days it's mostly toys and clothes for her young daughters, but Katherine's really looking forward to the day when her girls are old enough to join her in wild robotic-textile mash-ups, and she dreams of getting a family booth at Maker Faire with her awesome maker husband.
www.oneinchworld.com

Kathy Stowell

* Obi Belt, page 366

Kathy lives with her husband, Craig, and two small children, Edie and Kale, in a cozy strawbale house nestled in the mountains of British Columbia. It is here that she whips up sewing, spinning, and knitting projects during nap times. Kathy sells some of the resulting art yarn and handmade clothing at her online sites.
www.whiletangerinedreams.com

Katie Steuernagle

* Umbrella Redo, page 260

Katie's first craft projects were piñatas that she made for friends' birthday parties. By fifth grade, she had a business selling hand-painted pencils. In junior high school, she sewed custom poodle skirts for the '50s dance. Today, Katie still loves to hand craft beautiful and functional objects for everyday living. She has been a guest on the Martha Stewart Show, and her work has been featured in several publications. Katie lives in Minnesota with her husband and three kids.
matsutakeblog.blogspot.com

Katie Varela

* Roller Skate Romper, page 330

Katie is a wife, mother, and sewing enthusiast. She loves seeing things she likes in stores and trying to figure out how to make them on her own, usually for much cheaper and with much cuter fabrics!
www.katievarela.etsy.com

Keri McCarthy

* Portable Picnic, page 155

Keri's crafting and sewing satisfies and fuels her need to make all things, from her dog's collar to her kitchen shelves, look cute. She learned about all things crafty from her cake-decorating, mural-painting, clothes-making mom. As a mom-to-be, she's excited to delve into the world of nursery items and baby clothing. Keri is a New England child and family photographer and blog addict.
http://quaintandquirky.blogspot.com

Lauren Booth

* Gym Bag Set, page 257

Lauren is a molecular biology graduate student at University of California, San Francisco. She thanks her grandmother for fostering her love of arts and crafts at an early age, and has been crafting ever since!

Lauren Kurtz

* Smart Girl's Set, page 119

Lauren is a multitalented artist who teaches handbag design, jewelry making, and wire crochet. Her purses and jewelry are for sale in various boutiques in California and Oregon.
www.laurenkurtzdesign.com

Leigh Ann Tennant

* Cool Season Clutch, page 358

Leigh Ann, a former makeup artist, is now a freelance project designer for books and magazines. She enjoys working with vibrant color and unexpected texture and fabric combinations. Leigh Ann enjoys drawing and is currently working on her surface design portfolio.
www.spincushion.com

Lindsay Conner

* Hugh Manatee, page 308

A writer and editor by day, Lindsay sews stuffed toys and custom creations from her home in the Indianapolis area. She always thought a manatee would make a great pet, but her husband, Matt, and darling cat, Murph, disagree. You can keep tabs on her crafty ventures.
www.lindsaysews.com

Lisa Cox

* Personalized Garment Bag, page 78

Lisa is an occupational therapist by day, and an avid sewer, quilter, and crafter by night. Lisa attributes her passion for sewing, needlecrafts, and quilting to her mother and grandmother, who taught her the basics and encouraged her to develop her own style. Her designs have been published in several magazines. Lisa lives in Perth, Australia, with her husband, David, and their children, Brenton and Sarah. Lisa collaborates on a blog with her daughter, Sarah.
www.spoonfullofsugargirls.blogspot.com

Lisa Powers

* *Play Pants, page 215*
* *Sassy Dress, page 342*

Lisa is a fiber artist and designer with 30 years of sewing and knitting experience. Sewing and teaching are two of the things that make her happy, as well as her husband and two awesome little girls. Crafty Planet sweetly allows her to teach and hang out at their store in Minneapolis, Minnesota.

www.infantile.etsy.com

Lorraine Teigland

* *A-Line Skirt with Saddle Stitching, page 228*
* *Pig & Piglets, page 302*
* *Smocked Sundress, page 36*

Lorraine is a retired physics teacher and stay-at-home mother. She started sewing as a little girl, inspired by her mother, grandmother, and aunts, all amazing seamstresses. Now it is her three young daughters who inspire her with their sense of wonder, tendency to push limits, and their complete ignorance of the meaning of the word *impossible*. When Lorraine needs a break from sewing, she eats Nutella and makes toys with corrugated cardboard and electric circuit bits.

www.ikatbag.com

Madeline Warr

* *Smart Girl's Set, page 119*

Madeline fell in love with sewing at an early age and the flame is still burning brightly. She is inspired by modern fabrics and is passionate about keeping the art of sewing alive. In 2009 Madeline and her mom opened Maisonnette, a fabric boutique and online fabric shop in Oceanside, California. She also designs a clothing line for Maisonnette The Goods, an online shop featuring ready-made clothing, home goods, jewelry, and artwork.

www.maisonnetteoceanside.com

Marlene Gaige

* *Bunny Pillow, page 313*

Marlene learned to sew as a small child at her grandmother's feet and hasn't stopped. Dolls and bears, clothing and costumes, it really doesn't matter. Old or new, any textile will do! She has owned a store, had stuff in stores, been published, done shows, and taught classes all around the world, but she likes creating new patterns the best. With all of her boys mostly grown, creative time has become a part of savoring every day.

www.allmyown.etsy.com

Matt DeVries

* *Bicycle Panniers, page 268*

Matt and his wife, Patricia Hoskins, are co-owners of Crafty Planet, an independent craft shop in Minneapolis, Minnesota, specializing in the hippest fabrics, patterns, knitting, and other needlework. In his far-too-infrequent spare time, Matt enjoys riding and working on vintage motor scooters, pinball, and skateboarding. Matt will have you know he can survive on a steady diet of breakfast cereal and peanut butter and jelly sandwiches.

www.craftyplanet.com

Megan Risley

* *iPod Cozy (Jet Set), page 127*

Megan sews fabric accessories, including reversible belts, pet collars, iPod/MP3 player cases, cell phone cases, laptop covers, and other notions. She started out as a quilter and not a day goes by when she doesn't sew. Megan is motivated by color and patterns and derives great enjoyment from creating her own patterns. Her wares are sold at boutiques across the country and online.

www.megrnc.etsy.com

Melissa Haworth

* *Flat-Screen TV Cover, page 350*

Melissa's dad taught her how to sew when she was eight years old and she has been sewing ever since. She took quilting classes as a preteen and has continued quilting through the years. In 2007 when her husband, Rob, bought a football-worthy flat-screen TV, Melissa promptly designed the TV Cover to improve the look of their living room.

http://underconstructionblog.typepad.com

Michele Chisholm

* *Stroller Tote, page 143*

Michele happily works in her home studio, designing, sewing, and machine embroidering whatever is popular at the moment. A lifelong sewer and textile lover, Michele's hands are always busy, and she often carries around totes filled with yarn and her latest crochet projects. Michele lives in South Carolina with her husband and two college-age children.

http://calicodaisy.blogspot.com

Michelle Fante

✳ *Farmers' Market Tote, page 211*
✳ *Under-the-Sink Cleaning Stash, page 284*

Michelle, born and raised in Michigan, attended the Center for Creative Studies College of Art and Design in Detroit. With a degree in fiber design and seven years of corporate life, she decided that it was time to begin working for herself. Guided by her passion for fashion, Michelle is now an independent consultant and freelancer for the apparel industry. Michelle lives with her husband in Royal Oak and is always working on a new project whenever she gets a chance.

Nate Van Hofwegen

✳ *Airliner Bag, page 249*

Nate lives and works in Minneapolis, Minnesota. He started out hand-sewing patches on his hoodies and pants. From there, he handmade leather bags and hats and hosted sewing parties with friends. Nate is self-taught and pushes himself to tackle challenges; he has worked out patterns and processes for many different products and applications. Today, Nate makes handbags, motorcycle seats, classic car interiors, and vintage mod furniture.
www.natescustomsewing.com

Nicole Kaplan

✳ *Bright Bag Tag, Cheery Passport Cover, Travel Tissue Pack, and Vacation Valet Travel Tray (Jet Set), page 127*

Nicole lives in the Big Apple with her husband. As an attorney, she loves sewing and quilting to unwind after a long day. Nicole began sewing and crafting at an early age, and was given her first sewing machine at age 13 (one of the best, most useful presents she ever received)! Nicole especially enjoys making gifts and quilts for family and friends.
www.patchworkduck.com

Nina Martine Robinson

✳ *Camp Shirt, page 61*

Nina is a self-taught fiber artist who started sewing children's clothes and art dolls over 20 years ago. She has been published in Altered Couture magazine and has had her work at many local galleries and shops including the Textile Center of Minnesota and I like you, in Minneapolis. Nina works at a fabric boutique in St. Paul and lives with her son in Shoreview, Minnesota.

Pam McFerrin

✳ *Monster Backpack, page 219*
✳ *Petal Pillow, page 223*
✳ *Scruffle Scarf, page 34*

Pam was embroidering pillowcases and sewing on her mom's sea-foam green Sears Kenmore by the age of nine. A graphic designer by trade, with a love of color, patterns, textiles, and fashion, Pam has an overwhelming need to create and sewing has provided the solution. Pam resides in Southwest Minneapolis with her husband and two funny-looking bulldogs.
www.pamelamcferrin.com

Patricia Hoskins

✳ *Coupon Wallet, page 280*
✳ *Day of the Week Planner, page 266*
✳ *Lap Desk ("Work in Comfort" Travel Set) page 316*

Patricia (Trish) and her husband Matt are co-owners of Crafty Planet, a retail fabric and needlework store, plus craft workshop located in Minneapolis, Minnesota. Trish dabbles in all manner of all things crafty, including knitting, crocheting, spinning, sewing, quilting, embroidery, and cross-stitching. She unfortunately has yet to keep many completed projects for herself (she has yet to complete many projects, for that matter).
www.craftyplanet.com

Paula Ozier

✳ *Drawstring Tidy Caddy, page 75*

Paula graduated with a degree in textile design, specializing in woven and printed textiles, and began teaching college-prep textile courses. In August 2009, she teamed up with her sister, Michelle Ozier, to launch Paula Ozier Designs at the Festival of Quilts at the National Exhibition Centre. Paula and Michelle work together to produce original, exclusive quilting fabrics that are digitally printed onto 100% cotton fabric. Paula also designs and produces a wide range of gift products, patterns, and project kits.
www.paulaozierdesigns.com

Rachael Theis

✳ *Breezy Kite, page 276*
✳ *Superhero Cape & Shorts, page 273*

Rachael's grandmother gave her a bag of fabric scraps when she was five years old and she has been a fabric junkie ever since. In addition to sewing, Rachael likes to crochet, work in her garden, embroider, paint, and spin her own yarn. She is also a junk enthusiast and loves to reuse and recycle neat objects.
http://rachaelmade.blogspot.com

Rachel Knoblich

* 5-Gallon Garden Bucket Caddy, page 254
* Playday Frock, page 86

Rachel, a mother of four and grandmother to six, lives in Southern Wisconsin. Since childhood, Rachel has had a fascination with things that could be made and things that could be grown. She always loved going to the fabric store and has warm memories of her mother, Eleanor, sewing for the family. Several years ago Rachel started sewing and selling children's custom boutique clothing under her brand name, Googooagogo.
www.googooagogo.etsy.com

Rebecca Yaker

* Boxer Shorts, page 180
* Cap Sleeve Bolero, page 28
* Party Lamp Shade, page 42

Rebecca began sewing at age five. Today, she creates unexpected luxuries using all-American elements and icons in the most unpredictable ways. In 2005 Rebecca launched Hazel and Melvin's Room, and for five years she has created one-of-a-kind baby bedding and apparel for clients worldwide. Today, Rebecca is exploring new, creative opportunities using many of her honed craft skills. She is a seamstress, hand- and machine-knitter, crocheter, weaver, fabric printer, and design consultant, but you might know her large-scale sock monkey pieces best. More than anything, Rebecca enjoys spending time with her husband and son.
www.rebeccayaker.com

Sally Mortenson

* Ticket Portfolio and Vacation Valet Travel Tray (Jet Set), page 127

Sally hails from St. Paul, Minnesota, where she works as an attorney to help support her sewing habit. When Sally's daughter left for college, Sally decided to learn a new skill each year. The first year, she chose quilting, and was so hooked that she never went on to learn another skill. Sally especially appreciates her local quilt group, the Kellogg Quilters, and is thankful to her husband who agreed to relinquish their basement to her quilting passion.
Sally's e-mail address is morzil@tcq.net

Sarah Faix

* Liberty Lion & Blankie, page 193

Sarah loves dolls of all sorts and when her daughter was born, she wanted to give her daughter her first doll. She was disappointed when she couldn't find what she was looking for and settled for a generic pink doll. A few years later, Sarah gathered the confidence to create her own pattern. Once she started making dolls for her daughter, Bit of Whimsy Dolls was born. Sarah's daughter is still her inspiration and most of the patterns she creates are the result of a special request from her.
www.bitofwhimsydolls.com

Sarah Seitz

* Cheeky Panty & Cami Set, page 323

Sarah is a Seattle-based craft blogger who feels that every woman should have something pretty to wear under her clothes. After discovering how easy it is to make a pair of great-fitting panties and matching cami, she decided to share it with the world. Sarah enjoys offering sewing lessons at her church and hopes to eventually publish more patterns. Visit her crafting website for tutorials, challenges, giveaways, tips, and recipes.
www.comeandseetheseitz.com

Sharon Madsen

* Cupcake Apron, page 101

Sharon taught herself to sew after a brief introduction to the art at the age of eight. By the time she was 14 she was designing, with techniques that were more "by the seat of her pants" than "by the book," resulting in some hysterical moments in fashion. She presently spends enormous amounts of time sequestered in her studio dreaming and sewing, while surrounded by fabric, patterns, and her dogs.
www.sharonsews.blogspot.com

Stephanie Sterling

* Reverse Appliqué Baby Romper, page 338

Stephanie lives in Baltimore, Maryland, with her husband and two daughters who are the inspiration for her work. Stephanie has been blogging and sharing her ideas for nearly five years.
www.neurosesgalore.com

Sue Kim

* *Baby Overalls, page 146*
* *Bonnet and Mary Janes (Baby's Accessory Trio), page 184*
* *Charming Bag, page 116*
* *Chic Carryall, page 158*
* *The Day Out Bag, page 111*
* *Pajama Boots, page 294*
* *Retro Bag, page 50*

Sue lives in Toronto, Canada, with her three lovely children and husband. Sue has always had a passion for crafts and started sewing when she was 10 years old. She is the author of *The Modern Classics*, a book that includes over 20 of her bags and clutch patterns. Sue has also created patterns for Simplicity and sells her own patterns through her website, called *I think sew*.
www.ithinksew.com

Sue Walsh

* *On-the-Strap Camera Case, page 290*

Technical writer by day and maker of things stitched, knitted, and photographed by night, Sue is all about gifts that are beautiful, well made, and useful. They *must* be useful! She's grateful every day for her mom and grandmothers, who taught her to sew and knit at an early age. Born and raised in South Africa, Sue now lives in San Diego with her husband, son, her vintage, avocado-green Bernina 610, and a very unruly stash cupboard!
http://nobaddays.wordpress.com

Susan Byrd

* *Eight-Bottle Tote, page 172*

Using scraps from her nana's yarn collection, Susan started knitting clothes for her Barbie when she was eight years old. Susan's hobby quickly developed into a passion, and she finds herself knitting or sewing during every spare moment. Susan creates one-of-a-kind tote bags, playful accessories, home decor items, and more. She has a degree in graphic design and lives in Mississauga, Ontario, with her favorite person in the world, her very supportive husband, Gary.

Tanja and Suada Ivacic

* *The "O" Tunic, page 21*

Tanja and Suada are a mum-and-daughter team from Melbourne, Australia, who together form the Poppy and Lola design team. They design patterns for little ones that are feminine, funky, and most important, comfortable. Daughter Tanja is a passionate designer and crafter with experience in the graphic design industry. Mum Suada is an expert in apparel construction. They are very passionate about creating beautiful things for little ones, and the process of making nice clothing brings them great joy!
www.poppylola.etsy.com

Tina Michalik

* *Flirty Skirty, page 32*

Tina is a fabric hoarder in need of an intervention. She quilts and sews when her girls are sleeping and stalks sewing blogs mercilessly. Tina also writes about her vision of the perfect sewing world.
http://littlebluecottage.wordpress.com

Tracey Citron

* *Crayon Ammo Belt & Bag, page 93*

Tracey comes from a long line of accomplished sewists, but did not take up the craft until adulthood, under the careful guidance of her mom. A long-time knitter, Tracey enjoys the "instant gratification" of sewing, which is why she prefers to sew quick items like purses, pillows, and other accessories. Tracey lives in Eagan, Minnesota, with her husband, stepdaughter, two dogs, and ever-growing fabric collection.

Yasuko Shimamoto Solbes

* *Monkey Leggings, page 352*

Yasuko is passionate about drawing, designing, and making and wearing clothes, and often mixes Japanese and Western themes. As a mother of two boys, she came to realize how hard it is to find great designs for them, and so she strives to answer that challenge. She began her business in a flat in central London, but is now based in the traditional Kagurazaka district of Tokyo. Visit 'dans la lune' at her website.
www.atelierlalune.com

INDEX

Page numbers in **bold** indicate charts, page numbers in *italic* indicate illustrations.

C

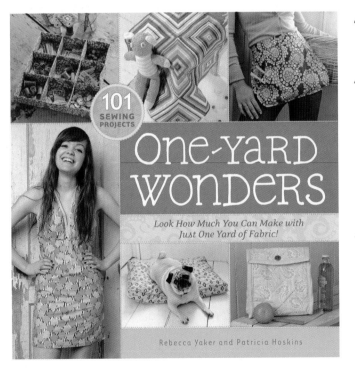